34.70

FIFTY
STATE
SYSTEMS OF
COMMUNITY COLLEGES:
MISSION, GOVERNANCE,
FUNDING AND
ACCOUNTABILITY

TERRENCE A. TOLLEFSON
RICK L. GARRETT
WILLIAM G. INGRAM
AND ASSOCIATES

The Overmountain Press

JOHNSON CITY, TENNESSEE

DEDICATION

We dedicate this book to Dr. Ben E. Fountain, Jr., President Emeritus of the North Carolina Community College System. He was the senior author and editor of the first book on state systems of community colleges in this series, which was published in 1989. He was co-editor and co-author of the second book in 1992, and he has written the introduction to this 1999 book. Ben Fountain has been a visionary leader and effective advocate of community colleges in his nearly 40-year career, which has included service as President of both Lenoir Community College and Isothermal Community College; President of the North Carolina Community College System, and as a faculty member at North Carolina State University.

In all of those capacities, he always was a wonderful scholar, gentleman, mentor, teacher, colleague and friend. He has been and still is an inspiration to us all. We appreciate you, Ben!

Terry Tollefson
Rick Garrett
Bill Ingram

CONTENTS

PREFACE AND ACKNOWLEDGEMENTS

When Ben Fountain suggested the first book in this series in 1987, he did so partly because he had read and admired Roger Yarrington's *Junior Colleges: 50 States/50 Years*, published by the American Association of Junior Colleges in 1969. All three of our books, published in 1989, 1992 and now in 1999, have followed the late Dr. Yarrington's lead in obtaining chapters whenever possible from community college leaders located within the states whose community colleges they have described. We have written chapters for only those states from which we could not find individuals who were both highly qualified and willing to write them.

The chief state-level community college officers or their designees wrote the chapters for most states in this book. Several exceptions have occurred in states where the executive directors or their staff members of statewide community college *associations* were the authors. In one state, a nationally prominent writer on community colleges was the author.

From its inception in November of 1996, this book has taken over two and one-half years to complete, because of the busy schedules of authors and editors. Some of the chapters were written for the first time only recently. Many chapters were written in 1997 or 1998 and updated in 1999, but in a few cases the authors were unavailable to revise their chapters from 1997 and 1998, and we decided to include them because the unique and irreplaceable "flavor" they provided outweighed the need for more current information. The result, which to a lesser degree also characterized our first two books, is that the most recent data included in a few chapters are up to three years old.

This book differs from the first two, in that the former were entirely descriptive in content. This book adds a chapter written by each of the three primary co-editors/co-authors that is analytical in nature. We also have added chapter sections on accountability and economic development to our third book.

We wish to acknowledge and express our gratitude to Dr. Louis W. Bender, Professor Emeritus of Florida State University, for his support of our first book while he was a member of the board of directors of the American Association of Community and Junior Colleges. Similarly, we thank Dr. David R. Pierce, President, American Association of Community Colleges, for his support of the second book. To Ms. Beth Wright, Editor,

Overmountain Press, we express our thanks for her support of our third book on state systems of community colleges. We thank Mrs. Rita Presnell for her patience and excellent typing and editorial work on the entire book.

To our employers, Durham Technical Community College, East Tennessee State University, and Mayland Community College, we express our appreciation for their support of our efforts to complete this book. Appreciation is also expressed to a former employer of Rick Garrett, Florence-Darlington Technical College, for its support of his national research.

Terrence A. Tollefson
Rick L. Garrett
William G. Ingram

INTRODUCTION

The publication of *Fifty State Systems Of Community Colleges: Mission, Governance, Funding and Accountability* is far more than an update of two similar predecessor books. The earlier volumes by former state community college directors Ben E. Fountain and Terrence A. Tollefson are titled *Community College Systems in the United States: Forty-Nine State Systems (1989)* and *Forty-Nine State Systems, 1992 Edition*. This new work continues the tradition of the earlier books by presenting timely descriptions of community college systems in the United States. Three new and important sections are included in this volume of what has evolved into a series of periodic accounts of state systems of community colleges.

The studies by Terrence A. Tollefson, Rick L. Garrett and William G. Ingram are major contributions to the body of community college education literature. First, Rick Garrett presents his recent study of levels of centralization of state governance of community colleges. This research replicates his earlier investigation and produces some surprising and interesting results.

Second, William Ingram presents a thoughtful analysis of the increasing role of community colleges in local and state economic development. He documents the growing importance of community colleges as they move from passive to active participation in economic growth strategies and practices.

Third, longtime coordinator, writer and editor of the community college state system series, Terrence Tollefson, includes a substantive overview of these state systems. He produces a summary of the current patterns and trends of state-level mission, governance, funding and accountability of community college operations.

These useful sections are followed by the entries for the individual community college systems. The reader will find for each state information on the origin, history, goals, programs, enrollment, funding and governance of the community system in that state.

The publication of this book is especially timely in 1999. Sharply increasing numbers of traditional college-age students in the United States are forcing higher education leaders and state policymakers to take steps to accommodate rising enrollments. Concurrently, the demands for continuing adult education are growing. Postsecondary education practitioners seeking answers to these and related challenges can turn to this volume to learn how others are coping.

Fifty State Systems of Community Colleges: Mission, Governance, Funding and Accountability was prepared with rigorous scholarship by seasoned and successful community college practitioners. The resultant book is a valuable resource to those persons seeking analytical and general information about state community college systems in the United States.

Ben E. Fountain, Jr.

President Emeritus

North Carolina Community College System

April, 1999

REFERENCES

Fountain, B. E. & Tollefson, T. A. (1989). *Community Colleges in the United States: Forty-Nine State Systems*. Washington, D.C.: American Association of Community and Junior Colleges.

Tollefson, T. A. & Fountain, B. E. (1992), *Forty-Nine State Systems, 1992 Edition*. Washington, D.C.: American Association of Community Colleges.

DEGREES OF CENTRALIZATION OF GOVERNANCE STRUCTURES IN STATE COMMUNITY COLLEGE SYSTEMS

Rick L. Garrett
Vice President of Instructional Services
Mayland Community College

In 1990, a survey was conducted among the state directors of community college systems for each of the 49 states with a system of publicly supported two-year postsecondary institutions. South Dakota is the one state that did not and still does not have a community college system. The purpose of the study was to establish empirically the degree to which the governance of each state community college system was centralized or decentralized so that benchmark data would be available on which to base decisions for changing governance structures in an effort to function more effectively and accountably. It was expected that organizations would continually change in order to improve profits, services, efficiency, etc. Thus, it was expected that community college systems would also change in response to the changing milieu. In order to identify possible changes among the governance structures of state community college systems over a seven-year period, the 1990 study (Garrett, 1992) was replicated in 1997.

The state directors of all of the 49 community college systems, plus the one in Puerto Rico, were surveyed and a 100% response rate was obtained. The original questionnaire, which was considered to be valid and reliable, was reconstructed and included the 29 function-questions with their subsumed centralization indicator-responses.

To ascertain the overall degree of centralization or decentralization of the governance structure of respective state community college systems, numerical values were assigned to each function of the degree indicators. For each of the 29 centralization-scale items in the questionnaire, the response could be categorized on an integer-continuum scale. For each of the 29 functions, the indicators of centralization were assigned high numerical values, while the indicators of decentralization were assigned low numerical values. Therefore, the response to each function-question equated to a numerical value. The centralization index for each state system represents the sum of the numerical values assigned to the response to each of the centralization-scale items in the questionnaire. However, because not every respondent answered all 29 function-questions, the total value of responses for each survey was averaged by the number of questions answered and then multiplied by 29 (the total possible number of responses) to obtain a summated score that could be appropriately compared to scores from the 1990 study. These scores provided a basis on which to rank state systems according to their respective centralization indexes, where a low score reflected a decentralized governance structure and a high score reflected a centralized governance structure.

Based on the numerical values assigned to the response categories in the questionnaire and on the number of responses to each question, the possible range of averaged centralization index values that could have been obtained was from 1.00, indicating a highly decentralized governance structure, to 4.07, indicating a highly centralized governance structure. However, the results of the summation of responses for state systems indicated a range from 1.43 for Pennsylvania to 3.79 for Connecticut. This compares to the 1990 range of 1.38 for Missouri to 3.69 for Connecticut (Garrett, 1992). The centralization index for Missouri in the 1997 study was 1.64. The average assessed centralization index in 1990 was 2.55, compared with 2.67 in 1997, while the mid-point of the centralization continuum for both studies was 2.54. Based on this mid-point, all state systems with assessed centralization-index values below 2.54 are considered to be decentralized, while all state systems with assessed centralization index values greater than 2.54 are considered to represent centralized governance structures. Two state systems (4%) are assessed as highly decentralized (Pennsylvania and Montana), while five state systems (10%) are assessed as functioning in a highly centralized manner (Colorado, Connecticut, Hawaii, Kentucky, and Tennessee). In 1990, three states were identified as highly decentralized and two states were identified to be highly centralized. Overall, 50% (25) of the state systems are decentralized and 50% (25) are assessed as being centralized. This is in contrast to the 1990 study (Garrett, 1992), where 45.5% of state community college system governance structures were assessed as being centralized and 54.5% were assessed as being decentralized.

In reference to the six categories of degrees of centralization, the largest proportion (15 state systems, or 30%) are considered to be centralized, followed by moderately decentralized and decentralized governance structures (with 12 state systems, or 24%, and 11 state systems (22%) in these categories, respectively). Similar results were obtained in 1990, though the percentages varied (Centralized = 29.5%, Moderately Decentralized = 25%, Decentralized = 22.7%).

Table 1
Degree of Centralization of State Systems

Degree of Centralization Categories	Range of Index Values	Mid-Point of Range	Number Of States in Category	Percentage of States In Category
1. Highly Decentralized	1.00-1.48	1.24	2	4
2. Decentralized	1.52-2.00	1.76	11	22
3. Moderately Decentralized	2.03-2.52	2.28	12	24
4. Moderately Centralized	2.55-3.03	2.79	5	10
5. Centralized	3.07-3.55	3.31	15	30
6. Highly Centralized	3.59-4.07	3.83	5	10
Total	1.00-4.07	2.54	50	100%

A second purpose of both the original and replicated studies of state community college system governance structures was to identify the characteristics of state systems that may be associated with the degree of centralization of governance. The literature suggests that several variables may be associated with the degree of centralization of governance structures for state community college systems. A 1990 study by Garrett (1993) found, in fact, that percentages of state and local funding were correlated with centralization or decentralization. Firstly, the type of governing board established upon initial legislative enactment of the state system may determine the system's degree of centralization or decentralization of control. Secondly, because the majority of community colleges are funded by both local and state funds, some authors assert that the degree of state or local control will be associated with the proportion of funding. Thirdly, the size of a community college system may necessitate establishing either a centralized or decentralized form of governance. Finally, the time at which a state system was established may reflect a tendency to create either a centralized or decentralized governance structure. The characteristics or variables investigated were: (1) Type of State-Level Board (Advisory, Coordinating, or Governing, as defined by Berdahl, (1971); (2) Percentage of State Funds that comprise the system's total operating budget; (3) Percentage of Local Funds that comprise the system's total annual operating budget; (4) Size of the systems in terms of the number of different local institutions; and (5) Years of Existence since legislative authorization for the system.

Based on the overall responses to the questions asked, inclusive equal-interval response categories were established. For each of the five independent variable characteristics, the following results were obtained and some comparisons have been made with the results from the 1990 study.

All of the state systems reported in this study are funded by some proportion of state funds. Seven state systems (16%) reported in 1997 that their total operating budgets were comprised of state funds equal to or less than 25.9%. This compares to 9.3% in the 1990 study. Fifty-three percent of the respondents indicated that state funds comprised 26%-55.9% of their budgets, while in 1990 that proportion was 34.9%. Thirty-one percent of the state systems reported that their total operating budgets included state funds equal to or greater than 56%. This compares to 56% of the state systems in 1990. Three states (7%) had annual budgets made up of 100% state funds.

Table 2
Percentage of State Funds

Percentage	Number	Percent
£25.9	7	16%
26-40.9	9	20%
41-55.9	15	33%
56-70.9	5	11%
71-85.9	6	13%
86-100	3	7%
Total	45	100%

Appendix II presents the percentage of state funds for each system's annual operating budget and a value for each state community college system that indicates the ranking of the system based on its percentage of state funding. As presented in Appendix II, the percentage of state funding ranged from 9.6% in Puerto Rico to 100% in Delaware, Utah, and Washington. The average proportion of state funding was 50.53%. This compares to a 60% average in the 1990 study.

Most state community college systems (63%) had operating budgets comprised of local funds of less than 21%. The largest proportion of state systems (47%) was funded by local funds totaling less than 11%. Only four state systems (9%) reported that the local proportion of their annual operating budgets equaled or exceeded 51%. As presented in Appendix II, 18 state systems (42%) had annual operating budgets comprised of no local funds (0%). The average proportion of local funding was 19.11%. Local funding proportions ranged from 0% in eighteen states to 60% in Illinois. The findings pertaining to proportion of local funding in the 1997 study are very similar to the findings in the 1990 study.

Table 3
Percentage of Local Funds

Percentage	Number	Percent
£10.9	20	47%
11-20.9	7	16%
21-30.9	4	9%
31-40.9	2	5%
41-50.9	6	14%
≥51	4	9%
Total	43	100%

State community college systems have been in existence for varying numbers of years. The greatest proportion (46%) of state systems in 1997 had existed between 31 and 35 years and 78% had existed for 31 or more years. Only three state systems (7%) reported that they had existed for 15 or fewer years, while 13 state systems (32%) had existed for 36 or more years. Based on the data presented in Appendix II, the number of years that community colleges had existed ranged from 11 for Maine to 90 years for California. The most frequent numbers of years of existence were 32 and 34, with six each having existed for each of these periods of time. The average number of years that state systems had existed was 36.85 in 1997.

Table 4
Years of Existence

Percentage	Number	Percent
£15	3	7%
16-20	1	2%
21-25	2	5%
26-30	3	7%
31-35	19	46%
≥36	13	32%
Total	41	100%

The number of local institutions represents different community colleges within respective states, not the number of districts or satellite centers. Based on the findings of this study, most state community college systems included local institutions ranging in number from 1 to 15 (53%). Nineteen percent of the state systems reported they had 5 or fewer local institutions and 4 states, or 8% (California, Illinois, North Carolina, and Texas) had more than 45 community colleges. Eighty percent of the state systems had 25 or fewer local colleges. The number of local institutions ranged from one in Alaska and Rhode Island to 106 in California. The average number of local community colleges per state was 19.67. The greatest proportion of state systems (34%) had between 6 and 15 local institutions.

Table 5
Number of Local Institutions

Institutions	Number	Percent
≤5	9	19%
6-15	16	34%
16-25	13	27%
26-35	5	10%
36-45	1	2%
>46	4	8%
Total	48	100%

State systems represented in this study were supervised at the state level by either coordinating boards or governing boards. Forty-three percent of the states were regulated by coordinating boards, while 57% were supervised by governing boards. No state system was reported to have a state-level board functioning in an advisory capacity. In comparison with the 1990 study, 41.5% of the state systems were supervised by coordinating boards and 58.5% were under state-level governing boards, so there was virtually no difference.

Table 6
Type of State-Level Board

Type	Number	Percent
Advisory	0	0%
Coordinating	19	43%
Governing	25	57%
Total	44	100%

Based on the centralization indexes assessed for state community college systems, correlational analyses were performed to identify associations between the assessed degrees of centralization and decentralization and other selected system characteristics that were analyzed in 1990 (Garrett, 1993). In addition, correlational analyses were performed to determine if there were any significant changes in the centralization indices and other variables between the 1990 and 1997 studies. For all analyses, a .05 level of significance was applied.

Correlation analyses indicated that there was a significant relationship between the degree of centralization of state system governance structure (centralization index) and each of three variables: percentage of state funding (p=.009), percentage of local funding (p=.000), and type of state-level board (p=.000). A relationship between the degree of centralization and the type of state-level board was not identified in the 1990 study. For the five correlation coefficients, four are reasonably close to the values from the 1990 study. However, the one for the type of state-level board is very different. In 1990, the value was -.039 and in 1997 it was .837.

Table 7
Correlations Between Centralization Indices and Independent Variables

	Correlation Coefficient	
Independent Variable	r-value	p-value
Percentage of State Funds	.3840*	.009
Percentage of Local Fund	.6176*	.000
Years of Existence	-.2795	.077
Number of Institutions	-.2707	.063
Type of State-Level Board	-.8376*	.000

*significant at the .05 level

A t-test for paired samples was conducted on each variable found to have a significant relationship with degree of centralization. As in the 1990 study, a high percentage of state funding in the 1997 study was associated with a high centralization index. Thus, as the percentage of state funding increases, the centralization index also increases. Regarding local funds, as the percentage of local funding increases, the centralization index decreases. Based on this study, as the proportion of local funding increases, the governance structure becomes more decentralized. Like the results from 1990, the percentage of local funds has the strongest relationship to degree of centralization, as the percentage of local funding predicts the degree of centralization more than any other variable.

In analyzing the type of state-level board with the degree of centralization by a comparison of the means, it was found that in the 1997 study, governing-type boards had an average centralization index of 3.21, while coordinating-type boards are in states with an average centralization index of 2.05. Thus, state systems that functioned in a centralized manner tended to be administered by governing-type state boards. Conversely, decentralized state systems were associated with coordinating-type boards.

Of particular interest for this study was to determine if there were any changes in the variables and in the degree of centralization between 1990 and 1997. Specifically, was there a trend toward more centralized or decentralized governance structures. Again, t-tests for paired samples were conducted. It is known that since 1990 several states have made changes in the governance structures of their community college systems. Thus, it might be expected that there would be a significant difference in the number of centralized or decentralized state systems identified in 1997. Moreover, a comparison of the data revealed that about five percent (5%) more of the states were assessed as being centralized in the 1997 study. In fact, the biggest change was in the "highly centralized" category, where in 1990, 4.6% of the state systems fell into this level and in 1997 the proportion was found to have increased to 10%. Nevertheless, no significant difference was found in the average centralization index between 1990 and 1997. The difference between the two means was only .0616.

In comparing the centralization indexes for both years for each state, it was determined that the index changed for every state system; some increased and some decreased. The two states that showed the greatest differences were New Jersey and Montana. The centralization index for New Jersey changed from 2.31 in 1990 (moderately decentralized) to 1.62 in 1997 (decentralized). For Montana, the centralization index in 1990 was 2.07 (moderately decentralized) and in 1997 was 1.46 (highly decentralized). The difference in centralization indexes for all other states was not nearly as great as for these two. For all states, change ranged from .69 for New Jersey to .04 for Hawaii, New York, North Carolina, and South Carolina, and the average was .21, compared with the possible centralization index range of 1.00 to 4.07, with a mid-point of 2.54. The mode was .07. Twenty state systems changed more than the average (.21) over the seven-year period between 1990 and 1997.

A significant difference was identified between the average proportions of state funding between 1990 and 1997. The average percentage of state funding for community colleges in 1990 was 60.74. In 1997, the average percentage was 51.42, for a difference of 9.32%. Thus, over this seven-year period, there was a significant decrease in the percentage of state funding (p=.010). The data show, however, that there was not a corresponding increase in the percentage of local funds. So, it is interesting to note that community colleges were being operated with additional funding sources in 1997.

Once again, the data show that the level of funding by funding source determines whether the state or local board controls local campuses. In particular, it was determined that the percentage of state funding was associated with degree of centralization, where the proportion of state funding increases with increases in centralization of governance structures. With a significant decrease in the proportion of state funding identified in 1997, one might expect to find a corresponding decrease in degree of centralization. However, there were no significant differences between centralization indexes. After the 1990 study, Garrett (1993) reported that research had noted shifts in the proportions of state and local funding among state community college systems. Specifically identified was a decrease in the proportion of local funding and an increase in the proportion of state funds. Based on this, it was concluded that there was a trend toward greater centralization of the governance of community college systems in the United States. Data from the 1997 study indicate that neither was the case; there was no decrease in percentage of local funding, nor increase in the percentage of state funding and there was no increase in the centralization index of state community college system governance structures.

Related to the proportions of funding and the degrees of centralization is the type of state-level board that exists and functions in either a "governing" or "coordinating" manner. It seemed reasonable to expect that a governing-type board would administer a centralized system and a coordinating-type board would administer a decentralized governance structure, as found in 1997. It is interesting, though, that this relationship did not appear in 1990.

In summary, there was no trend toward either more centralized or decentralized governance structures among state community college systems in the United States between 1990 and 1997. State systems in 1997 are supported by lower percentages of state dollars, while there was no proportional increase in local funding. There is still, however, a significant relationship between local funding and local control (decentralization) and between state funding and state control (centralization). Lastly, the type of state-level board (Governing or Coordinating) was associated in 1997 with the degree of centralization of state community college system governance structures; though this was different from the 1990 study. Why a significant relationship between type of state-level board and degree of centralization was identified in 1997 and not in 1990 is unknown. If this study had not been replicated, some conclusions could be drawn as was done in 1990, such as whether there is a national trend toward increased centralization or decentralization. However, after replicating the study, conclusions were unfounded. Perhaps the most profound realization was that the proportion of state funding of community colleges had decreased significantly. Of course, whether or not this will be a continuing trend is unknown, but it might be advisable for community colleges to react as if it will be. Now, more than ever before, it can be said that public community colleges have changed from being state-supported to being state-assisted. It would behoove community college leaders to become adept at identifying and procuring external funds in order to survive.

APPENDIX I
DEGREES OF CENTRALIZATION OF GOVERNANCE STRUCTURES OF STATE COMMUNITY COLLEGE SYSTEMS – 1997

State System	Averaged Centralization Index (Centralization Range= 1.00-4.07)	Rank	Degree of Centralization
1. Alabama	3.28	17.5	Cent.
2. Alaska	3.45	9	Cent.
3. Arizona	2.34	29.5	Mod. Decent.
4. Arkansas	2.10	36.5	Mod. Decent
5. California	2.41	28	Mod. Decent.
6. Colorado	3.66	2.5	Highly Cent.
7. Connecticut	3.79	1	Highly Cent.
8. Delaware	3.28	17.5	Cent.
9. Florida	2.25	33	Mod. Decent.
10. Georgia	3.25	19	Cent.
11. Hawaii	3.66	2.5	Highly Cent.
12. Idaho	1.86	42	Decent.
13. Illinois	2.31	32	Mod. Decent.
14. Indiana	3.34	15	Cent.
15. Iowa	2.00	38.5	Decent.
16. Kansas	1.93	40.5	Decent.
17. Kentucky	3.59	4.5	Highly Cent.
18. Louisiana	3.50	6.5	Cent.
19. Maine	3.17	20	Cent.
20. Maryland	1.79	43	Decent.
21. Massachusetts	2.34	29.5	Mod. Decent.
22. Michigan	1.76	44	Decent.
23. Minnesota	3.48	8	Cent.
24. Mississippi	2.00	38.5	Decent.
25. Missouri	1.64	47	Decent.
26. Montana	1.46	49	Highly Decent.
27. Nebraska	1.72	45.5	Decent.

28. Nevada	3.38	12.5	Cent.
29. New Hampshire	3.38	12.5	Cent.
30. New Jersey	1.62	48	Decent.
31. New Mexico	1.93	40.5	Decent.
32. New York	2.21	34.5	Mod. Decent.
33. North Carolina	2.62	25.5	Mod. Cent.
34. North Dakota	3.36	14	Mod. Decent.
35. Ohio	2.21	34.5	Mod. Decent.
36. Oklahoma	2.62	25.5	Mod. Cent.
37. Oregon	2.10	36.5	Mod. Decent.
38. Pennsylvania	1.43	50	Highly Decent.
39. Puerto Rico	3.43	10	Cent.
40. Rhode Island	3.50	6.5	Cent.
41. South Carolina	2.67	24	Mod. Cent.
42. Tennessee	3.59	4.5	Highly Cent.
43. Texas	1.72	45.5	Decent.
44. Utah	2.92	23	Mod. Cent.
45. Vermont	3.32	16	Cent.
46. Virginia	3.41	11	Cent.
47. Washington	2.93	22	Mod. Cent.
48. West Virginia	3.14	21	Cent.
49. Wisconsin	2.32	31	Mod. Decent.
50. Wyoming	2.52	27	Mod. Decent.

APPENDIX II

1997 STATE COMMUNITY COLLEGE SYSTEM DATA

State System (N=50)	% State Funding (N=45)	Rank Order	% Local Funding (N=43)	Rank Order	Years Exist. (N=41)	Rank Order	No. Of Inst. (N=48)	Rank order	Type of Board (N=46)
1. Alabama	49.2	21	0.0	34.5	34	18.5	32	8	Gov.
2. Alaska							1	47.5	Gov.
3. Arizona	24.0	40	59.0	2	37	11.5	19	17.5	Coor.
4. Arkansas							22	14.5	Coor.
5. California	45.0	26.5	50.0	5.5	90	1	106	1	Coor.
6. Colorado	49.0	22	0.0	34.5	32	25.5	16	22	Gov.
7. Connecticut	70.0	10.5	NA		32	25.5	12	31.5	Gov.
8. Delaware	100.0	2	0.0	34.5	31	30.5	4	42.5	Gov.
9. Florida	67.0	12	33.0	12	64	4	28	9.5	Coor.
10. Georgia	75.0	7.5	20.0	16.5	12	39.5	33	6.5	Gov.
11. Hawaii	80.0	6	0.0	34.5	33	22	7	35.5	Gov.
12. Idaho	36.0	32			34	18.5	2	45.5	Coor.
13. Illinois	30.0	36.5	60.0	1	32	25.5	49	4	Coor.
14. Indiana	75.0	7.5			34	18.5	22	14.5	Gov.
15. Iowa	47.0	24	6.5	25	32	25.5	15	25.5	Gov./Coor.
16. Kansas	27.0	38	46.0	7	78	2	19	17.5	Coor.
17. Kentucky	48.0	23	0.0	34.5	35	14.5	14	28.5	Gov.
18. Louisiana			0.0	34.5			6	38.5	NA
19. Maine	54.0	16	0.0	34.5	11	41	7	35.5	Gov.
20. Maryland									Coor.
21. Massachusetts	45.0	26.5	43.0	10	31	30.5	15	25.5	Coor.
22. Michigan	40.0	30.5	30.0	14.5	43	10	28	9.5	Coor.
23. Minnesota	45.0	26.5	0.0	34.5					
24. Mississippi	52.0	19.5	11.0	23	75	3	23	12	Coor.
25. Missouri	35.0	33	34.0	11	NA		12	31.5	Coor.
26. Montana	40-50	26.5	50-60	4	NA		3	44	
27. Nebraska	30.6	35	43.6	9	24	37	13	30	Coor.
28. Nevada	81.0	5	0.0	34.5	26	35	4	42.5	Gov.
29. New Hampshire	40.0	30.5	0.0	34.5	52	5	7	35.5	Gov.
30. New Jersey	22.8	41	30.2	13	35	14.5	19	17.5	Coor.
31. New Mexico	72.0	9	16.0	19	47	8.5	19	17.5	Coor.
32. New York	30.0	36.5	30.0	14.5	49	6.5	36		Gov.
33. N. Carolina	85.0	4	15.0	21	34	18.5	58	3	Gov.
34. N. Dakota	18.5	43	9.0	24	49	6.5	5	40.5	Gov.
35. Ohio					NA		23	12	Coor.
36. Oklahoma	53.0	17.5	18.0	18	NA		15	25.5	Coor.
37. Oregon	55.0	15	45.0	8	47	8.5	17	20	Gov.

1997 STATE COMMUNITY COLLEGE SYSTEM DATA

38. Pennsylvania	33.0	34	18-33	21	34	18.5	15	25.5	NA
39. Puerto Rico	9.6	45	0.0	34.5	31	30.5	6	38.5	Gov.
40. Rhode Island	58.0	14	0.0	34.5	37	11.5	1	47.5	Gov.
41. S. Carolina	53.0	17.5	20.0	16.5	16	38	16	22	Gov.
42. Tennessee	70.0	10.5	0.0	34.5	34	18.5	14	28.5	Gov.
43. Texas	43.0	29	57.0	3	32	25.5	84	2	Coor.
44. Utah	100.0	2	0.0	34.5	28	34	5	40.5	Gov.
45. Vermont	18.0	44	0.0	34.5	36	13	2	45.5	Gov.
46. Virginia	66.0	13	0.0	34.5	31	30.5	23	12	Gov.
47. Washington	100.0	2	0.0	34.5	30	33	33	6.5	Gov.
48. West Virginia	20.0	42	0.0	34.5	25	36	11	33	Gov.
49. Wisconsin	25.0	39	50.0	5.5	32	25.5	16	22	Gov./ Coor.
50. Wyoming	52.0	19.5	15.0	21	12	39.5	7	35.5	Coor.

REFERENCES

Berdahl, R. O. (1971) *Statewide Coordination Of Higher Education.* Washington, DC: American Council on Education.

Garrett, R. L. (1992). Degree of centralization of governance of state community college systems in the United States, 1990. *Community College Review*, 20(1), 7-13.

Garrett, R. L. (1993). A profile of state community college system characteristics and their relationship to degrees of centralization. *Community College Review*, 20(5), 6-15.

Mintzberg. H. (1979). *The Structuring Of Organizations: A Synthesis Of Research.* Englewood Cliffs, NJ: Prentice Hall.

Mintzberg, H. (1983). *Structures In Fives: Designing Effective Organizations.* Englewood Cliffs, NJ: Prentice-Hall.

ECONOMIC DEVELOPMENT IN STATE COMMUNITY COLLEGE SYSTEM

William G. Ingram
Senior Vice President and Chief Instructional Officer
Durham Technical Community College

INTRODUCTION

Virtually since its inception, the public community college has carried out a mission focused on meeting the educational needs of individual students. As early as 1925, Koos articulated a list of "special purposes" for the junior college. That list included (among other purposes) such items as giving "the first two years of curricula in liberal arts and preprofessional and professional work," providing "terminal general education for those who cannot or should not go on to higher levels of training," developing "lines of semiprofessional education," "[popularizing] higher education," and affording "more attention on the individual student" (cited in Diener, 1986).

More recently, Cohen and Brawer (1996) identified five "curricular functions" for public two-year institutions: academic transfer, vocational/technical education, continuing education, remedial education, and community service. These authors further asserted that these five functions were common to all public community colleges. The community service function, as described by Cohen and Brawer, encompasses civic and cultural activities offered or sponsored by institutions as well as short courses, workshops, and seminars. As was the case with Koos, the emphasis of the remaining four functions described by Cohen and Brawer was on the development and improvement of the individual student.

At present, virtually all state community college systems are involved in economic development efforts. This is not surprising, since the traditional mission of the community college includes postsecondary vocational and technical training, which in effect constitute passive economic development efforts. In addition, within the past ten years especially, political leaders in many states have turned to individual community colleges and increasingly to state community college systems to actively participate in such economic development efforts as business and industry recruitment, workforce development and training, small business development, and technology transfer. Melville and Chmura (1991) suggested that, in the mid-1980s, leaders in some states decided to "strategically align" economic development policy with the community college mission. These authors suggested that the flexibility and responsiveness to perceived needs inherent in the community college mission "created a climate of active and innovative service" necessary for successful economic development efforts.

In the 1997-99 period, the editors of this book asked state system leaders to describe the ways in which community colleges in their states were involved in economic development efforts. Thirty-five states responded to that request. This chapter includes a summary of those responses. It is not intended to be an exhaustive catalog of economic development efforts. Rather, it serves as a sampler of programs or services that state community college systems provide to enhance their states' economic activity.

TRADITIONAL EDUCATIONAL PROGRAMS

For the purposes of this chapter, economic development is defined as organized activities intended to promote, sustain, and/or enhance the economic vitality of a locality, region, or state. Using this definition, vocational and technical training initiatives of virtually every community college system are in effect passive economic development efforts. In 1984, the American Association of Community and Junior Colleges recommended that the associate in applied science (A.A.S.) degree be designated as the collegiate credential designed to prepare the individual student "for employment in a specific career." (Ignash, 1998). This recommendation has been broadly adopted across the country. In other words, the holder of the associate in applied science degree is at least ostensibly prepared for a successful and productive career.

The national "Tech-Prep" movement constitutes a more active means of using traditional community college programs for economic development. Intended to mirror the highly successful "College Prep" high school curriculum of the 1960s, "Tech Prep" was specifically designed to prepare high school students to enter technical career fields through the community college. Tech Prep encourages high schools and community colleges to form partnerships where faculty in both types of institutions work together to articulate technical or vocational curricula. All states are engaged in Tech Prep activities.

PARTNERSHIPS WITH BUSINESS AND INDUSTRY

In addition to the technical/vocational portion of their historic mission, many community colleges conduct other activities with the specific intent of enhancing economic vitality. For example, Grubb et al. (1997) suggested that community colleges should carry out economic development activities by fostering business and industry partnerships, facilitating technology transfer to small or medium-sized companies, or providing leadership skills training for business owners or operators. These authors identified environmental scanning and involvement in policy-setting as two other ways in which community colleges foster economic growth. Further, they pointed out that economic development recruiters can and do identify the services offered by a community college when attempting to attract new businesses or industries to a locality.

In virtually all states, community colleges have established or strengthened relationships with businesses and industries. These relationships are becoming increasingly complex and multidimensional. Community colleges frequently include business and industry representatives on advisory boards or councils intended to maintain the currency of vocational or technical programs. This advisory function enables businesses and industries to influence directly the content of diploma or "terminal" associate-degree programs and to ensure that graduates of those programs are exposed to skills that are in demand in the workplace.

Collaborative efforts with businesses or industries benefit the colleges in other ways, as well. Such efforts can result in the availability of state of-the-art equipment for a college (through gift-in-kind donations or lend-lease arrangements) and can provide professional renewal opportunities for college faculty. Another type of business-college relationship is workplace learning activities (such as cooperative education, internships, or apprenticeships). Such programs enable colleges to expand offerings and utilize instructional resources more efficiently and provide students with opportunities to apply theory in workplace settings and in some cases earn money while doing so (Rheams and Saint, 1991).

CUSTOMIZED TRAINING

In addition, community colleges in several states provide customized pre-employment or on-the-job training for businesses or industries. In 1996, the League for Innovation in the Community College and the National Association of Manufacturers reported that more than 96% of over 725 community colleges "provided workforce training for employees of business, government, and labor" (Johnson, 1996).

In North Carolina, for example, customized training may take several forms. In pre-employment training programs, a community college provides training to a group of prospective employees for a business or industry, which hires a subset after the training in completed. "In-plant" programs enable a community college to provide specialized training for a specific employer in the workplace. In special cases, the community college provides training for the employer's human resource development personnel, who then conduct the training program themselves. "Focused industrial training" provides special funds that enable a community college to provide highly specialized skills training for as few as one or two employees. "New and expanding industry" training serves as an incentive for employers to establish or expand work sites by providing them with training programs at little or no cost.

Although the typical customized training program for business or industry is not credit bearing, a number of community colleges also offer associate degree programs in conjunction with business partners or at job sites. In addition to North Carolina, Hawaii, Illinois, Kentucky, Massachusetts, Nebraska, New Hampshire, New Jersey, New Mexico, New York, Rhode Island, South Carolina, Wisconsin, and Wyoming all specifically indicated some form of customized training programs offered through community college systems. Moreover, states such as New Jersey and North Carolina provide skills retraining for workers who are displaced because of layoffs or plant closings.

TECHNOLOGY CENTERS

In many states, community colleges house "advanced technology centers." The specific purposes of these centers vary somewhat by locale. In general, however, their purpose is to bring resources together to support or enhance high-tech businesses or industrial enterprises. Often supported by special public funds or a combination of public and private funds, advanced technology centers enable community colleges to serve as focal points for credit programs, non-credit continuing education, and technology transfer in microelectronics, biotechnology, or other high-tech fields. For example, the Maricopa Community College District in Arizona houses the Maricopa Advanced Technology Center, which supports the semiconductor industry in the Phoenix area. Supported by a grant from the

National Science Foundation, the center includes as partners several semi-conductor manufacturing firms, Arizona State University, local secondary schools, and SEMATECH, "a national consortium of semiconductor businesses", as well as Maricopa Community College District (Messer, 1996). Other states in which community colleges are partners or hosts for technology centers include California, Colorado, Illinois, and New Mexico.

Along similar lines, several states report that community colleges house, host, or sponsor regional training centers. For example, through its community college system, California operates over 100 centers that focus training and educational resources on specific businesses or industries (such as advanced transportation technologies or media and entertainment). The development of these regional centers is often cited as a consequence of a "global" economy. In order to be competitive in such an economy, individual businesses and the communities in which they reside must form partnerships and share resources. Regional centers (whether focused on advanced technologies or not) serve as catalysts for these new business relationships. In addition to California, Maine, New Hampshire, New Jersey, Rhode Island and Virginia all report the establishment or support of regional training centers through their community college systems.

SMALL BUSINESS SERVICES

States such as New Mexico recognize that the majority of economic activity is derived from small business owners or operators. Therefore, community colleges in those states provide a variety of special services to small business owners or operators. Services for small businesses may include traditional courses (for credit or not) or seminars on various facets of operating a small business, specialized assistance in developing or modifying business plans, assistance in seeking financing, and referral to other agencies or entities who provide expertise.

In other states, the small business services remain centered on workforce preparation. For example, the state of Maine focuses resources on the needs of small business owners and operators through the Maine Quality Center Program. In this program, small businesses with similar human resource needs are organized into consortia so that specialized training can be delivered efficiently and effectively. Other states that provide small business services or service to entrepreneurs through their community college systems include Arizona, California, Illinois, New Jersey, North Carolina, and Wisconsin.

POLICY CONSIDERATIONS

States vary in the degree to which policies governing community colleges support economic development activities. In California, for example, the Board of Governors of California Community Colleges includes a standing committee on economic development and vocational education. In other states (such as Colorado and Wyoming), system mission statements include economic development activities. Moreover, some state community college systems (for example, North Carolina and South Carolina) were established primarily to enhance economic development (Tollefson, 1998).

Similarly, funding for economic development activities in state systems varies widely. In some states (such as Virginia) noncredit instruction at community colleges is not supported by state appropriations. As a result, businesses or industries that desire skills training for the workforce pay direct (and in some cases indirect) costs for that training. In other states, non-credit instruction is subsidized by tax dollars. Thus, in North Carolina, for example, enrollees in certain courses established to serve the business community are counted for funding purposes. In states such as South Carolina, special funds are set aside for economic development activities in two-year colleges. Such special funding is also provided in Arizona, Maine, and Nebraska.

CONCLUSIONS

Clearly, the expansion of the community college mission to include economic development activities is a national trend. However, it is not without controversy. For example, as reported in *The Chronicle of Higher Education* (1998, May 1) the Louisiana legislature recently acted to consolidate 46 existing technical and community colleges and four planned community colleges into a single "Technical and Community College System." Considerable debate continues over the purpose of this system. Supporters of the system point out the economic development benefits of the planned system and propose that the business community take an active role in the system's development. Others, however, fear that the new system will "relegate the community college to a vo-tech, trade-school classification" (Healy, p. A40). These critics are concerned that the system's economic development focus will divert resources and attention from more traditional educational programs such as transfer to four-year institutions.

The traditional mission of the comprehensive community college has emphasized service to individual students. In this tradition, colleges view their success in terms of the numbers of students who enroll, transfer, and graduate. The institution is student-centered. However, with the inclusion of economic development in the community college mission, the emphasis on programs or services shifts away from the student and to a business, an industry, or another employer. The success of the institution is measured in more complicated terms: the number of workers trained or the number of jobs created, the number of businesses attracted to a community, or the number of successful small business ventures initiated as a result of community college efforts.

In the higher education community, two-year colleges are at times criticized for attempting to be all things to all people. Indeed, the comprehensive mission of the community college is just that—comprehensive. As state leaders turn to community colleges to take on even more responsibilities in addition to those roles identified by Koos and restated by Cohen and Brawer, it is important that they bear in mind that community colleges will require adequate support to carry out those responsibilities well. While part of that support should be financial, a more important type of support is political in nature. Policy makers should provide a clarity of mission for community colleges in their states to enable them to do what is asked of them in serving all their constituents—both individuals and corporate entities.

REFERENCES

Cohen, A. M. and Brawer F.B. (1996) *The American Community College* (third edition). San Fransisco: Jossey-Bass.

Grubb, W.N. et al. (1997). *Workforce, Economic, and Community Development: The Changing Landscape of the Entrepreneurial Community College*. Mission Viejo, Ca: League for Innovation in the Community College.

Healy, P. (1998, May 1). Louisiana plans to meld 50 campuses into a coherent 2-year college system. *The Chronicle of Higher Education*. p. A40.

Ignash, J. (1998). Result of an investigation of state policies for the A.A.S. degree. In *Workplace*. 9(4). National Council for Occupational Education. pp. 1-20.

Johnson, L., Ed. (1996). *Common Ground: Exemplary Community College and Corporate Partnerships*. Mission Viejo, Ca: League for Innovation in the Community College.

Koos, L.V. (1925). The junior college movement. In Diener, T. (1986): *Growth of an American Invention: A Documentary History of the Community and Junior College Movement*. Westport, Ct.: Greenwood Press.

Melville, J.G. and Chmura, T.J. (1991). Strategic alignment of community colleges and state economic policy. In Waddell, G., Ed., *Economic and Workforce Development*. San Francisco, CA. Jossey-Bass.

Messer, J. (1996). Maricopa advanced technology education center to begin with aid of $4.5 million national science grant. In *Workplace*, 7(3). National Council for Occupational Education.

Rheams, P. and Saint, F. (1991). Renovating Cooperative Education Programs. In Waddell, G. (Ed.), *Economic and Workforce Development*. San Francisco, CA: Jossey-Bass. p. 50.

Tollefson, T.A. (1998). *The Expanding Mission of Economic Development in American Community Colleges*. Los Angeles, CA: ERIC Clearinghouse for Community Colleges.

MISSION, GOVERNANCE, FUNDING AND ACCOUNTABILITY TRENDS IN STATE SYSTEMS OF COMMUNITY COLLEGES

Terrence A. Tollefson
Professor, Department of Educational Leadership and Policy Analysis
East Tennessee State University

MISSION

From approximately 1900 to 1999, two generic public two-year post-secondary institutions have gradually converged. The public *junior colleges* that were established between 1900 and 1920 generally emphasized courses providing the first two years of traditional baccalaureate programs. For the next 20 years, public junior colleges characteristically shifted their emphasis toward so-called "terminal" programs that provided either entry-level vocational education or "general" education for improving health and citizenship (Frye, 1992). *Postsecondary vocational-technical institutes or colleges* in many states gradually added college-transfer programs, often only after being legislatively merged into two-year state systems of comprehensive community and technical colleges (Cox, Franklin, Howell, Lancaster, Oswald & Nespoli; in Tollefson, Garrett & Ingram, 1999).

The typical mission of the public community college has expanded in most states in the latter half of the 20th century to include associate-degree programs designed to lead *both* to immediate employment *and* to transfer to baccalaureate programs at four-year institutions, remedial/developmental education, noncredit continuing education, community service programs, financial and geographic access to equalize educational opportunity, special assistance for mentally and physically handicapped students, and, more recently, workforce and economic development (Breneman & Nelson, 1981; Brint & Karabel, 1989; Campbell, in Hoffman & Julias, 1994; Cross, 1981, in Diener, 1986; Frye, 1992; Ingram, 1999; Thornburg, 1988; Tollefson, 1994; Tollefson, 1998a).

The expanded missions of state systems of comprehensive community colleges have not been legislatively authorized—or funded—without long and arduous struggles, both within local, state and national community college and governmental leadership circles, and between community college leaders and leaders of other public and private educational sectors (Breneman & Nelson, 1981; Brint & Karabel, 1989; Finifter, Baldwin & Thelin, 1991; Vaughan & Associates, 1983).

Burton Clark (1978, in Altbach & Berdahl, 1981) concluded:

…There came into being a community college philosophy and a commitment to it, notably in the form of a "movement." Some leaders even became zealots, true believers, glassy eyes and all. Around the commitment, they developed strong interest groups with political muscle. Today, no one's patsy, they have a turf, the willingness and ability to defend it, and the drive and skill to explore such unoccupied territory as recurrent education and lifelong learning to see how much they can annex. When did we last hear about a state college movement? (pp. 323-324).

GOVERNANCE/COORDINATION

Lee Myers (in Tollefson, Garrett & Ingram, 1999) in his chapter on Pennsylvania's community colleges states:

Pennsylvania does not have a community college *system*. The fourteen community colleges and one technical institute, all organized under the Community College Act of 1963, operate as virtually independent, although publicly supported, institutions, responsible mainly to their communities and their "local sponsor" (p. 365).

One definition of a system is "a coordinated body of methods or a complex plan of procedures: *"a system of government"* (Webster's, 1996, p. 1444). By this definition, Pennsylvania, South Dakota and, at various times in recent years, several other states with decentralized or highly decentralized control could be said to lack state systems of community colleges. If the accepted definition of a community college is an institution whose highest degree awarded is an associate degree (Cohen & Brawer, 1996), then a number of states, including Georgia, Ohio, Pennsylvania, Texas, West Virginia and Wisconsin, each have two or even more state community college systems (See Barron & Heckman; Chin; Hudson; Myers; Skidmore, Smith; and Walton; in Tollefson, Garrett & Ingram, 1999).

The first nationwide classification of state-level governance and coordination of public junior and community colleges that I have found was

Martorana's 1963 study. Martorana reported that public junior colleges had been established in 38 states, and that state boards or agencies for elementary and secondary education provided state-level oversight in 26 of those states. He also said that 12 of the 38 states had no state-level coordinating agencies for junior colleges, 12 other states regulated junior colleges by state boards of higher education or state university boards, and that only six states had separate state-level coordinating and/or governing boards exclusively for junior colleges. That was a total of 44 boards in 26 states, as some states had more than one state-level coordinating board with overlapping jurisdictions (Martorana, in American Council on Education, 1963).

Robert Berdahl published his landmark book, *Statewide Coordination of Higher Education*, in 1971. He devised four categories for statewide coordination of senior public institutions of higher education, as follows: (I) states that had neither single statutory agencies nor any voluntary organizations that provided statewide coordination, (II) states with somewhat formal, voluntary coordination, (III) states with statewide coordinating boards that did not replace institutional governing boards, and (IV) states with single statewide governing boards. He reported that there were two states with neither state agencies nor voluntary associations, two with voluntary coordination, 27 with state-level coordinating boards, and 19 with "consolidated" governing boards (Berdahl, 1971). One implication of Berdahl's classification is that state-level coordination and governance are labels for different parts of the same continuum, with governance connoting more state control than coordination. That notion guides this report as well.

A 1989 classification of public community college state-level coordinating boards found that all states but South Dakota had public community colleges and state systems for coordinating them. In that study, Tollefson and Fountain (1992) compared their 1989 categorizations with those of Martorana in 1963. Their 1989 study found one state with no state-level coordinating board (South Dakota), seven states that coordinated community colleges through state boards and departments of education, 21 states with statewide boards of regents or boards of higher education, and 22 with separate state boards for community colleges.

As of late 1997, (See Tollefson, 1998b), the following five models of state-level coordination/governance of community colleges represented a large range of degrees of state control:

State Board of Education: Alabama, Idaho, Iowa, Kansas, Michigan, Oregon, and Pennsylvania. State boards of education generally exercise little control over community colleges, and they usually provide coordination in states with individual college boards of trustees.

State Higher Education Board or Commission: Arkansas, Maryland, Massachusetts, Missouri, Montana, Nebraska, New Jersey, New Mexico, New York (SUNY), Ohio, Pennsylvania and Texas. Several states have higher education boards or commissions, as well as local governing boards. Such boards or commissions often have degree/program approval and budget submission/recommendation authority.

Statewide Community College Coordinating Board: California, Colorado (for local district colleges), Florida, Michigan, Mississippi, New Hampshire, North Carolina, Oregon, South Carolina, Washington, Wisconsin, and Wyoming. These boards typically exercise moderate control primarily over budgets and programs.

State Community College Governing Board: Colorado (for state system colleges), Delaware, Kentucky, Maine and Minnesota. These governing boards hire and fire presidents, faculty and staff; hold title to land, buildings and equipment; and establish all policies for the state system.

State Board of Regents: Alaska, Georgia, Hawaii, Louisiana, Montana, Nevada, North Dakota, Rhode Island, Tennessee, Vermont, West Virginia and Puerto Rico. These boards typically are totally responsible for governing state universities, as well as community colleges.

Within the past two years, new state community college governing boards have been established by the legislatures in Kentucky, New Hampshire and Louisiana (Mayes; DuBois & Tollefson; and Tollefson; in Tollefson, Garrett & Ingram, 1999).

Several observations about the current status or recent changes should be made at this point.

First, South Dakota does have a number of two-year postsecondary technical institutes that fulfill community college functions and award associate degrees (See Keating, in Tollefson, Garrett & Ingram, 1999).

Second, several states have voluntary community college *associations* that perform state-level coordinating, and, in New Jersey, governance functions in funding (Oswald & Nespoli; in Tollefson, Garrett & Ingram, 1999). Other states with community college associations that are active in statewide coordination include Arkansas, Nebraska, New Mexico, and Pennsylvania (Franklin; Howell; Myers; and Renz; in Tollefson, Garrett & Ingram, 1999). All of these states are categorized by Garrett (in Tollefson, Garrett, & Ingram, 1999) as having either decentralized or highly decentralized state-level governance structures for community colleges. It appears that in some states, community college associations that perform voluntary coordinating functions have emerged in response to the need for better representation before the state executive and legislative branches of government. More research on this topic is needed to be conclusive.

A third observation is that the long-term trend of consolidating both state coordination/ governance of junior colleges emphasizing the first two years of baccalaureate programs and comprehensive community colleges, with postsecondary vocational-technical institutes or colleges has continued. In recent years, Connecticut, Arkansas and Minnesota have exemplified that trend, and Indiana is in the process. Only Georgia has a policy of maintaining two separate two-year systems, one academic and one vocational-technical, that appears to be durable for the foreseeable future (Cox; Franklin, Hudson, Tollefson, and Walton; in Tollefson, Garrett & Ingram, 1999).

Fourth, the trend toward increasing state centralization of control over community colleges has continued (See Tollefson & Fountain, 1992; and Tollefson, 1994).

FUNDING

State appropriations throughout the U.S. for community college operations increased 15.5%, from $6.96 billion in fiscal 1994-95 to $8.04 billion in fiscal 1996-97. California's half-a-billion-dollar, 44% two-year increase was by far the highest in absolute terms, but Oregon's 82% increase was proportionally the greatest increase. Community colleges actually lost state appropriations in current dollars in that same period in Alabama, Maryland and New York (Hines, E.R & Higham, J.R., III, 1997). Other states may have lost state appropriations in constant dollars (adjusted downward in recent years to adjust for inflation). Year-to-year variations in state funding for community colleges should not be over-emphasized, because idiosyncrasies in state economic cycles, as well as personal views of governors and key legislators, can obscure long-term trends. Much emphasis is given in this book to the role of community colleges in statewide economic and workforce development. Indeed, several state agencies for community colleges have added economic or workforce development to their names (West; and Keating; in Tollefson, Garrett & Ingram, 1999). There appears to be some evidence, though not conclusive, that state community college systems that successfully emphasize economic and workforce development are becoming better funded than their counterparts in other states that relegate economic and workforce development to minor roles. (Tollefson, 1998b).

Garrett found a decline in the average state share of community college operational support, from 60% in 1990 to 50.5% in 1997, with no corresponding increase in local funding. Tuition and fees and "other" (including private funds raised) increased. Garrett's conclusion, which I share, is that community college leaders need to become more effective at private fundraising (Garrett, in Tollefson, Garrett & Ingram, 1999).

Many early public junior colleges in California and elsewhere charged no tuition to residents of their districts (Witt, et al., 1994). By 1967, the national average tuition in public junior and community colleges was about $250 per year (Gleazer, E. J. & Houts, P. L., Eds, 1967). By 1968, only 18% of public junior and community colleges still did not charge any tuition, and most of these institutions were in California (Witt, et al., 1994). By 1992, in the aftermath of voter approval of Proposition 13, which dramatically reduced local property taxes, the California community colleges were required to charge at least five dollars per credit hour (Myers, in Fountain & Tollefson, 1989). By 1972, Thornton (cited in Witt et al., 1994) concluded that increased tuition costs were causing serious problems for poor students. By 1988-89, the national average annual tuition and fees at public two-year institutions was not quite $800. In the 1980 to 1990 period, tuition and fees for all types of postsecondary institutions rose at about double the rate of economic inflation (Hauptman, 1990).

From 1989-90 to 1996-97, the national average public community college tuition and fees rose from $758 to $1,283, a total increase of 69.3%. Public four-year institutions' average tuition and fees similarly climbed 67.6%, in the same period, from $1,781 to $2,986. Private four-year tuition and fees also increased in that time by 52.9%, from $8,446 to $12,920. Total average costs of tuition and fees, room and board, books, and transportation for commuter students in each of four types of institutions increases as follows:

Academic Year	Public 2-Year	Public 4-Year	Private 2-Year	Private 4-Year
1990-91	$4,654	$5,594	$8,214	$12,175
1991-92	4,913	6,036	9,006	13,893
1992-93	5,282	6,473	9,444	14,621
1993-94	5,372	6,809	10,190	15,200
1994-95	5,639	7,154	11,013	16,070
1995-96	5,752	7,449	10,835	16,910
Total Percentage Increase	23.6%	33.2%	31.9%	28.4%

Source: The nation, in *Chronicle of Higher Education Almanac Issues* for 1991, 1992, 1993, 1994, 1995, 1996 and 1998.

According to a national survey by the American Council on Education in July of 1996, the average public cost estimates of annual tuition and fees were $6,275 for public community colleges (compared with an actual cost of $1,194), $9,599 for public universities (compared with $2,982 actual cost), $13,824 for private liberal arts colleges (compared with $10,698 actual cost, and $20,410 for large private universities (compared with $14,510 actual cost) (Cvancara, 1996). The estimated-to-actual ratios were 5.3 to 1 for community colleges, 3.2 to 1 for public universities, 1.3 for private liberal arts colleges, and 1.4 for large private universities. Clearly, community college leaders in particular need to develop ways to communicate their relatively low actual costs much more effectively if they are to avoid scaring many potential low-income students away. The increasing availability of federally financed student aid for community college students also needs to be widely publicized.

ACCOUNTABILITY

Accountability is a term that has been increasingly used for community colleges, higher education, and state-funded organizations generally. As of 1997, 38 states used "performance measures" in higher education, and six others reported plans to do so. The three most commonly used performance measures were graduation rates, transfer rates, and faculty workload information. More than 40% of all states used performance measures in higher education budgeting, but the typical proportion of the budget represented by such "performance" based budgeting was from one-half of one percent to four percent. The exception was South Carolina, which was mandated to base 100% of the higher education budget on performance measures by the year 2000 (Christal, M. 1997, August 21-23). Tennessee, in 1999, provides performance funding up to 5.45% of total community college operating budgets (Phillips-Madson & Malo; in Tollefson, Garrett & Ingram, 1999).

REFERENCES

General References

Berdahl, R. O. (1971). *Statewide Coordination of Higher Education.* Washington, DC: American Council on Education.

Breneman, D. W. & Nelson, S. C. (1981). *Financing Public Community Colleges: An Economic Perspective.* Washington, DC: The Brookings Institution.

Brint, S. & Karabel, J. (1989). *The Diverted Dream: Community Colleges and the Promise of Educational Opportunity in America, 1900-1985.* New York, NY: Oxford University Press.

Campbell, D. F., in Hoffman, A. M. & Julius, D. J., Eds. *Managing Community and Junior Colleges: Perspectives for the Next Century.* Washington, D.C.: College and University Personnel Association.

Christal, J. (1997, August 21-23). *Preliminary Results from the SHEEO State Survey on Performance Measures.* Denver, CO: State Higher Education Executive Officers.

Clark, B. (1978), in Altbach, P. G. & Berdahl, R. O. (1981). *Higher Education in American Society,* Revised Edition. Buffalo, NY: Prometheus Books.

Cohen, A. M. & Brawer, F. B. (1996). *The American Community College,* Third Ed. San Francisco, CA: Jossey-Bass.

Cross, K. P. (1981). Where are the visions of the future?, in Diener, T. C. (1986). *Growth of An American Invention: A Documentary History of the Junior and Community college Movement.* New York, NY: Greenwood Press.

Cvancara, K. J., (1996, October 8). College is affordable, in *Community College Times* 8(19), pp. 1, 16.

Finifter, D. H.; Baldwin, R. G. & Thelin, J. R. (1991). *The Uneasy Public Policy Triangle in Higher Education.* New York, NY: American Council on Education.

Frye, J. H. (1992). *The Vision of the Public Junior College, 1900-1940: Professional Goals and Popular Aspirations* Westport, CT: Greenwood Press.

Fountain, B. E. & Tollefson, T. A. (1989). *Community Colleges in the United States: Forty-Nine State Systems.* Washington, DC: American Association of Community and Junior Colleges.

Hauptman, A. M. (1990). *The College Tuition Spiral.* Washington, DC: American Council on Education.

Hines, E. R. & Higham, J. R., III (1997, March). *State Higher Education Appropriations 1996-97.* Denver, CO: State Higher Education Executive Officers.

Martorana, S. V. (1963). The legal status of American public junior colleges. In *American Junior Colleges.* Washington, DC: American Council on Education.

Mayes, L. D. (1995). Measuring community college effectiveness: The Tennessee model. *Community College Review,* 23(1), pp. 13-22.

The nation, in *Chronicle of Higher Education Almanac Issues* for 1991, August 28; 1992, August 26; 1993, August 25; 1994, September 1; 1995, September 1; 1996, September 2; and 1998, August 28.

Thornburg, L. S. (1988). *A Comparative Analysis of Funding Priorities of Selected Community College Policy Makers and Administrators.* Unpublished doctoral dissertation, Raleigh, NC: North Carolina State University.

Tollefson, T. A. (1994). The evolution of state systems of community colleges in the United States, in Baker, G. A., III; Dudziak, J.; and Tyler, P., Eds. A *Handbook on the Community College in America: Its History, Mission and Management,* pp. 74-81. Westport, CT: Greenwood Press.

Tollefson, T. A. (1998a, April 24). The evolving community college mission in the context of state governance. Paper presented at the annual meeting of the Council of Universities and Colleges, Miami Beach, Florida.

Tollefson, T. A. (1998b, July 8). State-level governance and coordination of community colleges. Paper presented at the annual meeting of the Education Commission of the States, Portland, Oregon.

Tollefson, T. A. & Fountain, B. E. (1992, January-March). A quarter century of change in state-level coordinating structures for community colleges. *Community/Junior College Quarterly of Research and*

Practice, 16(1), pp. 9-14.

Tollefson, T.A. & Patton, M. (1998), The states, in *AACC Annual 1998-99*. Washington, DC: American Association of Community Colleges.

Vaughan, G. B. & Associates (1983). *Issues for Community College Leaders in a New Era*. San Francisco, CA: Jossey-Bass.

Webster's Encyclopedic Dictionary of the English Language (1996). New York, NY: Gramercy Press.

Witt, A. W.; Wattenbarger, J. L.; Gollatscheck, J. F. & Suppiger, J. E. (1994). *America's First Community Colleges: The First Century*. Washington, DC: American Association of Community Colleges.

References to Chapters in:

Tollefson, T. A.; Garrett, R. L. & Ingram, W. G. (1999), *Fifty State Systems of Community Colleges: Mission, Governance, Funding and Accountability*. Johnson City, TN: Overmountain Press:

Barron, G. O. & Heckman, L.; Texas.

Chin, E.; Wisconsin.

Cox, M. A. B.; Connecticut.

DuBois, G. & Tollefson, T. A.; New Hampshire.

Franklin, E. L.; Arkansas.

Garrett, R. L.; Degrees of centralization of governance structures in state community college systems.

Howell, S. J.; Nebraska.

Hudson, C. M.; Georgia community colleges.

Ingram, W. G.; The expanding role of community colleges in economic development.

Mayes, L. D.; Kentucky.

Myers, L. W.; Pennsylvania.

Oswald, J. M. & Nespoli, L. A.; New Jersey.

Phillips-Madson, L. & Malo, G.; Tennessee.

Renz, F. J.; New Mexico.

Skidmore, J. L.; West Virginia.

Tollefson, T. A.; Louisiana.

Walton, B. B.; Georgia technical institutes.

ALABAMA

Fred Gainous, Chancellor
Alabama Department of Postsecondary Education

OVERVIEW

The Alabama College System, consisting of public two-year community, junior, and technical colleges and an upper-division college, seeks to provide accessible quality educational opportunities, promote economic growth, and enhance the quality of life for the people of Alabama. The Alabama College System is comprised of nineteen community, nine technical and two junior colleges. Athens State University, the system's upper division university, the Alabama Industrial Development Training Institute (AIDT) and the Alabama Fire College are also among the system's many educational resources serving Alabama residents.

The Alabama College System was created in May, 1963, largely through the leadership of Governor George C. Wallace, who wanted to enhance the quality of life in Alabama by making postsecondary education accessible, affordable and responsive to the needs of Alabamians. Governance was placed with the Alabama State Board of Education and administrative responsibilities assigned to the state superintendent of education. The first organizational structure consisted of the Division of Research and Higher Education within the Alabama State Department of Education. Later, the administration of the two-year colleges was divided into junior and technical college branches, when the Division of Vocational and Higher Education was created. In recognition of the impact, growth and importance of the two-year college system, the state superintendent created a separate postsecondary division in 1976. At that time, all postsecondary education-oriented sections relating to two-year colleges were merged into one division, which became known as the Division of Postsecondary Education. On May 4, 1982, the Alabama Legislature enacted Act No. 82-486, which created the Alabama Department of Postsecondary Education and made it directly responsible to the Alabama State Board of Education. That Act provided the state board of education with the authority to appoint a chancellor to serve as the chief executive officer for the board, to assist the board in carrying out its responsibilities relating to the operation and management of two-year colleges. The chancellor is also the chief executive officer of the Alabama Department of Postsecondary Education. Dr. Howard Gundy served as chancellor from July, 1982 until his retirement in October, 1983. In December, 1983, Charles Payne became chancellor. Dr. Fred Gainous succeeded Mr. Payne, and has served as chancellor since March 12, 1988.

GOVERNANCE

The Alabama State Board of Education is composed of the governor, who serves as president, and eight other members who are elected from districts across the state. One of the members is elected by the board membership as vice president. Board members serve for four years. No more than one-half of the board members are elected during any given general election. They are qualified electors of the state of Alabama, and each member must be a resident of the district represented.

The Alabama State Board of Education, upon the recommendation of the chancellor, is authorized to perform the following functions: make rules and regulations for the governance of each college; prescribe the courses of study to be offered and the conditions for granting certificates, diplomas, and/or degrees; appoint the president, who is to serve at the pleasure of the board; direct and supervise the expenditure of legislative appropriations of each college; prescribe qualifications for faculty and establish a salary schedule and tenure requirements for faculty at each college; accept gifts, donations, and devises and bequests of money and real and personal property for the benefit of the system or any one of the colleges; and disseminate information concerning, and promote interest in the system among citizens of Alabama.

As chief executive officer of the Alabama College System, the chancellor is authorized to perform the following functions: execute, enforce and interpret the rules and regulations of the board governing the colleges; administer the office of the chancellor and appoint to positions of employment such professional, clerical, and other assistants on a full-time or part-time basis as may be needed to assist the chancellor in performing the duties of office; have the authority to take any and all actions necessary and proper to administer policies, rules and regulations of the board in carrying out its responsibility for the management and operation of the colleges; prepare and submit for approval and adoption an annual report to the board on the activities of the Alabama Department of Postsecondary Education; prepare and submit for approval by the board a budget; and prepare and submit for approval and adoption by the board the legislative matters that are needed for the further development and improvement of the Alabama College System.

FUNDING

The primary funding sources in fiscal year 1997-98 for the Alabama college system and the percent of total revenue from each source are listed as follows:

State Funds	48.3%
Tuition and Fees	21.2%
Auxiliary Revenues	5.9%
Federal Funds	21.3%
Other	3.3%

The Alabama College System receives approximately 21% of the state funds available to higher education in any given budget. There is no budgetary formula used in generating amounts for each college. The state of Alabama uses an incremental budgeting system; thus, each individual institution receives a proportionate share of available funds based on the prior year's allocation. In fiscal year 1997-98, the Alabama College System's state appropriation totaled $196,848,828. In that same year, tuition and fees totaled $92,220,443.

The state of Alabama does not have a cyclical capital funding process. Thus, there is no capital outlay budget within the state's education budget. The Alabama State Board of Education is authorized to issue general revenue bonds to fund capital projects on behalf of an individual college. Prior to board approval, each institution must demonstrate its capability of repaying the incurred indebtedness with institutional funds. The Alabama State Board of Education has no funds available to assist a college in terminating indebtedness. Occasionally, the state of Alabama issues bonds. However, state-sponsored bond issues have been very sporadic. In those instances, the state is responsible for the debt service.

PROGRAMS AND ENROLLMENTS

The Alabama College System provides the first two years of the university transfer programs as well as a full range of developmental, occupational, technical, and vocational programs. Special programs for industry training, personal enrichment, and continuing education are provided also. The colleges are the exclusive deliverers of educational services to the adults in Alabama's correctional facilities. Community and junior colleges offer associate in arts (A.A.) and associate in science (A.S.) degrees as university transfer programs. These institutions also offer associate in applied science (A.A.S.) degrees in occupational fields. Technical colleges and technical divisions within community colleges award associate in applied technology (A.A.T.) degrees. Community and technical colleges also offer short-term (less than 40 semester credit hours) and long-term certificate programs and diplomas in many technical fields.

The following is an enrollment summary for the Alabama College System for the fall term of academic year 1998-99.

	Credit Instruction	Non-Credit Instruction	Total Instruction
Headcouant	73,345	12,238	85,883
Full-time Equivalent	48,842	2,619	51,461

Typically, the percentages of credit-hour production in the major program categories in any given year are as follows:

Academic	51.0%
Occupational	42.0%
Remedial	7.0%

ECONOMIC DEVELOPMENT

The Alabama Industrial Development Training Institute's (AIDT) mission is to provide quality workforce development for Alabama's new and existing industry, and to expand the opportunities of its citizens through the jobs these industries create.

Instruction can be conducted in a company's plant, at one of AIDT's three training centers located strategically throughout the state, at leased facilities, or in one of more than 30 mobile training units that can be trucked to plant sites. All of these locations, including the mobile units, can be customized with the equipment and training materials needed to meet any company's needs for classroom and hands on training.

AIDT's services are available to any new or existing manufacturer that creates jobs through expansion or location of a plant in Alabama. Other programs, including management and supervisory training, ISO 9000, and business process re-engineering and technology transfer, may be made available to existing companies striving to remain competitive in today's global economy.

Workforce 21 is Alabama's long-range strategic plan for career/technical education. The strategic plan was developed with input from more than 600 stakeholders representing business, industry, education, labor, parents, students, community organizations and government.

Through regional and state meetings, focus groups, and position papers, stakeholders identified five "imperatives" with corresponding strategies and performance indicators for Alabama's career/technical education system. The imperatives and strategies were identified based on stakeholders' experience and knowledge and on economic, demographic, social, and political trends impacting education.

The imperatives require that the state's career/technical education system:

- Ensure that students attain the skills and knowledge they will need in the future workplace and for continued learning;
- Expand options for students to achieve career and education goals;
- Anticipate and respond quickly to changes in the workplace and in society;
- Continuously improve the quality of curriculum and instruction;
- Demonstrate accountability.

Examples of actions that will result from Workforce 21 are:

- Industry certification of programs and instructors;
- Leadership development for instructors and administrators;
- Comprehensive, systematic professional development;
- "One-stop" approach to assessment, counseling, linkage, training, and follow-up;
- Credentialing document for program completers;
- New instructor orientation;
- Long-term funding strategies for programs and equipment;
- State-wide public relations campaign;
- Instructor externships in industry;
- Work Keys academic, technological and employability competency assessments;
- Technical competency assessments;
- Competency-based curricula;
- Equipment upgrades;
- Articulation between secondary and postsecondary programs;

- Annual performance report to legislature and public;
- Computer literacy and employability skills in all programs;
- Computer networked campuses;
- Applied academics;
- Mentorships;
- Apprenticeships;
- Responsive, flexible programming;
- Guarantee of program completer skills;
- Effective completer/leaver follow up; and
- Shared facilities and equipment among secondary and postsecondary education and industry.

ACCOUNTABILITY

In order to ensure accountability, the Alabama State Board of Education has put the following accountability measures in place;

- Each college in The Alabama College System must communicate to public school superintendents of the districts in its service area aggregate placement/assessment examination results for the graduates of the school districts in order to improve articulation between the high schools and college;
- The instructional programs of each college undergo an instructional review at least once every five years, and more often if the effectiveness or efficiency of the program is impaired. The instructional program review for the colleges includes the following levels: Level I: A statistical review of pre-determined indices as defined by the chancellor is completed by the Alabama Department of Postsecondary Education and distributed to the colleges on an annual basis. Level II: A qualitative review of each instructional program is conducted by each college during a five-year cycle. Individual instructional program reviews may be required more frequently if warranted by the result of the Level I review or the impaired effectiveness or efficiency of the program. The chancellor provides each college with minimum standards for review, as well as appropriate procedures and forms on which to submit the findings of the review. Level III: A system-wide review of a specific instructional program or programs shall be initiated by the chancellor predicated upon the findings of instructional program reviews at Levels I and II. The chancellor may, however, use other factors to determine the need for a Level III instructional program review. This instructional pro-

gram review is conducted according to procedures as defined by the chancellor;

- Each college has developed and implemented an evaluation system whereby each instructor and staff member is evaluated at least annually by a supervisor with appropriate education and experience. Individual written records are maintained;
- Each college of the system has developed a three-year institutional management plan, which must be periodically up-dated. The institutional management plans have the following components: (1) new program development; (2) accreditation; (3) schedule of instructional program review; (4) inactive programs; (5) instructional equipment; (6) library holdings; (7) student services; (8) public relations; (9) economic development: (10) management information; (11) personnel; (12) acquisition, construction and modification projects; (13) deferred maintenance; (14) non-instructional equipment; (15) financial; (16) administration; (17) exemplary programs, services and projects; (18) summary of instructional program reviews; (19) outcomes assessment/institutional effectiveness. The chancellor reports to each college a summary evaluation of each college's institutional management plan; and
- Each college is required to provide placement services to help graduates and early leavers find employment and/or to enroll for further education. In order to determine instructional improvement needs, the colleges conduct follow-up evaluations of the performance of graduates. Each college is required to submit placement and follow-up data on an annual basis as determined by the chancellor.

In May, 1997, the Alabama State Board of Education appointed a task force to develop recommendations to guide the system's development and direction as it re-engineers itself to enhance services to its constituents. The recommendations of the task force, the Workforce Investment Act of 1998 and other changes in federal legislation, and the need for a skilled workforce statewide have all converged to serve as catalysts for change. The board's task force recommendations clearly parallel the Workforce Investment Act of 1998. That act allows the board to bring together the existing patchwork of fragmented and duplicative workforce training programs into a workforce development system for a new era of global competition. The new system unites postsecondary career technical training, adult education, the JTPA structure, the employment service structure, rehabilitation services, welfare services and other service providers with business and industry.

The board, by coordinating the task force recommendations with the Workforce Investment Act, will increase the employment, retention, and earnings of Alabama's workforce. It will improve the quality of the state's workforce, reduce welfare dependency, and enhance the productivity and competitiveness of the state.

FOR ADDITIONAL INFORMATION, PLEASE CONTACT:
Office of the Chancellor
Alabama Department of Postsecondary Education
401 Adams Avenue
Montgomery, AL 36130-2130
Telephone: (334) 242-2900

ALASKA

Robert L. Miller
Director, University of Alaska Public Affairs
and
Terrence A. Tollefson
Professor, Department of Educational Leadership and Policy Analysis
East Tennessee State University

OVERVIEW

Prince William Sound Community College is one of four institutions in the University of Alaska system. The other three are the University of Alaska Anchorage, the University of Alaska Fairbanks, and the University of Alaska Southeast, in Juneau. Each institution is accredited separately by the Northwest Association of Schools and Colleges. All four are open-admission institutions that fulfill a community college mission of providing academic (college-transfer), vocational-technical, developmental and community service programs. All three universities also offer upper-division baccalaureate and graduate programs. Nine branch campuses and several education centers in rural Alaska locations also provide programs leading to certificates, associate degrees, and, in a few locations, bachelor's and graduate degrees as well (Myers, in Tollefson & Fountain, 1992).

The Alaska Agricultural College and School of Mines was founded in 1917 as a land-grant institution. The legislature changed its name to the University of Alaska in 1935. Between 1954 and 1978, community colleges were established in Anchorage, Ketchikan, Juneau, Palmer, Sitka, Soldotna, Kodiak, Bethel, Fairbanks, Nome,Valdez and Kotzebue. In 1977, the University of Alaska Anchorage was founded, and in 1980 the University of Alaska Juneau was founded by merging Southeastern Senior College and Juneau-Douglas Community College. Each community college and university was required to be regionally accredited individually.

A rural education division was established to develop and provide both distance education and on-site courses in areas without access to community colleges. A process of decentralizing the university administration reached the point in 1982 that a chancellor was appointed to head each university campus (in Anchorage, Fairbanks and Juneau), the Division of Community Colleges, Rural Education, Extension, and Anchorage Community college (as an independent institution). In 1986, North Slope Borough and The University of Alaska Fairbanks collaborated to establish a college in Barrow that is now named Arctic Sivernnum Ilisagvic College. It provides both vocational and college-transfer programs. In response to an enormous decrease in state funding, the Alaska Board of Regents in 1987 merged 13 individually accredited postsecondary institutions into three multi-campus universities. Prince William Sound Community College retained its independent status because of a significant local funding commitment. The other community colleges became university branch campuses (Myers, in Tollefson & Fountain, 1992).

GOVERNANCE

The University of Alaska Board of Regents is an 11-person board that requires one full-time student to be a member. The governor appoints the student to a two-year term and the other 10 members to staggered eight-year terms. Appointments must be confirmed by the state legislature. The board of regents usually meets seven times per year. Its powers and duties include appointing a president, approving educational programs, adopting budget requests, and developing broad university system policies (Myers, in Tollefson & Fountain, 1992).

PROGRAMS

The University of Alaska system provides a comprehensive array of community college programs and services, including vocational, technical college transfer, developmental, job training partnership (JTPA), adult basic education (ABE), high school equivalency (GED) and other remedial instruction (Myers, in Tollefson & Fountain, 1992).

ENROLLMENT

Total headcount enrollment in the University of Alaska system has declined about 5 percent from 68,765 in the fall of 1993 to 65,476 in the fall of 1997. The "community college" proportion of those totals remained nearly constant, at about 48%. In the fall of 1997, 67.6% of the total systemwide student credit hours were in lower-division courses, and 3.4% were in developmental courses (Alaska Board of Regents, 1998).

FUNDING

The university receives financial assistance for both operations and designated capital improvements through appropriations by the state legislature. Appropriations to the university are for two types; operating and capital. Operating appropriations authorize expenditure of all current revenues and lapse at the end of the fiscal year. State-funded current revenues at this time include state general funds as well as funds from the Mental Health Trust Authority and the Alaska Science and Technology Foundation. Supplemental appropriations amend current-year appropriations of the prior legislative session. Capital appropriations are generally for facilities, equipment or specified projects, and have expiration dates beyond the end of the fiscal year. The greatest share of funding support comes from elsewhere in the system for services provided; interest income; dormitory, food, and auxiliary services; student tuition and fees; indirect cost recovery; and university receipts, which include city/borough appropriations. Prince William Sound Community College in Valdez maintained its community college status because of substantial community support (Miller, R., personal communication, 1999).

The Alaska Board of Regents has approved tuition rates for academic years 2000 and 2001 with no increases except for the Higher Education Price Index (HEPI) inflation adjustment of 3.1 percent for both years. Lower-division tuition rates will be $75 per credit hour in 2000 and $77 in 2001. Upper-division rates will be $84 per credit hour in 2000 and $87 in 2001; graduate charges will be $167 in 2000 and $172 in 2001; the nonresident surcharge will be $159 in 2000 and $164 in 2001. The consolidated fee was eliminated three years ago (Miller, R., personal communication, 1999).

REFERENCES

Myers, N., Alaska, in Tollefson, T. A. & Fountain, B. E. (1992). *Forty-Nine State Systems, 1992 Edition*, Washington, D.C.: American Association of Community Colleges.

University of Alaska, Office of Public Affairs, *UA in Review*, 1998, Fairbanks, Alaska: Author.

FOR ADDITIONAL INFORMATION, PLEASE CONTACT:
President Mark R. Hamilton
University of Alaska Statewide System
202 Butrovich Building
910 Yukon Drive

Fairbanks, AK 99775
Telephone: (907) 474-7311
Fax: (907) 474-7570
E-mail: sypres@alaska.edu

ARIZONA

Donald E. Puyear
Executive Director
and
Pete Gonzalez
Associate Executive Director for Community and
Governmental Relations
State Board of Directors for Community Colleges of Arizona

OVERVIEW

The philosophy of the Arizona community college system is a reflection of the purpose of a free democratic society: government of, by and for the people. This can be best achieved by an educated populace so that all may exercise intelligently and morally the rights, privileges and duties of self-government. This entails the affirmation that each individual has worth and dignity, must be afforded an opportunity to develop skills and talents, and must share the responsibilities of providing educational services with the community.

Further, the philosophy recognizes that education is a vital lifelong process that—like the society to which it responds—is never static nor completely realized. Education in a democratic society aims to equip all members with the knowledge and techniques necessary for coping with the economic, social and political dynamics affecting not only the individual but also the community.

It is therefore appropriate that the individual, the community and the state should share the financing and governance of the community college system. At the district level, fiscal and educational policy can be determined by local needs. At the state level, it is imperative to establish standards, and to assess and coordinate needs and services in the best interest of the state.

Because the communities in Arizona differ widely in demographic, economic and geographical characteristics, the community colleges of Arizona must be permitted relative autonomy and a variety of curricula. But each community college must be committed to the following general objectives:

1. To offer the first two years of baccalaureate—parallel or preprofessional courses of the highest quality, so that students enrolled in

transfer programs may complete study for the baccalaureate in four-year colleges and universities.

2. To provide occupational programs in technical, vocational and paraprofessional fields leading to an associate degree or a certificate, and to provide retraining and upgrading of skills in these fields, so that students enrolled in occupational programs are qualified to meet current needs of the labor market.

3. To provide appropriate general education for all citizens, so that they may performtheir personal and professional roles more effectively, and exercise their obligations and privileges as citizens more intelligently.

4. To offer programs in continuing education for those who wish to improve professional skills, acquire new ones, or expand their fields of knowledge and general interest.

5. To provide sound academic and occupational counseling, including job placement services, so that students may learn to define their goals clearly and pursue them realistically.

6. To provide cultural and community service programs for the enrichment of the community, and to encourage the use of community college facilities and services by all citizens of the community for educational and cultural purposes.

Finally, a democratic society prizes and values individual differences. The role of the community college is to encourage men and women of all ages to develop their skills and talents differently, each according to abilities and interests, so that collectively they contribute to the continuum of democracy (State Board of Directors for Community Colleges in Arizona, 1976, October 23).

History

In 1958, the Arizona Legislature appropriated funds to survey the higher education needs of the state. A year later, the study committee charged with this survey recommended the establishment of a state junior college system to assist the universities and state colleges in providing educational opportunities to the ever-growing Arizona population. Accordingly, in 1960, the legislature created the State Board of Directors for Junior Colleges and enacted legislation to create junior college districts supported by county and state funds.

Key leaders involved in the origination and development of the community college system were State Senator E. Blodwin Thode, who sponsored the enabling legislation; Governor Paul Fannin; and State Representatives Arthur B. Schellenberg, Thomas M. Knoles, Jr., and Polly Rosenbaum. Other influential leaders of that era included President Paul E. Guitteau of Eastern Arizona College, State Senator John Mickelson of Graham County, Executive Director John F. Prince (the first full-time executive director of the state board), and President Robert J. Hannelly of Phoenix College.

In 1962, two colleges, Eastern Arizona College and Phoenix College, were the first institutions to join the newly-created Junior College System. These community colleges have existed in Arizona since the 1920s. In fact, one, Eastern Arizona College, actually began as a private church-related institution in the 1880s. Another, Phoenix College, began in 1920 as part of the Phoenix Union High School district.

At the present time, there are ten community college districts with 19 community colleges.

GOVERNANCE

The community colleges in Arizona are governed at both the statewide level and the local district level. The State Board of Directors for Community Colleges of Arizona sets standards for establishing, developing, administering, operating, and accrediting community colleges in Arizona. The State Board oversees a system composed of 10 community college districts which provide educational services to all fifteen counties in the state. The State Board membership as defined in state law consists of fifteen members, one member from each county, appointed by the Governor and confirmed by the Arizona State Senate for a seven-year term. In addition, a representative from the Arizona Board of Regents and the Superintendent of Public Instruction or the superintendent's designee serve as members of the State Board.

The Executive Director is the chief executive officer as appointed by the State Board. At the present time, the State Board office has thirteen full-time staff members.

Each of the ten community college districts are governed by locally elected district governing board members who serve for a period of six years. There are five members elected to each of the ten district governing boards. The district boards manage the colleges, hire employees, set salaries, ensure quality instructional programs, and prepare district budgets. The respective powers and duties of the State Board and local dis-

trict boards are illustrated in the following matrix.
State Board And District Board Statutory Powers

General:
State Board
- Enact ordinances for the governance of the colleges under its jurisdiction. (§15-1425.1)
- Set standards for the establishment, development, administration, operation, and accreditation of colleges. (§15-1425.2)
- Approve intergovernmental agreements for providing service to unorganized counties. (§15-1470)
- File an Annual Report with the Governor. (§15-1427)
- Approve petitions to form a district. (§15-1403.C)

District Board
- Visit and examine college management, conditions, and needs. (§15.1444.A.3)
- Maintain colleges at least eight months per year. (§15-1444.A.1)

Academic and Student Services:
State Board
- Establish curricula and courses. (§15-1425.6)
- Set qualifications for student admission. (§15-1425.8, §15-1821)
- Fix student tuition and fees. (§15-1424.7, §15-1425.5)
- Approve offerings in unorganized counties. (§15-1470)
- With the State Board of Vocational & Technological Education, oversee vocational standards, planning, and funding priorities. (§15-1425.9-13)
- Determine open entry, open exit academic classes. (§15-1425.15)
- Adopt rules regarding the offering of credit courses outside a college district, including distance learning courses. (§15-1429)

District Boards
- Enforce the courses of study prescribed by the State Board. (§15-1444.A.2)
- Exclude partisan, sectarian, and denominational materials. (§15-1444.A.4)
- Award degrees, certificates, and diplomas. (§15-1444.A.8)

- Evaluate vocational education programs every five years, in the manner prescribed by the State Board. (§15-1447)

Personnel:
State Board
- Certify college faculty. (§15-1425.3 and 4)

District Board
- Determine salaries, and employ or remove staff when warranted. (§15-1444.A.5, 6 and 7)
- May participate in district health insurance plans. (§15-1450)
- May enter into multi-year employment contracts with chancellors, vice-chancellors, and presidents not to exceed five years. (§15-1444.A.5)

Finance:
State Board
- With the Auditor General, establish a uniform accounting system. (§15-1428)
- Contract with any person and establish regulations and limitations for contracting by districts. (§15-1424.4)
- Authorize district General Obligation bond elections. (§15-1465)
- Authorize revenue bonds. (§15-1482)
- Submit estimated number of full-time equivalent students to the economic estimates commission annually. (§15-1425.14)
- Allocate state aid to districts pursuant to Law. (§15-1467)
- Accept grants and donations. (§15-1424.J)

District Board
- Lease or sell personal property. (§15-1444.A.10)
- Contract, subject to regulations and limitations prescribed by the State Board. (§15-1444.B.3)
- Adopt annual budgets, and direct respective Boards of Supervisors to levy required property taxes. (§15-1461 and 1462)

Facilities:
State Board
- Determine location of college campuses. (§15-1424.C)
- Purchase, receive, hold, lease, or sell real property. (§15-1424.C and D)

- Adopt rules regarding minor construction and repair projects by districts without prior approval of the state board. (§15-1424.B.6)
- Approve major construction, remodeling, and repair projects. (§15-1424.C)
- Approve district rules concerning parking and control of vehicles. (§15-1449)

District Board
- Insure college buildings. (§15-1444.A.11)
- Accomplish minor construction or remodeling projects ($50,000 or less - adjusted annually for inflation.) (§15-1444.B.4 and 15-1424.B.6 and K)
- Lease-purchase real property upon authorization of the State Board. (§15-1444.B.2)
- Adopt rules for the control of parking and vehicles, subject to State Board approval. (§15-1449.A)

In 1992, the legislature passed Senate Bill 1454, Chapter 40, which removed the requirement that a community college district governing board enforce the use of textbooks prescribed by the State Board. This bill also removed the requirement that a community college district governing board obtain the State Board's consent to authorize, through an election, expenditures in excess of the district expenditure limitation.

Senate Bill 1080, Chapter 167, in 1993 required an educational institution wanting to use the term "community college" must be under the jurisdiction of the State Board of Directors for Community Colleges. The bill removed the Director of the Vocational and Technological Education from the membership of the State Board.

In 1996, the legislature passed House Bill 2439, Chapter 341, which established the Postsecondary Education Voucher Pilot Program to be administered by the Commission for Postsecondary Education. The bill requires the Commission to select up to 60 students per year who have obtained an associate's degree from an Arizona community college on or after July 1, 1996 to receive a tuition voucher of up to $1,500 annually for up to two years when enrolled full-time in a baccalaureate program at a private four year college or university in the state.

In addition, House Bill 2002, Chapter 1, Fifth Special Session 1996, called for an appropriation of $1.1 million to the State Board for technology assisted learning. The sum of $100,000 is for a one-time grant to design a statewide plan for interconnecting and consolidating community college, university and K-12 telecommunication video systems, voice and data and to tie individual community college districts' electronic delivery systems together. The remaining one million dollars is to be allocated by the State Board to college districts with priority to service in rural areas. This has resulted in the creation of Arizona Learning Systems (ALS). ALS is an alliance of Arizona's urban and rural community colleges whose purpose is to provide learner-centered education environments that build on the unique advantages that technology affords the learning process.

In 1996, House Bill 2472, was vetoed by the governor. The bill sought to transfer the ownership of community college buildings from the state to the community college district. The Governor's veto message stated he was concerned about a number of unanswered questions. "Primarily, it appears that no research has been done on the potential costs to local districts of transferring to them ownership of state property of sizable value."

Senate Bill 1109 was introduced in 1997 to address the concern of the limited access rural residents have to higher education. A provision included in this legislation permitted community colleges to offer courses beyond the two year level or to offer baccalaureate degrees. The bill was vetoed and a study committee was created and charged to ". . . determine unmet higher education baccalaureate needs, identify options, and develop specific recommendations for meeting these needs." A report from the study committee is due before the legislature reconvenes in January 1998.

Laws 1998, Chapter 6, House Bill 2192, extended the State Board of Directors for Community Colleges of Arizona for another ten years. This legislation was based on the recommendation of the Arizona Auditor General's Performance Audit of 1997.

Laws 1998, Chapter 129, House Bill 2505, authorized a $500,000 appropriation in fiscal year 1998-1999 and $500,000 for fiscal year 1999-2000 to the State Board for the purpose of establishing a community college campus in Benson, Arizona. This campus would be within the boundaries of Cochise County Community College District in the southeastern part of Arizona.

In the appropriations bill was found an appropriation of $300,000 to the State Board for use in support of transfer articulation activities.

The 1999 legislative session produced the following:

House Bill 2289—This legislation requires the State Board, on behalf of the ten community college districts, to include additional amounts for capital outlay in its budget submission. These requests are in addition to the current statutory formula for capital outlay state aid.

In addition, the legislation permits community college district governing boards to enter into employment contracts with chancellors, vice-chancellors, and presidents for a duration of more than one year but not more than five years.

The bill was signed by the Governor on May 13, 1999.

House Bill 2436— Authorizes community college districts to provide courses and services outside district boundaries.

Current statute grants general contracting authority to community college district (districts) under the rules adopted by the State Board of Directors for community colleges. In addition, statute grants specific authority to districts to enter into contracts to provide extension course work in counties that are without a community college district of their own. Currently, four counties (Apache, Gila, Greenlee and Santa Cruz) are without a district of their own. Known as "unorganized" counties, these four counties are served by existing community college districts through this statutory provision.

In addition to the ability to serve unorganized counties, HB 2436 grants a more general authority to districts to allow them to offer courses and services outside district boundaries. Specifies that courses and services offered must be in accordance with rules adopted by the State Board of Directors for Community Colleges.

The bill was amended to include language found in HB 2437 (provisional community college districts). HB 2437 is an effort to provide an opportunity to residents of Apache, Gila, Greenlee and Santa Cruz counties to decide whether a provisional community college district should be formed in their respective counties.

The Governor signed this legislation into law on May 19, 1999.

Senate Bill 1137— Appropriates $3,000,000 in FY 2000 the state general fund to the State Board of Directors for Community Colleges for community college district operations.

SB 1137 was signed into law by the Governor on May 19, 1999.

FUNDING

Source Of Funds

The major sources of funds in support of operating community colleges are:

Primary Tax Levy   *Tuition & Fees*

Formula State Aid   *Cash Balances*

Equalization Aid

How are these sources of revenue determined?

Primary tax levies are limited by the Arizona Constitution. The amount of revenue raised each year can increase by 2% over the preceding year, plus the amount raised by taxing new construction added to the tax roles.

Formula state aid for operations is specified by law. It is calculated by taking the prior year's appropriation for each district and adjusting it for the growth in full-time-equivalent students for the two most recent audited fiscal periods. In 1992, House Bill 2346, Chapter 345, implemented this new formula and the bill eliminated the three-tiered system of state aid which distributed a different per capita amount to districts depending on the number of enrolled FTSE. HB 2346 allows each community college district to use up to 20 percent of its total capital outlay aid appropriation for operating aid purposes or to use up to 20 percent of its operating aid for capital outlay purposes.

Equalization state aid is distinct and separate from formula state aid, and is appropriated to districts (five currently) that do not have enough assessed valuation to support a community college district. The minimum assessed value currently required to form a community college district is $564.3 million. Districts with less than that amount qualify for equalization state aid.

Tuition/registration fees, and all other charges to students, are set by the State Board, based upon the recommendation of local boards.

Cash balances carried forward each year, represent the excess of income over expenditures to that point in time. They are derived primarily from residual tuition and fee revenues.

Disposition of Funds

The amount of funds expended by community colleges is limited by the Arizona Constitution. The limitation, as calculated by the Arizona Department of Revenue-Economic Estimates Commission, is based upon expenditure levels in 1979-80, and is adjusted by the cumulative effects of enrollment growth and inflation, compounded to the current year.

Funding and expenditures for Arizona's community colleges in Fiscal Year 1997-1998 came from the following sources and for the following purposes:

DISTRICT SOURCES OF FUNDS		DISTRICT EXPENDITURES	
Fund Balance	$145,395,797	General Fund Expenditures	$411,385,330
District Tax Levy	$286,451,852	Capital Outlay Plant Fund	$111,441,270
State Aid	$118,263,690	Bond & Debt Redemption	$79,526,279
Tuition & Fees	$85,933,116	Bond & Debt Interest	$16,846,106
Contracts & Grants	$5,101,147	Total	$619,198,985
Tranfers & Other Revenues	$88,402,684		
Less Future Acquisition	($83,913,056)		
Total	$645,635,230		

ENROLLMENT

Arizona Community Colleges — Facts-At-A-Glance 1997-98

Enrollment FY 1997-1998			Enrollment By Ethnic or Race Group	Fall 1997	
Annual Full-Time Student Equivalent	85,1168		Non-Resident Alien	1,659	(1.1%)
Annual Unduplicatd Headcout	299,246		Black, non Hispanic	5,386	(3.5%)
Fall 1997 Headcount (credit)	155,689		American Indian or Alaskan Native	6.082	(3.9%)
Enrollment by Gender	Fall 1997		Asian or Pacific Islander	4,135	(2.7%)
Female	88,747	(57.0%)	Hispanic	27,637	(17.8%)
Male	64,819	(41.6%)	White, Non-Hispanic	102,878	(66.1%)
Undeclared	2,123	(1.4%)	Race/Ethnicity Unknown	7.922	(5.1%)
Total	155,689	(100.0%)	Total	155,689	(100.0%)
Enrollment Time or Part-Time	Fall 1997		Instructional Staff	Fall 1997	
Full-Time	36,023	(23.1%)	Full-Time Instructors	1,879	(23.7%)
Part-Time	119,666	(76.9)	Part-Time Instructors	6,054	(76.3%)
Total	155,689	(100.0%)	Total Faculty	7,933	(100.0%)

Headcount enrollments by age in the fall of 1997 were: 23.1% below 20 years of age; 24.1% between 20 and 24 years of age; 13.1% between 25 and 29 years of age; 17.6% between 30 and 39 years of age; 12.1% between 40 and 49 years of age; 8.5% over the age of 50, and 1.5% undeclared.

Over 71,035 students were enrolled in noncredit classes during FY 1997-98. In fall 1997, 40,890 students were enrolled in off-campus programs in 480 different locations.

In FY 1997-98, 3,026 academic degrees were awarded; 2,451 occupational degrees were awarded; and 1,019 other types of degrees were awarded in Arizona's community colleges. In addition, 8,774 certificates were awarded as follows: 1-15 hours (4,264), 16-30 hours (3,175), 31-45 hours (1,267) and 46 hours and over (68).

Tuition and fee charges for the FY 1997-1998 ranged from $652 to

$1,110 for 30 hours of study. Each of the ten community college districts has a different tuition rate as determined by the local district governing board and approved by the State Board.

In the fall of 1997, a total of 97,998 students were reported as continuing and/or returning students. In addition, 48,958 were first-time students, and 26,676 were higher education transfers.

Current Initiatives

To continue in the implementation of the Arizona Learning Systems in order to deliver quality distance and technology-assisted learning that integrates the services of community colleges with those of public education and other segments of higher education

To continue working with the legislature and policy leaders on examining the potential need for baccalaureate degrees at the community college level. This effort will continue through the Higher Education Study Committee

To continue monitoring the agreements focusing on Transfer/Articulation between community colleges and universities

To examine state funding of Arizona's Community Colleges with the assistance of the ten community college districts

To work with counties without community college districts to ensure the citizens of those counties are receiving the necessary community college services in their regions

To continue meeting and presenting the demonstrated needs of Arizona's Community Colleges to the Governor's Office and Legislature

FOR ADDITIONAL INFORMATION, PLEASE CONTACT:
State Board of Directors for Community Colleges of Arizona
3225 North Central Avenue, Suite 1220
Phoenix, AZ 85012-2411
Telephone: (602) 255-4037
Fax: (602) 279-3464
Web site address: <http://www.stbd.cc.az.us>

ARKANSAS

Edward L. Franklin
Executive Director, Arkansas Association of Two-Year Colleges

OVERVIEW

Arkansas has 23 two-year institutions. Of these, 12 are community colleges, which means that they have local taxes in addition to state revenue to support them, and they are governed by either an elected board or an appointed board. Three of the community colleges are part of the University of Arkansas system. Eight of the two-year colleges are technical colleges and have local boards appointed by the governor. Some have a sales tax in addition to state revenue. There are three additional campuses that are affiliated with Arkansas State University.

While there are three different categories of two-year campuses, all function as comprehensive community colleges. The mission of the two-year colleges is:

> Each college is a comprehensive two-year college dedicated primarily to meeting the educational needs of its service area. Each college offers a comprehensive education program including, but without limitation, technical occupational programs, speciality courses, continuing education courses, and business and industry training to meet the needs of the emerging and existing workforce.
>
> Each college is a student-centered college focusing on meeting the learning needs of the student through strong counseling, guidance, and comprehensive support services to meet the needs of all students including first generation, older, and traditional college-age students. Part-time and full-time students are valued equally.

In 1991, legislation changed 14 former vocational-technical schools to technical colleges. Eight have remained technical colleges while six have become community colleges or have merged with existing institutions. All 14 have received full accreditation by the North Central Association of Colleges and Schools and have experienced phenomenal growth in enrollments since becoming two-year colleges. The addition of these 14 colleges has created a geographically distributed statewide system of two-year colleges providing access to higher education throughout the state.

GOVERNANCE

At the state level, Arkansas has a single coordinating agency and board, the Arkansas Department of Higher Education (ADHE) and the Arkansas Higher Education Coordinating Board (AHECB). This agency and board works with all state institutions of higher education.

Legislation was passed in 1997 that changed the Arkansas State Board of Higher Education to the Arkansas Higher Education Coordinating Board. The composition of the board changed from 13 members to 12 members, each appointed for 10 year terms by the governor. Of those 12 members, three must have had experience on a four-year college board and three must have had experience on a two-year college board. The remaining six members are selected from business, industry, education, agriculturally-related industry, and medical services. At least one of these six must have a strong interest and commitment to economic and workforce development. The coordinating board selects its own officers and nominates the director, who is confirmed by the governor. A change in the 1997 legislation requires that the director have campus-based experience and that the nomination process should have input from the presidents and chancellors of all of the public colleges and universities in the state.

The state board meets quarterly and has other special meetings as necessary. As part of the 1997 legislation, an executive committee of the presidents and chancellors was created. This committee meets monthly and is composed of four two-year college presidents or chancellors and four presidents or chancellors from four-year colleges. The meetings are co-chaired by a two-year and a four-year representative. All items to go before the coordinating board are brought to the executive committee prior to being acted on by the coordinating board. While all presidents and chancellors can attend each monthly meeting, at least once a quarter a meeting is called for input from all presidents and chancellors. This committee provides input for all agenda items to go before the coordinating board and is used as a forum for issue development and discussion by the staff of ADHE. These new changes in the board and the provision of impact from the campuses through the executive committee have created a better working relationship with ADHE, the coordinating board, and the presidents and chancellors. This new structure allows input similar to the New Jersey governance structure, but leaves the ultimate coordinating authority to the appointed board of lay members.

Since half of the coordinating board members have had experience at the campus level by having served on a local college or university boards, there seems to be a much better understanding of local and statewide higher education issues than is typically experienced by an appointed lay board. This board experience, plus the executive committee of presidents and chancellors, has resulted in a more cooperative and less adversarial relationship than existed with the past board structure and may provide a model for replication in other states.

The Arkansas Department of Higher Education is a small agency of 35 employees. The responsibilities of the department are primarily coordinating responsibilities. The department recommends a single higher education budget with recommendations for each institution. The budget includes general operating as well as capital improvement and facility maintenance recommendations for each year of the biennial budget. The department operates several financial aid programs and makes recommendations for funding of state run scholarships.

In addition, ADHE has responsibility for reviewing proposed new programs and existing programs, maintaining a comprehensive data system and performing regular data analysis. The director, who is part of the governor's cabinet, is also responsible for carrying out, interpreting, and communicating the policy of the executive branch while maintaining close ties and gathering input from the legislative branch and the presidents and chancellors.

On the institutional level, each is governed by a board of trustees. For those colleges that are branches or part of a university system, they are governed by the same board that governs the university or the system. Community college boards are elected from their taxing district and technical college boards are appointed from the service area of the college by the governor. These boards have rule-making and policy authority and must approve programs prior to submission to the Arkansas Higher Education Coordinating Board.

A new entity on the scene was the expansion of the Arkansas Association of Two-Year Colleges (AATYC) by the hiring of an executive director and other staff. The Association has the following goals: 1) To provide information about the value and impact of the two-year colleges to the citizens of Arkansas. 2) To provide staff development opportunities to faculty and staff of two-year colleges, which would assist in constantly improving the quality of education. 3) To work with business and industry to provide partnerships with colleges, which will positively impact the economy of Arkansas. 4) To be a liaison with the various governmental and educational agencies, so that Arkansans will receive the highest quality two-year education and services possible.

The association has helped educate legislators about the role of two-year colleges in Arkansas. In addition, there have been numerous staff development activities and shareshops established.

The additional consortiums have been created through AATYC. These consortiums have been formed as divisions of AATYC. The first is the WorkForce Training Consortium (WFTC). This consortium was established to assist colleges in better meeting the needs of business and industry in their community. The consortium allows the sharing of people and training resources among the colleges thus serving each business through statewide shared resources that have expanded each colleges' local ability to meet every business's need for training of the existing workforce. This consortium was named one of the ten best workforce training programs by the 1999 Community College FUTURES Assembly.

The second consortium set up by AATYC is called ACCESS Arkansas which stands for "Access to College Courses for Every Student Statewide". This is a consortium that allows the colleges to share resources in developing and delivering Internet-based education programs.

FUNDING

A new formula for funding was developed for this legislative session (1999). The formula for higher education was divided into two different formulas. One formula for four-year institutions and one for two-year institutions. On a state level, 60% of the new general revenue dollars are to go to four-year colleges and 40% of the new dollars are to go to two-year colleges.

The portion of the formula for two-year colleges was developed by presidents and chancellors in conjunction with ADHE staff and subsequently was approved by the AHECB. The formula includes three categories: equity, FTE funding, and productivity funding. The formula assumes that all institutions keep their base funding , and thus the formula deals with the distribution of any new monies. Intrastate equity was given a high priority since the institutions that were established in 1991 are growing in enrollment faster than their financial support. By examining state subsidy per FTE, it was decided that 50% of new dollars would be distributed to seven colleges to raise their state subsidy per FTE, and to narrow the range between colleges. An additional 40% of new dollars would be distributed by FTE thus helping the faster growing institutions keep from falling further behind in state support. The last 10% of the formula was set aside for productivity. At this writing, the formula has not been approved by the legislature.

Funding for two-year colleges was substantially increased in the 1997 legislative session. Of a total of 47 million new general revenue dollars appropriated, almost 32 million went to the two-year colleges to assist in meeting growth needs and to help develop the infrastructure of the colleges. Total state funding for the last year of the 1997-1999 biennium for two-year colleges was $121.2 million. Tuition and revenues made up another 31,201,000 dollars or 20.5% of the revenue of the colleges.

An additional impact for all colleges and universities that helped the two-year colleges was the approval as part of the 1995 legislative session for the sale of college savings bonds to be used for construction of new buildings. The two-year colleges received $55.5 million over the last four years from this pool. This money plus $11.5 million capital improvement funds over the last biennium from the state and some grants from the Reynolds foundation have contributed to an expanded building and remodeling program on every campus. These buildings were needed to meet the expanding student body and for the updating of technology programs. In addition, some colleges have raised additional monies from local sales taxes.

Tuition and fees are determined by institutional governing boards. The standard tuition and fees for 1997-1999 ranged from $768 to $2,244 for in-state students. Out-of-state tuition and fees ranged from $1,140 to $4,214.

PROGRAMS AND ENROLLMENT

All of the two-year colleges are comprehensive colleges and offer A.A., A.S., and A.A.S. degrees. New degree programs are first approved by institutional boards and are then submitted to the AHECB.

Enrollment has been increasing dramatically since the expansion of the community and technical college system in 1991. Over the past five years, credit headcount enrollments at two-year colleges have increased by 40% to over 39,000 students, or slightly less than 40% of the total number of students in public higher education. These numbers are expected to rise as these new two-year colleges build capacity and more people recognize the access that they provide to higher education. Arkansas has the lowest percentage of population over the age of 25 with bachelors degree in the United States. In addition, Arkansas has 25% fewer persons enrolled in higher education than do the three states of similar population, which include Iowa, Kansas, and Mississippi.

Many Arkansans have not had an opportunity to attend a two-year college throughout the state in the past. Now they have that opportunity through their local two-year colleges. As technology demands more education and as people throughout the state continue to recognize the educational opportunities close to home, credit enrollments are projected continue to increase to between 55,000 and 60,000 students. This could mean another 50% growth in the next 5-7 years.

The ACCESS Arkansas distance learning initiative mentioned earlier will bring additional students to the system. The goal is to have all the core courses for an AA degree available through Internet-based courses by January of 2000. The model that is being used is unique to Arkansas. In most distance learning models, each college develops courses and then the student has to take classes from the college which developed the course or another model that is all courses are offered through a centralized electronic college. The ACCESS Arkansas model helps all of the colleges to work together to develop courses or lease courses. Through this model, the students are enrolled at their local two-year college and take the course from that college. It is believed that this model will produce a higher retention rate than most distance learning models. This model also allows the state to use fewer resources by colleges jointly leasing or developing courses that are shared. Workshops are being conducted to help instructors in developing their own courses. A standard course development software has been chosen which will allow instructors to share development techniques. This standard software will also mean that all courses will have the same look to students. A centralized server linked directly to the state backbone provides faster access and a central place for courses to reside.

An additional program that will be having a statewide impact is the partnership that has been established with Cisco. The Cisco company is a manufacturer of routers and switches for local area networks. The two-year colleges are partnering with Cisco to provide seven regional academies throughout the state. These seven regional academies will provide training for over 70 local academies at two-year colleges and high schools throughout the state. These local academies will be training students to work with switches and routers at businesses throughout the state, and high school students will be able to establish and manage networks at their own high school.

ECONOMIC DEVELOPMENT

The two-year colleges have been heavily involved with workforce development in the state. As was mentioned earlier, the 23 two-year colleges through AATYC have formed the WorkForce Training Consortium (WFTC) to share resources and meet the training needs of the existing workforce in the state. During 1997-1998, the two-year colleges provided non credit training to over 29,000 persons and provided credit training to another 8,000 existing workers. These workers represented over 50 companies which is a 55 percent increase over 1996-1997.

The colleges have been working closely with the Existing Workforce Training Program (EWTP) of the Arkansas Department of Economic Development (ADED). In fact, over 50% of all EWTP training was provided by the two-year colleges. The colleges through the WFTC continue to work closely with ADED and new legislation was passed in 1999 that allows a tax incentive for companies that will help pay for retraining workers.

The WFTC also has been working closely with the Arkansas State Chamber of Commerce, the Arkansas Hospitality Association, and the Arkansas Manufacturers Association to meet training needs through the development of common curriculums. The colleges have developed a common curriculum for workforce readiness and hospitality management and are currently working on a industrial maintenance curriculum. By colleges working together and working directly to obtain business input, curriculums are being developed that are available to every college in the state.

The colleges have refocused their mission statements to reflect this commitment to training of the existing, emerging, and transitional workforce. A workbook has been developed that lists all the customized training resources and capabilities of each college as well as the businesses with which they have worked. A website has also been established at http://www.access-ar.org/wftc.

Legislation has been passed to meet the federal mandates of the Workforce Investment Act, Welfare to Work, Adult Education, and Carl Perkins.

The commitment of two-year colleges and their actions over the last biennium have provided impetus for the colleges to be included as major partners for the implementation of this legislation in Arkansas.

ACCOUNTABILITY

Statewide productivity was eliminated from funding during the 1997 legislative session, after having been established in the 1995 session.

A committee of presidents and chancellors developed a formula for productivity that was recommended and approved by the AHECB. The formula involves four elements including student goal attainment, completion of developmental courses, completion of enrolled courses, and expansion of workforce training in the community.

Funding for this productivity formula was recommended at 10% of new monies. At this writing, it is not known if the productivity formula will be recommended or funded.

FOR ADDITIONAL INFORMATION, PLEASE CONTACT:
Office of the Director
Arkansas Department of Higher Education
114 East Capitol Avenue
Little Rock, AR 72201
Telephone: (501) 371-2000
Fax: (501) 371-2001
or
Dr. Edward L. Franklin
Executive Director
Arkansas Association of Two-Year Colleges
114 East Capitol Avenue
Little Rock, AR 72201
Telephone: (501) 371-2014

CALIFORNIA

Dorothy M. Knoell
California Postsecondary Education Commission (Retired)

OVERVIEW

Community colleges in California date back to the early 1890s, having been established by local governing boards of unified school districts, as extensions of the high school into grades 13 and 14. As such, they were regulated by the State Board of Education, under state statutes governing the public schools, and overseen by the State Superintendent of Instruction and his or her staff. In 1960 they were declared to be an integral part of the state's partite system of higher education, as part of its Master Plan encouraged but did not require the colleges to form their own districts, separate from unified school districts, with their own locally elected boards of trustees.

Still, it was not until 1968 that the colleges were removed by statute from the jurisdiction of the State Board of Education and placed under a new state Board of Governors for the California Community Colleges, whose members are appointed by the governor and confirmed by the Senate. However, they have not become a true "system of colleges" because of a strong insistence on autonomy and local control in most areas of operations. This insistence has continued, even in the face of the colleges' increased dependence on the State General Fund for their income which occurred after income from local property taxes was severely reduced following voter approval of Proposition 13 in 1978. Legislation enacted into statute in 1988 (Assembly Bill 1725) was designed to focus on the colleges as a system by strengthening and expanding the role of the Board of Governors in giving statewide leadership and direction. At the same time, this statute created a "shared governance" model for both the state and the districts, and has led to the formation of a state-level "consultation council," with representation from the major community college organizations.

The 106 colleges are currently organized into 71 community college

Editor's Note: The author requested our note to emphasize that this chapter is more than a year out of date in the spring of 1999.

districts. The chief executive officers of the districts are called chancellors/superintendent; the colleges CCO's are called presidents, except in single-college districts where they are also chancellors/ superintendents. Twenty districts have more than one accredited college, with one district having a total of nine. Most colleges have one or more off-campus centers, many of which operate in permanent facilities, are approved by the state board, and in some instances are evolving into comprehensive colleges within their districts.

The colleges' mission is broad and continues to expand as new and pressing state and local needs emerge, particularly in the area of workforce training and economic development. They offer associate degree and certificate programs, together with non-credit adult education, community service courses and programs, and, increasingly, contract education with business and industry. Their overall mission includes general education, lower-division coursework for transfer to baccalaureate degree-granting institutions, vocational/technical education, remediation, basic skills acquisition and English as a second language, continuing education for adults, and economic development. They also offer strong support services for students in need. Admission to the college is open to all high school graduates and others who are able to profit from the instruction they offer. They also offer opportunities for high school students to enroll in college-level courses for credit, and in articulated two-plus-two and "tech/prep" programs leading to an associate degree.

GOVERNANCE

Since 1968, the colleges have been governed at the state level by the Board of Governors of the California Community Colleges, appointed by the governor, for the most part for four-year terms. The board comprises 16 members, with 11 members representing the public, two local trustees, two tenured faculty members (appointed for two-year terms), and one student (appointed for a one-year term). Its officers are a president and vice president, who are elected annually by the board. Its offices are located at 1107 Ninth Street in Sacramento (95814), and most of its bi-montly meetings are held in Sacramento. The board has seven standing committees: Budget and Finance; Legislation; Economic Development and Vocational Education; Student Services and Special Programs; Equity, diversity, and Human Resources; Educational Policy; and the Community Colleges Foundation. Together with members of the Board of Education, three members serve on a Joint Advisory Committee on Vocational Education. At the present time, three members also serve on an Adult Education Task Force, together with members of the Board of Education, and three members serve on a California State University Joint Standing Committee. In addition, the board elects annually one member and an alternate to represent it on the California Postsecondary Education Commission.

The board selects a chancellor for the system who, in turn, appoints vice chancellors for governmental relations and external affairs, educational services and economic development, fiscal policy, human resources, student services and special programs, and policy analysis and management information services. Pending some reorganization, the executive-level staff also includes a general counsel and a director of system advancement and resource development. The approximately 180 authorized positions below this level include clerical, technical, professional, and other support staff who are civil service employees.

Under a statute enacted in 1968, the colleges were separated from the jurisdiction of the California State Board (and Department) of Education – an action which was taken for the California State University system as part of the state's master plan of 1960. Initially, there were no restrictions on or specifications of the board's membership, although the intent of the legislature was that it include local trustees and others with knowledge of the two-year colleges. Subsequent to the 1968 statute, amendments were adopted that mandated representation from local trustees, faculty, and students. The creation of a state-level board for community colleges brought about relatively little change in the way the colleges were governed locally, although a very important change in governance during this period was their separation from unified school districts, so as to form their own community college districts, with their own elected boards and chancellors/superintendents.

Changes in statutes that were a part of Assembly Bill 1725, adopted in 1988, were intended both to create a "statewide community college system" and to institute a process of "shared governance" at the state and local levels. "Shared governance" was to involve both faculty and students with local boards in policy and decisionmaking about local operations. For shared governance at the state level, the board adopted a process known as "consultation," through which representatives of 14 organizations advise the chancellor on policies and regulations that he or she will subsequently recommend to the board for adoption. These representatives include chief executive officers, academic senate members, chief student services administrators, chief business officers, student body government officers, and members of other community college groups. The consultation council meets monthly with the chancellor and appropriate staff, and reports of its deliberations are provided to the board in its bi-monthly agendas. The chancellor is not required to accept the advice or recommendations of the council, but, instead, in instances where there is disagreement, he or she is obligated to inform the board about the council's points of view, when making his or her recommendations. Shared governance, including the consultation process, has not yet achieved its optimum state, and proposals may be expected to emerge that will modify procedures, while maintaining its basic thrust.

No proposals for changing the governance of the colleges have yet been formulated, as of January 1998, but there is quite widespread agreement that change may be necessary in order for the system to make best use of the resources available to it. The California Postsecondary Education Commission, in implementing the recommendations of its 1995 report, The Challenge of the Century: Planning for Record Student Enrollment and Improved Outcomes in California Postsecondary Education, established an Ad Hoc Committee on Community Colleges to review the system's governance, in order to identify how it can become better integrated. The work of this committee has proceeded slowly, in part because of the complexity of its assigned task. Meanwhile, the board has taken action related to governance issues by contracting for an inquiry into problems and possible solutions, and for the rewriting/reduction of the Education Code—a volume of statutes that the legislature has adopted and the governor has signed over the years—that dictate in great and often outmoded detail how the colleges must operate.

The broad functions of the board of governors are quite easily described and rather unlikely to change dramatically in the future. Briefly, the board sets policy and provides leadership and guidance to the districts and colleges, while formally interacting with state and federal officials, other state boards and commissions, and state organizations for community colleges. Specifically, the board must adopt regulations to implement statutes that have been enacted into the Education code by the legislature. These regulations appear in Title 5 of the Administrative Code, which also contains regulations adopted by the Trustees of the State University and the Board of Education for the public schools. They are intended to have the force of law but are in many cases unenforceable because of a lack of clarity about how to "punish" districts and their trustees or administrators who ignore or do not adhere to particular regulations.

Theoretically, the board is constrained by the education code. Still, it goes beyond its regulatory role by adopting guidelines and other non-binding policies that give both direction and flexibility to the colleges, as they respond to local community needs and characteristics. Among its major policy documents is The Basic Agenda: Policy Directions and Priorities for the Nineties, related to which it publishes an annual report on the implementation of its goals and objectives.

The board is mandated in statute to develop minimum standards in various areas of college operations, while maintaining local control and authority to the maximum degree possible. A few areas of minimum standards are the following: (1) grading standards and graduation requirements; (2) conditions of employment of administrative and academic staff; (3) establishment of new community colleges, districts, and certain off-campus centers; (4) space and utilization standards; (5) distance learning; and (6) the offering of new degree programs and credit courses that are not part of such programs. Beyond establishing minimum standards, the board's responsibility differs for various areas of college operations. For example, the board leaves to the districts the appointment of their chancellors and presidents and other staff and the setting of their salaries. In the area of new program and course approval, it delegates this responsibility to the chancellor and his or her staff. However, in the area of facilities, the board must approve (1) the establishment of new colleges and certain off-campus centers, in order for them to qualify for state funding for construction—an action that the California Postsecondary Education Commission must then review and affirm, and (2) an annual capital outlay plan/budget for the colleges and districts. The board also must prepare and adopt a proposed budget and allocation plan for submission to the governor and the department of finance. Finally, the board, through the chancellor, solicits a large number of plans and statistical reports in such areas as vocational/technical education, equal educational opportunity, enrollments, and finance. It has attempted in recent years to reduce the number of such plans and reports, by either combining related plans and reports or eliminating those that cannot be generated routinely from existing management information systems—or are beyond what staff is able to review.

The board has supported two major planning exercises during the 1990s, in anticipation of large future growth in enrollment demand. The first was the appointment in the early 1990s of an external Commission on Innovation, whose charge was to examine options regarding how access might be provided for the vastly increased numbers of Californians who are expected to enroll in the coming years, with an assumption that full funding may not be provided by the state. More recently, the board created a special Task Force for the Chancellor's Consultation Council that was charged with recommending actions that will be necessary from now, 1998, until the year 2005, to meet the challenge of accommodating what is called Tidal Wave II—a college and university enrollment of between 450,000 and 650,000 additional students, most of whom are expected to be served by the community colleges. The task force report—"2005", containing a variety of "solutions" and possible alternatives, was presented to the board for discussion at its January 1998 meeting. No action is being taken to adopt the report but, instead, it is intended for use in giving direction to the chancellor and his staff as they develop a policy/vision statement for the early 21st century, for later adoption by the board. Finally four technical reports were prepared by staff in he areas of access, funding patterns, funding, scenarios, and trends, to assist the task force in its deliberations.

Statutory changes in the finance and governance of the community colleges have not significantly reduced the strength and powers of the locally elected boards. While their ability to tax was eliminated with the passage of Proposition 13 in 1978, they retain considerable authority to decide how to spend the money that is provided in the governor's budget, including setting employee salaries and benefits, and allocating funds for administration versus instruction and student services (except for an outmoded law that caps non-instructional expenditures at no more than 50 percent of the support budget).

At this juncture, no one can predict with any degree of certainty when, how, or even if, in the near future, there will be significant changes in community college governance at the state and local levels—or in the governance of California public higher education, generally. Some dissatisfaction continues to persist, while the model of shared governance continues to evolve, that the colleges are not a true system and that the state plays too strong a role in local operations. In any case, it appears likely that the status quo will be preferred by the field to any potentially significant changes in state and local relations.

FUNDING

The current estimate is that the 1997-98 community colleges' ongoing support budget from the state will amount to approximately $363.6 million, with an additional $128.5 million for one-time funding for instructional equipment, deferred maintenance, and child care facilities. The board had requested an ongoing support budget of $472.4 million for the colleges for 1998-99, plus $146.9 million for one-time funding. The governor's proposed budget, announced in January, provides an increase of only $288 million, or a 6.4 percent increase, that includes a 10.35 percent share of Proposition 98 revenue (the remaining 89.65 percent going to the public schools). The proposed budget would support approximately 26,000 additional students in the colleges. For the past three years, the colleges have attempted to obtain restoration of the loss of about 9,000 course sections and 180,000 students that had resulted from earlier reductions in state revenue.

Some of the major categories of funding in the ongoing support budget are General Fund Apportionment (including growth, COLA, and equalization). Partnership for Excellence (an incentive fund for allocation to the colleges on the basis of progress toward outcomes such as successful course completions, transfer to four-year institutions, and associate degrees awarded). Foster Care Education Program (training for foster parents), and the California Virtual University (for program development centers).

The budget for the operation of the chancellor's office is separate from the systemwide budget for the colleges. The 1997 Budget Act authorized 190 positions for the office, for a total of $17.6 million in salaries and benefits, and operating expenses and equipment. An additional 15 positions would be authorized under the governor's proposed budget for 1998-99, for an increase of 5 percent.

Colleges are funded on the basis of full-time-equivalent student enrollment, but actual funding in recent years has been less than that which enrollment would produce. Only partially successful efforts have been made to move the colleges into a program-based funding mode, and all credit courses are funded at the same level. The state budget also provides categorical funding for a variety of programs and services, for example, matriculation services and the Extended Opportunity Program and Services for disadvantaged students.

The federal government is another source of funding for both the colleges and the chancellor's office, under the Carl D. Perkins Vocational and Applied Technology Act—funding that the colleges share with the California Department of Education and the public schools in a ratio of about 40 to 60 percent, through their State Plan for Vocational/Technical Education. The most recent estimated expenditure plan for 1998-99 would provide more than $2.8 million to the chancellor's office for state administration and technical assistance, with a total of approximately $48 million for the colleges. Continuing uncertainty about the future of federal programs and funding for workforce training surrounds this budget item, although recent congressional attempts to change the administration and delivery systems in the states have been unsuccessful.

The colleges' funding for capital outlay continues to fall far short of their need, in the absence of legislative and/or voter approval of new bond issues. To apply for capital outlay funds, community college districts submit proposals annually to the chancellor's office for review to determine whether justification is adequate for supporting each project. Projects are prioritized into categories under board-approved criteria, with highest priority given to completing projects that have been approved earlier and funded for working drawings. Highest priority has been given in recent years to health and safety projects, especially to projects to remove hazardous materials and architectural barriers that affect students with disabilities. Annually, a prioritized list of approved projects is submitted to the board for it review and approval before being submitted to the California Department of Finance and the Legislative Analyst's Office for possible inclusion in the governor's budget, subject to the availability for capital outlay. General obligation bonds must be approved by the voters, and the defeat of the Higher Education Bond Act of 1994 resulted in few funds being allocated for capital outlay. In 1996, the voters approved a bond issue that provided community colleges with $300 million to use in meeting over $1.8 billion in approved projects. At issue now is (1) the inclusion (or exclusion) of higher education needs from initiatives for new bond issues, and (2) the division of funds from any new bond issue among the community colleges, the California State University, and the University of California. In any case, the outlook is rather bleak with regard to the state and its voters being willing and able to provide the funds to meet the facilities needs of the Tidal Wave II enrollments that are projected.

PROGRAMS AND ENROLLMENTS

The primary degree that the California community colleges award is the associate in arts (A.A.) degree. Although degree requirements may differ for students in liberal arts/transfer, occupational, and general studies programs, no distinction is made in the type of degree awarded and students in some technical programs may transfer to the state university without a major loss of credit. As noted in the section on accountability, the colleges award relatively few associate degrees, in part because there is no requirement or incentive for students who intend to transfer to obtain a degree before doing so. Before enrollment pressures increased in the state universities, students were permitted to transfer with as many as 56 (or fewer) transferable semester units; now the expectation is that students will have completed all requirements for junior standing before transfer, although possession of an associate degree still does not give the transfer applicant any special consideration.

Total fall enrollment in 1966—in both credit and noncredit classes—is estimated to be about 1.4 million headcount students. This is less than in the early 1990s, but reverses a downward trend that had occurred in recent years. The colleges measure their success in providing access for California adults by computing a participation rate: fall enrollment per 1,000 adult population. Except for three prior years, when the participation rate was slightly lower, the fall 1996 rate of 59.1 was the lowest since 1969. The highest rate was achieved in 1977, when it reached 85.3. the rate has fluctuated over time with changes in enrollment fees and budget reductions that led to enrollment caps and elimination of certain courses and sections. About 35% of recent California high school graduates enroll in the colleges as freshmen.

Approximately 70% of the students are enrolled part-time, that is, for fewer than 12 units. The full-time equivalent student attendance figure is about 800,000. Nearly 200,000 headcount students were enrolled exclusively in noncredit classes in fall 1996. Actual enrollment for that term exceeds 500,000, because students enroll in multiple classes each semester. Each noncredit full-time equivalent represents 526 hours of actual attendance. Adult schools that are part of unified school districts share this mission with the colleges and enroll as many as 1.35 million students in 1995-96. An unknown number of adults participate in community service courses and programs that must be self-supporting, with no direct state funding.

Women outnumber men in the colleges by a ratio of 5.6 to 4.4. About 54% of the students are age 25 or older, with the average age about 27. About half of the students reported their race/ethnicity to be white, while 23% checked the Hispanic category. The third largest group is Asian/Pacific Islander, with 14%; followed by Black, with 8%; Filipino, with 3.5%; and American Indian/Alaskan, with 1%.

The colleges awarded fewer than 54,000 associate degrees in 1994-95, and the number appears to be decreasing. Six disciplines accounted for 64% of the degrees awarded, as follows: liberal arts and sciences, 34%; business, 10%; general studies, 9%; nursing, 6%; social services, 3%; and administration of justice, 2%.

The community colleges award certificates for completion of programs of varying length: 60 or more units, 30 to 59 units, fewer than 30 units, and "other." Slightly more than 24,000 certificates were awarded in 1994-95, 14% of them in programs of at least 60 units, 44% in programs of between 30 and 59 units, and 34% in programs of fewer than 30 units. The largest number of certificates was awarded to students in nursing (2,371), followed by administration of justice (1,825), and child development (1,119). Other fields among those with the largest numbers of recipients were secretarial studies, accounting, electronics, cosmetology, medical assisting, and fire control and safety.

Among the 1.4 million students enrolled in 1994-95, 48% of those with stated goals indicated that their goal was to transfer to a four-year institution. The goal of occupational preparation was stated by 30%, while 6% said, "improve basic skills," and 16% had some other goal. However, 26 percent did not state a goal. While almost 478,000 stated transfer as a goal, fewer than 60,000 were known to transfer to a four-year institution that same year. While the number of transfer students is small, students who have had some work in a California community college are awarded at least half of the baccalaureate degrees granted by the California State University, and about 20% of those granted by the University of California.

ECONOMIC DEVELOPMENT

Economic development, defined in statute as "quality education and services focusing on continuous work force improvement, technology deployment, and business development," has become a major part of the mission of the California community colleges. The program began in

1987, as the Economic Development Network (Ed>Net) under the guidance of a field-based steering committee, and was codified in 1991 (Assembly Bill 1497) as a part of the community college mission, with the goal of advancing California's growth and global competitiveness. Amendments in 1995 established a 27-member executive committee and numerous reporting requirements. Legislation enacted in 1996 further clarified the goals of the program; defined regional planning, priority setting, and coordination; and added accountability and audit requirements. Finally, legislation enacted in 1997 expanded the scope of regional centers, and added regional collaboratives and job development incentive funding.

The colleges' Regional Business Resource, Assistance, and Innovation Networks that were established in statute represent an emerging approach to meeting the challenge of transforming existing delivery systems into regional structures that link communities and regions to the global economy.

There are four components to the program: (1) regional centers; (2) statewide network leadership, organizational development, coordination, and information and support; (3) regional collaboratives; and (4) job development incentive training. Total state funding for 1997-98 amounted to more than $29 million for 103 centers (for example, for Advanced Transportation Technologies, International Trade Development, Small Business Development, and New Media/Multimedia/Entertainment); 16 projects related to statewide network leadership and related activities (for example, the Economic Development Coordination Network, and Strategic Priority, Leadership, Coordination, and Technical Assistance); an estimated 94 regional business resource, assistance, and innovation network collaboratives (for example, Industry-Driven Regional Education and Training Cooperatives, and Planning, Priority Setting, and Coordination of Service Providers); and 20 to 30 job development incentive training projects. The governor did not include in his proposed budget for 1998-99 the additional $10 million that the board of governors had requested.

The governor's budget for economic development by the community colleges is only a fraction of the total amount spent in this area, but no total figures are available. Other sources of revenue include business and industry, other state agencies, and the federal government. Another expanding area of activity is workforce training through contract education, with employers paying for the programs. Enrollees in such programs are not counted for enrollment purposes, except in cases where they wish to earn college credit.

ACCOUNTABILITY

Legislation enacted into statute in 1968 (Assembly Bill 1725) included a mandate for the board and its staff to embark upon the development of a statewide accountability system that involves the centralized collection and reporting of data in such areas as student access, student success, student satisfaction, staff composition, and fiscal condition. Started in July, 1990, when the board adopted a preliminary planning report for accountability, the system may still be characterized as in a developmental stage.

Further impetus was given to its development in the Higher Education Accountability Program Act of 1991 (Assembly Bill 1808), which required the California Postsecondary Education Commission to develop and adopt a format for an annual report on the performance of the state's public colleges and universities. Still other calls for improved accountability measures include provisions in the federal Carl D. Perkins Vocational and Applied Technology Act, National Collegiate Athletic Association regulations, and the Federal Student Right-to-Know Act.

There is widespread agreement that any accountability structure should be based on outcomes, rather than input measures such as library holdings and qualifications of the faculty, as have often been reflected in accreditation standards in the past. The community colleges are facing at least two major issues in developing an accountability structure, both of which were in a sense previewed during the period when the state was attempting to develop standards under the now-defunct federal State Postsecondary Review Entity (SPRE) in the mid-1990s. First, number of degrees and certificates awarded is a logical output measure in any accountability scheme, but the California colleges grant a relatively small number of degrees and certificates, given the magnitude of their enrollment. Similarly, the number of transfer students to the state universities is another important output measure, but the California colleges transfer a relatively small percentage of their students who enroll for credit. There are problems in measuring the success of students who complete occupational programs, in terms of placement in entry-level jobs related to their preparation; many students are older, already gainfully employed, and enrolled without an intent to complete a degree or certificate program. Instead, their goal is to upgrade or update their skills, or to explore a different occupational area, often for personal reasons.

A second issue in developing accountability measures, as anticipated in statute, is whether any output measures can be developed that are relevant and valid for both the community colleges and the state universities. There are important differences among California's three systems, in mission, governance, demographics, and other characteristics—as well as among the community colleges—that may mediate against adopting common measures.

Drawing upon existing management information systems data, the colleges are now able to report annually on student performance in at least two major areas: student access and student success. The former includes the following: (1) the college participation rate for recent high school graduates and for the state's total adult population; (2) enrollment by gender and race/ethnicity, compared with the state's adult population, and (3) number of course sections taught by discipline. Current information also includes the following: (1) student-declared goals, as reflected in the colleges' historic mission; (2) credit course enrollments by letter grade; (3) course retention and successful course completion, by gender and race/ethnicity; (4) persistence rate from fall to spring term, by gender and race/ethnicity; (5) persistence rate from fall to spring term, by gender and race/ethnicity; (5) numbers of transfers to the state university university system; and (6) changes in earnings and employment rates from last year in college to third year after leaving college, for selected occupational education students.

Accountability ranks among the very top priorities on the board's action agenda for 1998, together with access, funding, and governance.

REFERENCES

Breneman, D. W. (1995). *A State of Emergency? Higher Education in California* (A report prepared for the California Higher Education Policy Center). San Jose, CA: The California Higher Education Policy Center.

California Postsecondary Education Commission. (1995a) *The Challenge of the Century: Planning for Record Student Enrollment and Improved Outcomes in California Postsecondary Education*, (Report 95-1). Sacramento, CA: Author

California Postsecondary Education Commission, (1995b). *A New State Policy on Community College Student Charges*. (Report 95-1).

Sacramento, CA: Author

California State Department of Education. (1960). *A Master Plan For Higher Education In California, 1960-1975.* Sacramento, CA: Author

Commission on Innovation. (1993). Choosing *Its Future: An Action Agenda For The California Community Colleges: A Report To The Board Of Governors.* Sacramento, CA: Chancellor's Office: Author

Fountain, B. E. & Tollefson, T. A. (1989). *Community colleges in the United States: Forty-Nine systems.* Washington, DC: The American Association of Community Colleges.

Henry, N. B., Ed. (1956). *The public junior college: The Fifty-Fifth Yearbook of the National Society for the Study of Education.* Chicago: University of Chicago Press.

FOR ADDITIONAL INFORMATION, PLEASE CONTACT:
Dorothy M. Knoell, Ph.D.
Consultant in Higher Education
605 Woodside Sierra, #2
Sacramento, CA 95825

COLORADO

Richard A. Voorhees
Associate Vice President for Educational Support Services
Colorado Community College and Occupational Education System

OVERVIEW

The legal title of the system is the State Board for Community Colleges and Occupational Education. The administrative agency of the board is known as the Colorado Community College and Occupational Education System (CCOES).

The system encompasses 13 state system community colleges, three local district colleges, and four legislated area vocational schools. The board governs the 13 state system colleges. In addition, the board, through the system, regulates and administers federal and state vocational education funds distributed to the local district colleges, the legislated area vocational schools, and the public secondary institutions using vocational funds. CCCOES administrators all Carl Perkins Vocational and Advanced Technology dollars in Colorado.

The Colorado General Assembly in the Community College and Occupational Education Act of 1967 charged the state board ì...to develop and establish state policy for occupational education and to govern the state system of community colleges... The board shall assure a system of two-year program delivery throughout the state coordinated, where appropriate, with the local district colleges.î The 1967 Act also ì...provided for the establishment of local councils to advise the board on the operation of individual community colleges from a local perspective:

> The function of the two-college system is to conduct occupational, technical, and community service programs with no term limitations and general education, including college transfer programs with unrestricted admissions. It is further the intent of this article to develop appropriate occupational education and adult education programs in the elementary and secondary schools of the state, permitting local school districts already having vocational schools to continue to operate them, and to develop work study and on-the-job training programs designed to acquaint youth with the world of work and to train and retrain youth and adults for employment. The

General Assembly intends that state agencies concerned with occupational education in the public schools shall cooperate with the board in planning and implementing occupational education programs, to the end that the state of Colorado has complete and well-balanced occupational and adult education programs available to the people of Colorado at all education levels.

The statutory goal and mission of the state system of community colleges are: There is hereby established a state system of community and technical colleges which shall be under the management and jurisdiction of the State Board for Community Colleges and Occupational Education. Each college shall be a two-year institution offering a broad range of general, personal, vocational and technical education programs. No college shall impose admission requirements upon any student. The objectives of the community and technical colleges shall be to provide educational programs to fill the occupational needs of youth and adults in technical and vocational fields, provide two-year transfer education programs to qualify students for admission to the junior year at other colleges and universities, and to provide a broad range of programs of personal and vocational education for adults.

The state board was created in 1967. The administrative agency existed with two separate divisions, the Division of Community Colleges and the Division of Occupational Education, until 1986. At that time the existing board was abolished by legislative fiat, and a new board was constituted with different criteria for membership. The new board restructured the agency into an integrated system under which there is a Division of Educational Services and a Division of Administration. Each division administers the governing function over the state system community colleges as well as the occupational education regulatory functions.

GOVERNANCE

The board consists of nine members who are appointed for staggered four-year terms by the governor, with the consent of the state senate. No more than five appointed members at any time may be members of any one political party, and each Congressional district shall have at least one member of the board. No appointed member may be employed by any junior, community, or technical college, state or private institution of higher education, school district, or agency receiving vocational funds allocated by the state board. No appointed member of the state board shall be an official of the governing board of any state-supported institution of higher education or an elected or appointed official of the state of Colorado.

Two advisory members to the state board are elected annually by and from their respective groups of students and faculty of state-system colleges.

Duties of the state board with respect to the state system and local district colleges are prescribed by statute:

Duties of Board with Respect to the State System

(1)   With respect to the community and technical colleges within the state system, the board has the authority, responsibility, rights, privileges, powers, and duties customarily exercised by the governing boards of institutions of higher education, including the following:

    (a) To recommend to the Commission on Higher Education and the general assembly the location and priorities for establishment of new community and technical colleges;

    (b) To construct, lease, or otherwise provide facilities needed for the community and technical colleges as authorized by the General Assembly; to issue, in the name of the board, revenue bonds and other revenue obligations, in the manner and for the purposes, subject to the provisions provided by the law for state education institutions under Article 5 of this Title or for junior college districts; and to refund, in the name of the board, revenue bonds and other revenue obligations transferred to the board or incurred by the board as provided in this article; such refunding to be undertaken pursuant to Article 54 of Title 11, Colorado Revised Statutes, 1973;

    (c) To fix the tuition and fees to be charged in the community and technical colleges. The board shall fix tuition in accordance with the level of appropriations set by the general assembly for such institutions;

    (d) To appoint the chief administrative officer of each community and technical college;

    (e) To recommend and review proposals for the establishment of curricula and for major changes in curriculum, subject only to the review function of the Commission on Higher Education relating to formal academic programs;

(f) To define the requirements of appropriate degrees and certificates and to authorize the award thereof in the community and technical colleges, subject only to the review function of the Commission on Higher Education relating to formal academic programs;

(g) To develop a plan with the governing boards of baccalaureate-degree-granting universities and colleges of the state, which will assure maximum freedom of transfer of students between local junior colleges and community and technical colleges under the direct control of the board and such universities and colleges;

(h) To receive, review, and transmit with recommendations to the Commission on Higher Education and the general assembly both operating and capital budget requests of the community and technical colleges;

(i) To plan, in cooperation with other state agencies, the allocation of federal funds for instructional programs and student services, including funds for vocational and technical education and retraining;

(j) To determine policies pertaining to the community and technical colleges, subject only to the functions and powers assigned by law to the Commission on Higher Education relating to formal academic programs;

(k) To control the direction of funds and appropriations to the colleges in the system;

(l) To receive, demand, and hold for the uses and purposes of the colleges in the system such monies, lands, or other properties as may be donated, devised, leased, or conveyed, and to apply the same in such manner as will best serve the objects and interests of the colleges in the system;

(m) To develop and implement, in coordination with four-year institutions and under the direction of the Colorado Commission on Higher Education, a core transfer program for students wishing to obtain a baccalaureate degree after transferring from the state system to a four-year institution, which program shall be implemented within the state system by September 15, 1978.

<u>Duties of Board with Respect to Local Junior Colleges</u>

With respect to local junior colleges operating under the provisions of Articles 70 to 72 of Title 22, Colorado Revised Statues, 1973, the board shall:

(a) Exercise all powers and perform all duties vested prior to July 1, 1967, in the State Board of Education or in the commissioner of education with respect to local junior colleges;

(b) Review and make recommendations concerning requests by any local junior college for appropriations for capital construction before such requests are submitted to the Commission on Higher Education and the General Assembly;

(c) Provide such junior colleges with such technical assistance as they may request.

FUNDING

State operational support for two-year state system colleges, local district colleges, and area vocational schools is based on FTE enrollment, where one FTE is calculated by dividing the number of eligible semester hours generated annually by 30, or the number of annual quarter hours by 45. In the fall 1998, system colleges enrolled a total of 60,000 headcount students. Total FTE enrollment for the 1997-98 fiscal year was 34,850. The legislative appropriation for system colleges was $105,955,975; when combined with $75,616,074 in augmenting revenues, total expenditures were $181,572,049.

PROGRAMS

Types of Degrees

Associate of Arts (A.A.)

Associate of Science (A.S.)

Associate of General Studies (A.G.S.)

(1) Each college can offer one degree in each of the above with areas of emphasis in A.A. and A.S. degree programs.

(2) Community colleges adhere to CCHE's "Policy and General Procedures for State-Level Review of Proposals for New Academic Degree Programs..."

(3) Colleges must submit a letter of intent to CCHE prior to submitting a proposal.

(4) SBCCOE takes action on all state system community college degrees and forwards them to CCHE for final approval prior to implementation.

(5) For local district colleges, SBCCOE, in its coordinating role, recommends an approval to CCHE; CCHE has ultimate approval authority prior to implementation of the degree.

(6) Once CCHE receives the proposal, action is to be taken within 120 days, with option of a 40-day extension for approval, if needed.

(7) All state system community colleges have approval of A.A., A.S., and A.G.S. degrees.

Associate of Applied Science (A.A.S.)

(1) Each college offers a number of A.A.S. programs based on specific occupational needs.

(2) All colleges, state system, and local district, adhere to the CCHE/SBCCOE agreement (February 1985) regarding approval of A.A.S. degrees.

(3) CCCOES staff has developed an internal process for review and approval of A.A.S. degrees.

(4) SBCCOE takes action on all state system community college AAS degrees and forwards them to CCHE; the CCHE executive director has final approval authority prior to implementation.

(5) For local district colleges, SBCCOE, in its coordinating role, recommends approval to the CCHE executive director, who has final approval authority prior to implementation.

Types of Associate Degrees

(1) Associate of Arts is intended to prepare students for transfer to four-year institutions. Requires completion of the Core Transfer Program of general education\courses. Students' emphasis of study is in arts, communication, and/or social sciences.

(2) Associate of Science is intended to prepare students for transfer to four-year institutions. Requires completion of the Core Transfer Program of general education courses. Students' emphasis of study is in science or mathematics.

(3) Associate of General Studies provides a broad program of courses without constraints of specialization. The A.G.S. requires 30 semester hours of prescribed general education courses.

(4) Associate of Applied Science prepares students for entry-level employment or for upgrading or re-training. The A.G.S. requires 15 semester hours of general education.

ACCOUNTABILITY

CCCOES has been a national leader in the development of community college effectiveness indicators. Adopting the AACC indicators in 1995, CCCOES was the first governing board in Colorado to publish an accountability document focusing on these indicators. Subsequently, Colorado has legislated a Quality Indicator System (HB 1219) which requires each governing board to report data similar in content to the CCCOES model. The first governing board reports under the new legislation will be made public in September 1998. In addition to participating in the statewide indicator effort, CCCOES will continue to refine its own core indicators of effectiveness and report them periodically.

CCCOES also maintains a longstanding accountability effort in career and technical education programs approved by the board. After initial approval, each career and technical program is reviewed by state staff every five years for compliance with Colorado Standards and Measures. These measures include: basic and advanced academic skills, general occupational skills, specific occupational skills, program completion and persistence, continuation of education or occupational placement, client satisfaction, gender/ethnicity equity, and equal access for special populations. The vocational database maintained by the system dates to 1976, providing a rich source for tracking Colorado's history in career and technical education.

ECONOMIC DEVELOPMENT

CCCOES' mission is to promote economic development for Colorado. This mission is accomplished in a variety of ways, including provision of traditional career and technical education, transfer education, and opportunities for citizens to upgrade their skills. In recent years, the system has become a national leader in applied educational technology and advanced technology applications in high tech areas. CCCOES established the Higher Education Advanced Technology (HEAT) Center at the former Lowry Air Force Base in the mid-nineties.

The HEAT Center is dedicated to evolving technology and its application to the Colorado workforce. The HEAT Center is home to the Rocky Mountain Manufacturing Academy, wherein CCCOES colleges collaborate to offer degrees and in machine technology, robotics, advanced joining, photonics and vacuums, metrology, and biotechnology. Innovative partnerships have been formed with four-year colleges and universities, both from the private and public sector, to offer seamless advanced technology education to the baccalaureate degree.

CCCOES also created the Colorado Electronic Community College (CECC) in 1994 to provide wider accessibility to associate degrees. The twelfth system college, CECC enrolls students from across the United States as well as internationally. Recent developments for CECC include offering an associate degree in business solely through the Internet, with the first classes scheduled to begin in January, 1988.

FOR ADDITIONAL INFORMATION PLEASE CONTACT:
Richard A. Voorhees, Ph.D.
Associate Vice President for Educational Support Services
Colorado Community College and Occupational Education System
State Board for Community Colleges and Occupational Education
1391 North Speer Boulevard, Suite 600
Denver, CO 80204
Telephone: (303) 620-4000
Fax: (303) 534-4832

CONNECTICUT

Mary Anne B. Cox
Assistant to the Chancellor for Communications and Advancement
Connecticut Community-Technical College System

OVERVIEW

The Community-Technical Colleges of Connecticut are twelve two-year, public institutions of higher education that share a mission to make educational excellence and the opportunity for lifelong learning affordable and accessible to all Connecticut citizens. The colleges seek to enrich the intellectual, cultural and social lives of the communities they serve. They support the economic growth of the state and its citizens through programs that supply business and industry with a skilled, well-trained work force.

The colleges are accredited by the New England Association of Schools and Colleges, the Board of Governors for Higher Education, and numerous other national accrediting agencies, such as the American Medical Association (AMA), the American Bar Association (ABA), the National League of Nursing (NLN), and the Technology Accreditation Commission of the Accreditation Board for Engineering and Technology (TAC/ABET) for specialized programs. The colleges are administered by an 18-member board of trustees, two of whom are elected by the students at the 12 colleges. The Community-Technical Colleges of Connecticut award certificates and associate degrees in more than 100 areas.

The primary responsibilities of the colleges are to provide occupational, vocational, technical, and career education designed as training for immediate employment, job retraining or upgrading of skills to meet individual, community and state manpower needs; to provide programs of general study including remediation, general and adult education, and continuing education; to provide programs of study for college transfer representing the first two-years of baccalaureate education; to provide community service programs, i.e., educational, cultural, recreational and community-directed programs; and to provide student support services including admissions, counseling, testing, placement, individualized instruction and instruction for students with special needs.

The five consolidated colleges in the system, formed by 1992 merger legislation combining the community and technical colleges in the shared geographic areas of Hartford, New Haven, Norwalk, Norwich and Water-bury, also provide associate degree and certificate programs that focus on the principles of basic science and technology, with emphasis on engineering and engineering technology, integrating theoretical and applied mathematics, basic science and applied science in order to meet the needs of the state's businesses and industries for a highly skilled, technically literate workforce. All twelve colleges share the responsibility for providing courses and degree programs in response to emerging technologies and have the primary responsibility for responding to the needs of the state's workforce as they relate to maintaining currency with job requirements, changing technology and providing continuing education opportunities for those wishing to upgrade their basic technical skills. The colleges in the system strive to address the needs of the state in areas of technology vital to the state's economic development. Cooperative ventures emphasizing the sharing of resources and expertise between community and technical colleges were initiated even before merger and the development of a strategic plan for technical education, following legislation that consolidated administration of the community and technical college systems in 1989. In 1992, following the full merger of the colleges according to P.A. 92-126, the development of the concept of the College of Technology expanded the resource-sharing capability of the colleges and supported the further development of technical programs by creating a curriculum pathway that would allow a student to begin a degree program in engineering or technology at any community-technical college. Upon completing the associate degree requirements, the student can complete the baccalaureate-level courses at the University of Connecticut's School of Engineering or at Central Connecticut State University's School of Technology.

The present system of community and technical colleges was formed in 1992 by P.A. 92-126, which merged the community and technical colleges in five shared geographic areas, Hartford, New Haven, Norwalk, Norwich, and Waterbury, to form five comprehensive community-technical colleges. The remaining seven colleges in the system also assume responsibility for meeting the needs of Connecticut for two-year higher education in technical, liberal arts, and career areas. Prior to this, in 1989, P.A. 89-260 consolidated the two pre-existing separate systems of community and technical colleges under the administration of a single board of trustees. This legislation renamed the Board of Trustees of Community Colleges to become the Board of Trustees of Community-Technical Colleges and temporarily expanded the membership of the board from 16 to 24 members, in order to include additional representatives of business, industry, labor and the technical occupations. Administration of the 12 community colleges continued to be the responsibility of the expanded board, and the five technical colleges were added to their responsibilities, according to this legislation. At present, the board of trustees comprises 18 members, 16 of whom, including the chair, are appointed by the governor for six-year terms. Two members are elected by the system's students to serve two-year terms.

Initially, in 1965, the community colleges were established as a system when the Connecticut General Assembly acted to establish a state system of two-year colleges for Connecticut in response to the recommendations of a special study commission on higher education, which advocated making the opportunity for higher education available to all Connecticut citizens. At the time of the system's inception, two community colleges, Norwalk and Manchester, had already been established and a third, Northwestern Connecticut, was about to open in response to local initiatives. These were incorporated into the Community College System and were joined shortly, according to a regional development plan, by Housatonic Community College, founded as a branch of Norwalk in Stratford in 1966, and, in the same year, by Middlesex Community College in Middletown, operating as a branch of Manchester, and Mattatuck Community College, which was established in Waterbury in 1967, along with Greater Hartford Community College in Hartford. In 1968, South Central Community College was established in New Haven, followed in 1970 by Tunxis and Mohegan Community Colleges in Farmington and Norwich, respectively. Quinebaug Valley Community College was founded in Danielson in 1971 and, with the founding of Asnuntuck Community college in 1972 in Enfield, the total number of community colleges was brought to 12.

The history of the technical colleges began with the establishment of the Connecticut Engineering Institute in 1946. The Institute was developed to meet the needs of Connecticut's manufacturers, following World War II, for competent technicians. The Institute was renamed Hartford State Technical College in 1955, and, in the following decade, three more technical institutes were established in Norwalk (1961), Norwich (1963), and Waterbury (1964). In 1967, the four state technical institutes were included in the state's system of two-year higher education and were renamed state technical colleges. The general assembly established a separate governing board of trustees for this system in 1974. A fifth state technical college, Greater New Haven State Technical College, was established in 1977 to fill the need for engineering technologies in the New Haven area's businesses and industries.

The remaining years demonstrated an effort on the part of both community and technical colleges to serve new and diverse student populations in order to fulfill their common commitment to access and opportunity through affordable and accessible higher education. An instructional television network was established at the community colleges in 1983 as an alternative educational delivery system attracting a new audience of nontraditional students including the homebound and the handicapped. This network now operates in cooperation with 18 cable television systems in the state and is available to the more than 500,000 homes served by these systems. In the fall of 1998, compressed-video pilot projects have been initiated at three system colleges and on-line programs are offered at several colleges, expanding the system's delivery capabilities through distance learning technology.

The Business Services Network and Traces, which are educational outreach initiatives developed to meet the needs of the state's businesses and industries for employee training and educational services, were established independently by the community and technical college systems in 1986. Collaborative efforts between these divisions, begun even before the consolidation of the systems in 1989, were strengthened by that consolidation. The operation of Traces was integrated with that of the Business Services Network to form what became the Business and Industry Services Network. The Network, now called The Learning Alliance, serves as a statewide link connecting business with education and state government and uses the resources and expertise of the twelve colleges in the system to meet the education and training needs of business and industry throughout the state. In 1996, the general assembly recognized and reinforced the contribution of the Connecticut Community-Technical College System to economic development by formally implementing an alliance that links the colleges with the Connecticut Departments of Labor and Economic and Community Development in providing training and education for new and existing employers to build Connecticut's economy.

By 1988, childcare centers had been established at all twelve community colleges to meet the needs of the college's predominately older, female student body. The centers are essential to ensuring access to higher education for parents of young children and they provide a high quality educational environment for the children of students, faculty, staff and area residents. At several colleges the centers serve as learning laboratories for direct observation, experience and research in child psychology, as part of early childhood education programs. These centers are now available, on a priority basis, to the children of students of the community-technical colleges.

The system's commitment to educational service and to outreach received added support from the development of a strategic plan for technical education in 1990 and of a revised mission statement, approved by the board of trustees in 1992. The primary thrust of both the plan and the mission statement was to expand opportunities in technical education and to enhance the role of the comprehensive community-technical colleges in responding to a rapidly changing technological and demographic environment. The strategic plan for technical education emphasized the importance of technical education to the state's economy and focused on expanding opportunities in technical education to every region of the state. Attracting new student markets, specifically minorities, women and other underserved populations, to technical education and increasing the availability of support services needed to ensure academic success for these students were among the overarching goals of the plan. Other goals included: improving the system's response to the state's technical education needs; improving academic excellence within existing programs and placing increased emphasis on the development of the students; ensuring that the colleges have the resources to effect the mission for which they are responsible, including the highest quality faculty and support staff and appropriate facilities; marketing technical programs aggressively to ensure that an increasing number of students choose technical education as preparation for entry into, or for upgrading in, technical careers.

These goals were subsumed into the 1992 revised mission statement in order to continue the strategic focus on enhancing and expanding access to technical education throughout the state through the system of twelve comprehensive community-technical colleges created by P.A. 92-126. More recently the colleges' mission statement has been redrafted to emphasize the leading role played by the colleges in creating academic, cultural, and economic development partnerships to serve the diverse groups and student populations within their communities. This revised statement was approved by the board of trustees in March, 1997, to serve as the foundation of a systemwide transformation focused on 21st century education and economic development involving strategic initiatives that include planning, technology, financing, and marketing.

GOVERNANCE

The chancellor of the Connecticut Community-Technical Colleges, as the chief agent of the board of trustees, is responsible for providing for proper functioning of the board and its committees, which deal with primary areas of responsibility including budget and facilities, personnel, academic policies and student affairs, marketing, and planning. The staff of the chancellor's office supports the efforts of the board of trustees and the chancellor in overseeing system compliance with state mandates and Board policy in each of these areas. The board itself consists of 18 members, including a chairperson, appointed by the governor for six-year terms. Two members are elected by the students at the colleges each fall for alternating two-year terms, and at least two members are alumni of the colleges

Systemwide councils provide intercollege and interdivisional communication and coordination among community-technical college administrators. The Council of Academic Deans meets monthly with the chancellor. Councils of Learning, Student Development Deans, Administrative Deans, Deans of Continuing Education/Community Services, and a Chancellor's Marketing Committee meet on a regular basis with chancellor's office staff liaisons.

As a state agency, the Connecticut Community-Technical College System works with a variety of other state agencies including the State Department of Public Works in its role of facilities development and with the State Department of Administrative Services, through its Division of Personnel, which deals with classified state employees. The former community college professional employees are represented by the Congress of Connecticut Community Colleges (4 Cs). Both teaching and nonteaching faculty, as well as administrative personnel, who are not excluded as part of management, are combined within this single union. The former technical college faculty, counselors and librarians are included in a bargaining unit represented by the American Federation of Teachers. The remaining professional, nonmanagerial employees are represented by the American Federation of State, County, and Municipal Employees (AFSCME). The

Community-Technical College System is funded by appropriations made by the General Assembly of Connecticut as part of the state budgetary process. Every two years, the chancellor, the deputy chancellor and the fiscal staff work with the Council of Presidents and the colleges' fiscal officers to develop system guidelines for preparing the agency budget request for the ensuing two fiscal years. These guidelines, which address both systemwide needs and individual campus needs, comply with state guidelines established by the state's Office of Policy and Management and the Board of Governors for Higher Education.

The budget request is developed by the chancellor's office of the board of trustees. It includes the use of formulas in the areas of instruction, library, physical plant operations and maintenance. All other areas of the budget are developed by function and program based upon the prioritized needs identified by each college and consistent with system guidelines.

Appropriations are made by the legislature to the board of trustees for the two-year budget cycle. The board in turn has the responsibility of allocating funds among the colleges in the system. The allocation of funds is based on a resource allocation model that provides for an equitable distribution of the funds available and in accord with priorities established by the board of trustees with regard to enrollment expansion, new program development and quality improvement.

Once allocations have been made, each college has significant discretion in the management of its budget within the specific categories of personnel, equipment and other operating expenses. In 1991, the general assembly enacted legislation creating an operating fund that is composed of tuition, auxiliary and extension accounts. All tuition and fee revenue collected is retained by the system and is budgeted for expenditure to provide services as colleges determine necessary within board policy. The legislation creating the operating fund provides greater flexibility in the area of purchasing, allowing adjustments between budget categories during the fiscal year and carry-over of revenue beyond the fiscal year.

Board of governors policy dictates that tuition levels be set to support 25 to 30 percent of operating expenses of the previous year for all constituent units of public higher education in Connecticut. In accord, with the board's commitment to ensuring access to higher education through affordable tuition, the board of trustees' policy maintains tuition at the lowest possible level within board of governors guidelines. In the spring of 1993, community college tuition and technical college tuition were equalized so that in-state students throughout the system paid $47 per credit for general fund courses. Prior to this equalization, technical college students had traditionally paid a higher rate tuition. By removing this financial barrier to choosing technical programs, the Board demonstrated its commitment to increasing enrollments in technical areas. In 1992, the board also committed $1.5 million dollars to a special fund to support the development of new technical programs throughout the system. This fund to support new program development has continued in place since that time. In 1997-98, students throughout the system paid $67 per semester hour. Since 1989-90, tuition and fee rates for full-time students have increased by 129%, from $880 to $1,814 annually, due in large part to declining general fund allocations to the system. Since 1989-90, the portion of the state's budget allocated to the Community-Technical Colleges has declined from 1.48% to .91%. During this same period, the state's general fund increased by 47.1% overall. In 1996-97, the Community-Technical College System received $2 million less from the general fund than it received in 1989-90, without the inclusion of collective bargaining increases. In the 1997 legislative session, the appropriation made to the college system for 1997-98 increased to $92.9 million, approximately $1.5 million below the level for the 1996-97 fiscal year. Tuition and fees, grants, and extension fund revenues contributed another $87.5 million to the system's budget for a total of $171.2. An early retirement incentive offered by the State of Connecticut in the summer of 1997 was accepted by approximately 12% of the college system's employees (nearly 15% of the faculty). While positions in higher education were refilled, budget limitations required agency savings and accommodation of the budget shortfall for that year.

In December, 1997, the board of trustees voted to freeze annual full-time tuition for the next year at the 1997-98 level: $1,814. The Connecticut General Assembly supported this action and expanded the tuition freeze to all of public higher education, covering the increased cost for the freeze through a special appropriation. Currently, continuing the freeze on tuition and other incentives to ensure affordability and encourage enrollment at public colleges are being reviewed in the 1999 legislative session.

PROGRAMS

The Community-Technical Colleges award certificates and associate degrees in over 100 career areas. (See attached program list.) Courses of study may lead to associate degrees, certificates, or the acquisition of career or personal skills. A core curriculum of general education courses is required in every degree program, making a community-technical college education a combination of the career training and the liberal arts essential in today's complex and changing society. General studies programs allow students the flexibility to work for a college degree and for personal enrichment, to meet individual educational goals, or to meet requirements for transfer to specialized major fields at four-year colleges and universities.

Responding to changing educational mandates and to challenges presented by the needs of students and the local service area is an underlying principle of system and program planning. Programs must possess internal coherence and integrity and must respond to external needs. Employment projections provide an important basis for program decisions throughout the planning process.

In response to their missions, community and technical colleges strive:

- To provide associate-degree and certificate programs of occupational, vocational and technical education to provide training for immediate employment, job retraining and upgrading of employment skills to meet individual, community and state needs;
- To promote general programs including remediation, general and adult education and continuing education designed to meet individual student goals;
- To provide programs that facilitate transfer to or continuation in other degree programs;
- To provide community service programs; and
- To provide student support services such as admissions, counseling, testing, placement, individualized instruction and services for non-traditional students and students with special needs.

The board of trustees has established specific procedures for system coordination of the planning and development of new academic programs, consistent with the Connecticut General Statutes and Board of Governors Regulations for Licensure and Accreditation. New program plans are initiated by individual institutions, while the board of trustees, in concert with the board of governors, is responsible for system planning, coordination, and review. The board of trustees may also initiate new programs or alter existing programs.

Each program is subject to several separate stages of review. The System Evaluation of Occupational Programs was established by the board of trustees in 1976 as a mechanism for continual assessment of the results and outcomes of programs. The evaluation process requires a comprehensive self-study, a visit by an evaluation team including members representing employers, graduates, specialists in the field. The team's final written report includes recognition of program strengths and recommendations for any needed improvements in the program. Each year, each community college evaluates twenty percent of its occupational program offerings with respect to program objectives, progress and effectiveness, operations, and output, including information on graduates, placements and employer reactions.

A significant portion of community college curricula exists apart from the occupational program areas and is evaluated according to the board's System for Evaluation of Special Areas, as a supplement to the Occupational Program Evaluation. This mechanism provides a more comprehensive and regular assessment of college operations in areas such as English/communications, ESL, social science, science, math, music, art, interdisciplinary courses and non-occupational degree or certificate programs.

In an effort to serve students throughout the state efficiently, share resources, and reduce costs, several programs are offered on a systemwide cooperative or consortium model. Most recently, a physical therapist assistant program has been implemented with one college, Naugatuck Valley, serving as the host college providing the specialized courses, and four other colleges in the system offering the general education component of the two-year degree program. Another cooperative model for program delivery is the Connecticut Safety Institute. Students may begin their studies at any of the twelve colleges in the system and then pursue specialization for degrees in fire technology and administration at five colleges, EMT/paramedic studies at Capital Community-Technical College in Hartford, or criminal justice at three colleges within the system.

ENROLLMENT AND FULL-TIME EQUIVALENCE

The community-technical colleges enrolled 39,366 students in the fall of 1998. This represented a decline of 1.5 percent in full-time equivalent enrollments across the system from the previous year.

Enrollments at the community-technical colleges grew to an all time high of 45,655 in 1992, following consolidation of the colleges in shared geographic regions. This growth was largely the result of increased operational efficiencies throughout the system as duplicate offices and redundant positions created by the merger were eliminated. An early retirement incentive offered to state employees in early 1992 allowed the system to replace employees displaced by merger into vacant positions created by retirements. Since that time, restricted funding due to the fiscal crisis which continues to beset the state of Connecticut and declining state appropriations, as discussed previously, have prevented the addition of course sections to meet student demand. In effect, a financial limit has been placed on enrollments.

More than 75% of the students enrolled are studying part time, and 24.5% full time. Sixty percent of the students at the twelve colleges are women. More than two-thirds of the African-American and Hispanic students enrolled in public higher education in Connecticut were enrolled in the community-technical colleges in 1998. The colleges' total minority enrollment equaled approximately 17.6% in 1991, grew to 19% in 1992, and to 23% in 1998. Nearly 60% of the colleges' students were 25 years old or older.

The proportion number of community-technical college degrees awarded in 1998 to graduates of occupational programs was 69.4% of the total of 3,495 degrees awarded in the system. The remaining 30% were in liberal arts and sciences and general preparation programs. Business and data processing programs continued to provide the single largest group of graduates (24.1%) in 1997-98, with health-related programs a close second, with 20.4% of the degrees that year.

FOR ADDITIONAL INFORMATION, PLEASE CONTACT:
Office of the Chancellor
Connecticut Community-Technical College System
61 Woodland Street
Hartford, CT 06105
Telephone: (860) 725-6601
Fax: (860) 566-6624

DELAWARE

Orlando J. George, Jr.
President, Delaware Technical and Community College

OVERVIEW

Delaware Technical and Community College is an open-access statewide institution with four campuses that are well positioned throughout the state.

The college curricula are primarily job-oriented. Additionally, Corporate and Community Programs provide a full range of ongoing and custom tailored training programs for the employees of area companies. College campuses use distance learning technology to enhance the instructional process by downlinking teleconferences from national and international sites and using a fiber optic network to link the campuses. The college offers both credit and non-credit telecourses developed by various community college networks, as well as by Delaware Tech faculty in the instructional television studios of the Stanton Campus. The college is fully licensed by the FCC for satellite uplinks worldwide.

General education programs are offered to help students develop the broader responsibilities of citizenship. These programs include courses in English as a Second Language and is offered in each county to non-english speaking students. The courses are designed to meet students' need to carry out every day communications with Americans and to prepare those having the interest and potential to continue into a degree program.

In 1967 the board of trustees selected Paul K. Weatherly as its first president. The board and its new president developed an integrated statewide plan for a four-campus system, with each institution to be administratively autonomous. The plan included the following goals, which are still in effect today (Kotula & Kubala, in Tollefson & Fountain, 1992):

- Provide for the constantly changing educational needs of a constantly changing community;
- Provide curriculum closely related to the economic and professional realities of the community;
- Develop a comprehensive community college with strong emphasis on occupational-technical skills and knowledge;
- Insure that individuals of all ability levels have access to all programs;

- Establish the college's identity as a significant member of the community;
- Develop the individual's ability to contribute to the enrichment of the economic base of the community;
- Promote interdisciplinary mix to facilitate student reactions and changing interests;
- Establish in the minds of the community that the college belongs to them;
- Develop a strong guidance system; direct the student to realistic, useable educational goals; and
- Develop strong emphasis on attitude and motivation training.

Four campus sites were selected, and facilities were built and programs developed and offered in the 1967-78 term of Dr. Weatherly's presidential service, from 1967 to 1976. Each campus obtaining accreditation from the Middle States Association of Colleges and Schools during this period (Kotula & Kubala, in Tollefson & Fountain, 1992).

Dr. John R. Kotula succeeded Dr. Weatherly as president in 1978. In his 14-year term, Delaware Tech developed a broadly participative three-year planning cycle to facilitate the fulfillment of the college's goals. Under Dr. Kotula's leadership, the college also increased its efforts in the areas of marketing, recruitment, resource development and industrial training (Kotula & Kubala in Tollefson & Fountain, 1992).

When Dr. Kotula retired in 1992, the board appointed Thomas S. Kubala to the presidency, a position he had until 1995. Under Dr. Kubala's leadership, Delaware Tech has undertaken strategic planning, increased cultural diversity, improved its management information system, emphasized institutional assessment and intensified its business and industrial training and service (Kubala & Kotula, in Tollefson & Fountain, 1995).

On July 1, 1995, Dr. Orlando J. George, Jr. became the college's fourth president. Since first being employed by the college in 1969 as a mathematics instructor, George has held various positions in the college, including dean of instruction, assistant campus director, and vice president and campus director of the Stanton/Wilmington campus. Under George's leadership, the college has emphasized increased partnerships with business, industry, and government; increased articulation agreements; educational technology and innovation; collegewide effectiveness, including an organizational structure supporting a one-college concept; and a supportive college environment.

GOVERNANCE

The Board of Trustees of Delaware Technical and Community College is the governing body of the institution. Trustees are appointed by the governor with the consent of a majority of the members elected to the State Senate of Delaware. The president of Delaware Tech represents the board of trustees as its state director for community colleges.

Six trustees are appointed for three-year terms. The city of Wilmington, New Castle County, Kent County, and Sussex County each have one resident on the board. The other two members may reside anywhere in the state. The seventh member may reside anywhere in the state, will serve at the pleasure of the governor, and will be chairman of the board. The vice chairman is selected by the board. No more than four trustees may be members of the same political party. Each trustee must be a citizen of the United States, a qualified Delaware voter, and a Delaware resident for at least three years preceding appointment. A trustee must continue to reside in the political subdivision of which he or she was a resident at the time of appointment.

The general powers and duties of the board are as follows:

(a) The board may establish institutions of learning throughout the state as may be necessary to effectuate the purposes of the Delaware Code;

(b) The board shall have custody of and be responsible for the property of the institutions and shall be responsible for the management and control of these institutions;

(c) The board has the following powers:

    (1) To select such officers, except the chairman, as it may deem desirable, from among its own membership;

    (2) To adopt or change the name of the institutions established by it;

    (3) To adopt and use a seal;

    (4) To sue and be sued, within the indemnification statues;

    (5) To determine the educational program of the institutions;

    (6) To appoint members of the administrative and teaching staffs of the institutions and to fix their compensation and terms of employment.

    (7) To appoint or employ such other officers of the institutions, agents, and employees as may be required to carry out this chapter and to fix and determine their qualifications, duties,

compensation, terms of office or employment, and all other terms and conditions of employment;

(8) To fix schedules of tuition rates and fees for educational services at the institutions;

(9) To grant diplomas, certificates, or degrees;

(10) To enter into contracts;

(11) To accept grants or contributions of money or property (conditional or otherwise) from government agencies or other sources, which the board may use for its purposes;

(12) To acquire (by gift, purchase, condemnation, or otherwise), own, lease, use, and operate property, whether real, personal, or mixed, or any interest therein, which is necessary or desirable for educational purposes;

(13) To determine that any property owned by the college is no longer necessary for educational purposes and to dispose of the same in such manner and upon such terms and conditions as shall be established by it;

(14) To make and promulgate such rules and regulations, not inconsistent with this chapter, that are necessary and proper for the administration and operation of the institutions and for the conduct of the business of the board;

(15) To exercise all other powers not inconsistent with this chapter, which may be reasonably necessary or incidental to the establishment, maintenance, and operation of higher learning institutions; and

(16) To employ such persons as deemed desirable.

The board meets a minimum of four times a year, varying its meeting places to include all five college locations, i.e., the office of the president and the four campuses. Four members of the board are required to achieve a quorum, and a board decision requires a majority vote. The administrative assistant to the president takes and keeps board minutes which are a public records and that are available upon request.

The Council of Presidents is an organization, that includes the presidents of the University of Delaware, Delaware State University, and Delaware Tech. The council coordinates relationships among the three institutions. The president of Delaware Tech also serves as a member of the Delaware Postsecondary Education Commission, whose purpose is to improve postsecondary education in the state of Delaware. The president of Delaware Tech also coordinated activities with the Delaware State Board of Education.

FUNDING

Budget (Fiscal Year 1999)

Operating Budget (includes credit, non-credit, Corporate & Community Programs, Special Programs, and State-funded debt service)	$78,530,900
Federal Funding	9,940,200
Capital Funding	8,000,000
Debt Service (State funded)	6,313,700

Percent of Budget

State Funding	62.6%
Federal Funding	9.7%
Tuition	13.1%
Special Funding	14.6%

Funding Methods

As an agency of the state of Delaware, the college is subject to the Delaware Code, to administrative rulings and policies set forth by the Department of Finance, State Treasurer, Controller General, Budget Director, and the Attorney General, and to annual budget provisions legislated by the General Assembly. The state uses no specific funding formula for institutions of higher education.

Each campus has instituted a formalized budget process and budget committee. The budget committee solicits from all divisions of the campus, budget requests which are linked to the college's strategic plan. Each campus holds open budget hearings on the budget requests from the various divisions. Individual campus budgets are submitted to the central fiscal office of the college and are combined to formulate the annual budget request for the college. The college's annual budget request is presented at an open hearing before the State Budget Director in the fall of each year. In the spring of the following year, the budget is presented at an open hearing before the Joint Finance Committee of the General Assembly which is responsible for preparing the state's final budget based on estimated revenues. The fiscal year period for the State of Delaware is from July 1 through June 30.

Tuition and Fees

Tuition:

In-state tuition	$57.50 per credit hour
Full-time (12+ credits)	$690 plus fees per semester
Out-of-state tuition	$143.75 per credit hour
Full-time (12+ credits)	$1,725 plus fees per semester

Fees:

Application Fee (for new students taking credit courses): $10.

Lab Fees: Fees vary. $7.50 per lab hour up to a maximum of 6 hours, or $45 per course. Industrial education course lab fees are determined by the specialized equipment utilized in the course. Some courses have additional lab fees.

Late Registration Fee (for students registering after the open registration period, and during the time set aside for late registration): $25.

Materials Fee (to defray cost of course materials): $4.50 per course.

Parking Fee (annual): $2, Stanton Campus; $7, Wilmington Campus.

Student Services Fee (for students taking credit courses): $15 per semester for full-time students and $6 per semester for part-time students; fee is non-refundable. Senior citizens are exempt from paying this fee.

PROGRAMS AND ENROLLMENTS

Delaware Technical and Community College enrolls students in five distinctly different types of offerings: courses leading to associate degrees, diplomas, or certificates; courses in association with the University of Delaware which encompass the first two years of study at the University; special interest non-credit continuing education courses; contract and workforce training courses in Corporate and Community Programs offered in conjunction with business, industry and public agencies; and courses leading to high school general equivalency diplomas (GED).

In the 1997-1998 academic year, 16,588 students were enrolled in degree, diploma, or certificate programs; 1,348 in the University of Delaware program; 10,465 in contract and workforce training, and 17,992 in special interest courses. It should be noted that 2,806 students were able to register in more than one of the college's academic divisions. The unduplicated number of students enrolled during the year was 43,535.

There are a large number of curricular offerings leading to degrees, diplomas, or certificates, and many offering options. For example: allied health, business administration, office systems technology, and heavy equipment operation offer courses of study in specific programs. Curricular offerings are added or deleted from time-to-time when advisory committees identify technologies which are "cutting edge", or when it becomes obvious that there is no longer a need for training in certain technologies which have become obsolete or for which employment opportunities have declined. Each program at each campus has an active advisory committee comprising a wide representation of the community interested in the specific program field. Recommendations obtained from the respective program advisory committees are considered in the development of all courses, technical and nontechnical. The advisory committees are very sensitive to the needs of the service areas of each campus. One of Delaware's three counties is highly industrialized, one serves as the location of many of the State's governmental offices, and the third has agricultural and resort areas with many specialized job opportunities.

Student demographics reflect the population of the state of Delaware in terms of race and gender. One notable trend is that the proportion of students enrolling part-time has increased each year for over a decade. Other than the program offered in conjunction with the University of Delaware, all of the programs offered at the college are designed for graduates to secure employment in their area of training, and/or transfer to a senior institution. Over 40% of our students plan to continue their education after graduation. The average age of the degree-seeking students is 28 years, and the college serves many women who return to school to prepare themselves for re-entry into the workforce.

Although it is possible to complete a program of study leading to an associate degree in as few as two years, over 65% of the students are part-time and supplement their income with full- or part-time jobs. The college has an "open-door" admission policy; however, many of its students require remediation in reading, writing skills, or mathematics prior to being accepted into a technology. This is especially true for students who have been away from school for a period of time. The actual time between admission and graduation approaches five years for the majority of students.

The availability of financial aid has not been a problem for the college. In addition to federal grants and loans, there are a wide variety of state grants, scholarships and loans, as well as private scholarships. The college does not offer housing or meal plans to any of its students, most of whom commute by public transportation or automobile. Tuition and fees for full-time students at the college are reasonably priced.

The fastest growing program area at the college is in Corporate and Community Programs. Some of the courses offered in Corporate and Community Programs are developed in cooperation with the State of Delaware Economic Development Office in an effort to attract new businesses which may require employees with specific training. Existing business, industry, and state agencies have well-developed partnerships with the college to maintain or upgrade the skills of their employees.

In addition to traditional classroom instruction, new distance learning technologies are in place at each of the college's campuses and these greatly enhance the educational offerings at each site. Many of the courses of study also offer clinical experiences, work-study opportunities, and internships with business and industry. Individualized instruction, computer labs, career counseling, placement offices, and many other student services are available at each campus.

Enrollments for the years 1996-1998 in courses leading to degrees, diplomas, and certificates are shown below. As was mentioned previously, several of the curricular areas, such as allied health, business administration, office systems technology, and heavy equipment operation offer specific programs. For example, allied health includes dental hygiene, diagnostic sonography, histotechnology, medical assisting, medical laboratory technology, veterinary technology, phlebotomy, nuclear medicine, occupational therapy, physical therapy, radiologic technology, respiratory care, emergency medical technology, exercise science technology, and health information technology. Catalogs are available upon request which describe the offerings at each campus, and within each technology.

Opening Fall Enrollment Collegewide by Technology—1996-1998

Technology	1996	1997	1998
Architectural Engineering	287	222	213
Agricultural-Business	56	57	67
Allied Health	1,251	1,362	1,492
Aeronautical Science**	24	22	6
Automotive Engineering	29	34	59
Bioscience	65	64	73
Business	1,252	1,343	1,348

Computer Aided Drafting	71	70	73	
Computer Engineering	55	51	52	
Computer Information Systems	570	608	691	
Computer Network Engineering	55	170	252	*
Civil Engineering	78	77	79	
Chemical Process Operator	—	—	394	*
Chemistry	49	48	44	
Construction Management	17	31	29	
Communications	49	40	41	
Criminal Justice	799	746	803	
Culinary Arts	52	49	51	*
Early Childhood Education	567	600	670	*
Educational Technology- Advanced Certificate	—	—	37	*
Engineering Drafting	10	6	8	
Electrical/Electronic Engineering	345	328	346	
Electromechanical Engineering	16	12	7	
EMT-Paramedic	15	15	7	
Environmental	42	38	47	
Fire Protection Engineering	74	78	75	
Food Service Management	71	64	60	
Engineering (General)	36	50	48	
Heavy Equipment Studies	42	42	0	
Human Services	758	714	660	
HVAC Engineering	22	20	13	
Industrial Engineering	141	147	138	
Mechanical Engineering	128	150	148	
Nursing/Practical Nursing	804	776	839	
Office Systems	290	270	238	
Poultry	22	14	9	
Refrigeration/Heating/Air	34	49	48	
Sign Language (American)	76	76	79	
Safety Management	24	18	21	
Specialized Occupations	146	161	173	
Visual Communication/Ad Design	—	68	84	*
Technology students	8,432	8,690	9,552	
Undeclared students	2,484	2,592	2,812	
Total enrollment	10,916	11,282	12,334	

*Programs implemented within the past three years.

ECONOMIC DEVELOPMENT

Delaware Technical and Community College is a recognized leader in economic and work force development. Through partnerships with business, industry, and various state agencies, the college serves over 700 companies and trains over 6,000 employees annually. In recent years, the college has allocated significant resources to develop initiatives to meet the needs of an increasingly technical, multi-skilled, and service oriented work force.

It is notable that within the past five years, Delaware Technical and Community College has been repeatedly recognized by the Delaware business community and state and local governments for exemplary efforts in serving special populations and addressing community needs that directly impact local economies. These recognitions are a testament to the college's focus on and effectiveness in finding innovative ways to serve. This spirit of innovation, fueled by the development and maintenance of strong partnerships with business, government, and industry, supports the delivery of high quality programming. Among the more important current thrusts of the college focused on developing the state's economy and its work force are:

- Outreach efforts to economically disadvantaged and educationally unprepared residents of the state provided through special courses and programs, many supported through state and federal funding;
- Targeted training programs that provide start-up training for newly located businesses, opportunities for companies to upgrade the skills of current employees, and retraining for current and potential employees. Among the audiences served by these programs are the small business community, established companies, businesses that have recently located to the state, and numerous state agencies;
- Maintenance of a team of statewide specialists who work directly with companies, trade associations, and economic development organizations to develop custom training initiatives that are delivered either on site or at one of the conveniently located campuses throughout the state;
- Providing leadership in the use of state-of-the art distance learning technologies to expand access to instructional programs, including access to the services of a fiber optic instructional network and satellite down-link capabilities. Technology is also being used to enhance instructional content and effectiveness by incorporating

computer and multi-media applications into both new and existing offerings; and

- Development of the Educational Technology Certificate program, designed to respond to important public educational reform initiatives in the state. Courses in this program help teachers, kindergarten through college levels, explore and become adept at using computers as a teaching tool.

In short, Delaware Technical and Community College is positioned as an influential and effective leader in economic and work force development within the state of Delaware and is a key contributor to its continued strong economy.

REFERENCES

Kotula, J. R. & Kubala, T. S. Delaware, in Tollefson, T. A. & Fountain, Ben B. E. (1992). *Forty-Nine State Systems, 1992 Edition*. Washington, D.C.: American Association of Community Colleges.

FOR ADDITIONAL INFORMATION, PLEASE CONTACT:
Office of the President
Delaware Technical and Community College
P.O. Box 897
Dover, DE 19903
Telephone: (302) 739-4621
Fax: (302) 739-3345

FLORIDA

J. David Armstrong, Jr.
Executive Director, Florida Community College System

OVERVIEW

Florida has become an international model for the orderly development of a statewide system of public community colleges. Indonesia, Russia and South Africa, among others, have sought to apply the governing principles of local autonomy and state coordination that comprise the bedrock of the Florida system.

Established by the legislature in accordance with a master plan developed in 1957 by the Community College Council, the system aims to provide post-high school education within a one-hour commuting distance of 99% of Florida's population. Its "open-door" policy and thorough "2 + 2" articulation plan with the state university system are hallmarks of the Florida Community College System.

Approximately 750,000 students are served annually at more than 200 learning sites in 28 community college districts. The state budget supporting the colleges—for all services including facilities—tops $1-billion, including student fees. Of that amount, only $4.7 million is spent on administration of the Division of Community Colleges. The student share is an average annual resident tuition cost of about $1,225 per student (32nd in the U.S.) and represents about 25% of direct cost per year. The Florida system ranks among the nation's largest in total statewide community college enrollment.

The primary mission of Florida's community colleges is to respond to community needs for postsecondary academic education and continuing career education. Community colleges are authorized to provide programs and services in the areas of:

- Lower-level undergraduate instruction and awarding associate degrees;
- Preparation for vocations that require less than baccalaureate degrees;
- Promotion of economic development of the state within the college service district; and
- Community services, adult pre-college education, recreational and

leisure services, general education developmental examinations (GED), and other programs and courses necessary to fulfill the mission.

In 1998, 63% of students in the upper division of Florida's universities received their lower-level undergraduate education at community colleges. In addition, a broad range of associate-degree and vocational certificate programs provide a trained workforce for Florida business and industry.

Community colleges emphasize both academic performance and preparation for the workplace. In addition to offering a complete range of degree programs, community colleges offer vocational and occupational education programs designed to prepare the students for the advanced technological demands of business and industry. Regardless of their career goals, community college students receive a quality education and are equipped for the challenges of four-year institutions.

GOVERNANCE

A strategic balance of local control and state coordination has been struck in Florida since 1983, when the legislature established the Florida State Board of Community Colleges (SBCC). The operation of each college is under the direction of a local board of trustees that is constituted as a corporate body and is assigned, by law, with specific duties and powers to carry out its responsibilities. These trustees are appointed by the governor, approved by the Florida State Board of Education, and confirmed by the Florida Senate. Boards range in size from five to nine members, depending on the geography of their service district. (The 28 college districts cover all 67 Florida counties.)

Among the powers and duties of the boards of trustees are the approval of programs and budgets, selection of the president and annual presidential evaluation. This local control has produced 28 distinctive colleges reflective of their communities. With approximately 250 programs operating collectively, the profile of each college is as different as Marianna is to Miami, as distinctive as Key West and St. Petersburg, as burgeoning as Orlando and Fort Lauderdale. These local boards eliminated more than 396 outdated programs between 1990-91 and 1996-97 and added 575 programs in response to community needs.

The 13 members of the state board are also appointed the governor and confirmed by the state senate. Their collective responsibility is to coordinate and oversee the operation of the locally controlled community col-

leges. Primary aspects of this role include:
- Developing statewide policy;
- Approving legislative budget requests;
- Reviewing and evaluating programs;
- Information sharing; and
- Advocating community colleges.

The SBCC serves as the director of the Division of Community Colleges within the Florida Department of Education. The SBCC appoints an executive director for the system, who serves as the executive officer and secretary to the SBCC and is responsible for leading the system, and recommending and implementing the rules and policies established by the SBCC. The executive director is in charge of the office of the SBCC and is responsible for appointing the staff of the Division of Community Colleges.

While the SBCC oversees the system, the successful governance of the colleges derives from local boards of trustees that know the educational and cultural needs of their local communities and can respond accordingly. This structure has resulted in the system's ability to meet its goals established in strategic plans and accountability plans at the state and local institution levels.

A recent illustration of the coordinative governance structure of the Florida system has been the handling of distance learning programs. As electronic delivery of courses and programs has expanded, and competing public and private forces seek to provide programs across traditional district boundaries, the state board created the Florida Distance Learning Consortium to provide guidance. Composed of a representative from each college, and chaired by one of the 28 presidents, the consortium recommends both to the Council of Presidents and to the state board. By the spring of 1999, it had developed a common-course database of more than 1,500 courses delivered by some mode of distance learning.

The total governance can be viewed as a three-legged stool (local boards and state oversight), with the third leg being the legislature itself serving as "finance committee" for each college and for the system as a whole. The legislature, of course, also sets policy and authorizes new initiatives (see "ACCOUNTABILITY" below).

Community colleges also must relate to the Florida Postsecondary Education Planning Commission (PEPC), which gives broad policy planning direction to all of the state's higher education systems. For example, local college plans for a new campus must be approved by PEPC on a decision path that leads to the SBCC. In 1999, the legislature considered giving PEPC authority to approve the delivery of baccalaureate degrees by a community college, if, after reasonable consideration, the state's university system had not provided access to a given B.A. program in a specific geographic area of the state.

Another critical aspect of governance in Florida is a body of laws, court rulings and attorneys general rulings collectively described as "the Sunshine Law." In sum, the public's business must be conducted in public view, and public transactions are public record. Of course, student records are federally protected, and most personnel records are confidential. Most, but not all, believe the Sunshine Law, while affecting presidential selection processes, has had a healthy effect on governance.

FUNDING

Florida community colleges are heavily dependent upon the state for operating funds and fixed capital outlay appropriations. Local property taxes are not a source of revenue for the Florida system of community colleges. The disequalization caused by local property taxes in funding per student was the principal reason the Florida Legislature chose to prohibit this revenue source in 1968.

State funds constitute approximately 69% of the collective colleges' operating budgets, while student fees represent 26.4%. If all funds are considered, the state share is 56.4%, student fees 19.1%, federal assistance 13.8% (primarily student financial aid), with sales, services and other receipts providing 10.6%. These revenues include interest earnings, sales commissions and rents, as well as indirect costs recovered from other governmental sources.

State appropriations for both state general revenue and lottery funds are allocated to each college in the Annual General Appropriations Act. Although Florida law provides for a funding process, the legislature does not use a consistent methodology in determining the allocation of state appropriations for each college. The unreliability of the budget formulas used in the appropriations process disadvantages meaningful long-term financial planning efforts at the colleges.

The Florida State Board of Community Colleges submits an annual legislative budget request for the collective needs of the 28 colleges within the system. This process of budget development includes the identification of statewide issues and a recommendation by the Council of Presidents, which serves as an advisory body to the SBCC. Local boards of trustees are briefed at regional meetings on the details of the legislative budget request. The Florida Association of Community Colleges is an important partner in disseminating information on the budget request and soliciting public support.

In the past, budget requests for the basic operating fund of each college (known as the Community College Program Fund) included an issue related to enrollment workload, which requested changes in state funding based on the actual FTE (full-time-equivalent) student enrollment of the prior year. Thus, as the enrollment of a college went up or down, the expectation of state funding would go, belatedly, in a similar direction.

Several years ago, in response to a public outcry for more accountability in state government, the Florida Legislature passed initiatives that required future legislatures to fund state agencies on the basis of outcomes or outputs (performance) instead of inputs. To implement the initiatives, the legislature chose to phase in the new performance-based budgeting requirements for two or three state agencies at a time over a period of several years. Community colleges were targeted for the 1996-97 fiscal year and were also targeted as the first educational agency in the state required to adopt performance-based budgeting initiatives. As a result, the colleges began working with the governor's office and the house and senate leadership to identify performance measures and a method to fund community colleges on the basis of these measures. This initial effort culminated with a community college system appropriation that provided $12-million in performance-based budgeting funds, which the colleges earn by "performing" defined "outcomes."

These incentive dollars have been allocated to colleges based on the achievement of specified individual student outcomes. Under the specified outcomes for the current year, the colleges earn incentive funds for each student who successfully completes an associate in arts degree, an associate in science degree, or a vocational program certificate. Other factors include rewards for each student completer who is successfully remediated, economically disadvantaged, disabled, licensed in a profession or placed in a job.

These incentive funds are earned by a college in the form of new state funding that is eventually added to its current funding level. This "base-plus" method provides both a reality check and a transitional period for colleges to adjust their priorities, internal resource allocations and management techniques to reflect the targeted outcomes. Since there are no restrictions on the use of these "incentive" funds, the entire college can share and benefit from the earnings generated. Such benefits may include additional faculty, specialized equipment, new programs or salary increases.

In the Annual Appropriations Act, the legislature establishes a standard tuition fee for resident and non-resident students. For 1998-99, the median standard fee for residents is $37.25 per credit hour, and the median standard fee for non-residents is an additional $111.42 per credit hour. Each college board of trustees may establish a tuition fee that varies no more than 10% above or below the standard fee established by the legislature. In addition to tuition fees, colleges also have discretion in charging application, transcript and laboratory fees to support their operating budgets.

Nearly all the revenues for fixed capital outlay come from the state. Generally speaking, community colleges do not have the authority to incur long-term debt. Lease-purchase agreements must be subject to the availability of annual appropriations.

For community college fixed capital outlay, there are two dedicated state tax sources. The first source is motor vehicle license tag revenue, a constitutional guarantee. Approximately $10-million per year is generated for community colleges from this state tax. These funds are allocated based on the annual number of full-time-equivalent (FTE) students served by each college. Local boards of trustees have the option of pledging their future receipts for the next 30 years as part of a state bond sale (which includes the public schools), or receiving the actual cash generated.

The primary source of revenue for fixed capital outlay is the state gross receipts tax, a 2.5% levy on electricity and telephone bills. Each year, the legislature authorizes the sale of 30-year revenue bonds, and the bond proceeds and other cash revenues are deposited in the Public Education Capital Outlay Trust Fund. Established for higher education purposes, the trust fund now allocates 20% of the total funds available to community colleges, a similar amount to universities and the majority to public schools.

Annually, each community college submits a five-year capital improvement plan by specific project to the Florida State Board of Community Colleges. The SBCC approves a three-year list of projects based on the projections of funds available to the system and a formula based on the relative need for space by college campus. In 1996-97, an amount of $125 million was appropriated by project to the colleges, and an additional $10.7 million was appropriated for maintenance. This amount is determined by a depreciation formula.

Primarily due to the diversion of funds for equipment needs, the 28 colleges have accumulated $173.7 million in deferred maintenance projects as of March,1999.

PROGRAMS AND ENROLLMENTS

Program planning and authorization is conducted in coordinated efforts among the colleges and the SBCC, primarily through a state Articulation Coordinating Council. An SBCC State Strategic Plan is developed in cooperation with the colleges. When adopted by the state board, it becomes a strong operating guide for the entire system. Local boards, of course, still can respond to special community needs in coordination with the state board.

In order to carry out the mission for Florida's community colleges, a variety of program areas are offered. These different areas are addressed through associate in arts (A.A.) degree programs, associate in science (A.S.) degree programs, Postsecondary Adult Vocational (PSAV) certificate programs, Postsecondary Vocational certificate programs, supplemental vocational, adult education and college preparatory courses, and recreation and leisure activities.

Each degree program consists of a designed course of study that leads to either the A.A. degree, which is the university parallel program, or the A.S. degree for persons going directly into the world of work. A.A. degree recipients are assured entrance into the State University System (SUS) under an articulation agreement. A.S. degree holders may also transfer to the SUS, but their coursework is evaluated on an individual basis.

Certificate programs are courses of study that take less than two years and prepare students for specific vocational fields. People who already hold A.S. degrees, certificates, or have on-the-job training may enhance their skills through continuing education or supplemental vocational courses.

Adult education enrolls persons who are no longer willing or able to attend regular high schools and moves them toward high school completion. For some, this means attaining basic or functional literacy while for others the outcome is an adult high school diploma, or the general equivalency diploma (GED).

Persons who have completed high school but are not yet academically ready for college are served by the college preparatory program. This program provides instruction in reading, English, mathematics and English Language. Many of the students in this program are older and have been out of high school for several years. The program allows students to refresh their skills and then proceed with college level work.

The final mission section is community service. One method of fulfilling this component is through the programmatic areas of recreation and leisure (R&L). The program consists of a vocational activity such as creating stained glass. This type of instruction is fully self-supporting and is not included in the enrollment calculation of the colleges for state funding purposes.

Between 1991-92 and 1997-98, the 28 colleges in the Florida Community College System increased their productivity by 22%. In 1997-98, they awarded the following degrees and certificates:

A.A. degrees	28,368
A.S. degrees	9,339
Certificates	11,547
TOTAL	49,254

The average age of students attending Florida's community colleges is 30 years. Three program areas have the following age breakdown: A.A. degree students – 26 years; A.S. degree students – 33 years; and PSAV certificate students – 31 years.

In recent research conducted by the Office of Educational Services and Research in the Division of Community Colleges entitled A Comparison of Community College Student Demographics By Program Areas, the following conclusion was stated:

...As one considers the demographics of these various [program] areas, it is clear there is an underlying relationship between the purpose of the areas and the students served. It is also apparent that students are moving among the different areas of need. This is a strong indication that the system is serving the needs of the students and not placing artificial barriers in their way. This movement among areas should be kept in mind when considering changes in programs or types of courses offered.

REFORM, REFORM, REFORM

Multiple and sweeping reforms initiated by the legislature substantially have reshaped what community colleges do and the way they do their work. Among the reforms and practices assimilated in the 1990s were:

- A legislatively mandated cap of 60 credit hours required for the associate in arts degree (down from 64);
- A legislatively mandated cap on general education core requirements at 36 credit hours (down from a state average of 42);
- Creation of an Occupational Forecasting Conference. In 1993, the Florida Legislature established this as one of eight consensus conferences that develop official information used for planning and budgeting the state's resources. This conference determines if the education system is training employees sufficiently to meet the state's employment needs, using labor marker information such as job openings, wages, and growth rates to identify needed training programs. The conference produces a list of "targeted" occupations at the state level and for each of the 28 college regions. The local lists are reviewed and validated by the local community college to identify their own targeted areas. Florida's community colleges provide training in nine of the top ten fastest growing occupations in Florida;
- Performance Based Incentive Funding. Traditional funding formulas do not give the colleges the incentive to terminate programs, or to create new programs. Looking at the situation from the college's perspective, terminating a program means firing a tenured faculty member. Creating new programs means having to absorb start-up costs and having to market the program to encourage student enrollment. Because shifting students and programs is such a difficult task, Florida created an incentive program – the Performance Based Incentive Funding (PBIF) program. PBIF rewards colleges for completing and placing student, if the training addresses one of the occupations targeted by the occupational forecasting process. Rewards are doubled if the student is a public assistance recipient. PBIF has shown tremendous potential in the community colleges and vocational centers during the first year, as follows:
- The number of economically disadvantaged enrolled in the targeted programs increased 46.6%, from 10,900 to 17,400. Non-targeted vocational programs were terminated, and program length has been reduced, because completing students increases earnings.

Quality was kept in line by paying for job placement, insuring that students have received the skills they need to be employed;

- Overhaul of Florida workforce development systems. In 1994, the Jobs and Education Partnership (JEP) of Enterprise Florida was established – Enterprise Florida is the privatized economic development agency for Florida. The mission of the JEP is to ensure that as jobs are created, personnel are trained to fill those jobs. JEP maintains oversight of the Occupational Forecasting Process and PBIF. The JEP was also charged with strategic planning, policy coordination and evaluation of Florida's workforce system; and

- In August, 1995, the JEP resolved the redesign of the Florida system, to be ready for a redesigned federal system. The Florida redesign began with the following premises:

    1. Systems must be locally designed and controlled;
    2. Duplication must be eliminated;
    3. Administrative costs and layers must be reduced; and
    4. Local business must be in the lead.

In October of 1995, the JEP recruited the economic development agencies in the state to take the lead in the local redesign. The JEP provided general design specifications, but left broad latitude and flexibility to the local areas. Systems are to reward outcomes that stress employment, increase wages, reduce public assistance and employer dissatisfaction. Systems are to be user friendly, for the economically disadvantaged and for business.

Since October of 1995, 24 geographic areas have been designated, reflecting labor market areas and patterns of commerce, as well as college boundaries. More than 1,000 representatives of business, economic development, education, job training, and social services are involved in creating the local systems, and eliminating duplication. Competitive procurement will ensure a valid return on investment, and cooperative efforts to share data are being created.

ECONOMIC DEVELOPMENT

These efforts, in combination, have created a community college system that is an integral part of the economic development system in Florida. The bottom line is that the leaders in local communities know best what their respective communities need. The systems are designed to meet those needs, not the needs of the funding categories.

The linkage between economic development and education is exceptionally strong and visible in Florida. The community colleges conduct training programs that meet the needs of employers, conduct continuing education and customized training for employees and employers, and are strongly involved in workforce development policy and programming at the local level.

ACCOUNTABILITY

In 1992, the Florida Legislature passed a bill establishing the community college accountability process (s. 240.324, Florida Statutes). This process required the adoption of an accountability plan, which established measures and goals, for five major categories: graduation rates; minority student enrollment and retention rates; student performance measures; job placement rates; and student progression rates. Each of the 28 community colleges adopted a separate accountability plan that contained college goals based on the statewide measures. The Statewide Accountability Plan, adopted in 1994, contained aggregate goals for the system. Since 1994, annual reports have been submitted to the legislature on the progress toward meeting the goals.

The accountability process is based on a five-year cycle. While institutions may adopt a new program to reach their accountability goals, the results cannot be measured for several years. This has been a criticism of the accountability process and has resulted in the creation of the Government Performance and Accountability Act of 1994 (s. 216.0172, Florida Statutes).

The 1994 act also requires the identification of accountability programs and measures, but a key difference in this act and the legislation passed in 1992, is that the measures must link directly back to the budget. In other words, the dollars appropriated to the various agencies must be appropriated according to the performance measures. (See also Issues In Brief # 4, April 1999.) The Florida Community College System was the first educational sector to tackle the difficult process of establishing Performance-Based Budgeting (See FINANCE section for more details on this issue). While representing only a small portion of the entire budget for the system, the program has stimulated the colleges to rethink how they do business. Barriers that stood in the way of students completing their education are being removed. The availability of student support services, particularly academic advising, has gained higher priority, and career counseling and job placement efforts have been re-energized, to name a few. Efforts are being made to expand to include universities and public schools. If all three sectors of education were to be funded on performance, the one guarantee is that "business-as-usual" would no longer exist. It's already that way in the Florida Community College System. Institutions are finding new and innovative ways to serve students and be more productive while maintaining quality education.

FOR ADDITIONAL INFORMATION, PLEASE CONTACT:
J. David Armstrong, Jr.
Executive Director
State Community College System
325 West Gaines Street
Suite 1314, Turlington Building
Tallahassee, FL 32399-0400
Telephone: (850) 488-1721
Fax: (850) 488-9763
Website: http://www.dcc.firn.edu

GEORGIA COMMUNITY COLLEGES

Cathie Mayes Hudson
Associate Vice Chancellor for Planning and Policy Analysis
Board of Regents of the University of Georgia System

OVERVIEW

Georgia's 13 two-year colleges are governed by the Board of Regents of the University System of Georgia. All 13 colleges offer transfer and career programs, and three of them also offer vocational-technical programs. Four of the two-year colleges are residential. Two additional colleges function as two-year colleges in their areas but also offer a limited number of baccalaureate programs. A separate system of 33 technical institutes and 17 satellite campuses operates under the Georgia Department of Technical and Adult Education.

The first Georgia junior college, Middle Georgia College, was established in 1884. The next two, Gordon Junior College and South Georgia College, were founded in 1927. The 1931 Reorganization Act, created the Board of Regents of the University System of Georgia. Other junior colleges were added in 1933, 1961, 1965, 1968, and 1970. Georgia Perimeter College was founded in 1964 (originally named DeKalb Junior College), was not transferred into the University System of Georgia until 1986. In recent years "junior colleges have eliminated the word "junior" from their names. In 1995, a systemwide initiative prompted each institution to study its mission in light of its distinctiveness as well as its members in the two-year sector of the system. As a result of this study, one two-year college changed its name to include the words "community college"; however, there are no community colleges in Georgia (with local funding) comparable to those in other states.

GOVERNANCE

The Board of Regents of the University system of Georgia is a constitutional body defined by the Georgia constitution, with 16 members. Five are from the state at large, and eleven are selected from their respective congressional districts. Members are appointed by the governor and confirmed by the senate to serve staggered seven-year terms. The chancellor is appointed by the board of regents and serves at its pleasure. The board employs standing and special committees that are not specialized by type of institution.

The administrative staff reporting to the chancellor are similarly organized under senior vice chancellors for academic affairs, fiscal affairs and facilities, and external affairs and human resources. There is no separate governance or administration for two-year institutions.

FUNDING

General operating revenues for the Georgia two-year institutions in the 1997-98 fiscal year totaled approximately $197 million. By policy, 75 percent of that total was from state appropriations, and 25 percent consisted of student fees, gifts, grants and miscellaneous revenues.

Matriculation fees in the 1998-99 fiscal year for all Georgia resident two-year college students were $573 per semester for full-time students and $48 per semester credit hour for part-time students. Full-time, non-residents paid $1,587 per semester, and part-time non-resident students paid $132 per semester credit hour. Other required fees ranged from $18 to $323 per semester per student at the two-year colleges. (The higher figure represents a mandatory laptop computer fee at one institution.) Georgia Perimeter College has a unique tuition and fee schedule of $39 per semester hour for Georgia residents and $92 per credit hour for non-residents.

PROGRAMS

All Georgia two-year colleges offer programs leading to associate degrees, and 13 institutions also offer certificate programs. The 5,807 associate degrees conferred from the summer of 1997 through the spring of 1998 by all Georgia two-year and senior colleges included 3,512 in liberal arts/general studies (in preparation for transfer), 1,513 in health professions, 250 in business, 128 in technical trades, 96 in agriculture, 134 in public affairs/social services/recreation, 45 in computer science, and 37 in engineering fields.

All two-year and senior colleges in Georgia participate in the Regents Testing Program (RTP). Since 1973, passing the test has been a requirement for graduation from all associate and baccalaureate programs. The RTP consists of a multiple-choice test based on reading passages and an assigned one-hour essay. Each essay is graded by three independent raters who do not know the names of the students or the institutions they represent. Students must pass both parts of the test by the time 45 semester credit hours have been completed or take non-degree credit courses in remedial reading or writing. In 1997-98, the percentage of students passing the RTP on their first attempt ranged from 41.0 percent to 79.9 percent in Georgia's two-year institutions.

All Georgia two-year and senior colleges offer a core curriculum in the freshman and sophomore years, which applies to two-year college students in transfer programs. The subject areas and required number of credit hours in each are as follows:

Area	Semester Credit Hours
A. Essential Skills (English, algebra)	9
B. Institutional Options (general education)	4-5
C. Humanities/Fine Arts	6
D. Science, Mathematics and Technology	10-11
E. Social Sciences	12
F. Courses Related to Program of Study	18
TOTAL	60

A systemwide remedial studies program (called learning support) has been implemented since 1974. Students scoring below 430 on the SAT-Verbal or 400 on SAT-Math (or comparable ACT scores), and students who have not completed the state's high school college preparatory curriculum in English or math or who do not meet their respective institutions' regular admissions standards, are required to take a basic skills examination (called the Collegiate Placement Exam, or COMPASS exam) to determine whether they must be placed into learning support courses. Such courses do not count toward a degree, and students must exit learning support through testing. Two-year colleges may play a larger role in providing remedial studies as the senior colleges and universities phase out learning support by the year 2001.

ENROLLMENT

Total headcount enrollment in Georgia two-year colleges increased from 35,709 in the fall of 1989 to 43,111 in the fall of 1998. Equated full-time enrollment grew over the same period from 25,595 to 27,223. The EFT figure is calculated by dividing the total credit hours by 15.

REFERENCES

Hudson, Cathie Mayes & Whitman, Susan, Eds., (1997, December). *University System of Georgia Information Digest, 1995-97*. Atlanta, GA:

Board of Regents of the University System. (http://www.usg.
edu/admin/pubs/infodig/infodig97).

University System of Georgia Academic Affairs Handbook (1998), Atlanta,
Georgia: Board of Regents of the University System of Georgia:
Author (http://www.usg.edu/admin /accaff/ handbook/section
2/2.04/2.04.html).

FOR ADDITIONAL INFORMATION, PLEASE CONTACT:
Dr. Cathie Mayes Hudson
Associate Vice Chancellor for Planning and Policy Analysis
Office of the Associate Vice Chancellor
Board of Regents
University System of Georgia
270 Washington St., NW
Atlanta, GA 30334
Telephone: (404) 656-2213

GEORGIA TECHNICAL INSTITUTES

Ben B. Walton
Director, Marketing and Program Improvement
Georgia Department of Technical and Adult Education

OVERVIEW

The mission of the Georgia Department of Technical and Adult Education is to contribute to the economic, educational, and community development of Georgia by providing quality technical education, public library services, adult literacy education, continuing education, and customized business and industry training. Accordingly, in addition to providing state support to 371 public libraries and 37 adult literacy service delivery areas, the agency provides credit and noncredit postsecondary technical education to Georgians through 37 institutions each with an assigned service area – 32 technical institutes directly governed by the Georgia State Board of Technical and Adult Education, one locally governed technical institute, and four vocational divisions of colleges in the University System of Georgia.

The first two institutions, North and South Georgia Technical Institutes, were established in 1943. In the 1960s, 20 institutes were established, and seven were established from 1970 to 1983. During this period, the system was under the jurisdiction of the Georgia State Board of Education. In 1984 the Georgia State Board of Postsecondary Vocational Education was established and the institutions placed under its jurisdiction. This board evolved into the current State Board of Technical and Adult Education. Since 1984, an additional four institutes have been established.

GOVERNANCE

The system of technical institutes and college vocational divisions is under the jurisdiction of the Georgia State Board of Technical and Adult Education and the Georgia Department of Technical and Adult Education. The board consists of 16 members appointed by the governor for three-year terms. Eleven members represent the state's congressional districts, and five are appointed at large. The state board approves the opening and closing of instructional programs, the curricula of programs, and the budget for the system as a whole. In addition, 32 of the institutes are directly governed by the state board. For these institutions, the board also approves the appointment of the state commissioner of the system and the institute presidents, as well as capital and operating contracts and purchases over $25,000.

These 32 institutions also have local boards which must also approve the fiscal and programmatic actions of the institution. The members of these local boards are appointed by the state board for three-year terms. The size of these boards depends upon the population and area of the service area of the institute, but each county in the service area must be represented on the board. Representation of counties is generally proportional to their population.

One technical institute is governed by a county board of education, and the four colleges are governed by the Board of Regents of the University System of Georgia.

When the system was put under the jurisdiction of the state board of technical and adult education in 1984, all the technical institutes were governed by local boards of education or local "area boards," except for two institutes directly governed by the state board of education. Since that time, gradually all but one of the institutions have been converted to direct state board governance as described above, with the two most recent conversions taking place in 1997.

FUNDING

The Georgia Department of Technical and Adult Education budget process is a zero-base budget request for each technical institute that is submitted to the Governor's Office of Planning and Budget in the fall for the next fiscal years' budget, which begins the following July. It is made up of two parts:

- The first part is a request for operating funds. This is based on prior year funding plus an amount for inflation and also enhancement funds for new programs; and
- The second part of the budget request is for Capital Outlay needs. This includes property acquisition and facility construction, renovation, and major repairs projects. Capital Outlay projects may be recommended for funding from various funding sources, including cash, bonds, or lottery funds.

Capital Outlay (Debt Service) FY99

	Bonds	Total
5 Year	$ 4,084,000	$ 4,084,000
20 Year	$ 62,170,000	$ 62,170,000
Total	$ 66,254,000	$ 66,254,000

Lottery Funds FY99

	Lottery	Total
Equipment	$ 20,809,346	$ 20,809,346
Repairs and Renovations	$ 6,000,000	$ 6,000,000
Total	$ 26,809,346	$ 26,809,346

The fiscal year 1999 operating budget information is included in the following table. In addition to state funds, each technical institute receives federal funds and local funds (generated by tuition, fees, etc.).

Department of Technical and Adult Education Operating Funds FY99

	Federal	State	Other*	Total
Personal Services Institutions	$ 8,243,869	$157,456,540	$ 22,934,516	$188,634,925
Operating Expenses – Institutions	$ 2,052,520	$ 23,874,171	$ 31,679,844	$ 57,606,535
Total	$ 10,296,389	$181,330,711	$ 54,614,844	$246,241,460
% of Total	4%	74%	22%	

* Includes $ 37,248,597 in anticipated tuition revenue

Currently, the department's annual appropriation is not formula driven. However, the new governor has created an education reform commission. This commission will address the issue of formula funding for the technical institutes, in addition to other educational items.

PROGRAMS AND ENROLLMENTS

The technical institutes offer programs resulting in technical certificates of credit, diplomas, and the associate of applied technology (A.A.T.)

degree. A technical certificate of credit program is one to three fulltime quarters in length, a diploma is four to eight quarters in length, and the A.A.T. is a minimum of 95 quarter credits, or at least six fulltime quarters. In FY 1998, 8,525 students received degrees or diplomas, and 6,186 received technical certificates of credit. Only 14 technical institutes are authorized to offer the A.A.T., but students at other institutes may pursue A.A.S. degrees through joint enrollment agreements with nearby colleges.

Enrollments in various categories for FY 1998 are shown on the attached charts. During the 1990s, enrollment has grown every year by an average of eight percent. Part-time enrollment is growing more rapidly than fulltime enrollment.

Georgia Department of Technical and Adult Education FY 98
End-of-Year Enrollment

PROGRAM	TOTAL ENROLLMENT	FTE
CREDIT PROGRAMS		
Engineering/Science	1,260	397
Technologies		
Industrial Technologies	21,965	9,874
Business Technologies	32,464	11,781
Health Technologies	15,589	7,130
Agriculture/Natural Resource	1,140	480
Technologies		
Personal/Public Service	6,441	3,157
Technologies		
Undeclared Majors	2,777	502
General Education	40,273	7,922
Developmental Studies	18,187	3,693
UNDUPLICATED TOTAL	88,801	44,934
NONCREDIT		
Adult Literacy/GED	67,979	
UNDUPLICATED – TOTAL	123,134	
CEU		
UNDUPLICATED TOTAL	27,723	

FTE = Full Time Equivalent-yearly credit hours divided by 45 quarter hours

FY 98 ENROLLMENT BY INSTITUTION

INSTITUTION	ENROLLMENT		
State Governed Technical Institutes	Total	Noncredit Courses	Certificate Diploma, Or Degree Programs
Albany Technical Institute	6,357	2,452	3,905
Altamaha Technical Institute	2,303	798	1,505
Athens Area Technical Institute	9,598	7,067	2,531
Atlanta Technical Institute	5,190	1,146	4,044
Augusta Technical Institute	9,481	4,871	4,610
Carroll Technical Institute	8,464	5,499	2,965
Chattahoochee Technical Institute	6,726	2,575	4,151
Columbus Technical Institute	5,117	2,190	2,927
Coosa Valley Technical Institute	6,381	3,776	2,605
DeKalb Technical Institute	26,300	21,665	4,635
East Central Technical Institute	5,285	3,328	1,957
Flint River Technical Institute	1,895	997	898
Griffin Technical Institute	4,423	2,269	2,154
Heart of Georgia Technical Institute	5,050	3,651	1,399
Lanier Technical Institute	8,891	6,679	2,212
Macon Technical Institute	11,541	6,912	4,629
Middle Georgia Technical Institute	5,996	3,477	2,519
Moultrie Area Technical Institute	4,331	2,657	1,674
North Georgia Technical Institute	6,869	5,110	1,759
North Metro Technical Institute	3,101	763	2,338
Northwestern Technical Institute*	5,333	3,195	2,138
Ogeechee Technical Institute	6,524	4,151	2,373
Okefenokee Technical Institute	3,693	2,293	1,400
Pickens Technical Institute	6,603	5,359	1,244
Sandersville Regional Technical Institute	3,067	2,343	724
Savannah Technical Institute	5,697	2,082	3,615
South Georgia Technical Institute	4,395	2,690	1,705
Southeastern Technical Institute	3,260	1,904	1,356
Swainsboro Technical Institute	4,358	2,880	1,478
Thomas Technical Institute	6,657	4,832	1,825
Valdosta Technical Institute	9,307	6,522	2,785
West Georgia Technical Institute	5,017	3,301	1,716
Locally Governed Technical Institutes			
Gwinnett Technical Institute	17,110	11,179	5,931
College Technical Divisions			
Bainbridge College	2,144	1,352	792
Clayton College and State University	9,556	7,799	1,757
Coastal Georgia Community College	2,108	1,093	1,015
Dalton College	1,530	0	1,530
State Total	239,658	150,857	88,801

Formerly Walker Technical Institute

ECONOMIC DEVELOPMENT

The Office of Economic Development Programs includes Quick Start, Georgia's economic development incentive training program; customized training for existing industry; retraining tax credit administration; certified economic developer trainer (CEDT); and new program incubator. In operation for over 31 years, Quick Start has trained approximately 300,000 workers for 2,850 companies. A rapidly growing area is customized courses that serve more than 50,000 trainees a year for existing industry. Workforce initiatives such as Certified Manufacturing Specialist, Certified Customer Service Specialist and Certified Construction Worker continue to grow in response to industry-hiring requirements. Economic development programs provides a single point of contact for business and industry at each technical institute throughout the state.

DTAE's Quick Start and technical institute business and industry services offer quality training as an incentive to locate new or expanding businesses and maintain existing businesses in Georgia. Quick Start is internationally known for providing effective customized training and services that help to maintain and increase jobs for Georgia. Technical institutes have expanded continuing technical education and customized training services for business and industry to provide rapid response to evolving state and local employment requirements. In 1998, Quick Start conducted 251 projects and provided training to over 31,345 trainees. The economic development divisions of Georgia's technical institutes provided a wide range of customized training programs for Georgia's business and industry, serving 54,658 trainees with 852,000 hours of training. Through these cost-recovery services, the technical institutes support the workforce needs of Georgia's existing industries statewide.

The Georgia Business Expansion Support Act of 1994 authorized and directed DTAE to set standards and approve retraining programs. The costs of these programs may be taken as a credit against state income taxes. Economic Development Programs administers this program through the technical institutes. The objective of the retraining tax credit is to foster the profitability and competitiveness of Georgia's existing industry by encouraging workforce development through retraining tax incentives. Eligible retraining programs are those that provide job skills for employees otherwise unable to function effectively on the job due to skill deficiencies or who would otherwise be displaced because such skill deficiencies would inhibit them utilization of new technology.

As the foundation for Georgia's workforce-pool development the certified manufacturing specialist (CMS), certified customer service specialist (CCSS) and certified construction worker (CCW) programs are offering businesses a way not only to ensure that they are hiring qualified workers, but also a way to certify their existing workforce. Some businesses offer premiums if workers become certified, while others promise interviews to prospective employees who hold the certification. Since its inception approximately 18 months ago, CMS has certified 2,140 and CCSS has certified 894 individuals. The CCW program has just recently been implemented.

Economic development programs are reviewed both internally and externally to determine their effectiveness. Internal view is based on customer feedback evaluations. External reviews are conducted by third party evaluations. One example of our external reviews was a recent evaluation conducted by the Carl Vinson Institute of the University of Georgia. Major areas evaluated were satisfaction of Quick Start services, satisfaction of employers with technical institute graduates and satisfaction of employers with technical institute customized training. Over 4,000 employers were surveyed and satisfaction ratings were all in the "high level of satisfaction."

ACCOUNTABILITY

The Georgia Department of Technical and Adult Education is currently piloting its new Performance Assessment System (PAS). PAS is unique in that it ties program assessment, community needs assessment, planning, and budgeting.

Program assessment is divided into two sections: Level 1 and Level 2. The purpose of the annual program evaluation in Level 1 is to promote quality and excellence in technical education and training. This evaluation includes a review of program standards developed by the Georgia Department of Technical and Adult Education. An improvement plan must be written for each standard that is not met by the program grouping. Benchmarks for achievement in enrollment, graduation, and placement constitute the cornerstone of the evaluation. Because PAS was developed based on the concept of no pass, no play, program performance becomes vitally important to the institution.

Level 1 analysis will be conducted annually by all program groupings at each campus. A program grouping may contain a degree, diploma, and technical certificates of credit within the same subject area. Groupings are identified by GDTAE. A program grouping will be measured on six performance measures: Annual Enrollment, Enrollment Trend, Annual Graduation, Graduation Trend, Annual Placement, and Placement Trend. To remain in Level 1, an institute must pass at least four of the performance measures. An improvement plan will be required for program groupings in Level 2 after the first pilot year. New program groupings will be exempt for three years from meeting performance standards.

Those program groupings that fail to meet the benchmarks outlined in Level 1 must respond to the Level 2 Credit Program Performance Improvement Plan. Since a major goal of these program groupings is to focus on improvement of performance, the institute and the program faculty must develop an organized plan for improvement. After a viable strategy for the process has been identified, a written plan including areas selected for improvement, description of improvement project, desired results, tasks to be completed, completion date, and leader responsible should be constructed. If the program grouping appears in Level 2 for three fiscal years, the institute must submit a proposal to justify keeping the program open.

Each year every institute must complete a community needs assessment. Through this process, each institute:

- Responds to significant changes in the community environment;
- Supports major changes in the planning section, especially requests for new or expanded programs not included in previous plans in the cycle; and
- Completes an Employment Demand Survey.

The planning section requires that each institute complete a campus master plan and a classroom and lab facility evaluation. Also, new program requests are made in this section. Improvement budget items are tied to planning.

FOR ADDITIONAL INFORMATION, PLEASE CONTACT:
Georgia Board of Technical and Adult Education
1800 Century Place, NE – Suite 400
Atlanta, GA 30345
Telephone: (404) 679-1600
Fax: (404) 679-1610
Web site: www.dtae.org

Daniel B. Rather, Chair
George L. Bowen, Vice Chair

Kenneth H. Breeden, Ph.D.
Commissioner
Georgia Department of Technical and Adult Education
1800 Century Place, NE – Suite 400
Atlanta, GA 30345
Telephone: (404) 679-1601
Fax: (404) 679-1610
E-mail: Kbreeden@dtae.org

Helen W. Mathis
Executive Secretary to State Board
1800 Century Place, NE – Suite 400
Atlanta, GA 303045
Telephone: (404) 679-1612
Fax: (404) 679-1610
E-mail: Hmathis@dtae.org

HAWAII

Joyce S. Tsunoda
Senior Vice-President, University of Hawaii, and
Chancellor for Community Colleges

OVERVIEW

In Hawaii, the Community College System consists of seven comprehensive campuses throughout the state, plus the Employment Training Center. This entire system, in turn, is a subsystem of the University of Hawaii. The University of Hawaii, therefore, is a ten-campus statewide system; seven of these ten campuses are community colleges.

The University of Hawaii Community College (UHCC) System was established by Act 139 of the Hawaii State Legislature in 1964. At that time, four existing state vocational schools were enfolded into the University. On O'ahu, two of these became Honolulu Community College and Kapi'olani Community College. On Kaua'i and Maui, respectively, they became Kaua'i Community College and Maui Community College. In 1969, the vocational school in Hilo on the Big Island of Hawaii became Hawaii Community College. From 1969-78, it operated separately from the University of Hawaii at Hilo; then from 1978-90, as a part of UH-Hilo. Two additional community colleges were added on the island of O'ahu: Leeward Community College in 1968 and Windward Community College in 1972. The Employment Training Center, which provides noncredit transitional training throughout the state to students at risk, and which had been established in 1962 as the Manpower Training Office, became part of the UH Community College System in 1968. Finally, in 1990, Hawaii Community College separated from the University of Hawaii at Hilo and became the seventh campus of the University of Hawaii Community College System..

The philosophical cornerstones of our UHCC System were laid down by the University's Board of Regents in their 1970 Policy Statement on Community Colleges, which implemented Act 139:

> *The goals of the Community Colleges of the University of Hawaii are comprehensive programs, low tuition, open-door admission, education guidance, quality teaching, and responsiveness to the community which each college serves.*

As part of the University of Hawaii, the community colleges are committed to the mission of the total University:

> To provide all qualified people in Hawaii an equal opportunity for quality college and university education; to create knowledge and gain insight through research and scholarship; to preserve and contribute to the artistic and cultural heritage of the community; and to provide public service through the dissemination of current and new ideas and techniques. In pursuing its charter, the University of Hawaii is committed to the development of the state's greatest asset, its people.

Within this context, the community colleges of the University of Hawaii have as their special mission:

1. To broaden access to postsecondary education in the state of Hawaii by providing the opportunity for any high school graduate or adult aged 18 or older to enter quality educational programs within his or her community.
2. To specialize in the effective teaching of diverse liberal arts and sciences so that community college graduates are prepared to enter the workplace or advance with confidence toward baccalaureate degrees;
3. To provide vocational and technical training that prepares students for immediate employment and supplies the paraprofessionals, technicians, and craftspeople needed by Hawaii's business and industry; and
4. To offer continuing education in the form of general and customized employment training, as well as non-credit instruction that emphasizes personal enrichment, occupational advancement, and career mobility.

GOVERNANCE

The University of Hawaii is governed as a system by a 15-member Board of Regents. Regents are appointed by the governor and confirmed by the state senate. Each island in the state is represented on the board. Although no student serves as a regent, non-voting student members serve on each board committee. The constitution of the state of Hawaii defines the functions and powers of the board of regents to govern the university, including the community colleges. Policy set by the board is carried out by the executive officer of the board, the president of the university. The board regularly reviews existing policy, modifies it, and adopts new policy as needed. It takes an active role in the management of the affairs of the university, determining the establishment and termination of programs, approving the university budget, and overseeing expenditures. The board has established direction to the community college system by mandating the development of comprehensive programs, low tuition, open-door admission, educational guidance, quality teaching, and responsiveness to the community which each college serves.

The committee on community colleges is one of eight standing committees of the board. The other committees are: academic affairs, finances, personnel relations, physical facilities, student affairs, university relations, and budget/long-range planning.

Within the past ten years, a major adaptation of the university's governance structure has involved the top-level administrative positions. The President of the University of Hawaii now also serves as the Chancellor of the Mánoa campus, which is the comprehensive undergraduate, graduate, and research campus of the system. The two baccalaureate campuses (UH-Hilo and UH-West O'ahu) are headed by a chancellor who is also a senior vice-president of the UH System. Similarly, the chancellor of the seven UH community college campuses also serves as a senior vice-president of the university system, with systemwide responsibility for international programs.

Within the community college system, a central chancellor's office staff coordinates the work of the seven comprehensive campuses and the Employment Training Center. Three vice chancellors for academic affairs, administrative affairs, and student/community affairs lead the central office staff and report directly to the chancellor. Also reporting directly to the chancellor are the CEO's of the seven community college campuses known as provosts and the CEO of the Employment Training Center, whose title is State Director.

FUNDING

As a public institution, the university's operating budget is funded primarily through appropriated general funds derived from tax revenues. Additionally, special funds, revolving funds, and federal funds supplement the operating budget. In addition to appropriated funds, each campus receives extramural funds from a variety of sources to supplement the development of innovative programs and to expand services to special student target populations.

Financial planning and resource allocation of state general funds is conducted in conjunction with institutional planning as defined in each campus academic development plan, a comprehensive statement of functions, goals and objectives, and resource requirements for a six-year period of time. These plans are developed with input from all segments of the institutional community. Each campus budget is submitted to the Chancellor for Community Colleges for review and possible adaptation before going on to the administration of the University of Hawaii System and the Board of Regents, then to the Hawaii Department of Budget and Finance, then the governor, and ultimately to the Hawaii state legislature. Funds released to the University of Hawaii are then directed to the campuses.

Over the past decade, the legislature and governor have provided the University with increased administrative and budget flexibility. Before 1995, tuition revenues for credit/degree programs were deposited into the state's general fund. Act 161, SLH 1995 altered the University's funding source by allowing the University to retain the tuition and fee revenues while continuing to receive a reduced general fund appropriation. The tuition and fees revenues, which offset part of the general fund reductions, are combined with the general fund to support the credit instruction program and academic, student, and institutional support programs.

The intent of Act 161 was to give the University additional fiscal autonomy. This would enable the University to adopt an integrated plan for the development of its programs, combining legislative allocations with the generation of income. Other provisions of Act 161 established a base level of general fund appropriations for the University, assured a minimal level of access to higher education and a minimal level of quality in instruction, and provided safeguards against financially overburdening students through tuition increases.

For fiscal 1996-97	Allocation	% of allocation
General fund	$ 60,710,975	63
Tuition & fees special fund (TFSF)	14,150,000	15
Special fund (excludes TFSF)	10,414,894	11
Revolving funds	7,303,408	8
Federal Funds	3,540,928	3
TOTAL	$ 96,120,204	100

PROGRAMS AND ENROLLMENT

The community colleges enroll more than 25,000 regular credit students in a typical semester, representing over half of the enrollment in the entire University of Hawaii System. Headcount enrollment of all regular students, classified and unclassified, in credit programs dropped slightly in the 1996-97 year. This drop of about 5% was not unexpected, given the tuition increase at all campuses.

Fall 1996 total enrollment was 25, 472 students. For spring 1997, the total was 23, 518. This translates to FTE enrollments of 15,510 for fall, 1996; 14, 342 for spring, 1997. Each semester, our campuses serve more than 18,000 additional students through noncredit programs.

Program areas of Fall 96 credit students are indicated below. This sort of breakdown is not yet available for Spring 97:

General Education		14, 745	
Vocational Education		8, 812	
includes			
Business Ed	— 2,967		
Food Services	— 920		
Health Services	— 894		
Public Services	— 1,549		
Technology	2,482		
	Unclassified		1,899
Not Indicated		16	
TOTAL		25,472	

The UH Community College System awards four types of degrees and five types of certificates:

1. Associate in Arts (A.A.) degree: A two-year liberal arts degree, consisting of at least 60 semester credits, which provides students with skills and competencies essential for successful completion of a baccalaureate degree, entirely at the baccalaureate level. The issuance of an A.A. degree requires that the student must earn a GPA of 2.0 or better for all courses applicable toward the degree.

2. Associate in Science (A.S.) degree: A two-year technical-occupational-professional degree, consisting of at least 60 semester credits, which provides students with skills and competencies for gainful employment, entirely at the baccalaureate level. The issuance of an A.S. degree requires that the student must earn a GPA of 2.0 or better for all courses applicable toward the degree.

3. Associate in Applied Science (A.A.S.) degree: A two-year technical-occupational professional degree, consisting of at least 60 semester credits, which provides students with skills and compe-

tencies for gainful employment. This degree is not intended nor designed for transfer directly into a baccalaureate program. A.A.S. programs may, however, include some baccalaureate level course offerings. The issuance of an A.A.S. degree requires that the student must earn a GPA of 2.0 or better for all courses applicable toward the degree.

4. Associate in Technical Studies (A.T.S.) degree: A two-year technical-occupational professional degree, consisting of at least 60 semester credits, which provides students with skills and competencies for gainful employment. This degree must be customized by using courses from two or more existing approved programs and is intended to target emerging career areas which cross traditional boundaries. This degree must have educational objectives which are clearly defined and recognized by business, industry, or employers who have needs for specialized training for a limited number of employees. This degree must have advanced approval, and cannot be requested based upon previously completed coursework. The issuance of an A.T.S. degree requires that the student must earn a GPA of 2.0 or better for all courses applicable toward the degree.

5. Certificate of Achievement: A college credential for students who have successfully completed designated medium-term technical-occupational-professional education credit course sequences which provide them with entry-level skills or job upgrading. These course sequences shall be at least 24 credit hours, but may not exceed 45 credit hours (unless external employment requirements exceed this number). The issuance of a Certificate of Achievement requires that the student must earn a GPA of 2.0 or better for all courses required in the certificate.

6. Certificate of Completion: A college credential for students who have successfully completed designated short-term technical-occupational-professional education credit course sequences which provide them with entry-level skills, or job upgrading. These course sequences shall be at least 10 credit hours, but may not exceed 23 credit hours. The issuance of a Certificate of Completion requires that the student must earn a GPA of 2.0 or better for all courses required in the certificate.

7. Academic Subject Certificate: A college credential for students who have successfully completed a specific sequence of credit courses

from the A.A. curriculum. The sequence must fit within the structure of the A.A. degree, may not extend the credits required for the A.A. degree, and shall be at least 12 credit hours. The issuance of the Academic Subject Certificate requires that the student must earn a GPA of 2.0 or better for all courses required in the certificate.

8. Certificate of Competence: A college credential for students who have successfully completed designated short-term credit or non-credit courses which provide them with job upgrading or entry-level skills. Credit course sequences shall not exceed 9 credit hours. The issuance of a Certificate of Competence requires that the students work has been evaluated and determined to be satisfactory. In a credit course sequence the student must earn a GPA of 2.0 or better for all courses required in the certificate.

9. Certificate of Attendance: A document issued to students who have attended credit or non-credit courses or activities which do not meet the requirements for other certificates or degrees. This certificate does not reflect academic performance and no performance evaluation is implied by its issuance.

In terms of enrollment trends over the past ten years, the following are noteworthy:

- 1985 was the last year in which the majority of students majored in vocational education programs;
- Average class size in both liberal arts and vocational programs has increased every year since the Fall 1991;
- Percentage of female students has increased; and
- Hawaiian and Filipino student enrollment has increased significantly in response to concerted efforts at reducing barriers to minority enrollment.

ECONOMIC DEVELOPMENT

Hawaii's economic future and the future of the community college system are mutually dependent. The trained workforce of the twenty-first century will increasingly require post-secondary education; and the fiscal resources available to the state's colleges are increasingly dependent upon a healthy state economy.

Timely, customized responses to community needs are one way the UH Community Colleges prepare the state to effectively handle change. Within the past decade, Hawaii has lost its main agricultural economies of pineapple and sugar cane production, as well as a good portion of the garment production industry. In addition, on the island of Kaua'i, the tourism industry was brought to a standstill following the 1992 devastation of Hurricane Iniki. In every instance, the community colleges have stepped in to provide short-term, non-credit instruction to help prepare workers for new career fields.

Hawaii is attempting to diversify and strengthen its economy, and the success of this effort will depend to a great degree upon the availability of appropriate retraining and extended education. Research by the state department of labor indicates that one quarter to one third of Hawaii's current workforce will need significant retraining over the next decade, while at least a third of the state's new jobs will require extensive postsecondary education.

To help meet these needs, the University of Hawaii Community Colleges are working cooperatively with the state's secondary schools and Hawaii's businesses on programs such as Tech-Prep and School-to-Work. But the role of the community colleges in economic development is not limited solely to short-term programs. The community colleges are also working with other arms of the university and with the state legislature to create more long-range educational opportunities in fields which will be vital to the economic growth of this Pacific island chain—air and water transportation research, agricultural and marine research, research in the health sciences, and communications and technological research.

In 1996, the university's board of regents approved a policy creating University Centers at three neighbor island sites. University Centers facilitate delivery of instructional programs and student support services from any of the university's ten campuses. These university centers — established on community college campuses on the islands of Hawaii, Kaua'i and Maui — are enabling neighbor island residents to access some of the upper-division and graduate-level instruction necessary to further their careers in education, health care or social work. This outreach, in combination with various forms of technologically-supported distance education, is allowing Hawaii's residents to improve their educational levels — and ultimately, their economic levels — without a need to disrupt their lives relocating from a neighbor island to O'ahu.

Hawaii's state legislature has recognized the role that the community colleges are playing and can continue to play. Various bills introduced for consideration by the 1997 legislature deal with the involvement of the community colleges in economic development activities.

ACCOUNTABILITY

The ten-year (1997—2007) strategic plan of the community colleges has five major goals. There is an accountability component to each.

1. Provide access to quality educational experiences and service to the state Accountability measures include monitoring of student transfer progress among the various campuses. The colleges will pursue strategies and actions that increase retention and graduation rates and shorten time to degree for all students. This includes better articulation with feeder schools, as well as with the baccalaureate programs to which community college graduates transfer. Responsiveness to state needs will be enhanced by a closer integration of credit and noncredit learning, expanded/strengthened partnerships with the business sector as well as other educational agencies, and utilization of distance education technology to reach more students;

2. Implement differentiated campus missions and function as a system Accountability measures include development of policies and procedures to facilitate concurrent registration across multiple campuses, termination/consolidation of low demand programs, and facilitation of open entry/open exit programs for basic skills instruction;

3. Continue to champion diversity and respect for differences Accountability measures include increased recruitment/retention efforts targeted to underserved populations, especially Native Hawaiians — both among students and among faculty/staff;

4. Strengthen the University as a premier resource in Hawaiian, Asian and Pacific affairs, and advance its international leadership role. Accountability measures include expanded course offerings and increased student enrollment in such courses about the languages, history and cultures of Hawaii, Asia and the Pacific. Also, provision of educational experience with an international dimension C whether arranging travel/study opportunities for Hawaii's students or attracting to Hawaii students from the Pacific Basin and Asia who can benefit from programs in fields where the community colleges have special strengths; and

5. Acquire resources and manage them with accountability and responsiveness For human resources, accountability measures include sup-

port of professional development activities and enhancements to student services. For fiscal resources, accountability measures include development and implementation of a multi-year fiscal plan to provide a sustainable resource base, as well as a plan to increase community financial support.

In conjunction with this strategic plan, a benchmark document identifies a series of performance indicators to monitor progress toward goals.

Not all accountability measures are connected to the strategic plan, however. Ongoing measures throughout the community college system include measures of program centrality, program efficiency, and program effectiveness. The criterion of program centrality subsumes variables which reflect the mission and priorities of the system, student enrollment demands, or (in the case of vocational programs) the external economic needs of the state of Hawaii. Program efficiency measures student utilization relative to program resources (average class size, class enrollment vs. capacity, student-to-counselor ratio, faculty teaching load, etc.). Program effectiveness measures the extent to which the community colleges' mission and goals have been attained — successful transfers to baccalaureate programs, success in chosen occupational field. Program reviews and indicators of program health are ongoing constantly, with analyses of data conducted jointly by the campuses and the chancellor's office.

FOR ADDITIONAL INFORMATION, PLEASE CONTACT:
Office of the Chancellor for Community Colleges
2327 Dole Street
Honolulu, HI 96822
Telephone: (808) 956-5883
Fax: (808) 956-8061
E-mail: jtsunoda@cccada.ccc.hawaii.edu
WWW: http://www.hawaii.edu/admin/tsunoda.html

IDAHO

Terrence A. Tollefson
Professor, Department of Educational Leadership and Policy Analysis
East Tennessee State University

OVERVIEW

Idaho's first two junior colleges were private and religiously affiliated: Ricks College, established in 1880 in Rexburg by the Church of Jesus Christ of the Latter Day Saints; and Boise Junior College, established by the Episcopal Diocese of Idaho. The state's first venture into public two-year college education was through North Idaho College, founded in 1933 in Coeur d'Alene. It was a private institution supported by public funds until 1939, when the Idaho legislature passed the Junior College Act authorizing public two-year institutions. The state's only other public community college is the College of Southern Idaho, founded in Twin Falls in 1964 after the enactment of House Bill 363 a year earlier, which created six community college districts in Idaho. There also is a public technical institute (Tollefson & Patton, 1998). Boise State University, Idaho State University, and Lewis-Clark State College also provide community college programs within their regions of the state (Barton, 1997).

GOVERNANCE

The Idaho State Board of Education is authorized to approve community college educational programs and make budget recommendations to the governor and legislature. Each community college has a board of trustees that appoints the president, hires faculty members, holds title to property, and sets policies and salaries (Barton, 1997).

FUNDING

Each community college board of trustees has the authority to levy a local property tax of up to $0.80 per $100 of assessed valuation for college operations, and up to one-half a mil on each dollar of assessed valuation for maintaining the college's grounds and gymnasium. Portions of state liquor revenues also are allocated to the community colleges (Barton, 1997). The state provided an 11% budget increase to the Idaho community colleges in the 1998-99 fiscal year, substantially to fund faculty salary increases (Tollefson & Patton, 1998).

PROGRAMS AND ENROLLMENT

The 1963 "junior college" act defined the colleges as "...intermediate institutions of higher education above grade twelve", that "...give instruction in academic subjects, and in such nonacademic subjects as shall be authorized by its board of trustees" (Barton, 1997, p. 148). Both community colleges provide comprehensive educational programs and services, including academic, vocational and technical, adult education and community services (Barton, 1997).

The two public community colleges and three senior public institutions enrolled over 29,000 headcount students in "community college" programs in the fall of 1996, of whom 42% were male and 58% female. Average tuition at public community colleges was $1,045 and at public four-year institutions it was 1,973 (Tollefson & Patton, 1998).

WORKFORCE DEVELOPMENT

A workforce training center funded by a foundation operates near the College of Northern Idaho. Business and technology programs also are expanding very rapidly (Tollefson & Patton, 1998).

REFERENCES

Barton, R. (1997, March). Community Colleges in Idaho, in Community College Journal of
Research and Practice, 21 (2), pp. 147-158.
Tollefson, T. A. & Patton, M. (1998). Idaho, in AACC Annual 1997-98, pp. 40-41. Washington, DC: American Association of Community Colleges.

FOR ADDITIONAL INFORMATON, PLEASE CONTACT:

Office of the Executive Director
Idaho State Board of Education
LBJ Building, Room 307
650 West State Street
Boise, ID 83702
Telephone: (208) 334-2270

ILLINOIS

Ivan J. Lach
Vice President (Retired)
and
Virginia K. Mcmillan
Executive Vice President
Illinois Community College Board

OVERVIEW

Illinois is prominently identified with the early history of the community and junior college movement in the United States. Joliet Junior College, established in 1901in Joliet, Illinois, was the first public junior college in the nation. Illinois adopted its first junior college legislation in 1931, which permitted the Board of Education of Chicago to establish, manage, and provide for the maintenance of one junior college offering two years of college work beyond the high school level as part of the public school system of the city.

The first Illinois Junior College Act became law on July 1, 1937, and provided for the development of the junior college system as a part of the public school system. It made no provision for the charging of tuition, nor did it stipulate that educational opportunities available through the junior colleges would be provided without charge to the students. Other provisions of the law allowed establishment of junior colleges by board resolution in districts with a population between 25,000 and 250,000, establishment of junior colleges in smaller districts by referendum, and validation of all operating districts established prior to 1937.

In 1943, legislation was adopted to hold referenda to set separate tax rates for both education and building funds to support junior college operations. State funding for junior colleges, however, was not established until 1955. Seven new public junior colleges were established in Illinois between 1955 and 1962, bringing the total to 18. Rock Island, Moline, and East Moline joined to form Black Hawk College in 1961, which was the first junior college created separately from a common school district.

In 1951, the Illinois General Assembly enacted legislation setting forth standards an procedures for establishing junior colleges. This action repealed the legislation that allowed establishment of junior colleges in districts with populations in excess of 25,000 by action of a resolution of the board of education. In 1959 separate junior college districts were authorized by allowing any compact and contiguous territory to be organized as a junior college district with an elected board of education having authority to maintain and operate the college and levy taxes for its operation. State funding for junior college operations was first appropriated in 1955.

As a result of recommendations of the Illinois Commission of Higher Education, legislation was adopted in 1961 creating the Illinois Board of Higher Education. According to the legislation, the Illinois Board of Higher Education had responsibility for conducting comprehensive studies on higher education needs; development of information systems; approval of new units of instruction, research, or public service in all public colleges and universities; budget review of public colleges and universities, with recommendations to the governor and generally assembly; approval of all capital improvements; surveys and evaluation of higher education; and preparation of "a master plan for the development, expansion, integration, coordination, and efficient utilization of the facilities, curricula, and standards of higher education in the areas of teaching, research, and public service." Although junior colleges were legally under the jurisdiction of the superintendent of public instruction at this time, a section of the enabling legislation for the Illinois Board of Higher Education contained the following statement concerning junior colleges:

> In the formulation of a master plan of higher education and in the discharge of its duties under this act, the board shall give consideration to the problems and attitudes of junior colleges...as they relate to the overall policies and problems of higher education.

In July 1964 the final draft of the higher education master plan was published. As a result, the Junior College Act of 1965, the foundation for today's system of public community colleges in Illinois, was adopted. The act contained the following key provisions:

- Provided that the junior colleges come under the jurisdiction of the Illinois Board of Higher Education rather than remaining part of the common school system;
- Provided for establishment of a system of locally initiated and administered comprehensive Class I junior college districts;
- Mandated that on August 1, 1965, all junior colleges operating in

school districts where separate educational and building fund tax levies had been established for the college become separate junior colleges, classified as Class II districts;

- Provided that school districts operating a junior college without a separate tax could continue to maintain the program as grades 13 and 14;
- Set forth procedures for converting Class II districts to Class I districts;
- Created a legal base for the establishment of public comprehensive districts with locally elected boards in a system coordinated and regulated by a State Junior College Board, which in turn related to the Illinois Board of Higher Education, as did the governing boards of the other public colleges and universities;
- Set forth the powers and duties of the Illinois Board of Higher Education, the Illinois Junior College Board, and the boards of the local junior college districts as individual entities and in relation to each other;
- Included provisions for local-state sharing of capital funding, acquisition of sites, operational funding, and annexations and disconnections of territory; and
- Made local and state financial support for junior college attendance applicable to all Illinois residents, whether they resided within the boundaries of a junior college or not.

On July 15, 1965, the Junior College Act became effective; and on August 1 the school boards of districts operating junior colleges with separate educational and building rates became the boards of the newly constituted Class II districts. Also in August of 1965, Governor Kerner appointed nine members of the first Illinois Junior College Board. In 1973, the term "junior" was changed to "community" in statute.

Currently, there are 39 public community college districts composed of 48 colleges and one multi-community college center. Thirty-seven of the districts have single colleges while two others are multi college districts. Since July 1990, the entire state has been included within community college district boundaries.

Mission. The mission of the Illinois Community College System is to provide high-quality, accessible, cost-effective educational opportunities for the individuals and communities it serves.

Focusing on individual educational needs requires a recognition of the diversity of individual student backgrounds and living environments. The colleges provide appropriate counseling, placement, and other types of support services to meet diverse student needs and goals.

Focusing on community educational needs requires extensive collaboration and cooperation with community agencies, government, business and industry, and other educational institutions in order to identify community needs and develop strategies to address them in a manner which is both educational and economically sound. The system recognized that the "community" it serves is multicultural, economically diverse, global, and changing.

Through the ongoing assessment of student and community needs and goals, it is the responsibility of each community college to provide (1) a broad range of educational programs, services, and delivery systems; (2) the necessary development of its staff, and (3) an appropriate learning environment to address these needs and goals.

The mission of the Illinois Community College Board (ICCB), as the state coordinating board for the community college system, is to administer the Public Community College Act in a manner that maximizes the ability of the community colleges to serve their communities, promotes collaboration within the system, and accommodates those state initiatives that are appropriate for community colleges.

GOVERNANCE

The governance structure of the Illinois Community College System consists of the state coordinating board (ICCB) and local governing boards of trustees for the 39 community college districts. Each of these local boards is elected by vote of the district residents with the exception of City Colleges of Chicago's board which is appointed by the mayor of Chicago.

The ICCB consists of 11 members appointed by the governor, with the consent of the state senate, and one nonvoting member selected by the Student Advisory Committee. Board members are appointed at large for six-year terms, with the chair appointed by the governor and the vice chair elected by board members. By statute, one of the 11 members appointed by the governor must be a senior citizen age 60 or older. The ICCB meets six to eight times a year.

The members of the board must be citizens and residents of the state of Illinois. A member of the board cannot engage in employment for which he or she receives a regular salary from public funds and cannot hold current membership on a school board or a board of trustees of a public or nonpublic college, university, or technical institute.

The ICCB has statutory responsibility for administration of the Public Community College Act (*Illinois Revised Statutes*, 1985, Chapter 122, articles I through VIII). The ICCB is empowered with regulatory as well as coordinating responsibilities. The following coordinating/regulatory powers and duties are assigned to the board in statute:

- Make and provide rules and regulations not inconsistent with the provisions of the Public Community College Act;
- Develop articulation procedures to the end that maximum freedom of transfer among community colleges and between community colleges and degree-granting institutions be available;
- Organize and conduct feasibility surveys for new community colleges or for the inclusion of existing institutions as community colleges and the location of new institutions;
- Approve all locally funded capital projects;
- Cooperate with the community colleges in continuing studies of student characteristics, admission standards, grading policies, performance of transfer students, qualification and certification of facilities, and any other problem of community college education;
- Enter into contracts with other governmental agencies and accept federal funds and plan with other state agencies for the allocation of such federal funds;
- Determine efficient and adequate standards for community colleges for the physical plant, heating, lighting, ventilation, sanitation, safety, equipment and supplies, instruction and teaching, curriculum, library, operation, maintenance, administration, and supervision;
- Determine the standards for establishment of community colleges and the proper location of the site in relation to existing institutions of higher education;
- Approve or disapprove new units of instruction, research, and public service;
- Participate and assist in the coordination of programs of interinstitutional cooperation with other public and nonpublic institutions of higher education and establish guidelines regarding sabbatical leaves;
- Establish guidelines for the admission into special, appropriate

programs conducted or created by community colleges for elementary and secondary school dropouts;

- Grant recognition to community colleges that maintain equipment, courses of study, standards of scholarship, and other requirements set by the state board;
- Prepare and submit to the state comptroller vouchers for credit hour grants, special populations grants, economic development grants, equalization grants, advanced technology equipment grants, and retirees health insurance grants, and distribute such other special grants as may be authorized by the General Assembly;
- Establish uniform financial accounting and reporting standards and principles for community colleges and develop procedures and systems for reporting financial data; and

The Illinois Board of Higher Education is the coordinating administrative agency with responsibility for all higher education sectors in Illinois. As such, it approves the instructional programs, capital projects, and systemwide operating and capital budgets for the public community college system after action by the ICCB.

FUNDING

Illinois public community colleges receive funding from three major sources: local property taxes, student tuition and fees, and state appropriations.

The state appropriation process begins with the ICCB submitting a fiscal-year system operating budget request to the Illinois Board of Higher Education, which evaluates the community college system request while considering the state's total higher education priorities. Requests for state funding for the community college system are introduced in the state legislature, usually at the level recommended by the Illinois Board of Higher Education.

Early in the legislative session the governor proposes a state budget. The Illinois Board of Higher Education, with input from the higher education system, then allocates the governor's higher education budget among the state's higher education institutions if the governor's budget for higher education differs from its own. It is then the responsibility of the legislature to appropriate funds at the level it desires and to authorize the distribution mechanism for its appropriations. The process is completed when the governor signs the appropriation passed by the legislature.

Conceptually, the community college state appropriation is equal to an estimate of funds needed, less an estimate of funds available to the community college system. The estimate of funds available to the community college system centers on four sources of revenue: local property tax receipts, student tuition and fees, other state grants, and federal and other miscellaneous revenues.

Local property tax estimates are determined by multiplying the statewide total community college projected equalized assessed valuation by an average tax rate. This amount, less adjustments for collection losses and equalization, yields estimated local tax receipts.

Statutorily, community colleges cannot charge tuition and fees that exceed one-third of their per capita cost. Actual tuition and fee rates range from $34 to $53 per semester credit hour. A statewide average tuition and fees calculation is used in the funding formula.

Community colleges receive additional revenue from a number of other sources. For example, the Illinois State Board of Education distributes grants for adult education and vocational education in support of specific instructional programs. In addition, the corporate personal property tax revenues eliminated in 1979 as part of local property taxes have been replaced by revenues from new taxes on corporations, partnerships, and utilities. The revenues generated from these taxes are distributed to community college districts. In addition, community college districts receive funds from a variety of other federal, state, and local sources. Given the difficulty of making accurate projections of this revenue, the community college funding plan provides that miscellaneous revenue is projected based on the percentage it represented of all revenue for the most recent historical year.

The estimate of funds needed by the system is determined by adjusting the most recent actual expenditures for anticipated cost increases. The final appropriation to the ICCB is then distributed in the form of grants to the community college.

There are a number of state appropriated categorical grants to colleges that flow through the ICCB. Base Operating Grants are based on enrollments and square footage. The major portion of this grant is allocated to colleges based on the credit hour enrollment in six instructional funding categories. The credit hour rate for each instructional category is determined by calculating the unit cost of that category and subtracting the system's other available resources from the projected unit cost in each instructional category. Frequently program improvement dollars are added to the formula in such areas as technology, staff development and training, adult education/remedial development support, and deferred maintenance. In fiscal year 1999 this grant was expanded to include an allocation based on the gross square footage at the colleges.

Small college grants are distributed to districts with less than 2,500 non-correctional full-time equivalent students. This grant is intended to help small colleges afford some of the fixed costs of operating a community college.

Equalization grants attempt to reduce the disparity in local funds available per student among districts. A state average of equalized assessed valuations per full-time equivalent student, multiplied by a weighted average local tax rate, determines an amount of expected local tax revenues per student. Any community college district that is below this amount when applying a standard tax rate to its equalized assessed valuation per full-time equivalent student receives additional state funding.

A Performance-based Incentive System was implemented in fiscal year 1999. A statewide planning committee met throughout 1997 and 1998 in order to develop a system that defines outcomes and measures for use in the community college performance-based incentive system. The grant focuses on the teaching/learning process and seeks funding of up to 2% of the prior year's appropriated grants to colleges. The allocation is based on performance in seven areas: (1) student satisfaction, (2) student educational advancement, (3) student success in employment/continuing education, (4) student transfer, (5) population served, (6) remedial course completion rate, and (7) a district-defined goal.

The state also distributes grants to support programs and services for special populations, workforce preparation activities, technology, and training. These grants are held in a restricted account by the college and used only for their specified purposes.

PROGRAMS AND ENROLLMENTS

Programs. Each of the 48 public community colleges is a comprehensive college providing extensive instructional and student support services to serve the needs of individuals as well as public services to address the needs of the community. The instruction available includes the first two years of baccalaureate education to prepare students to transfer to four-year colleges and universities; remedial/developmental education for individuals needing basic education skills in order to seek employment or pursue further education; and occupational education from among over 240 specialties for employment training or retraining. The 48 community colleges provide approximately 3,500 associate-degree and certificate programs.

All associate-degree programs offered within the community college system must be approved by the ICCB and Illinois Board of Higher Education on the basis of need, quality, and cost. Certificate programs require only ICCB approval. To qualify for federal vocational education funding, occupational programs also must be approved by the Illinois State Board of Education, the administering agency for the Carl D. Perkins Vocational and Applied Technology Education Act. Community colleges have the flexibility to create additional certificates and degrees that are closely related to these board-approved programs, and to modify programs as needed to keep them up to date. Beginning in 1999, a new approval process has been put in place to assist colleges in implementing programs more quickly. Temporary approval is granted upon submission of stated goals of the program with permanent approval granted pending the outcomes of the new program. The ICCB requires that each community college evaluate each of its existing education programs and services following a five-year cycle to ensure that the programs continue to be justified on the basis of need, quality, and cost.

The range of total number of credit hours required for completion of an associate degree curriculum must be within the following parameters:

- For the associate in arts (A.A.) degree and the associate in science degree, a total requirement of not less than 60 semester credit hours nor more than 64 semester credit hours or the quarter credit hour equivalent;
- For the associate in fine arts (A.F.A.) degree and the associate in engineering science (A.E.S.) degree, a total requirement of not less than 60 semester credit hours nor more than 68 semester credit hours or the quarter credit hour equivalent;
- For the associate in applied science (A.A.S.) degree, a total requirement of not less than 60 semester credit hours nor more than 72 semester credit hours or the quarter credit hour equivalent, including a minimum of 15 semester credit hours of general education. Programs may exceed 72 hours in such occupational fields in which it can be demonstrated that accreditation or licensure requires addi-

tional coursework; and

- For the associate in general studies (A.G.S.) degree, a total requirement of not less than 60 semester credit hours nor more than 64
semester credit hours or the quarter credit hour equivalent, including at least 20 semester credit hours of general education.

Transfer degrees meet Illinois models for A.A., A.S., A.F.A., and
A.E.S. programs and use a common general education core and numerous
major-specific courses that are transferable to all public higher education
institutions in the state. Occupational degrees are designed to meet the
criteria for excellence in A.A.S. degrees established by the National Council for Occupational Education of the American Association of Community Colleges. A directory of Illinois community colleges' certificate and
degree programs is located in the ICCB web site at http://www.iccb.
state.il.us.

Enrollment. Each year Illinois community colleges enroll nearly one
million students in credit and noncredit courses. During fiscal year 1998,
the 48 public community colleges in Illinois enrolled 659,069 students in
instructional credit courses. This is a 4.8% decrease from the 1994 enrollment. The full-time equivalent enrollment for fiscal year 1998 was
217,310. These enrollments are 4.9% lower than they had been five years
earlier. However, phenomenal growth has occurred in noncredit course
enrollment. In fiscal year 1998, unduplicated enrollments in noncredit
courses totaled 298,746, an increase of 32% over five years ago.

The baccalaureate/transfer program is the largest instructional program offered in the Illinois community college system enrolling 35.4% of
the 1998 students. The second largest program, occupational, enrolled
26.5% of the students. The remaining enrollments are accounted for as follows: adult basic/adult secondary/ESL, 18%; vocational skills, 10%; general studies certificates, 5.6%; and general associate degree programs
4.4%. This distribution has remained relatively stable over the past five
years.

Three out of four students attended college on a part-time basis during
the fall and spring semesters of fiscal year 1998. 56%of the students were
women. 66%of the students were White, 14% were African American, and
13% were Hispanic. The median age of the students was 27.4 years with
a mean age of 31.5.

Exemplary Programs. In 1992, the ICCB established annual awards for
excellence in teaching/learning, workforce preparation, accountability, and

substance abuse prevention. Three community colleges have been recognized each year for their innovative methods of approaching teaching and learning challenges. Up to ten community colleges have been recognized annually for their outstanding alcohol abuse and drunk-driving prevention and traffic safety programs to proactively educate their students and communities.

ECONOMIC DEVELOPMENT

The Illinois community college system supports a business and industry center at each of its 48 colleges. These centers provide a comprehensive, market-driven range of services based on local needs. Services range from customized job training and entrepreneurship training to consulting services, government contract procurement assistance, and industrial attraction and retention. Several community colleges also support centers that offer a variety of services in international trade. The centers conduct seminars and offer counseling, resource, and research assistance.

Supporting and strengthening the manufacturing sector of the Illinois economy continues to be a priority for community colleges. In addition to offering manufacturing-related programs (e.g., automated manufacturing/robotics, computer-aided design, industrial production, and precision metalwork), several colleges are equipped with advanced technology centers. These centers can be used for training and education as well as research and design.

The ICCB has been designated as the Illinois affiliate office for the American Council on Education's (ACE) Program on Noncollegiate Sponsored Instruction (PONSI). ACE/ PONSI reviews education and training being provided by noncollegiate organizations and, if appropriate, college credit recommendations are made for the courses. The college credit recommendations may be accepted by colleges and universities across the country motivating employees to either continue or begin college degree programs and save their companies money through tuition reimbursement costs. With noncollegiate education and training continuing to increase and the desire of organizations to have a better trained workforce in order to remain competitive, the demand for ACE/PONSI services is expected to increase.

Exemplary Programs. The ICCB established annual awards for excellence in workforce preparation in 1992. Three to four community colleges have been recognized each year for their efforts to improve the employment and job training needs of their communities.

ACCOUNTABILITY

In partnership with the colleges, the ICCB is actively involved in evaluating system performance. In *Vision 2000*, the System's Statewide Strategic Plan, the community college system reaffirmed its commitment to cooperatively develop local and statewide accountability measures that assess student outcomes and institutional effectiveness. Accordingly, there are numerous accountability initiatives in the Illinois community college system addressing both educational programs and financial management including:

- Accountability/Program Review/Priorities, Quality and Productivity processes;
- The Inventory of State-Level Accountability Measures;
- Program Oversight;
- Performance-Based Funding;
- Uniform Financial Reporting System;
- Occupational Follow-up Survey;
- Former/Nonreturning Student Survey;
- Recognition Process;
- Educational Guarantees;
- The Competitive ICCB Accountability Awards program;
- The Modified Employment Tracking System with the Department of Employment Security;
- Community College and Public University Shared Enrollment and Degree Files; and
- The Workforce Common Performance Management System.

Accountability/Program Review. Through the Program Review process colleges examine all academic, administrative, and support units in terms of need, quality, and cost effectiveness. Specified occupational reviews occur according to a five-year schedule. The combined Accountability/ Program Review process emphasizes reinvesting in essential priorities, increasing cost effectiveness, improving outcomes, and promoting collegewide involvement in strategic planning. Topics addressed through the process have stressed teaching and learning, minority student achievement, affordability, workforce preparation, and enhancing undergraduate education. As a part of the combined process, colleges provide Priorities Statements that guide institutional decision making in planning, budget development, internal budget allocation, program review, and program development.

Program Oversight. By statute, the ICCB is responsible for approving new units of instruction offered by community colleges. Through the Program Approval Process colleges must document the need, quality, and cost of proposed new offerings. In September 1992 legislation assigned additional duties and powers to the ICCB including the ability to: discontinue programs which fail to adequately address an area's educational needs; approve or disapprove cooperative agreements between community colleges and other institutions; and establish uniform financial reporting standards.

Inventory of State-Level Accountability Measures. The ICCB developed an Inventory of State-Level Accountability Measures, which includes major outcome focuses in student achievement, programs, diversity profile, cost/revenue comparisons, accreditation, staffing, and facilities. The 35 inventory descriptions include the area being measured, a brief definition, and the source(s) of data.

Selected Fiscal Accountability Initiatives. A computerized Uniform Financial Reporting System (UFRS) is being put into operation, which allows more detailed comparisons and analysis of fiscal data. Audited uniform financial data are accessible via the Internet. The system provides a series of standardized reports and has the capability for users to create customized queries. The system also has the ability to display data using graphs. The Illinois community college system is in the process of examining an incentive performance-based funding program. The intent of the program is to promote quality performance based on a "value added" approach.

Currently, colleges are required to have audits conducted annually by external independent auditors. Required guidelines for the audit report from this process are provided by the ICCB. Colleges are required to reconcile unit cost submission data with their audits and explain discrepancies. State grants are also reviewed as a part of the ICCB recognition process. Inadequate documentation or improper expenditures of funds has resulted in repayment of state funds to the ICCB.

Recognition. The recognition process is a primary accountability tool for the community college system. A college must meet the recognition criteria to receive state funding. The recognition process is based on standards for community colleges that focus on curriculum/ programs, instruction, awarding of degrees and certificates, policies and procedures, administration and supervision, finance, and the physical plant. Site visits are part of the process.

Workforce Common Performance Management System. The project promotes superior performance in workforce development systems and focuses on programs for school-to-work transition, retraining dislocated workers, and assisting disadvantaged adults to enter/reenter the workforce. The purpose of the project is to develop a performance management system which supports integrated service delivery that meets the needs of employers, workers, and those preparing to enter the workforce. Key features of the system are goals and outcomes which transcend individual programs, information systems that track progress and performance across programs, and a blending of accountability and continuous improvement processes.

Educational Guarantees. The ICCB adopted the "Plan for Implementation of Educational Guarantees" which address both transfer oriented and occupational courses and programs. Students must typically meet with an advisor or other college official to set up an agreed upon program of study. Students encountering difficulties are either offered refunds or additional training. Guidelines are available for the initiative.

Exemplary Accountability Initiatives. The mission of the Illinois community college system is to provide high-quality, accessible, cost-effective educational programs and services to individuals and communities. Accountability initiatives play a critical role in fulfilling this mission. As such, the ICCB established annual awards for excellence in accountability in 1992. Three to five community colleges have been recognized each year for their accountability initiatives in cost effectiveness, institutional quality, student outcomes, strategic planning, and program review.

FOR ADDITIONAL INFORMATION, PLEASE CONTACT:
Joseph J. Cipfl, Ph.D.
President/CEO
Illinois Community College Board
401 East Capitol Avenue
Springfield, IL 62701-1711
Telephone: (217) 785-0123
Fax: (217) 524-4981

INDIANA
William G. Ingram
Senior Vice President and Chief Instructional Officer
Durham Technical Community College

GOVERNANCE

Public two-year institutions in Indiana include a 13-campus system of vocational and technical institutions (IVY Tech) and Vincennes University, a comprehensive community college. The IVY Tech System is governed by a 13-member board appointed by the governor. Board responsibilities include hiring the president for each college in the system, approving programs and awarding credentials, establishing tuition and fees, approving budgets, acquiring and disposing of real property and approving capital contracts for improvements to college property. Vincennes University is also governed by a board appointed by the governor (Ivy Technical College System, 1999; and Vincennes University, 1998).

Planning and data collection for postsecondary education in Indiana are carried out by the Indiana Commission for Higher Education. The commission includes 12 lay members who are appointed by the governor to serve four-year terms, and a student member and a faculty member who both serve two-year terms. The commission employs a staff of approximately 20 persons (Indiana Commission for Higher Education, 1998).

In January, 1999, in an attempt to streamline public two-year institutions in the state, Governor Frank O'Bannon suggested the establishment of a stronger partnership between Vincennes University and IVY Tech system institutions (Selingo, 1999).

FUNDING

In 1997-98, the state allocation to Vincennes University was approximately $27,800,000, which represented a one-percent increase over the state allocation for the previous year. Approximately two-thirds of the institution's total operating budget comes from state sources. Tuition and fees for a full-time resident at Vincennes totalled $2,455 (based on 30 semester credit hours per year). In 1997-98, the state allocation to the IVY Tech system was approximately $74.7 million, which represented a four-percent increase over the state allocation for the previous year. Tuition and fees per full-time student at IVY Tech students were $1,937 (Schmidt, 1998).

PROGRAMS AND ENROLLMENTS

As a comprehensive community college, Vincennes University offers approximately 150 major areas of study in transfer, technical, and vocational fields. Institutions in the IVY Tech System offer programs leading to associate degrees in a variety of technical and vocational areas. Enrollments in the state's 13 IVY Tech System institutions totaled 20,867 full-time-equivalent (FTE) students in the 1996-97 academic year. This figure represented an increase of 6.7% over the 1994-95 academic year and an 8.2% increase over the 1991-92 academic year. Enrollments at specific colleges ranged from 560 FTE students at the Southeast Campus to 3,202 at the Central Indiana Campus. Enrollment at Vincennes University in 1996-97 was 6,708 FTE students, which represented a decrease of 9.5% from the 1994-95 academic year and a decrease of 14% from the 1991-92 academic year (Ivy Tech, 1999; Vincennes University, 1998).

The combined 1996-97 enrollments in two-year public institutions (27,575 FTE) represented 15.3% of the total FTE enrollment in Indiana public postsecondary institutions. The percentage enrollment growth at the IVY Tech colleges represented the largest such growth in Indiana public institutions over both the two-year and five-year terms (Indiana Commission on Higher Education, 1998, August 24).

REFERENCES

Selingo, J., Technical colleges at a crossroads (1999, March 12). Chronicle of Higher Education, 45(26), pp. A26-A28.

Schmidt, P., (1998, November 27). State spending rises 6.7% n 1998-99 to a total of $52.8-billion, Chronicle of Higher Education, 45(13).

Indiana Commission for Higher Education (1998, March 16 and 1998, August 24). www.che.state.in.us

Ivy Technical College System (1999, March 23). www.ivey.tec.in.us

Vincennes University (1998, March 16). www.vinu.edu

FOR ADDITIONAL INFORMATION, PLEASE CONTACT:

Indiana Commission of Higher Education
101 West Ohio Street, Suite 550
Indianapolis, IN 46204-1971

Telephone: (317) 464-4400
Fax: (317) 464-4410
Internet: www.che.state.in.us

IOWA

Janice N. Friedel
Administrator
Division of Community Colleges and Workforce preparation
Iowa Department of Education

OVERVIEW

The first two-year postsecondary educational institution in Iowa was established by the Mason City schools in 1918. Mason City Junior College proved to be successful and was accredited by the North Central Association of Colleges and Schools in 1919. Additional public junior colleges were organized beginning in 1920. The movement spread rapidly, until, by 1930, at least 32 towns and cities in Iowa had organized public junior colleges as part of their public school systems.

Between the years 1918 and 1953, 35 different public junior colleges were established through the operation of public school districts. Some of these colleges closed, although 10 of the closed colleges later reopened. The enrollment trend steadily increased over the years, with the exception of the World War II years. During the 1955-66 decade, which immediately preceded the initiation of a community college system, enrollment almost quadrupled.

By 1965, 16 public junior colleges were operating in Iowa and the total enrollment during the fall semester of the 1965-66 school year was 9,110. These institutions offered college-parallel programs equivalent to the first two years of baccalaureate programs and a limited number of occupational programs and adult education opportunities.

The Iowa General Assembly in 1965 enacted legislation that permitted the development of a statewide system of two-year postsecondary educational institutions, identified as "merged area schools." The Iowa department of education was to direct the operation of the development of merged area schools as either community colleges or area vocational schools. This legislation was enthusiastically received and the Department of Education received the first plan for a community college on July 5, 1965, one day after the legislation was effective. Plans for the other community colleges followed in quick succession. Fourteen community colleges were approved and organized in 1966, and a 15th in January of

1967. Fourteen of these community colleges began operation during the 1966-67 school year.

The statement of policy describing the educational opportunities and services to be provided by community colleges is included in Section 260C.1 of the Iowa Code. This statement of policy identifies the following as services that should be included in a community college's mission:

- The first two years of college work, including pre-professional education;
- Vocational and technical training;
- Programs for inservice training and retraining of workers;
- Programs for high school completion for students of post-high school age;
- Programs for all students of high school age who may best serve themselves by enrolling in vocational and technical training while also enrolled in a local high school, public or private;
- Programs for students of high school age that provide advanced college placement courses not taught at a student's high school while the student is also enrolled in the high school;
- Student personnel services;
- Community services;
- Vocational education for persons who have academic, socioeconomic, or other handicaps that prevent succeeding in regular vocational education programs.
- Training, retraining, and all necessary preparation for productive employment of all citizens;
- Vocational and technical training for persons who are not enrolled in a high school and who have not completed high school; and
- Developmental education for persons who are academically or personally underprepared to succeed in their program of study.

Currently, 10 of the 15 community colleges are operated as multi-campus institutions; resulting in a total of 30 major campuses. The colleges also operate courses and programs at numerous other sites in their districts. Credit programs are offered at a total of 73 different sites throughout the state. Additionally, all community colleges have expanded access to lifelong learning through the Iowa Communications Network (ICN).

All Iowa community colleges have a variety of educational service contracts with other public and private educational institutions, including many agreements to provide instructional programs to clients from human service agencies. Each of the community colleges cooperates with local school districts within its merged area to identify and to offer needed academic and vocational programs for students from the local districts.

GOVERNANCE

Each community college is governed by a local board of directors elected from director districts of equal population within each merged area. These local boards vary from five to nine members who serve terms of three years. A local board has the responsibility for the operation of the college, and developing and enforcing local policies and rules, determining the curriculum to be offered, and appointing the president of the college.

At the state level, the regulation and coordination of community colleges is the responsibility of the Iowa State Board of Education and the Iowa Department of Education. The state board of education is a chosen-member board appointed by the governor and subject to confirmation by the senate.

In 1990, the 72nd Iowa General Assembly created the Community Colleges Council, a council of the state board to provide greater attention to community college issues.

The State Board has specific responsibilities for approval of Community College instructional programs, college budgets, and facilities. In addition, the state board determines the continued state-level accreditation of each college. The Iowa State Board of Education is also responsible for the regulation and coordination of elementary and secondary education school districts, the intermediate area education agencies that provide services to local school districts, and their operation of vocational rehabilitation services statewide.

The director of the Iowa Department of Education, a gubernatorial appointee, has specific responsibilities for community colleges. These include approval of changes in boundaries; the administration of the allocation and disbursement of federal and state funds for acquiring sites and constructing facilities; the administration of the allocation and disbursement of federal and state funds for operating costs of community colleges; the approval of sites and buildings; the approval of a uniform system of accounting; the approval of lease agreements; and the approval of instructional programs.

The Division of Community Colleges and Workforce Preparation is the unit within the department of education that has the major role in implementing the responsibilities of the department of education for community colleges. These responsibilities include the administration of state and federal funds for community colleges, the approval of instructional programs, the review of community college budgets, coordination of road construction projects with the department of transportation, administration of the state approval process of community colleges, and the responsibility for such other activities and services relating to community colleges that may be delegated to the department. The two bureaus within the division are the Bureau of Community Colleges and the Bureau of Technical and Vocational Education, the latter of which has responsibility for regulating both secondary and postsecondary vocational education.

FUNDING

Revenues

Community colleges have three primary sources of revenue in their general operating budgets: state general aid, property tax, and student tuition and fees. Over the past few years the percentage of total revenue derived from federal reimbursement programs (such as the Carl Perkins Act) has constantly decreased. Local taxes for community colleges are at the maximums allowed by law, and state general aid has not kept up with rising costs of operation. Increasingly, the colleges are forced to look to student tuition and fees as a means of providing revenue for college operations. Tuition and fees for each community college are determined locally by their board of directors. The following tables show the increasing reliance of the general operating fund on tuition and fees.

Revenue by Source as a
Percent of Total General Operating Fund Revenues*
in Iowa Community Colleges

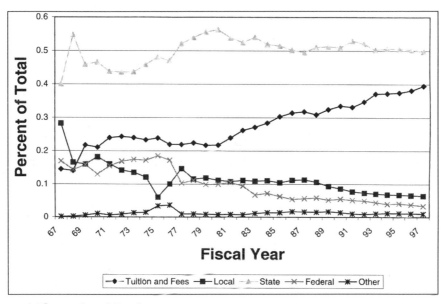

* Unrestricted Portion

Source: Iowa Department of Education, Bureau of Community Colleges

The rise in dependence on tuition and fees can also be demonstrated by the changes in tuition over the past few years. Since 1990 the average annual tuition for 12 credit hours has risen $334, from $1,024 to $1,358; a 32.6% increase. The following graph demonstrates changes in the highest, lowest, and average community college tuition from the 1989-90 school year to the 1997-98 school year.

Changes in Low, Average and High Tuition Rates at
Iowa Community Colleges from 1989-90 through 1997-98

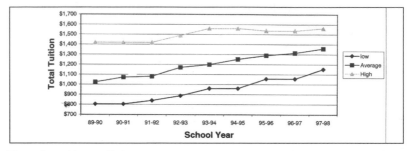

Based on 12 credit hours per term

Source: Iowa Community College Tuition and Fees, Iowa Department
of Education, Bureau of Community Colleges.

The following chart illustrates the expenditures by function of community colleges for the unrestricted portion of the general operating fund for fiscal year 1997. Expenditures for vocational-technical programs constituted approximately 26%, while expenditures for arts and science programs were approximately 21% of the community colleges' total operating budgets for fiscal year 1997. Approximately 5% is spent on administration.

General Operating Fund Expenditures* by Function and Category, Fiscal Year 1997

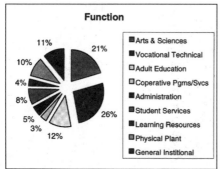
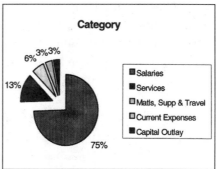

*Unrestricted Portion

Source: AS15E, Iowa Department of Education, Bureau of Community
Colleges

The major categories of expenditures for fiscal year 1997 for the unrestricted portion of the
*Unrestricted Portion
Source: AS15E, Iowa Department of Education, Bureau of Community Colleges.

The major categories of expenditures for fiscal year 1997 for the unrestricted portion of the general operating fund are identified below. In fiscal year 1997, approximately 75% of the total expenditures were devoted to salaries and benefits.

The major instructional programs offered by Iowa community colleges include:

1. Adult basic education and high school completion courses that are intended to provide basic literacy skills for under-educated adults.;
2. Continuing and general education courses;
3. Recertification and relicensure courses;
4. Supplementary vocational courses that are designed to upgrade skills of employed individuals, including related education courses for apprenticeship programs;
5. Arts and sciences (college parallel) courses intended to transfer as the first two years of a baccalaureate degree program, and "career option" programs that provide immediate entry level employment skills as well as the option of transferring into baccalaureate degree programs;
6. Preparatory vocational programs, many of which incorporate options such as short-term certificate programs, one-year diploma programs, and two-year A.A.A. or A.A.S. degree programs. The purpose of these programs is to prepare students for entry-level employment. Many options are available to part-time as well as full-time students;
7. Special needs programs and services designed to assist disadvantaged students and students with disabilities;
8. Customized training programs designed to prepare employees for new and expanding industries;
9. Courses and programs offered for students in local secondary school districts, including exploratory and preparatory vocational programs as well as courses in academic disciplines;
10. Avocational and recreational courses;

11. Courses and programs for individuals who are institutionalized in correctional, health care, or custodial facilities; and

12. Community service programs and services such as workshops, meetings, festivals, cultural events, speaker bureaus, and seminars.

Community colleges are authorized to offer five degrees. They are also authorized to offer diplomas for completion of programs not less than 12 weeks in length that do not lead toward associate degrees and certificates for other short-term programs. The associate in arts degree awarded by all community colleges is articulated with the three state universities to ensure transfer of college credit. Community colleges have also established articulation agreements with independent colleges.

Number of Awards Granted by Iowa's Community Colleges in Fiscal Year 1997

Associate in Arts	3,126
Associate in Applied Arts	69
Associate in Applied Sciences	3,348
Associate in Sciences	54
Associate in General Studies	734
Certificate	1,172
Diploma	2,630
Total	11,133

Source: Degrees Granted, Iowa Department of Education, Bureau of Community Colleges

The Community College Student

Fifty-two percent of the new freshmen in all Iowa colleges and universities in the fall of 1997 were enrolled at public community colleges. Ninety-four percent of community college students enrolled in the fall of 1997 were Iowa residents, compared to 75% at the regents universities (Fall 1997 Iowa College and University Enrollments). In addition, 84% of all known community college alumni have continued their residency in the state (Iowa College Student Aid Commission). These facts illustrate the critical role that community colleges play in the development of Iowa's workforce and the enhancement of Iowa's population, issues vital to Iowa's continued economic viability and growth.

Enrollments in community college credit programs have grown steadily throughout their history, and today, total unduplicated head count is more than 60,000, making community colleges the largest provider of undergraduate-level education in the state. Total enrollments in Iowa's community colleges surpassed the total undergraduates enrolled in Iowa's regents universities in 1991, and have continued to exceed the annual undergraduate enrollment of Iowa's independent two- and four-year colleges.

Students enroll in four types of credit programs in the community college system: 1) arts and science programs that are designed as college parallel programs and transfer to four-year colleges and universities, 2) vocational-technical programs that prepare graduates for direct entry into selected careers, 3) career option programs that are designed to meet the objectives of both arts and science and vocational-technical programs in that they prepare the graduate for direct entry into work and are articulated to specific four-year colleges and universities, and 4) high school cooperative programs that are jointly administered programs between the community college and local school district and enroll high school students.

Approximately 56% of credit (excluding adult and continuing education) students are enrolled in arts and science programs, 32% in vocational-technical, 8% in career-option, and 4% in secondary programs. The average student in the fall of 1997 was 26 years old.

Iowa's community colleges serve thousands of other Iowans in adult basic education and high school completion programs; 46,210 Iowans were served in these programs in fiscal year 1997 alone. In that year community colleges issued, either themselves or in conjunction with a local school district, approximately one of seven high school diplomas granted in Iowa.

In 1997, 8,566 candidates were tested in Iowa for the General Equivalency Diploma (GED) through the community colleges. 91.4% (7,829) passed by Iowa state standards on the initial test or on the retest. This pass rate was third in the nation, surpassed only by Nebraska and Maine. Iowa's goal is to reach 96%. This high pass rate is an excellent testimony to the effectiveness of Iowa's Adult Basic Education/GED instructional and GED testing delivery system through the community colleges. Due to the success of the program, the number of GED awards granted has been slowly decreasing over the past few years. The long-range objective is to continually decrease this number through making Adult Basic Education/GED instruction so available that all interested adults will have obtained their certificates and the only people remaining to reach will be recent dropouts.

As educational institutions with open-door policies, community colleges have been impacted by increasing numbers of adults pursuing educational opportunities who are not prepared to enter and successfully complete college level work. Thousands of students annually receive special services and support at the community colleges. These students may be academically disadvantaged, economically disadvantaged, or in need of developmental education.

In addition to credit enrollment, community colleges enroll thousands of Iowans in adult and continuing education courses, which also include avocational and recreational courses. In Fiscal 1997, total enrollments in adult and continuing education classes at community colleges exceeded 539,000. (Note: These are enrollments, not individuals served; individuals may enroll in more than one class; classes range in length from one to 120 hours each.)

ECONOMIC DEVELOPMENT

Each community college has an economic development division which offers customized training programs for business and industry. These programs are designed to provide training and retraining services on-site or at any location, at any time of the day or night, seven days per week. The programming is flexible, responsive to the needs of the customer. It is focused on the learner, using innovative and non-traditional approaches as necessary to provide quality services.

Community colleges also have the responsibility for operating the Iowa New Jobs Training Program and the Iowa Jobs Training Program, which provide customized training for new or expanding industries. The Iowa New Jobs Training Program, for employees in newly created positions for which their employer pays Iowa withholding tax, is funded through resources derived from certificates that are later repaid from a part of the withholding tax from wages of new employees and from incremental property taxes, and from resources deposited into the Workforce Development Fund. Since its inception in 1983, it has funded 1,266 projects statewide at an investment of $321,087,808 to train a projected 97,819 workers (Norm Nielsen, Kirkwood Community College, August 1997).

The Iowa Jobs Training Program funds education and training services for new employees of small Iowa business and for current employees of businesses which are retooling. It is funded through an annual appropriation from the Iowa Workforce Development Fund. In FY 1999 this fund will provide over 6.5 million dollars to fund the Iowa Jobs Training Program, apprentice programs, innovative skill development activities and targeted industry training.

FOR ADDITIONAL INFORMATION, PLEASE CONTACT:
Janice Nahua Friedel, Ph.D.
Administrator
Division of Community Colleges and Workforce Preparation
Iowa Department of Education
Grimes State Office Building
Des Moines, IA 50319-0146
Telephone: (515) 281-8280
Fax: (515) 281-6544

KANSAS

Merlyne Hines-Starr
Team Leader
Community Colleges/Technical Education
Kansas State Department of Education

OVERVIEW

Kansas public community colleges were organized as junior colleges in 1917, when the legislature first authorized the upward extension of high school for the purpose of offering freshman and sophomore college courses. Within the 1917 act, provisions were made for an election, giving patrons the ability to vote on a tax levy to the extent of two mills for this course work. By 1938, 16 junior colleges were organized. Two institutions, Holton and Marysville, closed due to low enrollment. By 1937, enrollments in junior colleges had increased to a total of 3,531, placing Kansas sixth nationally in number of students enrolled in public junior colleges. As authorized by the legislature, these new institutions offered college-level instruction on the freshman and sophomore levels, a mission which the institutions accomplished well, although accreditation and transfer of credits at first represented a major problem.

By the beginning of the 1930s, there was a noticeable shift in the philosophy of the colleges as they began to add vocational courses. This shift reflected both the desire of some students to receive vocational training and the intent of the colleges to offer some type of alternative for students who did not intend to complete four-year university programs. The trend of expanding vocational opportunities continued over the next two decades and, by the 1950s, the junior colleges were enrolling students in over 65 different vocational programs. By the 1966-67 school year, the enrollment of students in vocational programs had grown to 1,300 students, 15% of the total enrollment in the community-junior colleges.

Although the 1917 Act was a significant piece of legislation, the dynamic growth of Kansas community college education came after the enactment of the Community College Act of 1965. The enrollment in 1965, which totaled 9,404 students (8,667 full-time equivalents), increased by 1998 to 63,212 (31,208 full-time equivalents). The significant enrollment increase was due, in part, to the organization of three new community colleges since 1965. In addition, the expansion of the mission of the community college has resulted in the substantial growth of vocational-technical, adult, and especially continuing education programs at the colleges. The role of the Kansas community colleges in the overall economic development of the state has begun to receive unprecedented but well-deserved recognition. Kansas community colleges provided training for over 60,000 employees from more than 700 businesses during the recent past years.

Following are the community colleges listed by their year of establishment:

1.	Garden City Community College	1919
2.	Fort Scott Community College	1919
3.	Cowley County Community College	1922
4.	Allen County Community College	1923
5.	Coffeyville Community College	1923
6.	Kansas City, Kansas, Community College	1923
7.	Labette Community College	1923
8.	Independence Community College	1925
9.	Butler County Community College	1927
10.	Hutchinson Community College	1928
11.	Dodge City Community College	1935
12.	Neosho County Community College	1936
13.	Highland Community College	1937
14.	Pratt Community College	1938
15.	Colby Community College	1964
16.	Cloud County Community College	1965
17.	Barton County Community College	1968
18.	Johnson County Community College	1968
19.	Seward County Community College	1968

GOVERNANCE AND FUNDING

Under the Community college Act of 1965, the modern era for Kansas community colleges was ushered in. This act also put into place the present governance structure of local boards under the general supervision of the state board of education. Each of the community colleges receives the largest share of its funding from its county or taxing district, and the college's board of trustees is elected by voters of the county.

Counties without community colleges are relatively free of financial obligation to the colleges except through paying out-district tuition for residents of their county who are attending community colleges. The community colleges bill these out-district counties directly for the payment, providing a record of the student's name and credit hour enrollments. Out-district tuition is, therefore, not tuition charged to the student, but a special tax charged to the county.

At the state level, the Division of Lifelong Learning is the state board of education's primary contact with the community colleges. The Division of Lifelong Learning has a Community/Technical Education Team that is responsible for monitoring compliance by community colleges with state board regulations and policies.

State aid to community colleges is based on a credit-hour funding formula and is enrollment driven. To be eligible for state aid, courses must be approved by the state board of education. A master Course List of approved courses and programs is maintained in the Community College/Technical Education Team. Vocationally funded courses are paid at 1.5 times the rate of academic courses, (which are those that are part of a transfer curriculum) except for Pratt Community College, Cowley County Community College, Hutchinson Community College, Johnson County Community College, and Dodge City Community College. These five institutions are designated as area vocational-technical schools and their vocational courses are paid at 2.0 times the state aid per credit hour for academic courses. The state also pays out-district state aid, which is equal to the amount the colleges receive in out-district tuition.

Funding History. Four year before the 1965 Community College Act, the Kansas legislature made a financial commitment to the community colleges by authorizing state aid at $3.00 per credit hour. The next important development in state aid occurred in 1973, when the legislature, in essence, split the out-district liability with the counties, picking up 50% of the cost. In 1978, the legislature established a categorical credit-hour reimbursement rate, reimbursing courses that were a part of an approved vocational program at 1.5 times the rate of academic courses, except where community colleges were also designated as area vocational-technical schools, when the reimbursement for vocational courses was 2.0 times that of academic courses. Also, in 1978, the rate of out-district state aid and tuition was changed from an amount based on the average credit-hour cost of each institution to a flat rate.

Due to the financial exigencies the state faced in the early 1980s, the 1983 legislature froze payments to community colleges in FY1984 at the

FY1983 levels. In 1986, the legislature initiated a "general state aid" program based on FTE and the community college's adjusted valuation per student. The funds were to be distributed inversely to the valuation; in other words, they were a type of equalization payment. This new payment system did not replace the credit hour state aid payment, it only supplemented it. The 1988 state legislature established, in statute, $28 per credit hour as the reimbursement rate for academically funded community college credit hours. This amount is dependent upon full funding of enrollment growth.

KANSAS COMMUNITY COLLEGES
1996-97 BUDGETED SOURCES OF REVENUE

REVENUE SOURCE	AMOUNT	PERCENT OF TOTAL
STATE	$ 58,192,296	28.92%
COUNTY OUT-DISTRICT	$ 9,416,555	4.68%
FEDERAL	$ 1,212,096	6%
LOCAL	$ 82,012,835	40.76%
TUITION & FEES	$ 42,982,846	21.36%
OTHER	$ 7,377,028	3.68%
TOTAL	$201,194,847	100.00%

PROGRAMS AND ENROLLMENT

Kansas community college regulations require that all courses and programs be classified into one of several categories. These are (1) university parallel/transfer; (2) occupational; (3) developmental (4) community education; (5) continuing education; or (6) adult education/general education development. The associate in arts, associate in science, associate in applied science, and associate in general studies degrees are conferred at the state's 19 community colleges. A variety of occupational certificates are also available. The majority of the adult basic education/GED programs of the state are housed in all of the 19 community colleges as well as several unified school districts and community-based organizations. Below are the enrollment figures for FY 97-98 for community colleges and adult basic education/GED centers.

Community College Full-Time and Part-Time Resident/Nonresident Headcount and FTE

	Resident	Non-resident	Headcount	FTE
Full Time	16,527	1,581	18,108	
Part Time	43,310	1,794	45,104	
Total	59,837	3,375	63,212	31,208

Community College Headcount Enrollment by Student Classification

	Freshman	Sophomore	Other	Total
Fall	36,010	15,560	11,444	63,344
Spring	36,305	15,893	11,014	63,212

Community College FTE by Student Classification

	Freshman	Sophomore	Other	Total
Fall	17,168	9,965	3,833	31,043
Spring	17,932	9,630	3,694	31,208

Community College Credit Hours by Classification

	Freshman	Sophomore	Other	Total
Fall	257,484	149,478	57,520	465,630
Spring	268,996	144,475	54,694	468,165

About 63 percent of the Adult Basic Education/GED population for the state are generated in centers that are housed in community colleges. Given below is the total ABE/GED enrollment for FY 97-98.

Enrollment by Program Category

Category	Program Type	Enrollment
Adult Basic Education	Beginning ABE	3,140 Students
	Intermediate ABE	5,465 Students
English as a Second Language	Beginning ESL	3.025 Students
	Intermediate ESL	1,311 Students
	Advanced ESL	547 Students
Adult High School Diploma	High School Diploma or GED	3,726 Students
Total enrollment		17,214 Students

These figures reflect a gender breakdown of 8,270 male students and 8,944 female students. The enrollment by age group is as follows:

16-24 years of age	9,047	25-44 years of age	6,363
45-59 years of age	1,341	60 and over	463

ECONOMIC DEVELOPMENT

The Business and Industry Service Program was approved by the Kansas State Board of Education in 1989 as a means to provide Kansas community colleges the flexibility to respond to requests from industry for customized training. Since its inception, over 1,000 courses have been approved. Presently all 19 Kansas public community colleges are providing courses under the Business and Industry Service Program. Customized training by credit hour and continuing education hours is available.

In addition to the B&I Service Program, all of the 19 community colleges offer courses and training that is part of the individual institutions' Master Course List. This affords all Kansas business and industries the full range of academic and/or vocational curriculum offered.

Kansas community colleges also assist business and industry by providing specific industrial customized training through the State's KIT/KIR programs. The Kansas Industrial Training Program/Kansas Industrial Retraining Program are cooperative efforts with the Kansas State Department of Education, the Kansas State Department of Commerce and Housing, and the Kansas Department of Human Resources. Through this cooperative, comprehensive training is available in customized applications for companies locating new facilities in Kansas or expanding existing facilities. Qualified instructors come from the company's supervisory staff, from Kansas area vocational-technical schools or from Kansas community colleges. Training might be offered in Kansas community colleges or area-vocational technical schools. The Kansas Industrial Retraining Program assists employees of restructuring industries, those people likely to be displaced because of obsolete or inadequate job skills and knowledge. The Kansas legislature provides funding so that vocational and occupational instructors in community colleges and area vocational technical schools can participate in internships that keep them up-to-date with the technology of their teaching areas.

ACCOUNTABILITY

As citizens and the legislators of Kansas seek greater accountability for the expenditure of both local and general fund dollars, and as colleges embark on developing long-range planning initiatives, the importance of having in place a data system measuring community college effectiveness is imperative. The community colleges, in partnership with the Kansas State Department of Education developed a framework for, and subsequently implementation of, a data management system that allows for the collection, aggregation, and reporting of information which documents the community colleges' success in meeting their role and mission.

In the summer of 1997, a task force sanctioned by the Council of Presidents of the Kansas Association of Community College Trustees was formed. The task force submitted and received a research grant from the Council of North Central Two-Year Colleges to support work on core indicator development. In December of 1997, a final set of core indicators was developed and a priority schedule was set.

Following approval by the Kansas State Board of Education, steps were taken to begin implementation of this project. An implementation plan has been developed that will address the first 4 of 13 core indicators of effectiveness for Kansas community colleges. It is expected that all 13 of these indicators will be addressed in accord with the established time line.

THE FUTURE OF KANSAS COMMUNITY COLLEGES

Over the last 26 years, various legislative committees have studied the issue of postsecondary governance in Kansas. Each year a report of findings has been published. During the 1999 session of the Kansas legislature, Senate Bill 345 was introduced. This bill proposes to move Kansas area vocational-technical schools, technical colleges, community colleges, proprietary schools, and adult basic education programs under the supervision of a revised Kansas State Board of Regents. The purpose of this proposed act is to bring the overall leadership, supervision, and coordination for postsecondary education institutions under one board to maximize all available resource and to eliminate costly and undesirable duplication in program and course offerings, faculties and physical facilities at postsecondary educational institution. If passed, this bill would require a reorganization of the current Kansas State Board of Regents to include three operating segments; one for the state's universities and colleges and the municipal university, one for the state's community colleges, and one for the state's area vocational-technical schools and technical colleges. This proposed change would begin July 1, 1999.

REFERENCES

Kansas State Plan for Community Colleges (1996). (Topeka, KS: Kansas State Department of Education.

Kansas State Annual Performance Report for FY97-98 (1998). Topeka, KS: Kansas State Department of Education.

Kansas Higher Education Enrollment Report No. 108: Spring 1998 (December, 1998). Kansas Legislative Research Department.

1998-1999 Statistical and Financial Information of Kansas Community Colleges (February, 1999) Topeka, KS: Kansas State Department of Education.

FOR ADDITIONAL INFORMATION, PLEASE CONTACT:
Dr. Merlyne Hines-Starr, Team Leader,
Community Colleges/Technical Education
Kansas State Department of Education
120 SE 10th Avenue
Topeka, KS 66612
Telephone: (785) 296-3048
Fax: (785) 296-3523
E-mail: mhines@ksbe.state.ks.us
Susan Peck, Community College Program Consultant
Kansas State Department of Education
120 SE 10th Avenue
Topeka, KS 66612
Telephone: (785) 296-4936
Fax: (785) 296-3523

KENTUCKY

Larry D. Mayes
Director of Institutional Research
University of Kentucky Community College System

OVERVIEW

In 1962, the Kentucky General Assembly enacted legislation mandating the formation of a system of community colleges and entrusted the Board of Trustees of the University of Kentucky with its operation. In 1964, acting under the authorization of the 1962 legislation, Kentucky's community college system was developed within the framework of the University of Kentucky. In that respect, the system was unique among state community college systems in the Southeast. In 1964, the total number of campuses under the new system was seven with a total enrollment that fall of 2,876 students. The community college system has experienced substantial growth since that time. In fact, the fourteenth and last campus was added in 1986, and enrollment peaked in 1993 at 48,370 students.

GOVERNANCE

In 1996, the General Assembly examined the entire governance structure of higher education in Kentucky, including whether the current governance arrangement of the community colleges was adequate to meet Kentucky's community-based education needs at the start of the 21st century. During the 1996 regular session, the Kentucky General Assembly, by resolution, created a Task Force on Postsecondary Education to study means of improving Kentucky's system. The task force issued an assessment of the state of higher education and educational attainment in Kentucky. Among its findings, the task force noted that low educational attainment, duplication of programs, lack of cooperation among postsecondary institutions, low persistence rates, low levels of research funding, lack of strategic planning, and low efficiencies were pervasive throughout Kentucky and its postsecondary system.

Consequently, on May 30, 1997, at the end of a special session of the Kentucky General Assembly, the Governor signed into law the Kentucky Postsecondary Education Reform Act, also known as House Bill 1 (HB 1). This historic legislation enacted into law specific goals to be achieved by Kentucky's system of postsecondary education. The overarching goal of HB 1 was for Kentucky to achieve by 2020 a postsecondary education system that is among the nation's best. Also among these goals was the development of a comprehensive community and technical college system with a mission that assures access for each potential student to a two-year course of study designed for transfer to a baccalaureate program, and the technical education necessary to develop a workforce with the skills to meet the new and existing needs of employers.

Specifically, HB 1 mandated that the management responsibility for the University of Kentucky Community College System be transferred by the university's board of trustees to the Board of Regents of the Kentucky Community and Technical College System (KCTCS). The University of Kentucky Community College System became one branch of the system, with the other being the technical system branch. The technical system is currently comprised of 24 postsecondary technical institutions that were, prior to the passage of HB 1, under the auspices of the Workforce Development Cabinet. The two systems were not merged. Each system functions as a distinct, separate academic unit. The existing University of Kentucky Community College System faculty governance structure (including the University of Kentucky Community College System Faculty Senate) is maintained intact with the University of Kentucky Community College System in the new structure. The law, however, charged the new Kentucky Community and Technical College System Board of Regents and the Council on Postsecondary Education with ensuring cooperation, coordination, and efficiency between the two branches. Each branch is headed by a chancellor who reports directly to the president of the Kentucky Community and Technical College System. The president serves at the pleasure of the Kentucky Community and Technical College System Board of Regents, and the chancellors serve at the pleasure of the Kentucky Community and Technical College System president. The Kentucky Community and Technical College System Board of Regents, in exercising its delegated personnel management responsibility, is responsible for the operating policies and procedures for the University of Kentucky employees in the community colleges and has the right to appoint and dismiss personnel.

House Bill 1 vests the government of the Kentucky Community and Technical College System in its Board of Regents. The authority for the new "governing board" is described within the existing statutory sections for the boards of regents of Kentucky's six regional universities, with the result that the attendant duties and powers of the Kentucky Community and Technical College System Board clearly encompass and, in some respects, exceed those of the other six governing boards. Among other duties and powers, the Kentucky Community and Technical College System Board has the authority to:

- Receive grants and bequests and expend the same for the use and benefit of the System or college;
- Adopt bylaws, rules, and regulations for the governance of its members, officers, agents and employees, and enforce obedience to such rules;
- Determine the number of divisions, departments, bureaus, offices, and agencies needed for the successful conduct of the affairs of the system or college;
- Develop and implement guidelines for the preparation of biennial budget requests;
- Adopt a biennial budget request for each branch of the Kentucky Community and Technical College System, upon the recommendation of the chancellor and the president of the system;
- Approve the annual operating budget for each community college;
- Assure that budget planning and implementation processes are consistent with the adopted strategic agenda, biennial budget, and the missions of the institutions;
- Require such reports from the president, officers, faculty, and employees as it deems necessary and proper;
- Evaluate periodically the institution's progress in implementing its missions, goals, and objectives to conform to the statewide postsecondary strategic agenda;
- Issue indebtedness and purchase liability insurance;
- Approve policies to implement medical and accident insurance programs for students enrolled in Kentucky Community and Technical College System institutions;
- Establish personnel policies, including the right to appoint and dismiss personnel, and set compensation for the employees;
- Develop a new personnel system for prospective employees, while grandfathering in the rights and benefits of current employees;
- Deduct dues from an employee's paycheck for employee membership organizations, upon receipt of a written authorization from the employee;

- Establish a personnel dispute resolution system that results in an independent third party appeal process for all Kentucky Community and Technical College employees;
- Select and employ the President of the Kentucky Community and Technical College System, involving the University of Kentucky Board of Trustees in appointing the search committee;
- Appoint the chancellors, upon recommendation of the President, to head the Community College System and the Technical Institutions' Branch;
- Approve academic policies and curricula (that do not involve University of Kentucky policies and curricula) developed by the University of Kentucky Community College System Faculty Senate and submitted to the board through the University of Kentucky Community College System chancellor and president of Kentucky Community and Technical College System; and
- Grant diplomas and confer degrees (that are not University of Kentucky degrees) upon the recommendation of the Kentucky Community and Technical College System president and faculty.

House Bill 1 further provided that, upon the completion of the regional accrediting agency's substantive change process, but not later than July 1, 1998, the University of Kentucky Board of Trustees must delegate to the Kentucky Community and Technical College System Board of Regents the management responsibility for the University of Kentucky Community College System, except for Lexington Community College. The substantive change prospectus was accepted on January 8, 1998, by the Commission on Colleges of the Southern Association of Colleges and Schools, and the subsequent transfer of management of the community college system occurred on January 14, 1998. This management responsibility includes, but is not limited to, management of facilities and grounds, assets, liabilities, revenues, personnel, programs, financial and accounting services, and support services. The board of regents in this capacity is charged with receipt and disbursement of funds and all financial matters. Section 19 of HB 1 also specifies that if any management conflict arises between the Kentucky Community and Technical College System Board of Regents and the University of Kentucky Board of Trustees, with respect to the delegation of management responsibilities for the University of Kentucky Community College System, then the Council on Postsecondary Education will resolve the conflict.

However, the University of Kentucky Board of Trustees retains several roles in the administration of the University of Kentucky Community College System.

- The University of Kentucky Board of Trustees will nominate individuals for four (4) seats on the Kentucky Community and Technical College System Board of Regents. For each vacancy, the University of Kentucky Board of Trustees is required to nominate three individuals from which the governor is to make the final appointment. The other four (4) appointed seats on the Kentucky Community and Technical College System Board of Regents are appointed by the governor from nominations submitted by the Governor's Postsecondary Education Nominating Committee. In addition, six (6) additional regents, each with a one-half (1/2) vote, are elected to represent the students, faculty, and staff of each branch.
- The University of Kentucky Board of Trustees is also charged with selecting six (6) representatives to function as a search committee for the president of the Kentucky Community and Technical College System.
- The University of Kentucky Board of Trustees reviews and makes recommendations on the University of Kentucky Community College System biennial budget request adopted by the Kentucky Community and Technical College System Board of Regents and forwards the request and recommendations to the Council on Postsecondary Education for its consideration.
- Section 140 of HB 1 specifies that the acquisition and disposition of real property and capital improvements in excess of $400,000 must be approved by the Kentucky Community and Technical College System Board of Regents and the University of Kentucky Board of Trustees. HB 1 specifies that the Kentucky Community and Technical College System is charged with approving these projects first and then passing the matter on to the University of Kentucky Board of Trustees for approval.
- The University of Kentucky Board of Trustees will oversee the quality of associate-degree programs awarding diplomas that bear the name of the University of Kentucky Community College System, and will notify the Kentucky Community and Technical College System and Council on Postsecondary Education of deficiencies in the University of Kentucky Community College

System associate-degree programs.

- The University of Kentucky Board of Trustees will also approve new associate-degree programs that are to bear the University of Kentucky name.
- University of Kentucky Community College System employees, as of the effective date of the transfer of management responsibility to the Kentucky Community and Technical College System continue to be governed by University of Kentucky Governing Regulations and by any subsequent changes to those regulations made by the University.
- Students enrolled in the University of Kentucky Community College System continue to have all the responsibilities, privileges, and rights accorded to University of Kentucky Community College System students, on the effective date of the transfer of management responsibility, to Kentucky Community and Technical College System.
- University of Kentucky Community College System bonds for existing and future facilities remain the responsibility of the University of Kentucky.
- The University of Kentucky Board of Trustees appoints half of the membership of the search committee for any future chancellor to head the University of Kentucky Community College System.
- The University of Kentucky Board of Trustees receives appropriations for the University of Kentucky Community College System and transfers and allots these funds to the Kentucky Community and Technical College System Board of Regents for the benefit of the University of Kentucky Community College System.

House Bill 1 also provides for the establishment of local boards of directors that are comprised of seven (7) gubernatorial appointees, one (1) faculty member, and one (1) student member. The fundamental purpose of these boards is to ensure local input and guidance to the institution and involves the following specific duties:

- If a vacancy exists, recommend one candidate for the community college president to the KCTCS from a list of three candidates supplied by the KCTCS president;
- Evaluate the performance of the community college president and advise the chancellor of the University of Kentucky Community College System;

- Approve budget requests for the community college before they are sent to the Kentucky Community and Technical College System for final approval;
- Adopt and amend an annual operating budget for the community college; and
- Approve and implement a strategic plan for the community college that is consistent with the statewide strategic agenda for postsecondary education, and that includes input from local employers and civic leaders.

FUNDING

For fiscal year 1998-99, the total University of Kentucky Community College System revised budget is approximately $201,943,700. The largest unrestricted budget item is instruction, with $65,254,900 (32%) allotted in this category, and approximately $37,487,600 (19%) of the restricted budget is allotted to Student Financial Aid.

Unrestricted expenditures for 1997-98 were expended for instruction (48%), academic support (10%), institutional support (11%), operations and maintenance (9%), mandatory transfers (9%), and student services (7%). The remaining categories (public service, libraries, and student aid) were each less than five percent. The restricted expenditures for 1997-98 were primarily student aid (75%), instruction (21%), academic support (2%), and public service (5%), with the other categories being one percent or less of the $41,342,800 total amount of dollars expended.

For the last two years, tuition for residents in the community college system has risen from $500 in 1996-97 to $510 in 1997-98 and on to the current rate of $530 in 1998-99. For non-residents, the tuition has increased from $1,500 in 1996-97 to $1,530 in 1997-98 and is currently $1,590 in 1998-99. There is also a $40 technology fee charged to both residents and non-residents to help the colleges upgrade computer labs and other technology.

PROGRAMS AND ENROLLMENTS

The community colleges are charged with offering curricula for the first two years of a baccalaureate program. Courses parallel university offerings and are transferable to four-year institutions—both public and private. Students who successfully complete 60 semester hours of work in major fields or professional curricula may be awarded associate in arts or associate in science degrees.

In 1996, the Kentucky General Assembly implemented a new statewide transfer policy known as Transfer Frameworks designed to improve the transferability of general education coursework among public colleges and universities. This general education core curriculum provides sufficient breadth and depth in the curriculum to meet the needs, interests, and abilities of all students, and ensures that the community college graduates are intellectually flexible, articulate, creative, and prepared for continuous growth and lifelong learning.

The community colleges are also committed to an expanded program of occupational career education to develop trained technicians to meet the workforce needs of the Commonwealth of Kentucky, especially in business, engineering, and health technologies. Over 30 career programs are currently offered that are usually completed in two years and lead to an associate in applied science degree.

The total headcount enrollment during the 1998 fall semester was 35,189. About half of the students (17,679) were enrolled part time, and almost 40 percent (13,287) were enrolled in occupational career education programs. Nearly two-thirds (23,314) were female and over 40 percent (15,387) were 25 years of age or older.

ECONOMIC DEVELOPMENT

From its inception, the community college system has focused a growing proportion of resources on the development of applied science curricula. By 1994, students in applied science programs accounted for 46 percent of the system's enrollment and 62 percent of its associate- degree graduates. By 1998, the community college system offered over 30 associate-in-applied- science degree programs, including engineering technologies, business and public service technologies, and allied health. In fact, Kentucky's community colleges have been particularly influential in the health care arena. From 1989 through 1994, for example, associate degree nursing programs across the system have produced nearly 5,000 graduates in response the state's prolonged nursing shortage.

Similar to the community colleges' efforts to create a stronger combination of technical programs was a growing determination to increase their role in local economic development. Business and industry services had been a focal point of activity since the mid-1980s and by 1997-98, the colleges provided job-specific training and retraining, consultation services and technical assistance to over 1,400 companies throughout the Commonwealth. Simultaneously, the colleges placed increasing emphasis on community partnerships in the business and industry arena, including tech-prep and school-to-work transition programs with vocational schools, high schools, and numerous businesses and industries.

Under Kentucky statutes, the community college system historically shared responsibility for technical education with a separate system of postsecondary technical and vocational schools. For more than a decade, the community college and vocational systems had attempted to differentiate their roles. The community colleges had sole authority under state law and through accreditation with the Commission on Colleges of the Southern Association of Colleges and Schools to offer associate degrees, and refrained from developing certificate programs; the vocational system was limited to certificate programs. Despite numerous successful efforts at coordination and cooperation, the existence of two delivery systems for technical education created confusion among the general public and particularly among policymakers. Consequently, one of the fundamental goals of the Kentucky Community and Technical College System, created by House Bill 1, was to ensure that the community colleges, in collaboration with the vocational system, would provide services to Kentucky's employers and the general public pertaining to continuing education and customized training, for purposes of improving the knowledge and skills of Kentucky workers and citizens in all regions of the state.

ACCOUNTABILITY

During the 1992 session, the General Assembly passed legislation mandating Kentucky's first accountability reporting process. However, House Bill 1 empowers the Council on Postsecondary Education to assume a much stronger role in statewide planning and evaluation including the development of a statewide strategic agenda. Moreover, House Bill 1 required the Council on Postsecondary Education to develop a new system of public accountability that provide for both statewide performance indicators and institutional accountability measures. These new accountability indicators, adopted in January 1998, supersede the 14 performance measures mandated in the 1992 legislation.

The current accountability model contains three main components: statewide performance indicators, institutional accountability indicators, and a status report on the implementation of the reform efforts during the

1997-98 academic year. The statewide segment involves a variety of student outcomes criteria including annual college-going rates of recent high school graduates, percentages of adults enrolled in credit-bearing courses, and annual college graduation rates. Institutional-level accountability indicators are divided into six primary dimensions: institutional profile information, in-depth analysis of educational quality measures and student outcomes data relative to student progress and advancement, information concerning institutional service to the community and workforce development, demonstration of efficient use of resources including room utilization and use of technology, and institutional commitment to equal employment opportunities. Also reported in the 1998 Accountability Report will be an analysis of the progress the community colleges have made toward implementing House Bill 1.

FOR ADDITIONAL INFORMATION, PLEASE CONTACT:
Larry D. Mayes
Director of Institutional Research
111 Breckinridge Hall
Lexington, KY 40506-0056
E-mail: LDMAYE1@pop.uky.edu
or
Anthony L. Newberry, Chancellor
University of Kentucky Community College System
Telephone: (606) 257-5039
Fax: (606) 257-5640

LOUISIANA

Terrence A. Tollefson
Professor, Department of Educational Leadership and Policy Analysis
East Tennessee State University

OVERVIEW

Louisiana historically has provided public two-year postsecondary education programs through various institutions, including Delgado Community College (governed by the Board of Trustees for State Colleges and Universities); Louisiana State University at Alexandria and Louisiana State University at Eunice; Southern University-Shreveport/Bossier City; and up to 46 trade-oriented postsecondary vocational-technical schools (Beard, S.E., in Tollefson & Fountain, 1992).

Louisiana State University Normal school, which trained elementary and secondary teachers, was established in 1889 as the first two-year college in Louisiana. In 1921, the Louisiana Constitution was amended to authorize the establishment of two-year colleges. In that same year, two public junior colleges were established. One was Hammond Junior College, which in 1937 became a four-year college and later was renamed Southeastern Louisiana University. The other was Delgado Central Trade School in New Orleans. The latter institution is now Delgado Community College (Woods, 1996).

In October of 1998, Louisiana conducted a referendum tat proposed to merge the governance of the public community college campuses with the 42 campus uses of what had become Louisiana Technical College (Tollefson & Patton, 1998). The voters approved the referendum and Governor Mike Foster appointed members to the newly established Louisiana Community and Technical College System Board of Trustees. As of July 1, 1999, all public two-year institutions will be governed by the new board. Wayne Brown has been chosen as interim president. The new 15-member board, which was appointed by Governor Foster in January, includes numerous high[level business and professional leaders whose charge includes expanding liberal arts and science transfer programs and bringing order out of a chaotic division of the state into "fiefdoms" (Giles, 1999).

FUNDING

Under Governor Foster's leadership, state appropriations for two-year postsecondary education increased sharply from $39.5 million in fiscal 1997 to $53.7 million in fiscal 1998, still leaving Louisiana as the last-ranked southern state in its support for higher education (Tollefson & Patton, 1998).

ACCOUNTABILITY

Governor Foster's announced plan is to develop a performance-based system that provides programs responsive to local needs.

REFERENCES

Beard, S. (1992). Louisiana, in Tollefson, T. A. & Fountain, B. E., *Forty-Nine State Systems, 1992 Edition*, p. 89. Washington, DC: American Association of Community Colleges.

Giles, D. (1999, January 26). Louisiana community and technical college system unveiled. *Community College Times*, 11(2), pp. 1,4.

Tollefson, T. A. & Patton, M. (1998). Louisiana, in *AACC Annual 1998-99, pp. 48-49*. Washington, DC: American Association of Community Colleges.

Woods, J. L. (1996, November-December). Louisiana's community colleges, in *Community College Journal of Research and Practice*, 20(6), pp. 539-544.

FOR ADDITIONAL INFORMATION, PLEASE CONTACT:
Office of the President
Louisiana Community and Technical College System Board of Supervision
150 Third Street, Suite 129
Baton Rouge, LA 70801
Telephone: (225) 219-4340
Fax: (225) 219-4683

MAINE

John Fitzsimmons, President
Maine Technical College System

OVERVIEW

Maine Vocational Technical Institute (MVTI) was established in Augusta by the Maine Legislature in 1946 to accommodate veterans of World war II who were supported by the so-called "G.I. Bill". In that year, 80 veterans participated in four vocational programs in the automotive, electrical, machine-tool and radio areas. In the ensuing years, MVTI enrollments expanded rapidly, and in 1952 it was relocated to the former site of Fort Pueblo in South Portland, and it subsequently was renamed Southern Maine Technical College (Fitzsimmons, 1999).

The Maine Department of Education published a state master plan in 1962 that recommended establishing three additional postsecondary vocational technical institutes (VTIs). The master plan also advocated establishing a number of secondary vocational education centers. Five additional VTIs were created in the 1960s, including Northeastern Maine Vocational Institute in Presque Isle (1961), Androscoggin State Vocational Institute in Lewiston (1963), Eastern Maine Vocational Technical Institute in Calais (1968) and Kennebec Valley Vocational Technical Institute in Waterville (1969). The legislature authorized York County Technical College in 1994 and it opened the following year (Fitzsimmons, 1999).

The guiding philosophy for the Maine Technical College System from its inception in 1946 has been to prepare students for entry-level employment and enable them to update and enhance their skills to allow them to grow in their careers. The Maine Technical College System's official mission statement includes the following:

> The basic mission of the Maine Technical College System is to provide associate degree, diploma and certificate programs directed at the educational, occupational and technical needs of the state's citizens and the workforce needs of the state's employers...to create an educated, skilled and adaptable labor force which is responsive to the changing needs of the economy of the state and to promote local, regional and statewide economic development. (Public Law, 20-A, Chapter 431).

All vocational institutes were renamed "vocational technical institutes" by the state legislature in 1965. In 1986, the VTIs were transferred from state government to the governance of the newly created Maine Vocational Technical Institute System. The new law established a state-level board of trustees to set policy and employ a chief executive officer in a new system office designed to provide staff support to the state board, as well as leadership, coordination and support to the VTIs. In 1989, the Maine Legislature redesignated the VTIs as "technical colleges" to differentiate them more sharply from secondary vocational schools and identify them more clearly as higher education institutions (Fitzsimmons, 1999).

Maine's voters approved a number of statewide bond referendums for the MTCS, including a $7 million issue in 1984, and others for $2.2 million (1985), $20 million (1989), and $5 million (1994). Those bond issues both reflected the respect of the voters for existing educational programs and enabled the technical colleges to build, equip and update state-of-the art facilities and equipment on each campus (Fitzsimmons, 1999).

GOVERNANCE

The MTCS Board of Trustees includes 13 voting members who are appointed for four-year terms by the governor and confirmed by the state senate. Twelve members are selected from business and industry, organized labor, education and the general public, as well as one student who serves a two-year term. There also are two ex-officio, non-voting members, including the Maine Commissioner of Education and the Maine Commissioner of Labor. Board members elect a chair and a vice chair annually. The MTCS president serves as secretary to the board. MTCS board meetings are held a minimum of six times per year, and the chair also may call special meetings as needed. A quorum of a majority of board members is required, and a majority of members also must be present and vote in favor of each issue for any proposed action to be approved. The MTCS Board of Trustees has been assigned the following types of authority and responsibility:

- Appointing the MTCS president;
- Developing and adopting a biennial budget request; and
- Developing, adopting and revising policies to govern the statewide system.

The system president provides leadership and coordination for the MTCS, carries out state board policies, recommends new presidential appointees, evaluates presidents and other system personnel. Individual college presidents implement state board policies, provide campus leadership and administration, hire and evaluate faculty and staff, and develop and submit campus budget proposals. The system president and the seven college presidents comprise the Presidents Council (Fitzsimmons, 1999).

PROGRAMS AND ENROLLMENTS

The Maine Technical College System enrolled approximately 8,000 students in the fall of 1998 in over 200 one- and two-year programs. Among the many fields of study are automotive technology, computer and environmental sciences, financial services, graphic arts, health care, marine sciences and manufacturing. Each technical college also has a continuing education division that provides both credit and non-credit courses in academic, occupational and personal enrichment subjects, with approximately 15,000 students enrolling in them each year. Continuing education courses are sometimes later converted and expanded into programs leading to associate degrees. Each technical college is responsive to the unique constellation of needs in its service area. Each college's programs include those that culminate in certificates, diplomas and associate degrees.

Maine Technical College System enrollments are growing rapidly, with approximately a 50% increase since 1990. The mean age of degree-seeking students is 27 years, and the student body is comprised of 56% females and 44% males. Approximately 85% of MTCS graduates are employed within one year of graduation, and another 7% transfer to four-year colleges and universities within that same period.

WORKFORCE DEVELOPMENT

Quality Centers, which began in 1994, have trained over 3,000 individuals for new jobs in customized programs for specific employers, at no cost to students or employers. Corporate investments in Maine exceeding a total of $1 billion are attributed to this program. The Tech Prep program in MTCS, funded by the federal Carl Perkins Act, provides "hands-on" education and training in math, science and English for over 4,000 high school students each year to enable them to understand the relationships between education and successful employment.

Maine Career Advantage (MCA), which began in 1992, is an internship program offered by MTCS institutions in over 100 Maine high schools in partnership with nearly 300 host business firms. Modeled upon Danish and German internship programs, MCA serves nearly 5,000 students per year and has become nationally acknowledged. The National Alliance of Business designated it as the 1993 "School-to-Work" Program of the Year, and the American Association of Community Colleges conferred an "Organizational Leadership Award" on MTCS for Maine Career Advantage in 1996.

FUNDING

The Maine Legislature appropriated $29 million in operational support to MTCS in 1997-98, and $34.1 million in 1998-99. The 1998-99 appropriation includes $3 million for equipment, technology and deferred maintenance that will not be continued in future years (Tollefson & Patton, 1998).

REFERENCES

Fitzsimmons, J. (1998, April-May). Maine Technical College System: "Building Communities" *Community College Journal of Research and Practice*, 23(3) pp. 227-242.

Maine Revised Statutes Annotated, Title 20-A, Chapter 431. Augusta, ME

Maine Technical College System (1998). *Progress Report on Maine Tech Prep*. Augusta, ME: Author

Maine Technical College System Board of Trustees (1997). *Report of the Tuition Task Force*. Augusta, ME: Author

Maine Technical College System (1997, June). Strategic Plan: July 1, 1997 to June 30, 2002. Augusta, ME: Author

Maine Technical College System data provided by MTCS System Office.

Tollefson, T.A. & Patton, M., (1998) Maine in *AACC Annual, 1998-99*. Washington, DC:American Association of Community Colleges.

Warren, W.C. (1997). The Development of Vocational Technical Institutes in Maine. Doctoral dissertation, Iowa State University.

FOR ADDITIONAL INFORMATION, PLEASE CONTACT:
Office of the President
Maine Technical College System
323 State Street
Augusta, ME 04330

Telephone: (207) 287-1070
Fax: (207) 287-1037

MARYLAND

David E. Sumler
Director of Academic Affairs
Maryland Higher Education Commission

OVERVIEW

The Maryland Community College System is composed of 16 comprehensive two-year institutions—three with three-campus systems. A statewide coordinating board oversees the activities of all of higher education, including the community colleges. In fiscal year 1998, around 388,000 Marylanders were enrolled in credit programs and continuing education courses.

The mission of Maryland's community colleges is to provide high quality transfer, associate-degree and occupational programs, continuing education courses, and community service programs at a reasonably low cost to students in response to local educational needs. The community college mission is unique in that it provides for low-cost, nonresidential, open-admission institutions, funded through a state and local partnership, offering associate degrees, certificates, customized training, and continuing education courses, certified by a faculty committed to teaching and scholarship but not to sponsored research.

The community colleges are woven into the social and economic fabric of the state and their local communities. The colleges are recognized for their responsiveness, their flexibility, and their ability to customize training for the special needs of business and industry.

GOVERNANCE

The first two Maryland community colleges opened in 1946, governed by local boards of education. Hagerstown Junior College occupied temporary quarters until 1966, when it moved to its own facilities. Montgomery College, which today has three campuses, began as the higher education division of the Montgomery County schools. One year later, in 1947, Baltimore Junior College was established by the school system in Baltimore City. These three institutions served as the forerunners of today's system of 16 comprehensive community colleges (22 separate campuses). Besides the first three community colleges, eight additional institutions were created between 1946 and 1961. From 1961 to 1970, five more community colleges were established. Two more institutions were added in 1975 (a regional college serving Maryland's lower Eastern Shore) and 1993 (Carroll Community College).

While no additional community colleges have been established in Maryland since 1993, efforts to increase geographic accessibility have continued. Branch campuses have opened in three counties. These branch campuses, operating under contract with existing community colleges, have been encouraged as examples of a cost-effective mechanism for assessing citizen interest while offering a core of needed programs. With the branch campuses and the state's two regional community colleges, services currently are offered in all of the state's 24 political subdivisions.

The most striking organizational change in the 1990s has been the evolution of local "systems." Montgomery College has been a three-campus system since 1975, but has reaffirmed its structure as "one college with three campuses" in a recent strategic plan. The three campuses of the Baltimore County system have undergone extreme centralization into a unified Community College of Baltimore County as recently as the summer of 1998. Finally, Charles County Community College has operated extension sites in Calvert County and St. Mary's County for over a decade. These sites have now matured into branch campuses, and the creation of a new legal entity recognizing the existence each of these regional colleges is now being considered by the state legislature.

Of the 16 community colleges, 15 are governed locally by county college boards appointed by the governor. One college, Baltimore City Community College, is a state institution. It was created in 1990 when the state assumed ownership of the formerly local Community College of Baltimore as part of a State attempt to improve the financial condition of Baltimore City.

The primary instructional purpose of the first community colleges was the transfer curriculum, preparing thousands of war veterans and other students for further study at four-year colleges. The community colleges were responsive to local needs in that they were able to provide high quality programs at a reasonable cost to students. The Maryland community colleges have continued to provide transfer curricula, as well as high quality career programs and continuing education courses for those citizens needing to upgrade their skills or seeking courses in self-improvement.

Except for their common mission, the 16 Maryland community colleges are as varied as the communities they serve. There are three colleges with multiple campuses, two regional colleges serving seven counties, and two colleges that serve multiple counties through special contractual relationships. There are small rural colleges, suburban colleges, an urban college, and colleges involved in the phenomenal growth of the Baltimore-Washington corridor.

Within the scope of their mission, community colleges serve a wide range of Marylanders, from high school students to gifted and talented programs to senior citizens. In general, community colleges reach out to citizens who might not otherwise have an opportunity to attend college.

The Maryland State Board for Community Colleges (SBCC) was established by the Maryland General Assembly in 1968 to coordinate a statewide system of locally governed community colleges. The SBCC lasted until 1990, when it was abolished; and most of its coordinating, planning and regulatory authority was transferred to the Maryland Higher Education Commission (MHEC). The MHEC is a statewide coordinating board with reponsibility for all postsecondary education.

The advocacy role of the SBCC was assumed by a new voluntary organization created by the community colleges. The Maryland Association of Community Colleges (MACC) is supported by a per-campus contribution that supports a small staff. The MACC executive board is composed of campus presidents and trustees. An equally important body is the MACC Council of Presidents. Each campus chief executive is a member, and policy issues are considered by the council before a public policy is announced. The most important role of MACC may be legislative relations during each year's general assembly session; but it also conducts research, publishes studies, and encourages inter-institutional collaboration and cooperative projects.   Direct governance of each college still resides with a local board of trustees appointed by the governor.

FUNDING

Maryland's 15 local community colleges receive their funding from four sources:

1) State funding through a funding formula;
2) Local funding through a negotiated budget process;
3) Students' tuition and fees; and
4) A small percentage from other sources.

Operating funds totaled $465.7 million in FY 1999. Approximately 27% of the unrestricted revenues (including state paid benefits) came from state funding, 34% from local funding, 36% from student tuition and fees, and 3% from other sources. The level of state support is based on (1) annual institutional enrollments two years prior, (2) a percentage of the per FTE amount going to specified 4-year public institutions, (3) the previous year's grant, and (4) a "small size factor" plus a grant per college board of trustees. The funding formula is provided by law. A hold-harmless provision is added to ensure that each community college will receive at least the amount of state funding received in the prior fiscal year. Each board of trustees sets tuition and fees. In fiscal year 1999, the systemwide average tuition and required fees per credit hour for a full-time student is $60.90. Because of their system of local governance, community college expenditure priorities are determined by local boards of trustees. The state provides no less than 50% but not more than 75 percent of the eligible costs of capital projects.

PROGRAMS AND ENROLLMENTS

Programs

The 16 Maryland community colleges are comprehensive institutions offering associate- degree transfer programs for students wishing to pursue baccalaureate degrees at four-year institutions and associate degree and certificate career programs for students seeking entry-level employment, skills enhancement, and career mobility. The curriculum emphasizes both the acquisition of a strong foundation in the liberal arts and a solid education in the technologies. Articulation agreements with Maryland public and private four-year colleges and universities have been developed to insure adequate preparation and to facilitate student transfer.

Occupational programs are designed primarily to prepare individuals for immediate job entry or to upgrade the skills of those already employed. They are intended to meet manpower requirements at two levels: management trainee and technician levels in such fields as health services, business and commerce, engineering, public service, agriculture, and high-technology fields, such as data processing and electronics; and artisan, trade, and service levels within each of these fields.

Associate degree programs must include not less than 60 and no more than 70 semester hours of credit. Associate of arts (A.A.) and associate of science (A.S.) degree programs require a minimum of 30 and maximum of 36 semester hours of "general education" courses distributed among the following areas: English composition, arts and humanities, natural sciences, mathematics, and the social sciences. This general education component is transferable as a block to four-year institutions. Associate of applied science (A.A.S.) degree programs require 20 hours of general education. One college offers an associate of fine arts (A.F.A.) degree, which requires 40 credit hours of studio courses.

Certificate programs must include 12 or more credit hours that stress the technical or skill requirements of an occupation. About 37% of the community college students are enrolled in one- and two-year occupational programs.

Maryland Community College Teleconsortium

Maryland community colleges entered into an innovative consortial agreement in summer 1998 to permit a student from any jurisdiction to take distance education courses originating at any of the 22 community college campuses at in-county tuition rates. The Maryland Community College TeleConsortium (MCCT) is a series of interrelated policies and procedures agreed upon by all 16 separate institutions concerning student tuition and fee sharing, registration and student records, transfer of credit, course scheduling, and other issues. The MCCT allows students to participate in courses offered by any "provider" campus, while receiving student support services and learning resources from their "home" institution. This provides Maryland residents with the advantages of a "virtual community college" without creating a new administrative structure or unit. The first courses were offered through the MCCT during the spring, 1999, semester.

Enrollment

The Maryland community colleges enrolled nearly 104,417 full-time and part-time students in credit programs in the fall of 1998. Forty-eight percent of the credit students were enrolled in transfer programs, and 36% were enrolled in career programs. Of the occupational students who were enrolled in programs designed to prepare them for immediate job entry or to upgrade their skills, the largest percentage were enrolled in the health services technology programs (30%), followed by business technology programs (28%), and public service programs (17%).

Sixty percent of all credit program students attend college part-time. Sixty-two percent of all credit students are women; 41% are minorities; and 27% are African-American. The average age of credit students is 28. Registrations in state-supported continuing education courses totaled 283,469 in fiscal year 1998.

ECONOMIC DEVELOPMENT

During the 1996 session of the Maryland General Assembly, initial funding was authorized to create Advanced Technology Centers (ATCs) in the several regions of the state to provide company-specific customized training, retraining, and upgrading of skills for existing, expanding and new businesses and industries. Each ATC is a cooperative effort of two or more community colleges. A significant feature is the collaboration of the community colleges, business and industry, and state and local government to respond to private sector needs for education and training. Currently, nine regional ATCs are operating in the state, bringing industry-driven training to businesses and adult workers in fields including manufacturing, agriculture and aquaculture, tourism, biothechnology, information technology and telecommunications, warehousing/distribution, and aerospace. As of October, 1998, the ATCs had delivered customized training to more than 650 companies and trained more than 29,000 workers.

In addition, community colleges provide a wide variety of noncredit and continuing education courses that meet the economic development, professional, technical, and environmental needs of the community. These include work-related courses for business and industry, apprenticeship training, preparation for licensure and certification, literacy training, and self-development courses that promote the quality of life.

ACCOUNTABILITY

In 1996, the Maryland Higher Education Commission, responding to the requirements of state law, approved a new accountability system for public higher education which measures campus performance on a series of key indicators that respond to concerns often expressed by State legislators. These indicators are grouped in 5 categories:

- *Quality* - how campuses can show whether they are doing a good job;
- *Effectiveness* - how campuses can demonstrate whether students are progressing and performing well;
- *Access* - how campuses can show whether the are accessible and are meeting the needs of students in all regions;
- *Diversity* - how campuses can evaluate whether students, faculty and staff reflect Maryland's gender and racial make-up; and
- *Efficiency/allocation of resources* - how campuses can determine how productively funds and facilities are being used.

For each indicator, the public campuses were required to develop benchmarks or goals to measure their performance. These benchmarks were prepared through a "bottom-up" process, meaning that each institution had the responsibility for identifying its own set of goals. The Maryland Higher Education Commission publishes a report each fall indicating each college's progress in achieving its goals on all indicators.

REFERENCES

Maryland Association of Community Colleges, *Databook.* (January 1999) Annapolis, MD: Author

Maryland Association of Community Colleges, *The Maryland Community College Teleconsortium* (May 1998). Annapolis, MD: Author

Maryland Higher Education Commission, *Data Book* (1999). Annapolis, MD: Author

Maryland Higher Education Commission, *1998 Opening Fall Enrollment.* (December 1998) Annapolis, MD: Author

Maryland Higher Education Commission, *Trend Book* (January 1999). Annapolis, MD: Author

Maryland Higher Education Commission, *1998 Performance Accountability Report, Maryland Public Colleges and Universities* (November 1998). Annapolis, MD: Author

FOR ADDITIONAL INFORMATION, PLEASE CONTACT:

Coordinator, Community Colleges
Maryland Higher Education Commission
16 Francis Street
Annapolis, MD 21401
Telephone: (410) 974-2971

MASSACHUSETTS

Janice C. Motta
Executive Officer
Massachusetts Community Colleges

OVERVIEW

The Massachusetts Public System of Higher Education is composed of 29 public colleges and universities. These institutions were established to ensure educational opportunities of high quality that are geographically accessible, affordable, and convenient.

Public colleges and universities have strong academic programs and are accredited by the New England Association of Schools and Colleges. Strategically located throughout nearly all regions of the state, these institutions serve the needs of the populace and are accessible to everyone in the commonwealth. To make education more affordable, tuition at public colleges and universities is set at reasonable levels, and financial aid programs are available to help needy students. Diversity in the system is assured through its 15 community colleges, seven comprehensive state colleges, two specialized professional colleges, and five university campuses.

Community colleges are comprehensive two-year institutions located in many regions of the state. These institutions offer associate degrees in the arts, sciences, and applied sciences, as well as an array of certificate programs that prepare students for transfer to four-year colleges and universities and for employment in a vocation.

Mission and Goals

Within the system of public higher education, the community colleges open pathways to baccalaureate education and to careers and career advancement. Their broad mission encompasses degree and certification programs, training for business and industry, serving as a resource for solving community problems, and enriching the quality of peoples' lives. Rooted in their communities, these colleges are open-admission institutions dedicated to serving an academically, economically, and culturally diverse population.

Given the breadth of their mission, the community colleges have the following purposes:

- Through the associate degree, provide the first two years of baccalaureate education equal in content and quality to the first two years of education at a four-year college or university;

- Through the associate degree or certification, provide programs for career-oriented students that emphasize the cognitive and technical skills needed to enter and advance in professional, technological, and service careers;
- Through partnerships with business and industry, provide job training, retraining, certification, and skills improvement to ensure a workforce equipped to meet the needs of a changing economy;
- Through partnerships with elementary and secondary schools, develop programs and initiatives to improve a student's ability to succeed in school and pursue higher education. Partnerships with vocational-technical high schools are especially important and should move beyond simple collaboration to establish formal "tech-prep" and "two-plus-two" arrangements; and
- Provide cultural activities and lifelong learning opportunities that enrich the communities served by the colleges.

In fulfilling their appropriate role within the system of higher education, the community colleges must carry out three important responsibilities:

- As the initial point of entry for many of the commonwealth's citizens, offer transfer programs leading to four-year college degrees. Development of educational "career ladders" in selected professions and specific transfer agreements with both public and independent baccalaureate institutions is especially encouraged.
- Provide educational programs that prepare individuals to directly enter the workforce in occupational and technical career areas; and
- Assume primary responsibility to offer courses, programs, and other educational services for individuals who seek to develop the skills necessary to successfully pursue collegiate study.

With a primary emphasis on classroom and laboratory instruction, the community colleges should:

- Conduct evaluations of institutional effectiveness and student achievement, demonstrating through verifiable means their attainment of purposes and objectives both inside and outside the classroom;
- Recognize and honor students' diversity in programs of study, academic and student support services and all aspects of college life;

- Provide an appropriate assortment of academic and personal support services, including services related to job placement and transfer, to assure that all students have a realistic opportunity to achieve academic and career success; and
- Foster the professional development of faculty and staff through the encouragement of research, curricular innovation, and new instructional methodologies.

The above Mission Statements were adopted by the Massachusetts Higher Education Coordinating Council in June, 1992.

The community college system developed relatively late in Massachusetts. The first initiative relative to community colleges occurred in March, 1958, in a report by the State Commission on Audit of State Needs, established under Chapter 38, Resolves of 1957, titled *Needs in Massachusetts Higher Education with Special References to Community Colleges*. The report recommended the establishment of a community college system to address a need for more diversity in, and access to, higher education in the commonwealth. The general court adopted the recommendation on August 1, 1958, in Chapter 605, Acts of 1958, and enabling legislation was signed by the governor on October 6, 1958.

The audit report submitted as evidence for the need for a community college system served as the foundation for suggesting regions around the state where these institutions should be located. In an effort to meet this need, the newly formed Board of Regional Community Colleges, between 1960 and 1965 established nine of the current 15 community colleges, as follows:

- Berkshire Community College   1960
- Massachusetts Bay Community College   1961
- Cape Cod Community College   1961
- Northern Essex Community College   1961
- Greenfield Community College   1962
- Quinsigamond Community College   1963
- Holyoke Community College   1964
- Mount Wachusett Community College   1964
- North Shore Community College   1965

Chapter 737, Act of 1964, which gave the community college system fiscal autonomy comparable to the University of Massachusetts and the state college system, was passed on July 3, 1964, and signed into law on July 9, 1964. Having used the audit report as a master plan since 1958, the community college board in the same year sought and acquired an appropriation of $100,000 under Chapter 640, Act of 1964 (item 8065.41 of the Commonwealth Capital Outlay Program), for the purpose of developing a master plan for community colleges and preparing preliminary plans for a community college in southeastern Massachusetts. The Willis-Harrington Act, Chapter 572, Act of 1965, which was significant legislation relating to community colleges, was approved by the legislature on June 21, 1965, and signed into law on June 28, 1965. This legislation, designed to reorganize the educational system in Massachusetts, did little to change the Board of Regional Community Colleges or its function except to bring the community college system and other entities of higher education under the jurisdiction of the newly formed coordinating board, the Massachusetts Board of Higher Education.

The new master plan that commenced in 1965 projected the need for community colleges by taking into account demography, the economic and social climate of Massachusetts, and the role these institutions should plan in effecting progress in the state. These projections extended to September, 1975, a period in which three additional community colleges (Bristol, Massasoit, and Springfield) were added to the system and at least four sites were recommended for the establishment of other community colleges.

The Willis-Harrington Act remained in effect for 15 years, during which time the final three community colleges (Bunker Hill, Roxbury, and Middlesex) were established.

The current Massachusetts Board of Higher Education was established on July 1, 1996, as part of a massive education reorganization by Governor William F. Weld and the Massachusetts legislature.

GOVERNANCE

The Massachusetts Board of Higher Education consists of 11 members appointed by the governor for five-year terms. No appointee can serve more than two consecutive terms. While the chair of the board is appointed by the governor, it is the board's responsibility to select a chancellor to administer the affairs of the state system of higher education.

The chancellor is the chief executive offer for the system and, with staff, provides oversight and governance for the system. Under the Office for Policy and Planning, the board's staff is divided into divisions headed by a chief academic officer, chief budget director and a director of institutional research.

Meetings of the board of higher education are held once a month, except in cases where the chairperson, with the board's approval, chooses to omit meetings in July and August. Eight members must be present to constitute a quorum, and eight votes are needed to make valid any business transacted during a board meeting. Issues and items for actions are transmitted from the board staff to the Academic Affairs Committee, Fiscal Affairs Committee and the Executive Committee to be approved, amended, or rejected; then the matter goes to the full board. Approval is the final stage for policy changes and new policies in the state system of higher education.

The major power, duties, and responsibilities of the board of higher education, as set forth in legislation creating the board, are to grant degrees and scholarships, approve new educational programs and activities; and to develop tuition policies and master plans.

Each institution has its own board of trustees. Acting as an immediate governing body to individual institutions, the board of trustees is made up of eight members, appointed by the governor. Members serve for five-year terms; however, no member is appointed for more than two consecutive terms.

FUNDING

In fiscal year 1999, $938,369,683 was appropriated by the legislature to public higher education, which includes five campuses of the University of Massachusetts, nine state colleges and 15 community colleges. Of that total state appropriation, the community colleges received $199, 399,469. This allocation represents approximately 47% of the total revenues required to operate the community colleges. Since there is no local tax base used to support public higher education in Massachusetts, the additional revenue is derived from other institutional support sources, including students fees, income from auxiliary enterprises, endowment income, grants and contracts.

PROGRAMS AND ENROLLMENT

All community colleges are considered comprehensive regional community colleges because they offer an array of programs leading to certificates and associate degrees, including a variety of vocational programs. These institutions are engaged in adult basic, adult continuing, and job training type educational programs. They develop affiliations with high schools and industry and develop unique job training programs. All Massachusetts' community colleges are accredited by the New England Association of Schools and Colleges.

Community colleges offer certificate programs for less than 30 hours that do not have to be approved by the board. Certificates for curricula of 30 hours or more require board approval. In addition to certificates, community colleges offer the Associate of Arts degree (A.A.), the associate of science (A.S.), and the associate of applied science (A.A.S.). All associate degrees require the completion of a minimum of 60 credit hours. Collectively, the state's 15 community colleges offer more than 150 different associate degree programs, 100 certificate programs and literally thousands of courses ranging from business, computer science, engineering technology, health care and human services to liberal arts and sciences. All programs stress and reinforce the development of cognitive skills that are essential if workers are to be prepared to adapt to changes in the workplace.

The Massachusetts community colleges are well positioned to be the Commonwealth's primary resource for workforce training and retraining. Jobs in the growth industries the Commonwealth seeks to attract and retain will require higher level cognitive, communication, computational and technical skills that cannot be acquired in the short-term skills oriented training programs which focus on entry level jobs.

ENROLLMENT

Nearly 170,000 full and part-time students are enrolled in Massachusetts public colleges and universities for the 1997-98 academic year. Of those, 72,347 were enrolled in credit courses at the community colleges in the fall of 1997.

Student enrollment information is maintained on total headcount (HC), full-time equivalent (FTE), and the Division of Continuing Education (DCE) enrollment. A full-time equivalent student is one who registers for 15 credit hours during any given semester. Students attending community colleges in the evening tend to be primarily registered on a part-time basis and are enrolled in the Division of Continuing Education. Therefore the number of FTEs in DCE is determined by dividing the total number of credits taken by students in DCE by 15 credit hours. Total number of credits taken by students in DCE/15 equals number of full-time equivalents.

Consequently, the number of FTEs in DCE would be only a fraction of the total DCE headcount. Moreover, the aggregate date are given by program enrolled rather than degree pursued. Thus, the numbers enrolled will represent thousand individuals registered in certificate programs as well as those pursuing A.S., A.A.S., and A.A. degrees.

In the last ten years, the number of Massachusetts high school graduates dropped approximately 20%, contributing to an overall public higher education enrollment decline of 9% during that period. However, between 1997 and 2007, the number of high school graduates is expected to increase by nearly 30% and, therefore, community college enrollment is expected to rise. In 1998, enrollments in community colleges increased by 7.5%. One goal of the Board of Higher Education is to encourage students to enroll at community colleges and, where appropriate, to transfer to a state college or university campus.

ECONOMIC DEVELOPMENT

An educated workforce is the commonwealth's greatest natural resource. The growth industries that Massachusetts must attract and support require a workforce with the skills needed to manage technology, think critically, and adapt to changing demands. Community colleges are the only training resources positioned to provide the sequential training opportunities that move unemployed workers into the workplace and current workers into more demanding and rewarding positions.

Virtually every Massachusetts resident lives within a 25-mile radius of a community college. Community colleges can and do serve adults as well as traditional age students; more than half of all community college students are 24 years of age or older. Many are working adults who wish to acquire the skills needed to advance on a career ladder or to maintain their current employment in view of new applications of technology. Community colleges also serve significant numbers of minority citizens and new immigrants who are project to make up a growing percentage of the workforce by the turn of the century.

Community colleges in Massachusetts are recognized by leading corporations as major providers of training for high technology occupations. Corporations contract with community colleges to provide training for their employees and invest in research and development initiative with their community college partners. In 1997, more than 600 companies entered into training partnerships with one or more of the community colleges. More than 100,000 individuals have participated in programs designed to upgrade the skills of current employees in the last three years

ACCOUNTABILITY

In June 1992, the Higher Education Coordinating council approved *The Mission of Public Higher Education in Massachusetts: The System*. Contained in this document are the mission statements for each of the public higher education segments.

The community college mission statement begins by stated that "within the system of public higher education, the community colleges open pathways to baccalaureate education and to careers and career advancement. Their broad mission encompasses degree and certification programs, training for business and industry, serving as a resource for solving community problems, and enriching the quality of people's lives. Rooted in their communities, these colleges are open-admissions institutions dedicated to serving an academically, economically, and culturally diverse population."

In order to determine the effectiveness of the Massachusetts community colleges, core indicators or outcomes that directly relate to the key components of the community college mission have been identified. The following core indicators also create a composite picture of the Massachusetts community colleges: student progress, career preparation, transfer preparation and developmental education.

REFERENCES

Mindpower in Massachusetts: The Commonwealth's Natural Resources - A Report on Public Higher Education in the Commonwealth, (1997).

Massachusetts Legislature. (1980) Boston, MA: *Massachusetts General Laws*, Chapter 15A:a: Author

Massachusetts Board of Regents. (1982). Boston, MA: *Long Range Plan for Public Higher Education in Massachusetts*: Author

FOR ADDITIONAL INFORMATION, PLEASE CONTACT:
Ms. Janice C. Motta
Executive Officer
Massachusetts Community Colleges
294 Washington Street
Boston, MA 02108
Telephone: (617) 542-2911

Fax: (617) 542-2904
or
Dr. Stanley Z. Koplik
Chancellor
Board of Higher Education
One Ashburton Place, Room 1401
Boston, MA 02114
Telephone: (617) 727-7785

MICHIGAN

James H. Folkening
Director, Postsecondary Services
and
Kenneth E. Snow
Consultant, Higher Education
Michigan Department of Education

OVERVIEW

Michigan has 28 public community colleges, with a total of 38 campuses. Access, quality and comprehensiveness are the hallmarks of Michigan's community colleges, are the hallmarks of Michigan's community colleges, and over 95% of the people in Michigan live within 40 miles of a community college campus. Over 500,000 students in 1996-97 were enrolled in credit and non-credit courses in the community colleges, and over 46% of all credit students in Michigan postsecondary institutions were attending community colleges.

The first public junior college in Michigan was Grand Rapids College, which was established in 1914. By 1940, a total of eight junior colleges had been established by school districts as extensions of public high schools, and by 1955, three more colleges were started within the same type of district. The state legislature passed Act 116 in 1954, which authorized the establishment of independent two-year college districts, and 18 were founded by 1968. Public Act 331 of 1966, the Comprehensive Community Act, established the independent recognition of public community colleges in Michigan (Folkening, in Tollefson & Fountain, 1992).

GOVERNANCE

Locally elected boards of trustees by law govern Michigan's community colleges. The Michigan State Board for Public Community Colleges was established by statute to advise the Michigan State Board of Education, a constitutionally created board of members elected on a statewide basis. The state board of education provides statewide planning, supervision and recommendations regarding state appropriations for public education at all levels, including postsecondary education. The state superintendent of public instruction is appointed by the state board of education, and the superintendent directs the staff of the Michigan Department of Education (Folkening, in Tollefson & Fountain, 1992). Within the department of education, staff members of the Community Colleges Service Unit, Office of Higher Education Management, provide support for the Michigan State Board for Community Colleges.

FUNDING

Approximately 96% of Michigan community colleges' operating support in 1996 came from three sources: state general fund appropriations (33%), local tax support (34%), tuition and fees (29%), with four percent obtained from other sources.

General appropriations to each community colleges are appropriated directly by the state legislature by means of a formula that includes factors for average costs, inflation, equalization of local effort and a minimum percentage increase totaling $275 million for 1997-98. Local community college boards of trustees set student tuition and fees charged by their respective colleges. Money for community college facilities planning and construction is provided by the legislature through the Capital Outlay Act, and state funds must be matched by locally obtained revenues. Local property tax levies are approved by voters in each community college district, for both operating and capital outlay purposes, and for the issuance and repayment of bonded indebtedness.

PROGRAMS

In the years since the first Michigan junior college was established in 1914, the two-year institutions have evolved into comprehensive institutions with common missions that include vocational-technical programs, college transfer and general education programs, noncredit continuing education programs, developmental courses, student support services, economic and community development and contracted training for business and industry employees. The state policy sets a minimum of 60 semester credit hours for each program leading to an associate degree, and local governing boards have the exclusive authority to approve educational programs in the Michigan community colleges.

INSTRUCTIONAL ACTIVITIES

The following instructional activities are reported by fiscal-year-equated students (FYES) and Contact Hours of Instruction. One FYES equals 13 semester credit hours.

In 1966 the distribution included:

Instructional Activity	Total FYES	Percent of FYES Instruction	Total Contact House	Percent of Contact Hour Instruction
General57,952	52.0%	32,782,411	48.9%	
Business24,329	22.0%	14,009,002	20.9%	
Trades 9,842	8.9%	6,880,481	10.3%	
Health Occupations	9,710	8.8%	8,218,813	12.3%
Developmental Education	8,399	7.6%	4,510,306	6.75
Human 718 Development	.7%	578,245	.9%	

Enrollment in Michigan community colleges, which peaked in 1993, leveled off to 110,949 FYES in 1996.

REFERENCES

Folkening, J.H., Michigan, in Tollefson, T.A. & Fountain, B.E. (1992) *Forty-Nine State Systems, 1992 Edition.* Washington, DC: American Association of Community Colleges.

FOR ADDITIONAL INFORMATION, PLEASE CONTACT:
Community College Services Unit
Department of Education
P. O. Box 300038
Lansing, MI 48909
Telephone: (517) 373-3360
Fax: (517) 373-2759
E-mail: folkenj@state.mi.us

MINNESOTA

Terrence A.Tollefson
Professor, Department of Educational Leadership and Policy Analysis
East Tennessee State University

OVERVIEW

Minnesota State Colleges and Universities is a system of 36 colleges and universities in Minnesota comprising 53 campuses and one institution in Japan. It was created by a statute adopted by the state legislature and governor in 1991 that required a new state board to merge three previous state systems of community colleges, technical colleges, and universities, excluding the University of Minnesota campuses (Minnesota State Colleges and Universities, 1999). The "MINSCU" system includes 29 two-year public institutions.

The first Minnesota public two-year college was established in 1914 by the Cloquet school district. In 1915, Rochester Junior College was opened (Christenson, in Tollefson & Fountain, 1992). Now named Rochester Community and Technical College, it is the oldest Minnesota community college still in operation (Minnesota State Colleges and Universities, 1999).

The Minnesota junior colleges operated as local institutions until July of 1964, when a new law established a state system of junior colleges. The new state board appointed Phillip C. Helland as its first chancellor, and Dr. Helland served in that capacity until 1983, when he was succeeded by Gerald W. Christenson (Christenson, in Tollefson & Fountain, 1992).

The first 10 campuses were all moved to new sites and eight new colleges (six of them in the Twin Cities Metropolitan Area) were established by 1970 (Christenson, in Tollefson & Fountain, 1992).

The evolving MINSIU system had two interim chancellors, Mary Rieder and Jay Noven, from 1991 to 1993 and 1993 to 1995, respectively. In 1995, Judith Eaton became the first permanent chancellor. When Dr. Eaton resigned in 1997, Morris J. Anderson, who was then a trustee, was appointed as chancellor, a position he still holds (Minnesota State Colleges and Universities, 1999).

PROGRAMS AND ENROLLMENTS

The Minnesota community and technical colleges offer a wide range of courses and programs in vocational, technical and college-transfer areas, as well as placing a considerable emphasis on workforce training. Credit enrollment in the 1998 fall semester was estimated at 93,100 students (Taylor, personal communication, 1998).

FUNDING

The Minnesota state legislature appropriated $269.6 million for operational purposes to the community and technical colleges in fiscal 1998-99, and some additional appropriations were anticipated (Taylor, K., personal communication, 1998).

ACCOUNTABILITY

The board of trustees recently developed a preliminary funding formula to create incentives for improving educational quality and productivity (Minnesota State Colleges and Universities, 1999).

REFERENCES

Christenson, G.W., Minnesota, in Tollefson, T.A. & Fountain, B.E. (1992) *Forty-Nine State Systems, 1992*, Washington, DC: American Association of Community Colleges. Edition. Washington, DC: American Association of Community Colleges.

Minnesota State Colleges and Universities (1998). St. Paul, Minnesota: Author. *A Decade of Accomplishments, 1991-1999 (1999)*. St. Paul, Minnesota: Minnesota State Colleges and Universities: Author.

FOR ADDITIONAL INFORMATION, PLEASE CONTACT:

Morris J. Anderson, Chancellor
Minnesota State Colleges and Universities
500 World Trade Center
30 East Seventh Street
St. Paul, MN 55101
Telephone (General Number): (651) 296-8012
Telephone (Information Line): (888) MNSCU-4-U
Fax: (651) 296-7087

MISSISSIPPI

Rick L. Garrett
Vice President of Instructional Services
Mayland Community College

OVERVIEW

Mississippi's two-year college system evolved from the state's agricultural high schools, which started in 1908 in response to the need to organize secondary schools in rural areas of the state where sparsity of population and inadequate roads were prevalent. According to Howell (1996), 1922 legislation authorized the agricultural high schools to expand their instructional programs to include freshman-level college courses. A statewide system of junior colleges began in 1928, with the passing of the Public Junior College legislation. As a result, course offerings at agricultural high schools and municipal school districts were authorized to expand to include the first two years of college work.

This legislative authorization gave Mississippi claim to having the first state system of two-year colleges in the country. Howell (1996) reported that "…the junior college mission was to offer academic coursework that paralleled the freshman and sophomore years of university work. The State Department of Education was the state agency with responsibilities for the junior colleges" (p. 547) and the Junior College Commission functioned under its authority. The Mississippi State Board for Community and Junior Colleges was established through legislation in 1986 as an independent board to coordinate, set standards, and provide guidance for the operation of the 15 community college districts. " Mississippi's public 2-year colleges are the largest single sector of the state's postsecondary education system, providing education and training in three general categories: university parallel, vocational-technical, and noncredit educational service programs" (Howell 1996, p. 549). However, the primary mission is still to provide university-parallel programs.

GOVERNANCE

There are 15 community college districts with 23 different local public institutions. The Mississippi State Board for Community and Junior Colleges serves a coordinating role in overseeing the 15 community college districts (Garrett, 1999). The board has 10 members who are appointed by the governor, two from each congressional district with initial terms of appointment from two to five years (Howell, 1996; and Moody & Ray, in Tollefson & Fountain, 1992.) "The institutions are governed by local boards of trustees who employ, dismiss, budget, own property, and establish policies" (Moody & Ray, in Tollefson & Fountain, 1992, p. 113).

FUNDING

The 15 Mississippi community college districts received a total of $152.7 million in state funding for fiscal year 1998 (Tollefson & Patton, 1998). The following funding sources and proportions financed Mississippi community colleges during 1995-96: state funds, 49%; local funds, 8%; federal funds, 17%; tuition 14%; and other, 11%. Expenditures per FTE totaled $7,755 and the average tuition and fees paid per student in 1996-97 was $952 (Tollefson & Patton, 1998). "Capital improvements are financed mostly from local property tax revenues, federal vocational act funds, and negotiated state appropriations" (Moody & Ray, in Tollefson & Fountain 1992, p. 118). Tuition and fees are set for each college district by the local boards of trustees (Tollefson & Fountain, 1992).

PROGRAMS AND ENROLLMENTS

More vocational courses and evening hours have been offered at Mississippi community colleges resulting in increased system-wide enrollments. The 1996 fall credit headcount was 54,522 (Tollefson & Patton, 1998). Total enrollment for 1995-96 was 76,229 of which 68.7% were full-time and 31.3% were part-time. Male enrollment comprised 41.0% of the students while female enrollment was 59.0% of the total. Minority students accounted for 30.7% of the total student body at public two-year institutions. There were a total of 5,519 associate degrees awarded among the community colleges during 1997-98. The fastest growing age group is students 35 years of age and older; 20% of the total student body. A significant number of full-time students in vocational and technical programs hold baccalaureate degrees (6%) (*Chronicle of Higher Education 1997-98 Almanac Issue,* (1998). New full-time technical and vocational programs require state board approval (Howell, 1996). "The Mississippi public junior colleges offer academic (university-parallel), technical, vocational, adult basic education, adult continuing education, general educational development, job training partnership and industry related" (Moody

& Ray, in Tollefson & Fountain 1992, p. 118).

ECONOMIC DEVELOPMENT

Mississippi's two-year colleges impact state economic development by training people for jobs, helping to create and retain jobs, offering startup training for new industries, and retraining for existing industries. The Mississippi Workforce and Education Act of 1994 expanded the state's two-year college's role in economic development. This act established a system for the delivery of workforce training that includes the organization of one-stop career centers at each two-year college campus to provide workforce training and related services to industries and individuals. Moreover, advanced technology centers at two community colleges provide high-skill/high performance training in electronics and manufacturing (Howell, 1996). The Workforce Education Act of 1994 includes the following mission statement:

> "…to provide for the creation and development of a regionally based system in Mississippi for education and training which: responds to the needs of Mississippi's workforce and employers; is driven by the demands of industry and a competitive economy; makes maximum use of limited resources; and provides for continuing improvement through constant assessment of the results of education for individual workers and employers" (Mississippi State Board for Community and Junior Colleges, 1999) (http://www.sbcjc.cc.ms.us/94act.htm).

REFERENCES

Garrett, R. L. (1999). Degrees of centralization of governance structures in state community college systems. In Tollefson, T. A.; Garrett, R. L.; Ingram, W. G. and Associates, *Fifty State Systems of Community Colleges: Mission, Governance, Funding and Accountability*: Johnson City, TN: Overmountain Press.

Howell, W. G., Mississippi, in *Community College Journal of Research and Practice* (1996, November-December, pp. 545-555).

Mississippi State Board for Community and Junior Colleges (1999, April 28). http/www.sbcjc.cc.ms.us

Mississippi. in *Chronicle of Higher Education 1997-98 Almanac Issue*, (1998, August 28, 45(1), pp. 80-81).

Moody, G. V. & Ray, O., Mississippi, in Tollefson, T. A. & Fountain, B. E.,

Eds. (1992). *Forty-Nine State Systems, 1992 Edition*. Washington, DC: American Association of Community Colleges.

Tollefson, T. A. & Patton, M. (1998, pp. 56-57), Mississippi, in *AACC Annual 1998-99*, Washington DC: American Association of Community Colleges.

MISSOURI

Kala Stroup
Commissioner of Higher Education
Missouri Coordinating Board for Higher Education

OVERVIEW

The Missouri community college system includes 12 locally controlled taxing districts with a total of 17 main campuses and 10 state-appropriated off-campus, out-of-taxing-district outreach centers. The three St. Louis and four Kansas City campuses are in multi-campus institutions. A locally elected board of six trustees, composed of district residents governs each college. Although district resident students are the first priority of the community colleges within the districts, anyone may attend because all are "open enrollment" institutions. However, a tuition differential does exist for out-of-district and out-of-state students. The Missouri Coordinating Board for Higher Education (CBHE) provides statewide coordination through mission review, mission enhancement, funding for results, program approval and review process, and budget recommendation responsibilities. The coordinating board also has the authority to call elections to form new districts, based on appropriate local petitions when received.

Although the Missouri community college system is not designed with a centralized governance structure, the CBHE Blueprint for Missouri Higher Education(1996) states that providing such access was a primary reason for establishing a system of community colleges in Missouri. Access, in geographic, programmatic, and financial terms, is a statewide goal of Missouri community colleges. The delivery of quality programs and services is another common goal of the institutions, thereby offering the community the best possible educational value. Finally, the "community" colleges are committed to serving the unique educational needs of their local service regions by providing innovative programs and services in the communities they serve. Other common goals include responding to unique local needs with high quality and innovative programs and sources (Aery & McClain, in Tollefson & Fountain, 1992).

The 1961 act built upon Missouri's long tradition of providing post-secondary education in two-year institutions. That tradition began in 1915, when Kansas City Polytechnic Institute commenced operations. The tradition gained momentum from a 1927 statute that authorized existing school districts to add courses at grade levels 13 and 14 when appropriate petitions signed by district residents were presented to the Missouri State Board of Education. The 1927 law set the precedent for state-level oversight of public two-year junior colleges. The 1927 act also authorized school districts to charge tuition for instruction in grades 13 and 14, and by 1949 eight districts were providing such junior college instruction. Under the 1927 legislation, local school districts were authorized to charge tuition for grades 13 and 14 but they were not eligible either to receive state funds for that purpose or to levy additional local taxes for junior college instruction. Each junior college district was limited in size to the boundaries of the affiliated school district(s), thus limiting both potential student bodies and local tax revenues that could be reallocated by the school districts to their respective affiliated junior colleges. In the 1950s, several state conferences on higher education, in the context of a predicted doubling of college enrollments by the 1970s, viewed the operation of junior colleges in borrowed high school buildings as viable low-cost alternatives to the construction of greatly expanded senior institutions. The lack of state and local tax funding and district size limitations resulted in many school districts eliminating their early efforts to provide junior college instruction (Aery & McClain, in Tollefson & Fountain, 1992).

In 1960, Governor James T. Blair appointed Ward E. Barnes, a school superintendent in the St. Louis area, to chair the Committee on Education Beyond High School. This committee recommended creating a state system of junior college districts, in which each new college could be authorized, only after an affirmative vote by the district residents, to levy local taxes for operating the college. The committee also recommended authorizing the state legislature to appropriate state tax revenues to supplement local tax and tuition revenues. Senator Earl R. Blackwell, of Hillsboro, submitted a bill based partly on the committee's recommendation. The Blackwell bill was ratified by both houses of the state legislature and signed into law by Governor John M. Dalton in July of 1961. The 1961 statute provided for the establishment of larger college districts after successful votes of the people, with the authority to levy property taxes and to receive state appropriations as well. The law allowed any school district or combination of geographically connected districts to create a junior college district after a positive vote of the electors within the district. The state department of education kept the supervisory authority that had been assigned to it by the 1927 statute. The 1961 law expanded the junior colleges' revenue-raising capacity, which allowed them to broaden the scope of their offerings beyond the traditional college-transfer programs, and thereby enabled them to become comprehensive community colleges (Aery & McClain, in Tollefson & Fountain, 1992).

Seven previously existing junior college districts were authorized to receive state appropriations under the new law, and after considerable local and statewide competition, the first new district was established in St. Louis City and County in April of 1962. Two additional colleges were authorized in 1963, and the Missouri Higher Education Commission was established in that same year to coordinate all postsecondary education in the state. The state board and department of education retained their previous administrative authority (Aery & McClain, in Tollefson & Fountain, 1992).

In 1964, the existing Joplin Junior College District expanded to encompass all of Jasper County, and the Kansas City Junior College District was expanded to include eight school districts in three counties. Public junior college enrollments increased from about 6,700 students in 1961 to more than 10,000 in 1964. By 1968, nearly half of Missouri's high school students lived within the 12 junior college districts. The Missouri junior colleges became identified with the goal to expand the availability of postsecondary education (Aery & McClain, in Tollefson & Fountain, 1992).

The Missouri Commission on Higher Education recommended in its state higher education master plan in 1972 that administrative oversight of junior colleges be transferred from the state department of education to the commission, and the state legislature subsequently made that change. The reason stated to support the transfer was that the previous division of authority had limited the enrollment growth of junior colleges, even though enrollment had exceeded 43,000 students by 1973. The state legislature subsequently transferred that authority from the state board of education to the new Missouri Coordinating Board of Higher Education, effective in 1974 (Aery & McClain, in Tollefson & Fountain, 1992).

In the years since 1974, the state-level administrative structure for community colleges has remained intact, but two new college districts have been established, and several other districts have changed the way that their trustees are elected to comply with a decision of the Missouri

Supreme Court that the one-man, one-vote rule must be applied to junior college district trustee elections. St. Charles Community College, in a rapidly expanding county, near the western edge of St. Louis, was established in 1986. Heart of the Ozarks Community College was established in 1990 to include all or part of 14 contiguous school districts. It later shortened its name to Ozarks Technical Community College (Aery & McClain, in Tollefson & Fountain, 1992).

From the onset of the first three junior colleges in the early 1920s to the late 1980s, the Missouri General Assembly gave very little attention to state policy regarding the nature, scope and equity among community college taxing districts. Policy conversations over the years perhaps should have included:

- The equitable distribution of state general revenue dollars to support local community colleges;
- The number and location of community colleges;
- Mandated service regions versus autonomous taxing districts;
- State-wide accessibility of the first two years of postsecondary education; and
- Annexation incentives, to create a geographically and financially balanced system of community colleges.

Consequently, Missouri's 12 publicly supported community college taxing districts (with 17 campuses) can be described as a confederation of regional two-year institutions that have generally evolved from the K-12 public school district statutes into 13th- and 14th-grade junior college operations. Over the years, Missouri's community college taxing districts have taken on many shapes and sizes. Although some taxing districts have retained their original single, public school district junior college taxing authority from the 1920s, others have grown strategically to encompass 5 or 6 counties and 25-30 school districts each. In general, community college boards of trustees, as well as past and current presidents, have been dedicated to providing educational services to communities outside the existing taxing districts, and have prioritized the need to increase the local revenue sources by making their taxing districts larger.

Despite the best of intentions by most of the Missouri community colleges' efforts to annex new contiguous public school districts to bring in local support through new and increased property tax revenues, results and accomplishments have varied. Voter apathy and anti-tax moods and sour local economies have often shaped annexation and property tax referendums. It is generally conceded that, over time, Missouri's community college taxing districts and derived tax revenues are the result of considerable local autonomy and control, rather than from the benefits of a well-thought-out statewide public policy.

In September of 1993, the Missouri Community College Association submitted for the coordinating board's approval a proposal for establishing non-statutory out-of-taxing district service regions for each of the 12 community college districts in Missouri. These 12 service regions, collectively, cover the entire state and are intended to facilitate the coordination and delivery of postsecondary instructional opportunities—principally for vocational/technical education and Tech Prep programming—available through the primary stewardship of Missouri's community colleges. The proposal was developed in full cooperation with the Missouri Department of Elementary and Secondary Education and representatives of the state's area vocational schools.

In 1995, the Coordinating Board for Higher Education adopted its *Blueprint for the Future of Missouri Higher Education*. The *Blueprint* integrated the goals recommended to the board by the Task Force on Critical Choices in 1992. These goals reaffirmed the values of access, quality, and efficiency for the state's system of higher education that were officially approved by the board in June 1996. To build on Missouri's strengths and address the new challenges and opportunities facing higher education, a vision statement acknowledges at least the two following characteristics:

- A coordinated, balanced, and cost-effective delivery system; and
- A range of vocational, academic, and professional programs that are affordable and accessible to all citizens with the preparation and ability to benefit from the programs.

Further, the coordinating board declared certain value statements, including access (financial, geographic, programmatic, and access to academic success), quality (of teaching, learning, research, and service), and efficiency (that is performance based, maximizes the impact of funding, minimizes unnecessary duplication, and maximizes the sharing of resources). These value statements guided the board's public policy framework and the strategic initiatives, strategies, and outcomes included in the Integrated Strategic Plan for the Missouri Department of Higher Education and the state's system of higher education.

The Missouri Coordinating Board for Higher Education affirmed these vision and values statements under the provisions of sections 163.191.3,

173.005.2(3) and 173.030(4), RSMo. These statutes authorized the board to include selected off-campus and out-of-district instructional activities in its appropriation recommendations and to place funding in the core budgets of selected institutions operating in areas where the coordinating board has established prior need.

The community college presidents and chancellors are commended for bringing a 1993 plan to the coordinating board that divided the state into 12 geographic service regions, and thereby enhanced the accessibility of postsecondary education. However, in doing so, the extent that the community colleges have annexed more school districts in their service region into the community college taxing district has been very limited. In fact, only about 62% of the people of the state have accessibility to the taxing district of a regional community college. This figure is somewhat misleading when comparing urban and suburban community colleges to rural community colleges. In each of six rural community colleges, the population of the taxing district, averages only 15% of the population of the service region. Clearly, the rural community college taxing districts serve a very small proportion of the total population residing in their respective voluntary service regions. The rural community colleges of Missouri certainly could benefit, and should be encouraged to take advantage of, the new "Hop-over" legislation designed to annex additional school district populations into the tax paying community college district. "Hop-over" legislation created in SB 553 in 1998 authorizes community colleges to annex additional public school districts to an existing community college taxing district while ignoring the previously required contiguous location factor. In theory, this statute enables annexation among likely public school districts without the necessity of wooing poorer, apathetic school districts lying between the existing community college taxing district and the school districts optimistically voting to annex. This legislation is important and beneficial, because it allows the public school district(s) desiring to annex to the community college taxing district to "hop-over" intervening school districts and begin enjoying the advantages of belonging to a community college district. In most cases, economically challenged public school districts lying contiguous to the community college taxing district would probably demonstrate little to no chance of ever desiring to join a community college taxing district. Under the old statutes, responsive and progressive school districts were blocked from being annexed, and the community college were permanently prohibited from raising new local property taxes to supplement revenue sources.

Critics of the "hop-over" legislation applaud its intent and potentiality to help strengthen local property tax revenue streams for community college taxing districts. Nevertheless, community college leadership remains tentative and appears to be reluctant to seriously consider using the features and benefits of SB 553 (1998). The reasons vary, but they seem to point toward the degree of difficulty involved in selling an annexation vote to the residents of neighboring communities. Second, it is believed that Missouri residents are not prone to tax themselves any more than they already are, given their own public school initiatives, local library taxes, local recreation levies, and other issues important to their communities. And third, residents of communities desiring to annex to the community college taxing district must agree to be taxed at the preexisting community college taxing rates (e.g., 43 cents or 33 cents/ $100 assessed valuation). In some rural Missouri farming school districts, these tax rates are prohibitive, and, in all probability, would be voted down.

Section 178.637 RSMo (Senate Bill 101, 1995), directed the CBHE, in cooperation with the Missouri Department of Elementary and Secondary Education, to implement a comprehensive system for advancing geographic and programmatic initiatives in postsecondary technical education throughout Missouri. On June 11, 1996, Governor Carnahan signed House Bill 1003, which provided the first $5,000,000 in general revenue funds to the Missouri Department of Higher Education to begin developing and enhancing capacity and infrastructure for advanced technological education and training as defined by The State Plan for Postsecondary Technical Education. The goal of The State Plan for Postsecondary Technical Education is to strengthen the state's associate of applied science degree delivery system and to enhance the delivery of postsecondary technical education among Missouri's community colleges.

At its October 10, 1996 meeting, the coordinating board approved the distribution of the FY 1997 (Year 1) $5,000,000 appropriation to the community colleges' Regional Technical Education Councils (RTECs) for the initial implementation of the State Plan for Postsecondary Technical Education. At its February 12, 1997, meeting, the coordinating board approved the FY 1998 (Year 2) funding distributions of $9,925,000. Finally, at its October 9, 1997, meeting the board approved the budget recommendation and proposed distribution of funds for FY 2000

GOVERNANCE

State-level coordination of community colleges is provided by the Missouri Coordinating Board for Higher Education, acting through a commissioner and his staff in the Missouri Department of Higher Education. The board has a combination of governance and coordination powers, including statewide planning, providing information and advice on policy to the governor and the state legislature of reviewing and approving educational programs, and making budget recommendations. The members of the nine-member board are appointed for staggered six-year terms by the governor, subject to the consent of the state senate. Only one board member can be from each congressional district, and the maximum number of board members from one political party is five. The coordinating board is required by law to meet at least four times annually (Aery & McClain, in Tollefson & Fountain, 1992).

FUNDING

State law limits the state share of financial operating support to a maximum of 50% of the total operating expenditures of all community colleges combined. The actual share per college district varies considerably from one district to another.

By 1996, an estimated 38 of Missouri's 114 counties (33%) were annexed into community college taxing districts. These annexed counties accounted for about 3.6 million (71%) of the state's population. By 1996, local citizens paying property tax to their respective community colleges account for only about 62% of Missouri's total population. These data reconfirmed that roughly five million Missouri citizens to community colleges. Conversely, the remaining two million persons (of all ages) theoretically do not have geographic and programmatic accessibility to postsecondary two-year education and training.

The following table shows the 1996 distribution of population among the 12 voluntary community college service regions. The table also shows the percentage of citizens residing in taxing districts as a proportion of the total population of the service region:

TABLE 1

1996 Distribution of Missouri Population Residing in Community College Service Regions and Taxing Districts

College	1996 Service Area Population Estimate	Percent of Total Missouri Population	Population of Taxing District	Percent of Taxing District Population to Service Region Population
Crowder College	272,894	5.3%	15,861	5.1%
East Central College	152,501	3.0%	45,018	29.5%
Jefferson College	181,871	3.5%	181,871	100.0%
Metropolitan CC	1,106,479	21.5%	806,724	72.9%
Mineral Area College	144,677	2.8%	64.362	44.5%
Moberly Area CC	310,705	6.0%	15,861	5.1%
North Central MO Coll.	121,654	2.4%	7,318	6.0%
Ozarks Tech. Com. C	471,912	9.2%	280,694	59.5%
St. Charles Co CC	326,104	6.3%	248,564	76.2%
St. Louis Com. Coll.	1,384,360	26.9%	1,384,360	100.0%
State Fair Com. Coll.	339,861	6.6%	51,167	15.1%
Three Rivers Com. Coll	333,216	6.5%	51,167	15.1%
Total	5,146,234	100.0%	3,213,818	62.4%

At present, the community college taxing districts' assessed valuation is unevenly distributed. Assessed valuation ranges from $43 to 97 million at the lower end, $372 to $465 million in the middle, to $7 to 17 billion at the upper end. Furthermore, while relatively stable, the proportion of total state aid to total revenues has crept up to about 37%. The following table consolidates these data:

TABLE 2

FY 1997 Distribution of Community College
Assessed Valuation, Tax Rates, and Local Tax Revenue

College	Assessed Valuation	Tax Rate	Local Tax Revenue	Local Taxes as a Percent of E and G
Crowder College	$404,000,000	0.43	1,590,257	20.5%
East Central College	811,805,881	0.45	2,814,763	32.3%
		0.37 operating		
		0.08 debt service		.
Jefferson College	1,401,071,261	0.23	2,296,837	16.4%
		0.18 operating		
		0.05 debt service		
Metropolitan CC	7,574,048,595	0.22	17,855,451	24.4%
Mineral Area College	372,785,608	0.53	1,757,411	13.0%
		0.36 operating		
		0.17 debt service		
Moberly Area CC	97,175,130	0.33	332,990	5.4%
North Central MO Coll.	43,000,000	0.40	198,005	5.1%
Ozarks Tech. Com. C	2,359,539,889	0.15	2,125,443	11.2%
St. Charles Co CC	2,662,228,258	0.25	3,484,500	25.9%
		0.13 operating		
		0.12 debt service		
St. Louis Com. Coll.	17,453,698,966	0.24	41,639,055	37.9%
State Fair Com. Coll.	465,504,394	0.41	1,824,812	19.8%
Three Rivers Com. Coll	426,810,287	0.24	1,021,735	14.7%
Total	34,071,668,269	0.32 Avg.	76,941,259	27.1%

Over the past four years, full- and part-time students enrolled in credit certificate and associate degree programs have stabilized at around 70,000 unduplicated students. However, in FY 1998 the non-credit participation from workforce development and training programs designed specifically for employers and their employees exploded to over 200,000 duplicated individuals.

In FY 1999 state aid to community colleges reached nearly $136 million, up nearly $65 million from as recent as 1993, a 48% increase. For the 1999 Fiscal Year, state appropriations as a percent of Education and General (E & G) budgets averaged 42.1% among the 12 community college districts. Similarly, tuition and fees as a percent of E & G averaged 23%, while local property tax funds as a percentage of E & G averaged 26.4%. The following table details and compares the percentage differences among the 12 community colleges and proportion of funds received from state general revenue, tuition and fees, and local property tax:

TABLE 3

FY 1999
Distribution of State Appropriations, Tuition and Fees, and Local Property Tax
as a Percentage of E & G Budgets for
Missouri Community Colleges

Colleges	State Appropriations as a Percent of E & G	Tuition and Fees as a Percent of E & G	Local Property Taxes as a Percent of E & G
Crowder College	48.0%	22.4%	17.8%
East Central College	48.0%	21.0%	28.2%
Jefferson College	48.6%	24.3%	16.4%
Metropolitan CC	38.9%	25.5%	23.5%
Mineral Area College	42.0%	28.8%	11.9%
Moberly Area CC	68.7%	36.0%	4.9%
North Central MO Coll.	47.8%	30.2%	4.1%
Ozarks Tech. Com. C	39.1%	30.6%	10.4%
St. Charles Co CC	35.1%	30.3%	31.6%
St. Louis Com. Coll.	41.3%	18.7%	38.3%
State Fair Com. Coll.	44.1%	18.9%	17.1%
Three Rivers Com. Coll	50.6%	27.5%	14.4%
Total	42.1%	23.7%	26.4%

Over the years, shifting proportions coming from state general revenue, tuition and fees, and local property taxes has marked Missouri community college funding. As shown in Table 4, the trend in Missouri has been toward increased dependence on state general revenue and tuition. The major trend is that Missouri is picking up an increasingly larger share of total E & G support through state general revenues than the local districts do through local property taxes.

TABLE 4

Average Percentage of Income from Various Sources as a Proportion of E & G for Missouri Community Colleges

FY 1995-FY 1999 (planned)

Source	FY 1995	FY 1996	FY 1997	FY 1998 (estimated)	FY 1999 (planned)
State General Revenue	32.0%	35.4%	36.9%	38.6%	42.1%
Tuition and Fees	27.5%	25.5%	24.4%	23.4%	23.7%
Local Property Taxes	28.5%	27.6%	27.1%	26.8%	26.4%

The Missouri Higher Education Coordinating Board, Governor, legislators, and local community college presidents/chancellors and boards of trustees are exploring incentives to encourage more public school district residents to vote to annex to their regional public community college taxing district. Historically and fundamentally, community college finance in America has been founded on a revenue-allocation strategy of "one-thirds"—*one-third from local tuition, one-third from local property tax, and one-third of the revenue sources from state general aid*. Missouri has seen shifts in recent years away from the fundamentals of one-thirds. From as recently as FY 1994, local tuition has actually declined about five percentage points to about 24%. The proportion reserved for local property tax has declined to a level slightly above 26%, while state general revenue has seen about a 10 percent increase. At present state-aid to community colleges is over 42%.

TABLE 5
Comparison of a Model Community College Financing Allocation
to Actual Missouri Sources of Income

Source	Model Allocation	Missouri Distribution (planned FY 1999)
Local Tuition and Fees	33%	23.7%
Local Property Taxes	33%	26.4%
State General Revenue	33%	42.1%

Community College Resource Allocation Model

The state aid portion of community college revenues was on a reimbursement-per-credit- hour formula until 1991. Before 1991, each institution reported to the coordinating board the number of eligible credit hours generated the previous year, with the hours categorized as general or vocational. State funding was provided on a per-credit-year basis, the rate being set statewide and differentiated for each type of credit hour. The CBHE had the responsibility for recommending an amount for community colleges to the governor. Once the general assembly approved the appropriation and after the governor signed the legislation, the appropriation was allocated to the community colleges, through the CBHE, based on each one's proportion of total credit hours produced. If a community college experienced a decline in enrollment, its proportion of the appropriation would be reduced by the amount of its enrollment loss.

However, from the state perspective, providing state aid on a per-credit-hour basis tends to reinforce student recruitment and growth in relationship to other factors or objectives. Thus, the more students attending, the higher the proportion of state aid. The community colleges and the Missouri Coordinating Board for Higher Education requested a revision of the law by the Missouri General Assembly, and it won approval in December, 1991. House Bill 1102 revised the statute regarding funding of community colleges so that they would no longer receive state aid on the per-credit-hour basis, but rather based on a resource-allocation model. Section 163.191 (1) RSM, says that community college operating expenditures must be distributed according to a resource- allocation model developed and revised, as appropriate, cooperatively between the department of higher education and the community colleges, and adjusted annually for inflation, limited growth, and program improvements.

The current funding model, which was established in 1992, allows community colleges to request funding on the basis of several components, including a core appropriation that maintains funding of programs at existing levels, an inflation adjustment for educational and general expenses, program improvements and targeted enhancements, workforce preparation results, funding for results elements, instructional technology, maintenance and repair, out-of-district programs, and results and accomplishments from implementing initiatives in *The State Plan for Postsecondary Technical Education.*

Tuition rates, on the other hand, are a matter of institutional prerogative. Although the Missouri Coordinating Board for Higher Education makes recommendations concerning the proportion of the budget they should comprise, tuition is one of the few income sources over which the local community college board of trustees has complete control. Therefore, tuition rates vary widely from district to district. The 1998-99 range of unrestricted student fees for district residents is from $990 to $1,500 for a full-time student or from $33 to $50 per student credit hour, respectively. Out-of-district student tuition for full-time students ranges from $1,500 to $2,400. Unrestricted student fees are the charges incurred for one academic year and do not include restricted or designated fees for a specific purpose, such as health service, student activities, computer usage, or debt retirement.

PROGRAMS AND ENROLLMENTS

As was clear in the system history, enrollment numbers increased rapidly during the formative years of the system. Determining the exact level of growth is difficult, however credit (versus noncredit) enrollments continued to increase after 1973 until reaching a peak in the fall of 1983, exceeding 59,000 by student headcount and 32,000 full-time equivalents (both figures being on-campus and on-schedule counts). Since that time, credit enrollment changes at the community colleges have been uneven, with an overall decline of over 8%in FTE and a headcount reduction of nearly 7% between fall 1983 and fall 1986. Contrary to that trend, however, is the growth reported between 1987 and 1992 of approximately 30% in both categories, mostly due to suburban population growth, and increases in older and part-time students. In fall 1997, the full-time-equivalent credit enrollment in the state's public community colleges was 38,842, while the total headcount enrollment was 71,909, or 30.3% of the total credit enrollment in public institutions of higher education. Although

Missouri has experienced a tremendous growth in enrollment for credit, current trends indicate that community college on-campus and on-schedule credit enrollments have hit a plateau.

The current credit-based enrollment plateau can be explained, in part, by a smaller pool of graduating high school seniors and a robust Missouri economy where unemployment is at a record low. Graduates of associate degree and technical certificate programs contribute to the state's economy by either continuing their education in four-year institutions or entering the workforce directly. Non-credit workforce development, training and education is a major enrollment factor for Missouri community colleges. Through legislative initiatives and entrepreneurial savvy, the community colleges have captured a significant portion of the state's non-credit customized and contract training, continuing education, JTPA, and adult basic skills and employability literacy training. In FY 1998, it is estimated that Missouri community colleges trained 285,000 employees for the state's employers.

New program approval was authorized by the 1974 reorganization act that created the Missouri Coordinating Board for Higher Education. This power of approval of proposed new degree programs, which extends to both two- and four-year public institutions, is designed to promote effective and economical specialization among the institutions and to implement the coordinated plan for the development of higher education in the state. In 1983, the Coordinating Board of Higher education assumed the added role of reviewing existing degree programs on a five-year rotational basis.

All new community college associate degree (A.A., A.S., A.A.S.) and certificate programs must be submitted to the coordinating board for review and approval. In addition to submitting new programs for in-district offerings, a public community college must submit for approval programs offered outside the college-taxing district, but within its service region. Multicampus institutions must submit separate proposals for individual campuses. Each institution must implement an approved program within two years of approval or the proposal must be resubmitted with updated information. Changes in existing programs, such as adding or deleting options, also require approval by the coordination board.

The criteria for review of a proposal include the program's appropriateness to the institution's role and scope; the academic structure of the program; the regional, state, or national need for the program; adequacy of physical facilities and instructional equipment; administrative structure; performance goals; and suitability of financing arrangement (including institutional reallocation of funds and the financial costs and benefits resulting from the program). Since innovative programs may differ significantly from traditional practices, nontraditional proposals must provide information to justify that difference and assure that traditional quality will be maintained. Proposed programs are measured by the coordinating board against these standards and, after clarification of any problems or questions through communication with the institutions, are approved or rejected. Procedures have been established for an institution to request that the Missouri Coordinating Board for Higher Education reconsider its decision on a proposal.

Before 1961, the state's *junior colleges* (now community colleges) were concerned primarily with college transfer curricula for current high school graduates. Today, Missouri's community colleges are truly comprehensive institutions, offering a full range of certificate and associate-degree programs. These include the traditional A.A. academic programs geared toward credit transfer to four-year institutions, vocational and technical A.A.S. degree and certificate credit programs to prepare students for employment, some A.A.S. and A.S. degree programs that are transferable a four-year institutions, general education for all students, community services, adult basic education, continuing education (credit and non-credit), and remedial/developmental and ABE/GED instruction. In addition, all institutions are engaged in partnerships with industry to provide customized and contract job-related training and skills upgrading. All are providing activities to attract the nontraditional learner to higher education, especially with regard to older and minority students.

Before 1974, the Missouri Department of Elementary and Secondary Education accredited all public junior and community colleges. Because of state reorganization in 1974, statutory authority was transferred to the Missouri Coordinating Board for Higher Education, including the responsibility for accreditation, which is a prerequisite for receiving state funding. At that time, the Missouri Coordinating Board for Higher Education adopted the current policy, which accepts accreditation by the North Central Association of Colleges and Schools as prima facie evidence of acceptable standards. Authorization to establish a new college and the approval of the program of instruction constitutes initial accreditation for three years. After that time, in the absence of North Central accreditation, the coordinating board conducts accreditation visits under its adopted guidelines.

Neither the Missouri legislature nor the coordinating board sets graduation or degree standards for the state's community colleges. While the legislature has required the teaching of certain subjects, for example, U.S. and Missouri constitutional studies, the determination of the course requirements for degrees or certificates is considered the prerogative of the individual institutions. The Missouri Coordinating Board for Higher Education has some control in this area, through its power of approval of new programs, and critical issues identified in its *Blueprint for Missouri Higher Education*, such as access, quality, and efficiency.

ECONOMIC DEVELOPMENT

The system of public community colleges is a critical educational asset to Missouri's efforts to provide appropriate and adequate training and education for Missouri's workforce. In Missouri, the community college districts cover urban, suburban and rural areas of the state. They differ from four-year institutions in three distinct ways: (1) a part of their revenues derive from local property taxes; (2) entrance to the colleges is open to all who can benefit from the opportunities provided; (3) while credit courses and programs provide access to traditional 13th and 14th years of education, community colleges are "community-based" and, therefore, intensely related to the upgrading and retraining needs of employees working in regional businesses and industries.

Governor Carnahan took office in January, 1993, with a goal of renewing Missouri's economy and putting Missouri on the right track for economic development. Six years later, Missouri is a state with an economy that is clearly moving forward, with the creation of more than 350,000 new jobs. The unemployment rate for November, 1998, was only 3.3%, significantly below the national rate of 4.1%.

Governor Mel Carnahan has made significant improvements in geographic and programmatic accessibility of secondary and postsecondary vocational and technical education. According to Governor Carnahan's Missouri—*Meeting the Challenges of a New Century*, The Missouri Budget, Fiscal Year 2000, an estimated 125,000 Missourians were assisted by the state's workforce development system in Fiscal Year 1998. The governor believes Missouri citizens must have skills and knowledge to be effective, innovative, and competitive now and in the years to come.

A high degree of diversity among the community colleges serves not only the local needs but also reduces unnecessary program duplication and fosters program diversity throughout the state. The Missouri General Assembly passed Senate Bill 101 (1995) which directed the Missouri Coordinating Board of Higher Education to develop, in cooperation with the Missouri Department of Elementary and Secondary Education (DESE), a *State Plan for Postsecondary Technical Education*. The Plan promotes workforce development and training in advanced postsecondary technical education certificate, associate, and bachelor degree programs. Further the *State Plan for Postsecondary Education* encourages partnerships and collaboration among area vocational technical schools, community colleges, Linn State Technical College (two-year state technical college also authorized in SB 101, 1995), private career schools (proprietary schools), labor union apprenticeship training schools, and seven four-year baccalaureate institutions that offer associate and bachelor technology degrees. Missouri's community colleges, the primary deliverers of postsecondary technical education, have created Regional Technical Education Councils (RTECs) that encourage regional input on training programs needed for the service regions.

The governor issued an executive order in 1995 calling for cohesive planning among state agencies making up the workforce development system. The Missouri Departments of Labor and Industrial Relations, Economic Development, Social Services, Higher Education, and Elementary and Secondary Education have formed partnerships to increase responsiveness to employees and employers. The following table (Table 2), entitled *"Workforce Preparation—$28.2 Million Increase,"* describes the governor's FY 2000 budget recommendation for workforce development.

Since its inception in 1996, *The State Plan for Postsecondary Technical Education* continues to strengthen the state's postsecondary technical education capacity through the work of the RTECs. These 12 councils, representing the 12 community college service regions, include more than 400 members representing local employers, education, and community leaders. The RTECs are actively involved in identifying the types and locations of advanced-skill, and high-wage technical education programs needed for labor market training and education, in specific geographic areas across Missouri. In FY 2000, Governor Carnahan recommended increases of:

- $5 million to continue implementation of the State Plan for Postsecondary Technical Education. Combined with funding approved in FY 1997, FY 1998, and FY 1999, the budget to expand geographic and programmatic access to postsecondary technical education will total $19.6 million. This investment enables the state's public two-year community colleges to expand and strengthen student access and to build program capacity in technical education within taxing districts and at out-of-taxing-district sites;

- Funding through the CBHE mission enhancement initiative for Southwest Missouri State University—West Plains, Southeast Missouri State University, Central Missouri State University, Missouri Western State College, and University of Missouri—Rolla to strengthen their baccalaureate and master's degree programs in technical fields;
- $3 million to continue workforce preparation projects begun in Fiscal Year 1999 at public community colleges. This combines with $18.4 million in core workforce preparation funding for$21.4 million. core funding includes $2 million to assist Missouri's unemployed and underemployed citizens through Welfare Reform (or Temporary Assistance to Needing Families utilization plans);
- Over three years, 52 of 57 area vocational technical schools will be involved in partnerships with the 12 community college districts, including articulated high school credit toward an associate of applied science degree and/or certificate at the respective community college;
- After three years, a total of nearly 60 Missouri communities will have local access to postsecondary technical education provided by the state's community colleges and other public and private two- and four-year colleges and universities. This translates into 82 percent of the state's total square miles being accessible to postsecondary technical education;
- By the end of five years, at least 100 new associate of applied science degrees and certificates will be offered, pending CBHE approval, at both the campuses of existing community colleges and at community outreach sites. Proposed programs include moldmaking technology, precision machine technology, graphic design/illustration technology, industrial engineering technology, industrial management, industrial maintenance, electrical distribution, integrated manufacturing technology, manufacturing engineering technology, and industrial electronics;

- At the end of two years the numbers of students enrolled in post-secondary technical education targeted programs approaches nearly 10,000 students, while the number of associate of applied science degree graduates is well over 1000 students;
- The earnings potential for graduates of targeted postsecondary technical programs is exciting. Nearly all associate-degree graduates from engineering technology, computer information systems, precision production trades, mechanic and repairer occupations, and advanced level health occupations, can look forward to earnings averaging $27,000; and
- With the use of technical education (RTEC) funds, DESE vocational equipment enhancement funds, and the state appropriations to MOREnet, the ability to send and receive courses via electronic two-way compressed video and the Internet has been greatly enhanced.

Through the cooperative efforts of the Missouri Division of Job Development and Training (JDT), the Missouri Department of Elementary and Secondary Education (DESE), the Missouri Coordinating Board for Higher Education, the community colleges and the area vocational technical schools have received more than $20 million in customized/contract training investments in each of the last three years. Nearly 400 companies in Missouri have access to a wide range of training services designed to meet their specific needs. By combining the sources of funding and technical education delivery infrastructure, the agencies are serving roughly 65,000 employees annually. The Missouri Job Development Fund and the Community College New Jobs programs assist new, expanding and existing businesses that are making capital investments in manufacturing.

ACCOUNTABILITY

The Missouri Coordinating Board for Higher Education has the statutory responsibility to review proposed programs that are either new or are significant adjustment to the current programs of community colleges. Although each community college has responsibility for academic program development, the implementation of new programs and program changes are reviewed to ensure that the program is cost effective, efficient, and provides a balanced system of higher education in the state of Missouri.

Since 1994, Missouri's community colleges have been participating in the coordinating board's Funding for Results (FFR) program. Funding For Results is a major strategic initiative of the coordinating board, as outlined in its *Blueprint for Missouri Higher Education*. In designing a results-oriented agenda that builds on previous planning priorities, the board uses FFR as a funding strategy to both promote and acknowledge results. This innovative strategy continues a commitment by the coordinating board to link a portion of state appropriations to the achievement of statewide priorities. Through FFR, quality is reinforced; assessment is promoted; accountability is emphasized; improvements in teaching/learning are rewarded; and change is encouraged.

Missouri's public two-year institutions began to receive FFR money in FY 1995. The increase in FFR dollars for public two-year institutions through FY 1999 totaled $7,174,671, representing 13.4% of new money. Public two-year institutions annually receive approximately $1.5 million dollars, dedicated to teaching/learning improvement projects.

The enactment of Senate Bill 340 in June, 1995, (Section 173.030, paragraphs (7) and (8), RSMo) directed the board to review every five years the mission of the state's public two- and four-year colleges and universities. Included in that legislation is a provision authorizing the board to recommend an additional investment to enhance an institution's mission based on a mission implementation plan approved by the coordinating board. In 1996 the state's public community colleges and Linn State Technical College a (two-year public college) were included in the first phase of mission review as part of the development of a five-year master plan for Linn State Technical College, as required by Senate Bill 101, and The State Plan for Postsecondary Technical Education. From May to December, 1999, the coordinating board will review the state's investment in the community college system and the progress made in achieving those mission accountability associated with the community colleges' role in implementing The State Plan for Postsecondary Technical Education.

REFERENCES

Aery, S. & McClain, C.J., Missouri, in Tollefson, T.A. & Fountain, B.E. (1992), *Forty-nine State systems, 1992 Edition*. Washington, DC: American Association of Community Colleges.

Missouri Coordinating Board for Higher Education (1995). *Blueprint for Missouri Higher Education*. Jefferson City, MO: Author

Missouri General Assembly (1998). *Senate Bill 553*. Jefferson City, MO: Author

Missouri General Assembly (1995). *Senate Bill 101*. Jefferson City, MO: Author

Missouri General Assembly (1995). *House Bill 101*. Jefferson City, MO: Author

Missouri Coordinating Board for Higher Education (1995). *State Plan for Postsecondary Technical Education*. Jefferson City, MO: Author

Carnahan, Governor Mel (1998). Missouri-meeting the *Challenges of a New Century*. Jefferson City, MO: Office of the Governor.

FOR ADDITIONAL INFORMATION, PLEASE CONTACT:
Kala Stroup
Commissioner of Higher Education
Missouri Coordinating Board for Higher Education
3515 Amazonas Drive
Jefferson City, Missouri 65109-5717
Telephone: (573) 751-2361
Fax: (573) 751-6635

MONTANA

Rick L. Garrett
Vice President of Instructional Services
Mayland Community College

OVERVIEW

The Montana Board of Regents of Higher Education is responsible for all public higher education in the state. There are three publicly supported community colleges (Garrett, 1999) and five colleges of technology that are part of the Montana University System (Tollefson & Patton, 1998). Actually, there are three types of 2-year institutions in Montana; five colleges of technology, each associated with one of the units of the Montana University System; three community colleges, each with a local board of trustees; and seven tribal colleges operated by the various Native American tribes in Montana. The colleges of technology were originally created through legislation in 1939 as vocational training centers under the authority of the Montana State Board of Education. In 1987 the Montana Legislature transferred control to the Montana Board of Regents and in 1994 the centers were renamed colleges of technology (Crofts, 1997).

Enabling legislation passed in the Montana Legislature in 1939 to create community college districts. One community college was established in 1939, one in 1940 and the third in 1967 (Crofts, 1997).

According to Crofts (1997), Montana has the largest number of tribal colleges of any state in the country. A tribal college exists on each of Montana's seven Native American reservations.

GOVERNANCE

The Montana State Board of Regents is responsible for all public higher education in Montana. The three public community colleges are governed primarily by locally elected boards of trustees (Garrett, 1999). Members of local boards are appointed by the governor for three-year terms and provide a consultative and advisory service to local presidents (www.montana.edu).

Local presidents are appointed by the board of regents upon the recommendation of the commissioner of higher education. Local presidents are supervised by and responsible to the commissioner of higher education (Montana State Board of Regents, 1999)

FUNDING

Montana's public community colleges are funded as follows: state funds, (31%); local funds. (9%); federal funds, (33%); tuition, (16%); and other (11%). Also reported was that the expenditure per FTE was $8,449 in 1995-96, while the average tuition and fees paid per student in that year was $1,382. Annual budgets are presented to and reviewed by the Montana Board of Regents of Higher Education (Montana State Board of Regents, 1999). Student fees are approved by the commissioner of higher education (Montana State Board of Regents, 1999).

According to Crofts (1997, p. 225), "Montana's institutions of higher education have suffered financially in recent years because of economic downturn, budget shortfalls, and falling confidence in educational institutions. Many studies have suggested that Montana provides the lowest amount of state support for higher education students in the country." Rising tuition rates among the public community colleges are believed to be responsible for some students attending colleges in neighboring Wyoming and the Dakotas. Declining enrollments may result in the college's losing significant state financial support (Tollefson & Patton, 1998).

PROGRAMS AND ENROLLMENTS

Full-time enrollment in the eight public two-year institutions (three community colleges and five colleges of technology) during 1995 was 6,943; 4,280 full-time (62%) and 2,663 part-time (38%). Males accounted for 37% of the total student body (2,566), while females represented 63% of the total number of students (AACC Tollefson & Patton, 1998). There were 1,329 associate degrees awarded during 1997-98 (Chronicle of Higher Education Almanac, 1997-98). The Montana Board of Regents has the responsibility for establishing minimum entrance requirements and approving curricular offerings at all community colleges (Internet: www.montana.edu). Crofts (1997), reported that Montana students attend baccalaureate institutions in disproportionate numbers as there are not sufficient opportunities to attend two-year postsecondary institutions. Only one out of five students is enrolled at a two-year college.

ECONOMIC DEVELOPMENT

In order to address the need for greater emphasis on economic development, higher education in Montana took a more sophisticated approach to developing the state's workforce. Crofts (1997, p. 219) reported that "The Montana Department of Labor estimated that 80% of the jobs that will be created in the next decade will require more than a high school education, but less than a 4-year degree." The students should be prepared for the jobs in an anticipated information and knowledge-based economy. In January of 1995, the position of director of workforce development was created to coordinate "...the implementation of a wide variety of workforce preparation activities" (Crofts, 1997, p. 219).

ACCOUNTABILITY

Because sufficient opportunities were not provided for students to attend two-year postsecondary institutions, the board of regents of the Montana University System restructured the system during 1993/1994 in a effort to place greater emphasis on two-year programs and less on baccalaureate programs. Over a six-year period, the university system was allowed to grow 14.4%, while the colleges of technology were expected to grow 48.2%. Universities that exceeded enrollment projections would not be able to keep the state funds or tuition dollars paid by the additional students. The expected result was that colleges of technology enrollments would expand as universities were mandated a disincentive to recruit and enroll additional students (Crofts, 1997).

REFERENCES

Chronicle of Higher Education 1998-99 Almanac Issue (1998, August 28, 45(1)

Crofts, R.A. (1997, March). History of 2-Year Postsecondary Education in Montana, *Community College Journal of Research and Practice*.

Garrett, R. L. (1999). Degrees of centralization of governance structures in state community college systems. In Tollefson, T. A.; Garrett, R. L.; Ingram, W. G. and Associates, *Fifty State Systems of Community Colleges: Mission*, Governance, Funding, and Accountability: Johnson City, TN: Overmountain Press.

Montana Board of Regents (1999, April 15). Http://www.montana.edu/wochelp/borpol/

Tollefson, T.A. & Patton, M. (1998). Montana, in AACC *Annual 1997-98*:

Washington, DC, American Association of Community Colleges.

FOR ADDITIONAL INFORMATION, PLEASE CONTACT:
Office of the Commissioner
University of Montana System
2500 Broadway
Helena, MT 68509-5005
Telephone: (402) 471-2847

NEBRASKA

Sharon A. Howell, Assistant Director
Nebraska Community College Association

OVERVIEW

<u>Enabling Legislation</u>: The Nebraska community college system evolved from at least three separate sources: 1) local junior colleges, offering predominately academic transfer programs; 2) state vocational/technical colleges, awarding vocational/technical degrees; and 3) area vocational/technical schools. The latter two offered programs designed specifically for occupational job entry. In 1971, the Nebraska Legislature created one system of two-year institutions, and in 1975, established the six community college areas. Currently, the six areas are independent political subdivisions supported by a combination of revenues, including property taxes, state aid, tuition, and other miscellaneous funds. The six areas are Central with campuses at Columbus, Grand Island, and Hastings; Metropolitan with campuses at Elkhorn Valley, Fort Omaha, and South Omaha; Mid-Plains with campuses at McCook and North Platte; Northeast with a campus at Norfolk; Southeast with campuses at Beatrice, Lincoln, and Milford; and Western with a campus at Scottsbluff.

The community college areas were organized by the Legislature to continue the tradition of providing educational and public services adapted to local and regional community needs. The enabling legislation creating the areas stated:

> *The Legislature hereby declares that for a technical community college to be truly responsible to the people it serves, primary control of such colleges must be placed in the citizens within the local areas so served. It is the intent and purpose of sections 79-2636 to 79-2662 to create locally governed and locally supported technical community college areas with the major educational emphasis on occupational education. Each technical community college area is intended to be an independent, local, unique, and vital segment of higher education separate from both the established elementary and secondary school system and from other institutions of higher education, and not to be converted into four-year baccalaureate degree-*

granting institutions.

Current Role and Mission Statutes: In 1993, the legislature revised and expanded the original role and mission statutes for the community colleges. "It is the intent of the Legislature that the community colleges shall be student-centered, open-access institutions primarily devoted to quality instruction and public service, providing counseling and other student services intended to promote the success of a diverse student population, particularly those who have been traditionally underserved in other educational settings." The community colleges' role and mission priorities are: 1) applied technology and occupational education and, when necessary, foundations education; 2) transfer education, including general academic transfer programs, or applied technology and occupational programs which may be applicable to the first two years of a bachelor's degree program and, when necessary, foundations education; 3) public service, particularly adult continuing education for occupations and professions, economic and community development focused on customized occupational assessment and job training programs for business and communities, and avocational and personal development courses; and 4) applied research.

GOVERNANCE

Area Structure and Governance: As established by the Legislature, the fundamental organizing principle of the Nebraska community college system is local control. The elected, eleven-member area boards of governors have the ability to respond quickly and independently to the needs of their communities, citizens, businesses, and industries. Flexible response to local demands, promoted by local governance, is viewed by the areas as essential to meeting their educational and public service roles.

As independent political subdivisions, the six community college areas are responsible directly to their local constituents and indirectly to the Coordinating Commission and the state Legislature. Each area is divided into five electoral districts. Two individuals elected from each district and one person elected from the area at-large comprise the eleven-member board of governors for each area. Board members serve four-year terms, staggered so that the voters of each district elect one member every two years. State statutes grant a wide range of powers and duties to these governing boards, including: prescribing courses of study; employing an executive officer and staff; constructing and maintaining facilities; establishing fees and charges; granting diplomas, degrees, and certificates; entering into agreements for services, facilities, or equipment for the presentation of courses to students; and setting property tax levies necessary to carry out provisions of state law. The area president is the executive officer of the area and reports directly to the area board of governors. This individual is charged with implementing board policies and administering the college area.

State Coordination: Legislation passed in 1991, LB 663, gave strong coordinating powers to an agency placed in the Nebraska Constitution by voters in the November 1990 election. The Coordinating Commission for Postsecondary Education replaced a coordinating agency with a similar name, the Nebraska Coordinating Commission for Postsecondary Education, but, unlike its predecessor, this new commission has the authority to obtain compliance by public institutions of higher education. Legislation, based on the report of a study of higher education in the state, "Challenges and Opportunities for Nebraska Higher Education ... A Call to Action," November 1990, gave responsibility to the commission for program, budget, and facility review, and charged the agency with the task of developing a state plan for higher education.

The report revealed that the challenges to higher education in the state *"are of such magnitude that Nebraska's institutions will have to pull together in a coordinated statewide manner."* The report drew a clear distinction between governance, setting policy dealing with the day-to-day operational decisions of institutions of higher education, and coordination, setting policy to guide the overall shape of higher education in the state in accord with the commission's comprehensive statewide plan. Major concerns of the study report and the new commission are institutional efficiency and effectiveness regarding a reduction of overlapping and redundant services, and greater student access to higher education, through an increase in services to under-served populations. The duties and authorities outlined for the new commission in the report were embodied in the subsequent legislation:

> . . . *the commission shall establish an ongoing process to review, monitor, and approve or disapprove the new and existing programs of public institutions and proposed capital construction projects which use tax funds designated by the Legislature in order to provide compliance and consistency with the comprehensive statewide plan and to prevent unnec-*

essary duplication. . . . the commission shall review and modify,
if needed, to promote compliance and consistency with the com-
prehensive statewide plan and prevent unnecessary duplication,
the budget requests of the governing boards.

Additionally, the commission is charged with setting policy in a number of areas and to incorporate those in the statewide plan, including: credit transfer, admission standards, enrollment, tuition and fees, remediation, geographic and programmatic service areas, institutional peer groups, telecommunications, economic development activities, public service activities, and financial aid strategies.

Dr. David Powers is the executive director of the commission and can be reached at the Coordinating Commission for Postsecondary Education, P.O. Box 95005, Lincoln, NE 68509, (402) 471-2847.

System Coordination: For the first two years of the areas' independent operation after the state board for community colleges was abolished in 1975, the Nebraska Coordinating Commission for Technical Community Colleges existed as an advisory body to provide recommendations on area operations and policy. This commission was eliminated in 1977. Subsequently, the areas operated as six autonomous political subdivisions. However, the local governing boards recognized the desirability of voluntary coordination among the six community college areas and created the Nebraska Association of Community College Trustees (NACCT), a statewide organization for board members. This organization was superseded by the Nebraska Technical Community College Association (NTCCA) in 1980 and the Nebraska Community College Association in 1991, which functions, as did its predecessors, as a coordinating body for area governing boards. A change came in 1991 with the passage of LB 625, which established in statute "an association of community colleges" to act as a liaison with the new Coordinating Commission and with responsibility for coordination of the community college system in strategic planning, program needs assessment and articulation, and biennium budget requests. As a consequence of this legislation, the voluntary nature of association was abolished and membership in an association became mandatory.

As it now stands, the Nebraska Community College Association is a statutory, nonprofit corporation whose members are the six community college areas. The NCCA is governed by a 12-member board of directors composed of two representatives from each area board of governors. The goals of the organization, as set forth in its bylaws, are "to promote the welfare and common good of Nebraska's community college areas and to advance the concepts of technical community college education." Included in this broad scope are several specific responsibilities. The association has three primary functions: 1) to represent the six areas at the state level with agencies, the governor's office, the Legislature, and various ad hoc committees and commissions constituted from time to time by the state; 2) to promote coordination and cooperation among the areas and between the areas and other secondary and postsecondary education institutions, government agencies, and business and industry; and 3) to help provide the widest possible access to community college programs by assisting the areas in informing communities, businesses, and policy makers of the programs and activities available through the areas. Additional NCCA activities include collecting and analyzing data and statewide public relations activities. Bylaw changes in 1991 added the responsibilities of preparing and updating a statewide community college system strategic plan and conflict resolution between and among the six areas. The NCCA sanctions a Council of Chief Executive Officers, a Council of Business Officers, a Council of Instructional Officers, a Public Relations Council, and other inter-area coordinating bodies to facilitate statewide administration, policy development, and implementation.

Association Office: The association employs three full-time employees, an executive director, assistant director, and an administrative assistant. The association also contracts for lobbying services. The association produces periodic legislative newsletters, brochures, a membership directory, a policy manual, a board member handbook, an Educational Opportunities Guide (summary of courses of study offered at each area), and other publications. The office is located in Lincoln, two blocks west of the State Capitol. (See the end of this chapter for contact information.)

Potential Governance Changes: Ever since the mid 1980s, at least one senator was interested in removing the property tax levying authority from the community colleges and replacing those revenues with total state funding. Until the 1997 session, this "takeover" legislation had very little support. However, in light of Nebraska's property tax payer concerns, legislation introduced that year gained much more support, although it failed to come out of committee. In January, 1999, several bills and constitutional amendments dealing with the reorganization of higher education were introduced. Although none of the proposals specifically address the governance structure of the community colleges, one proposal calls for the creation of a "super board" that would replace the current Nebraska Coordinating Commission for Postsecondary Education. As drafted, one bill would give the super board governance and funding authority over a combined university and state college system. This super board would also have authority to review community college budgets, programs, and capital construction projects, and make recommendations to the Legislature. Several other bills and two constitutional amendment resolutions are variations on the same theme. It is anticipated that the outcome of this legislative session will produce an interim study on the overall governance structure of Nebraska's higher education system.

FUNDING

Nebraska's community colleges receive primary funding from three major sources: property taxes, levied by each area for operations and capital (including revenue bonds); state aid (for operations only), provided through three separate programs: 1) funds are distributed through an enrollment-driven formula in Program 51; 2) funds are distributed through an equalization formula in Program 152; and 3) funds are distributed through ag rant process in Program 99; and tuition established by each area board. Other sources of funds include monies from grants, foundations, and miscellaneous sources. In FY 97-98, property tax revenues represented 45.15%, state aid represented 31.97%, tuition and fees represent 22.50%, and other revenue represented 0.39 percent.

Property Tax

Fiscal Year	Property Tax Revenues
FY 1997-98 – Actual*	$55,049,839
FY 1998-99 – Projected**	$46,782,103
FY 1999-2000 – Projected***	$40,220,817

*FY 97-98 includes motor vehicle fee revenues
**FY 98-99 includes one-half year of motor vehicle fee revenues
***FY 99-00 does not include motor vehicle fee revenues

Prior to FY 98-99, the property tax levy limit for community colleges was 9 cents per$100 of property valuation (may exceed 9 cent limit up to 11.5 cents with 75% vote of board) for operations and 1.8 cents per $100 of property valuation for capital projects and revenue bonds. The college boards could also set a levy specifically for projects relating to the Americans With Disabilities Act and hazardous waste removal. In 1997, the legislature changed the levy limits for the community colleges by decreasing the operations levy to 7 cents per $100 and 1.0 cent for capital projects for fiscal years 1998-1999 and 1999-2000. In FY 2000-2001, the operations levy is projected to drop to 6 cents per $100. The capital levy will remain at 1 cent per $100. The boards retain the ability to levy a tax for ADA and hazardous waste removal projects.

In this legislation, LB 269, legislative intent language reaffirmed the original partnership among the state, local communities, and college constituents that was established when the system was created in the 1970s to provide high-quality, affordable two-year education. The intent language further states that this educational partnership would be reinforced through a funding partnership of 40% from the state, 40% from local property taxes; and the remaining 20% from tuition and other sources of revenue. In order for the state to contribute at least 40% of college revenues, a new funding program, the Community College Property Tax Equalization Program, was created. This new formula considers several factors including an area's ability to generate 40% of its revenue from local tax dollars. There is a dollar-for-dollar trade-off built into the formula.

Also in 1997, the legislature passed legislation limiting all budgets to a maximum 2% increase, plus an increase for growth in population (full-time enrollment for community colleges). The Legislature also adopted a bill that changed the motor vehicle tax collected by each county to a motor vehicle fee, which resulted in a small loss in revenue to the colleges. However, in November, 1998, the voters passed a constitutional amendment that changed the number of recipients of the motor vehicle fee. As of January, 1999, the community colleges and several other political subdivisions would no longer receive their proportional share of the motor vehicle fee receipts. This change, when implemented by state statute, effective July 1, 1999, will result in a loss of over $4 million per year for the colleges. Currently, the Nebraska Community College Association is working with the Revenue and Appropriations Committees of the legislature to replace this loss in revenue for the colleges. One scenario would be to replace the $4 million loss with additional state aid distributed through one of the formula programs. However, this infusion of state aid would shift the funding balance away from the 40/40/20 ration. Another scenario the system is investigating would be to leave the college property tax levy at

7 cents per $100 at least for the biennium. Given the current anti-property tax climate in the state, this option doesn't have much support. A third scenario would be for the colleges to absorb the loss. This option would be devastating to the system, forcing massive cutbacks in several of the smaller, more rural college areas. At this point, it appears that the Legislature will replace the lost revenue with an almost equal amount of state aid.

State Aid

Fiscal Year	Program 51	Program 152	Program 99*	Total State Aid
FY 97-98 Actual	$38,525,148	$0	$461,974	$38,987,122
FY 98-99 Projected	$39,403,744	$8,208,078	$547,498	$48,159,320
FY99-00 Projected	$40,790,756	$8,642,462	$1,288,591	$50,721,809

*In FY 97-98, Program 99 includes $450,000 for specific projects and Tech-Prep activities with the remainder for distance learning classrooms. In FY 98-99, Program 99 includes $450,000 for specific projects with the remainder for distance learning classrooms. In FY 99-00, Program 99 includes $650,000 for specific projects with the remainder for information technology projects.

State aid to the community colleges is appropriated by the Legislature through three program funds. Program 51 appropriations are allocated in a single amount for the system and are distributed according to the enrollment-based formula described below. Program 152 appropriations are allocated in a single amount for the system and are distributed according to an equalization formula described below. Program 99 appropriations are categorical funds appropriated to a grant program to be used primarily for faculty and staff training and development, equipment upgrading, and customized training for business and industry. Program 99 is also used as a mechanism to fund pilot programs and information technology projects.

Program 51 Allocation Formula:

1) 52% is allocated as follows:
    (a) In the same proportion as the first 1,775 audited reimbursable educational units or portion thereof of the three-year average for each community college area, calculated by taking the average of the audited reimbursable educational units for the three most recently completed fiscal years, is to the first 1,775 audited reimbursable educational units or portion thereof the

— 266 —

three-year average of all community college areas combined for such fiscal year;
2) 38% is distributed as follows:
   (a) In the same proportion as the three-year average of all audited reimbursable educational units in excess of 1,975 for each community college area, calculated by taking the average of the audited reimbursable educational units for the three most recently completed fiscal years, is to the audited reimbursable educational units in excess of 1,975 for all community college areas, calculated by taking such average, combined for such fiscal year; and
3) The balance of such funds for each fiscal year shall be distributed to the community college areas in inverse proportion to the amount of the three-year average valuation for taxable property in the community college area, calculated by taking the average of each community college area's three most recently completed fiscal years of county-certified property valuation, divided by the three-year average number of reported aid equivalent students in the community college area, calculated by taking the average of each community college area's three most recently completed fiscal years of reported aid equivalent students.

Program 152 Allocation Formula:
1) The Community College Property Tax Relief and Equalization Program is created. The legislature recognizes the need for a state and local partnership for the funding of community colleges. The legislature also understands that some community college areas have a better ability than other areas to raise revenue through property taxes because of larger and growing valuation bases.
2) It is the intent of the legislature to appropriate funds beginning with fiscal year 1998-99 to provide property tax relief to those areas that (a) have levied the maximum allowable property tax levy and cannot generate 40% of their operating revenue or (b) do not receive 40% of their operating revenue from state aid and levy the maximum allowable property tax levy or the greater of a minimum levy of six and three-tenths cents per one hundred dollars of valuation for fiscal year 1998-99 and fiscal year 1999-00 and five and three-tenths cents per $100 of valuation for fiscal year 1998-99 and fiscal year 1999-00 and five and three-tenths cents per $100 of

valuation for fiscal year 2000-01 and all subsequent fiscal years or a levy that raises 40% of its operating revenue.

3) Each eligible community college area which qualifies pursuant to subdivision (2)(a) of this section shall receive funds equal to the difference between the property tax revenue raised and 40% of its operating revenue. Each eligible community college area which qualifies pursuant to subdivision (2)(b) of this section shall receive funds equal to the difference between state aid pursuant to subdivisions (1)(a) and (b) of section 85-1536 and 40% of its operating revenue, and any community college area which raises in excess of 40% of its operating revenue from property tax shall have such excess serve as an offset to payments received from this program. Any community college area which qualifies under both subdivisions (2)(a) and (b) of this section shall receive funds as calculated for both subdivisions. The base year for calculating 40% of operating revenue shall be fiscal year 1997-98, with future adjustments reflecting increases equal to two percent plus the percentage increase, if any, in full-time-equivalent students eligible for state aid from the second year to the first year preceding the year for which the aid is being determined.....If the legislature fails to appropriate adequate funds for the program, the funds appropriated shall be apportioned on a pro rata basis to the areas that qualify.

Tuition and Other Revenue Sources

Tuition and fee rates are set annually by each of the six college areas, ranging from $39.50 to $41.25 for tuition per credit hour and "4.50 to $5.00 per credit hour for fees. Other revenue sources include federal and other restricted revenues. The greatest fear is that significantly raising tuition and fees will price many needy students out of a much needed educational advantage, thereby reducing access to a great number of individuals.

Tuition and fee revenues for FY 97-98 show a significant increase due to the changes in property tax levy limits discussed above, as area boards are forced to place more of the financial cost of higher education onto the students.

Fiscal Year	Tuition & Fees	Other Revenue
FY 97-98 Actual	$27,492,141	$2,568,891
FY 98-99 Projected	$27,612,180	$2,895,504
FY 99-00 Projected	$29,481,561	$2,902,868

PROGRAMS AND ENROLLMENTS

Unlike community colleges in other states, the Nebraska community college system was created primarily to prepare individuals for careers in vocational/technical (now applied technology) careers. Originally, only one campus per college area, generally the former junior college, was permitted to offer academic transfer courses. It wasn't until 1993 that academic transfer options were expanded to almost all other campuses. However, the system is committed to maintaining the high proportion of applied technology offerings as Nebraska moves into the next century, a time of increased expectations of a highly trained and skilled workforce.

FISCAL YEAR	ACADEMIC TRANSFER	APPLIED TECHNOLOGY FTE (Audited)	TOTAL REIMBURS- FTE (Audited) FTE (Audited)	HEAD- COUNT ABLE (Unaudited)
FY 97-98	3,116.89	19,133.91	22,250.80	137,314.00
% of Total	14.01%	85.99%	100.00%	

Nebraska's community colleges offer a wide range of programs in the following fields: agriculture occupations, auto and diesel occupations, business and office occupations, communication technology, construction occupations, electronic/electrical occupations, health occupations, manufacturing fabrications occupations, service occupations, and transportation occupations. Students may earn the following: A.A., A.S., A.A.S., A.S.N., A.D.N., diplomas or certificates. The colleges are also the primary providers of foundations education (ABE, GED, ESL, remedial/developmental, etc.). The colleges are also actively involved in economic development activities as the providers of almost all the customized job training and retraining for local business and industry.

The colleges tailor their offerings, filling critical needs within their areas. Several programs are only offered at one campus in the state, drawing students from across the state. Many programs are offered jointly by two or more areas and are delivered through an extensive telecommunications network located on almost all community college campuses. In addition to the 13 campus locations, the colleges offer courses at over 260 off-campus sites, representing 49% of all communities around the state. The outreach of Nebraska's community college system serves as a lifeline to rural America, offering affordable, high quality, and accessible educational opportunities.

Nebraska's community colleges have demonstrated a willingness and ability to adapt rapidly to changing needs and circumstances. Despite projections that enrollment would decline along with the drop in the 18-year-old population, Nebraska's community college full-time equivalent credit enrollment grew over 46.5% between 1981 and 1998, while headcount enrollment grew almost 136%. Much of the enrollment growth has resulted from programs that attracted older, part-time students, many single head-of-households who work full-time. The community college system expects continued growth based on this trend as well as increased demands for occupational assessment, job training and upgrading by business and industry in the state. According to A Factual Look at Higher Education in Nebraska, published by the Nebraska Coordinating Commission for Postsecondary Education in August 1997, using IPEDS (Integrated Postsecondary Education Data System) information, Nebraska's community college enrollment in the fall of 1996 was comprised of 56.04% female and 43.96% male students, of which 11.96 percent were from a minority race/ethnic group, the highest percentage of all Nebraska public and private postsecondary education institutions.

Also in the fall of 1997, the Commission reported the following statistics regarding age of students:

INSTITUTION	24 & YOUNGER	25-29 YEARS	30 & OLDER	TOTAL
Community Colleges	48.1%	12.1%	39.7%	100.00%
Independent Colleges & Universities	66.0%	12.3%	21.7%	100.00%
State Colleges	70.3%	8.1%	21.6%	100.00%
University of Nebraska	65.2%	15.9%	18.8%	100.00%

Clearly, the community colleges are serving the greatest number of students over the age of 30, yet have a substantial number of the traditional age college student, illustrating that community colleges efficiently reach a broad spectrum of Nebraska's population.

A report of community college enrollments would not be complete without information regarding the placement of students following completion of their course of study. In FY 97-98, the community colleges placed 98.27% of completers, 91.39% in Nebraska with 74.68% of those placements within the community college area, and 8.61% placed out-of-state. It is evident that Nebraska's community colleges do not contribute to the well-known brain-drain, but rather, offer Nebraska business and industry a well-trained, local workforce.

ECONOMIC DEVELOPMENT

Because of their strategic location throughout the state, Nebraska's community colleges are uniquely qualified to respond quickly to area needs, especially in service to business and industry, either by designing custom training programs or adapting course work to provide training, retraining, and skills upgrading for employees in businesses and industries of all sizes. The availability of these services has a significant impact on the state's economic development efforts. In 1997-98, the community colleges trained more than 27,000 workers in over 848 businesses, industries, and agencies. The demand is growing. Yet, over the years, funding has failed to keep pace with the demand.

In FY 1989-90, the Legislature created a separate fund, the Nebraska Community College Aid Cash Fund (Program 99), using revenues generated from interest from an unemployment security fund. Program 99 was designed for applied technology and occupational faculty training, instructional equipment upgrades, employee assessment, pre employment training, employment training, and dislocated worker programs. Funds ranging from $300,000 to $600,000 per year were distributed through a grant process. In FY 1994, funds in the unemployment security fund were depleted. Recognizing the importance of the service provided by these funds, the Legislature appropriated funds from the State General Fund into Program 99, although funding reached an all-time low of $175,000 in FY 96-97. However, in 1997, this categorical funding was increased from $175,000 to $450,000 per year for the upcoming biennium, to be specifically targeted toward business and industry assistance and Tech-Prep projects. In recognition of the partnership among the colleges, the state, and business and industry, the grant program now includes a minimum match of $40,000 from business and industry.

Nebraska's community colleges have been key players in the state's economic development activities. They have been instrumental in bringing several businesses and industries to the state which declared that the proximity and availability of services provided by the colleges were key elements of their decision to locate in Nebraska. Clearly, Nebraska's community colleges' ability to respond quickly and efficiently to local needs, the ability to provide state-of-the-art training and retraining, and the ability to provide lifelong services to the citizens of the state, has positioned Nebraska as an exemplary model for other states for the future.

FOR ADDITIONAL INFORMATION, PLEASE CONTACT:
Nebraska Community College Association
601 South 12th Street, Suite 200
Lincoln, NE 68508
Telephone: (402) 471-4685
Fax: (402) 471-4726
Dennis G. Baack, Executive Director
dbaack@ncca.state.ne.us
Sharon A. Howell, Assistant Director

NEVADA

Anthony D. Calabro
Assistant Vice Chancellor of Academic Affairs
University and Community College System of Nevada

OVERVIEW

The first community college in Nevada was established as a local college in Elko in 1967. In 1969, by action of the state legislature, Elko College became Northern Nevada Community College under the governance of the University of Nevada Board of Regents. The Board of Regents would oversee the administration and development of the universities, the community colleges, and the Desert Research Institute. These institutions now comprise the University and Community College System of Nevada. The addition of Western Nevada Community College in Reno and Carson City led to the establishment of a Community College Division. The Board of Regents adopted a *State Plan for Community Colleges*. The Plan defined a five-point mission: Occupational Education, University Transfer, Developmental Education, Community Services, Guidance Counseling.

Since the System was established in 1971, organization and planned development have responded to increased enrollment. In 1980, the Reno campus of Western Nevada Community College became Truckee Meadows Community College. The three other community colleges provide services through campuses and rural centers throughout their respective service areas.

Western Nevada Community College has a satellite campus in Fallon, Nevada, in addition to centers in seven other rural counties.

Northern Nevada Community College in Elko is now named Great Basin College. This name more adequately reflects the college service area of over 40,000 square miles. Great Basin College has instructional centers in rural communities such as Ely and Winnemucca.

The Community College of Southern Nevada has expanded to three campuses withadditional centers located throughout the Las Vegas area and southern Nevada.

Truckee Meadows Community College has established additional facilities by renovating a shopping mall in south Reno. In addition, the college offers instruction and services in public schools and other facilities throughout the college's Reno/Sparks service area. The College has expanded its service area to include the north shore of Lake Tahoe.

The community college mission has been revised to included economic development. The current mission is stated as follows:

> The mission of Nevada's community colleges, as institutions of the University and Community College System of Nevada, is to provide superior, student-centered educational opportunities for the citizens of the state within the designated service area of each college. The community colleges subscribe to an open-door policy, admitting high school graduates as well as others who have personal developmental needs and who can profit from this educational experience. The specific programs offered by each of the community colleges are responses to the identified needs of the state and, in particular, the communities to be served. The community college mission encompasses a belief that education and training are the chief means of developing human capital for investment in the economic health of the state of Nevada.

Each of the educational programs and support services provided through the community colleges is equally important. The colleges provide:

University Transfer Programs

> The colleges provide a broad range of courses to fulfill the requirements of an associate degree and the first two years of a baccalaureate degree aimed at preparing students for transfer to a four-year college or university.

Applied Science and Technology Programs

> The colleges provide programs necessary for the development of technical and occupational skills needed for immediate and meaningful employment. Individual courses for maintenance of a job's state-of-the-art skills, semester or one-year certificate programs, as well as two-year associate degrees are available.

Business and Industry Partnering Programs

> The colleges provide the planning and implementation of programs to be in partnership with the state's economic development effort. Customized training is tailored to meet a given business or industry need and offered at the work site, institute or college site, or any other appropriate location. This program is aimed at maintaining a competitive

work force within the state of Nevada.

Developmental Education Programs

The colleges provide, with individualized attention and special support programs, developmental education. The program is designed to develop and upgrade skills necessary to successfully compete in college courses. Students are provided an opportunity to acquire, improve and apply basic reading, writing, computational and language skills.

Community Service Programs

The colleges provide, through lectures, forums, concerts, plays, exhibits and short-term academic and practical instruction, a lifelong learning process and focus for each community's cultural, intellectual and recreational enrichment. The continuing education opportunity provides the state's citizens the ability to develop and experience a variety of lifetime skills and interests.

Student Support Service Programs

The colleges provide a variety of personal support services to students and to assist them in becoming more aware of their potential and in planning and achieving their educational goals. Students are provided counseling, academic advisement, placement testing, career planning, job placement, and financial assistance.

The University and Community College System of Nevada is committed to the support of the diverse and changing communities of the state. The community colleges provide an open academic environment where students of all ages and backgrounds can discover their potential and achieve their life goals. (UCCSN Planning Report, 1995-1999).

GOVERNANCE

The exclusive control and administration of the University and Community College System of Nevada (UCCSN) is vested by the Nevada Constitution of the State in an elected board of regents. The composition of the Board and terms of its members are prescribed by law. The members are elected for six-year terms, with each member representing an apportioned district within the state. Based upon results of the 1990 Census, the reapportionment resulted in increasing the board from nine to eleven members. The board officers consist of chairman, vice chairman and committee chairs. Meetings are held on a regular basis throughout the year approximately every six weeks, with special meetings scheduled when needed.

The board appoints the presidents and the chancellor of the system.

Each college has an advisory board whose members are recommended to the board of regents for approval. The advisory broads meet regularly with each college president to provide guidance regarding the unique needs of each college service area.

The board cooperates with any and all agencies of the state in the interest of serving the people and ensuring the maximum utilization of the state's resources. Joint meeting are held periodically with the state board of education which is responsible for K-12 education, and cooperative efforts are frequently undertaken.

FUNDING

The state legislature meets on a biennial basis: the fiscal year used by the system is July 1 through June 30. Systemwide, approximately 79% of funds are allocated through state appropriation. Nineteen percent is provided through registration fees, non-resident tuition and miscellaneous student fees. The remaining 2% is from miscellaneous sources. Standard student fees are $39.50 per credit, or an average of $1,185 per year for full-time enrollment, at each community college.

A funding formula is built upon two major components. The instructional area is based upon the number of full-time-equivalent students (FTE) enrolled or projected to be enrolled. A student/faculty ratio determines the number of full-time faculty authorized. The second area includes a support services formula which includes academic and institutional support, student services, and plant operation and maintenance.

Colleges make enrollment projections that serve as a basis for requesting state funds in the biennial budget request. State funding is based on student/faculty ratios and funding formulas. These ratios attempt to address the size of the institutions, and the population served:

	1995-97
Regular Ratio	23:1
Voc Tech Ratio	18:1
Rural Ratio	12:1
Nursing Ratio	7.5:1
Developmental Ratio	18:1
Classified Support Ratio	5:1

When a total number of faculty positions is determined by the ratios, 60% of the positions are funded according to an average full-time faculty salary. Forty percent are funded as part-time positions. These positions are funded at a reduced level that is less than half of the average amount for full-time positions.

This is in contrast to the universities that receive an average full-time salary for all faculty positions.

For example, if the student/faculty ratios generate 100 faculty positions for a community college, 60 positions may be funded at an average salary of $42,000. Forty positions would be funded at perhaps $20,000 per position. The expectation is to have 60 full-time faculty members, and to hire part-time instructors from the $800,000 pool generated by the part-time allocation.

Student services allocations are based on formulas that combine headcount and FTE students.

Community Colleges' operating budgets are funded from the following sources:

1998-99	Amount	Percent
State Appropriation	75,934,589	78.7%
Tuition and Fees	18,839,829	19.5%
Other Sources	1,712,535	1.8%
	96,486,953	100%

Nevada community colleges do not have a local funding source. Higher education competes for funding from the state general fund with K-12 education, prisons, and other state agencies. No state revenue sources are earmarked for higher education.

Each community college develops a two-year Academic Master Plan. The plans are revised in a cycle to coincide with the Biennial Budget Request that is submitted to the legislature. The Academic Master Plan includes accountability measures as well as planned program development. The plans are coordinated with the budgeting process.

PROGRAMS AND ENROLLMENT

Approximately 84% of Nevada community college students are part-time students. In addition to degree and certificate programs, many students are enrolled in one or two courses that meet their current educational goals.

The community colleges offer the following degrees and certificates:
        Associate of Arts Degree (A.A.)
        Associate of Applied Science Degree (A.A.S.)
        Associate of Business Degree (A.B.)

Associate of Science Degree (A.S.)
Associate of General Studies Degree
Certificate of Achievement
Certificate of Completion

Enrollment: (These categories are used in FTE (15 credits=1 FTE) computing allocation of funds)

Regular Programs	11,665
Vocational/Technical	4,285
Developmental	1,035
* Rural Programs	1,393
Dental Hygiene	84
Dental Assisting	23
Radiological Technician	15
Nursing	358
TOTAL	18,858

* Courses offered in designated rural areas are funded at a 12-to-1 student-faculty ratio.

The colleges have expanded course and program offerings throughout their respective service areas. This effect is enhanced through a variety of partnerships with public and private entities.

The colleges have articulation agreements with local school districts. These agreements allow students to demonstrate competencies while in high school that will apply to college course credits. High schools may also award high school credit. At the Community College of Southern Nevada and at the Truckee Meadows Community College, high school programs now are housed on the college campus.

Great Basin College has recently received approval by the board of regents to offer a limited number of baccalaureate programs. This is in response to meeting a need for four-year programs in the widely scattered small communities in Northeastern Nevada. Great Basin College serves an area of approximately 40,000 square miles.

In contrast, the Community College of Southern Nevada is faced with utilizing innovative partnerships, technology, and a variety of community resources in order to respond to the needs of the Las Vegas Area. Las Vegas is one of the fastest growing communities in the nation.

Truckee Meadows Community College has just dedicated a technical institute locate din Reno's industrial area. This campus will specialize in offering industrial programs that are focused on the needs of local economic diversification. Western Nevada Community College has also responded to the needs of industry through a variety of partnerships with the growing manufacturing base in the college's service area. This has resulted in additional facilities and equipment for WNCC.

All four community colleges have extensive contract education programs with local industry. Truckee Meadows Community College has an Institute for Business and Industry. The Center for Excellence at Western Nevada Community College provides contract education in Total Quality Management to private industry and public agencies. Great Basin College serves the extensive mining industry in northeastern Nevada. Through a partnership with the University of Nevada, Reno, the colleges participate in the Manufacturing Assistance Program (MAP). This program provides technical assistance and training to manufacturers. The program has now been expanded to include the construction and mining industries. The Community College of Southern Nevada customizes programs to directly support the incredible growth of the gaming and hospitality industry in Las Vegas.

In the Fall of 1997, the colleges served 63,028 students. 45,693 were enrolled in state supported classes. An additional 18,168 were enrolled in non-state funded courses. The enrollment increased seven percent from 1996 to 1997.

A Higher Education Distance Learning Network has been initiated. This network links instructional sites by interactive video and computer. Access to the instruction is extended to high school students. The board of regents has approved a twenty-five dollars per credit fee to encourage enrollment of high school students. Distance education and other instructional technology application also support the state's economic development efforts.

ECONOMIC DEVELOPMENT

The University and Community College System Board of Regents has approved a strategic direction to promote the economic health and growth of the state.

Nevada community colleges have responded by expanding their partnerships with business and industry. Private industry plays a greater role in planning and developing curriculum.

The State of Nevada has established a structure needed for workforce development. Higher education and specifically community colleges have had a key role in this effort. School to career partnerships are organized according to the service areas of the four community colleges.

The State Workforce Development Board appointed by the governor includes higher education representation. The State School to Careers Council also includes community college representation. Each college has incorporated a well defined tech prep program.

The State Employment Security Department either has offices or provides services at the community college campuses.

The Workforce Development initiatives position the community colleges to provide education and training support to Nevada's economic development efforts.

ACCOUNTABILITY

The cyclical planning process in Nevada's higher education establishes the benchmarks for accountability. The community colleges and universities prepare a biennial budget that is submitted to the legislature. The planning cycle is four years. In coordination with the budget proposal process, the institutions prepare Academic Master Plans that are revised with the development of each Biennial Budget Request. The Academic Master Plans reflect the strategic directions for higher education approved by the Board of Regents.

The colleges have a process for reviewing existing programs. This process helps insure that programs reflect current needs and requirements. This process also provides the information needed to add or eliminate programs.

The budget, academic planning, and review process provides an ongoing assessment and accountability to the legislature, governor, and other interested constituencies.

REFERENCES

State Plan for Community Colleges in the State of Nevada, 1971.

University and Community College System of Nevada Operating Budget, 1998-99.

University and Community College System of Nevada Planning Report, 1999-2003.

University and Community College System of Nevada Biennial Budget Request, 199-01.

Community College of Southern Nevada Academic Master Plan, 1997-99.

Great Basin College Academic Master Plan, 1998-00
Truckee Meadows Community College Academic Master Plan 1998-03..
Western Nevada Community College Academic Master Plan, 1997-99.
The Nevada Board of Regents Handbook.
The University and Community College System of Nevada Enrollment
*   Report, Fall 1997.*

FOR ADDITIONAL INFORMATION, PLEASE CONTACT:
University and Community College System of Nevada (UCCSN)
2601 Enterprise Way
Reno, Nevada 89512
Telephone: (702) 784-4901

NEW HAMPSHIRE

Glenn DuBois
Commissioner, New Hampshire Department of Community and
Technical Colleges
and
Terrence A. Tollefson
Professor, Department of Educational Leadership and Policy Analysis
East Tennessee State University

OVERVIEW

The first institution in the New Hampshire State Trade Schools, since renamed the New Hampshire Community Technical College System, opened in Portsmouth in 1945. That school's first programs were electricity, heating and air conditioning, machine shop operation and sheet metal working. Later that same year, the second postsecondary trade school in the state opened in Manchester. Both schools were in operation for 40 hours a week and 50 weeks per year. All students were male veterans supported by the GI Bill until 1949, when the first two female students were admitted. The original authorizing legislation directed the New Hampshire State Board of Education "...to provide trade and vocational training and retraining for the occupational adjustment of youths and adults, and particularly to provide trade school facilities for veterans demobilizing from the armed service." (Rafn, in Tollefson & Fountain, 1992, pp. 131-132).

The New Hampshire postsecondary trade schools expanded rapidly until 1949, when their names were changed to vocational and technical institutes. The two schools began providing programs for disabled and handicapped students in the early 1950s, including a machine tool program for blind students (Rafn, in Tollefson & Fountain, 1992).

By the beginning of the 1960s, the two New Hampshire technical institutes had become overcrowded with both veterans and the new majority of non-veterans, many of whom were recent high school graduates. In 1961, the state legislature authorized adding three more vocational institutes to the system, for a statewide total of five vocational institutes and one technical institute. The legislature also appropriated $1.65million to fund the additional institutes. In 1996, a new vocational institute was established in Berlin, the Portsmouth and Manchester institutes erected new buildings and sites were chosen for three more vocational institutes, to be established in Laconia, Claremont, and Nashua. In 1967, the New Hampshire State Board of Education authorized the vocational and technical institutes to begin awarding associate degrees (Rafn, in Tollefson & Fountain, 1992).

The New England Technical Institute obtained accreditation from the New England Association of Schools and Colleges in 1969, after earning specialized accreditation for several individual programs. Also in 1969, the state legislature redesignated the institutions as the New Hampshire Vocational-Technical Colleges. New health-related programs in dental hygiene, nursing and radiological technology ere added in the early 1970s, and each one received specialized accreditation (Rafn, in Tollefson & Fountain, 1992).

In 1972, the state department of education established the Division of Postsecondary Education. The vocational and technical colleges were assigned to its supervision and the state legislature charged the remaining colleges with obtaining regional accreditation as soon as possible, to enable them to become eligible to receive federal funds. In 1983, the Department of Postsecondary Vocational-Technical Education became a separate state department, and in 1988, its name was changed to the New Hampshire Department of Postsecondary Technical Education (Rafn, 1992).

The state legislature enacted a new law in 1998, which required establishing a 25-member board, nine of whom are ex-officio, of the redesignated New Hampshire Community Technical College System (CTCS). The new law was designed "...to create more leadership and to increase flexibility in the postsecondary technical education system". In August of 1998, the new board appointed Glenn DuBois as commissioner, to succeed an interim commissioner who had served for about a year.

The New Hampshire Community Technical College System's official mission is:

> To provide the highest possible level of technical, academic and professional preparation to all people in New Hampshire. Its mission is to prepare students to enter directly into the work force and to advance their chosen career as technicians and skilled workers, while preparing students for continuous educational and career mobility as well as full participation in community life. As an essential element in developing and

maintaining a strong economy, the department is committed to meeting the education and employment needs of existing and future New Hampshire employers. Each college serves as an educational, technical, and community resource. The department achieves its mission by holding its colleges accountable for responsiveness to all students and employers.

The CTCS now has seven colleges and 11 satellite centers throughout the state. The seven college campuses are in Berlin, Claremont, Concord, Laconia, Manchester, Nashua, Portsmouth, and Stratham. CTCS has grown to an open-access system that is the primary provider of highly skilled personnel for the state's business and industrial organizations. CTCS programs are competency-based, which involves clear standards of expected student performance (Westover, 1997, p. 2). The New Hampshire Community Technical College System currently is accredited by the Commission on Technical and Career Institutions of the New England Association of Schools and Colleges. It is in the process of obtaining accreditation of the New England Association's Commission on Institutions of Higher Education, which is intended to increase enrollment and facilitate student transfer to four-year institutions.

PROGRAM AND ENROLLMENT

With approximately 80 associate-degree programs and 170 shorter diploma and certificate programs, CTCS attained a total headcount enrollment of 8,918 students in credit programs in the fall of 1998, which translated into 5,728 full-time equated (FTE) students. Approximately 8,000 additional students also enrolled in non-credit courses in the 1998-99 academic year. New programs are being developed in health information technology, information systems technology, and mobile equipment and diesel technology.

WORKFORCE DEVELOPMENT

The CTCS is a truly open-access system, with all programs open to all students without regard to past performance. Access has increased even more in recent years for such special students as prison inmates and disabled and unemployed workers. Increasing proportions of all jobs require high-level skills, and CTCS strives to fill such needs by regular certificate and degree programs, Technology Development Centers (TDCs), and other partnerships with business and industry (DuBois, 1998). CTCS has developed a Training Challenge Grant program that provides matching grants to employers for employed training. Some employers have estimated they receive $30 for each dollar of investment in this programs (Westover, 1997).

FUNDING

The New Hampshire Community Technical College System's total budget for fiscal year 2000 is approximately $51.7 million, which will rise to about $52.4 million in FY 2001. Forty-three percent of that total is from the state's general fund, and 57% is from tuition and other sources.

The CTCS Foundation is being developed, as authorized by Senate Bill 503, which was enacted in 1998. The CTCS board and commissioner have established funding goals of $75,000 each year in FY 2000 and FY 2001 to "jump-start" the foundation.

ACCOUNTABILITY

A new automatic "triggering system" will lead to a thorough, systematic review of CTCS educational programs. Evaluation will be based upon enrollments, industry demand, and graduation rates. Programs that do not meet market demand will be phased out.

REFERENCES

DuBois, G. (1998, September 23). Presentation on National Public Radio.

Rafn, H.J. (1992). New Hampshire in Tollefson,T.A. & Fountain, B.E., Eds. *Forty-Nine State Systems, 1992 Edition*, pp. 337-344. Washington, DC: American Association of Community Colleges.

Westover, S. (1997). New Hampshire. Unpublished article. Concord, NH: New Hampshire Community Technical College System.

FOR ADDITIONAL INFORMATION, PLEASE CONTACT:
Office of the Commissioner
New Hampshire Department of Technical and Community Colleges
5 Institute Drive
Concord, NH 03301-7400
Telephone: (603) 271-2722
Fax: (603) 271-2725

NEW JERSEY

Jeanne M. Oswald
Deputy Executive Director
New Jersey Commission on Higher Education
and
Lawrence A. Nespoli, President
Council of County Colleges

OVERVIEW

The New Jersey State legislature created the framework for a statewide system of community colleges in 1962. Both the state and the counties in which they are located provide financial support. The first four community colleges began operations in fall 1966, and 10 more opened their doors before the end of the decade. Three were established during the 1970s, and the last two in 1982. (Three of the last five started as agencies providing services on a "brokerage" model and evolved to full-fledged colleges.) Today, all of the state's 21 counties operate community colleges; in two instances two counties jointly sponsor one college.

The statewide system of community colleges was established to meet the educational, cultural, and community needs of their respective counties. The colleges offer a wide array of associate degree programs, including both transfer and occupational curricula, and certificate programs in various occupational fields, as well as noncredit courses that serve participants' general interest or vocational skill needs; community service and cultural programs also are part of their missions. Community colleges prepare students to enter four-year institutions, train them to assume skilled positions in New Jersey's workforce, and offer other opportunities that enrich the quality of life for county residents.

New Jersey's community colleges have relatively low tuition, and they are open-access institutions, permitting anyone with a high school diploma or its equivalent or anyone over the age of 18 to enroll for courses. As such, they have greatly expanded higher education opportunities for new, nontraditional populations of students, which typically include larger proportions of minorities, women, older adults, and part-time students than is true at senior institutions.

The state's 19 community colleges form a sector within a 56-institution system that includes 12 other public and 25 nonpublic institutions. The other public colleges and universities include three research universities (Rutgers, The State University; New Jersey Institute of Technology; and the University of Medicine and Dentistry of New Jersey) and nine state colleges/universities. (One of these, Thomas Edison State College, offers degree programs through nontraditional methods, such as credit for life experience and portfolio assessment.) The 25 nonpublic institutions include 14 senior colleges and universities receiving state aid, eight religious institutions, and three degree-granting proprietary institutions.

GOVERNANCE

The New Jersey Higher Education Restructuring Act of 1994 created the Commission on Higher Education as the new state-level coordinating agency for New Jersey's system of higher education, and the Presidents' Council as a new systemwide advisory body. The restructuring act also established the Office of Student Assistance, previously part of the former new Jersey Department of Higher Education, as a separate entity to administer student financial aid programs. College and university boards of trustees continue to govern the individual institutions, but with increased autonomy, responsibility, and accountability.

The 1994 statute abolished the New Jersey Board and Department of Higher Education, created in 1966 and vested with broad regulatory, as well as coordinating, authority. The department, the board's administrative arm, consisted of the office of the chancellor and vice chancellor and four operating areas, each headed by an assistant chancellor. Dissolving these entities reduced the extent of state involvement in institutional matters, removed a level of bureaucratic review, and introduced a new, entrepreneurial management paradigm. Under restructuring, institutional trustee boards have sole and final authority in several matters that formerly were subject to various state review or approval processes, such as setting tuition and fees and making capital improvements. Contracting for services, materials, and supplies exemplifies how the restructuring act eliminated unnecessary state oversight of community colleges. A 1982 statute, the County College Contracts Law, governs procurement procedures for these colleges. Until 1994, this law included provisions subjecting the colleges also to regulation by the former Board of Higher Education. The restructuring act repealed these unnecessary additional requirements. Based upon further legislative restructuring in March of 1999, the governor appoints six members of the New Jersey Commission on Higher Education with the advice and consent of the state senate.

Commission on Higher Education: The governor appoints the New Jersey Commission on Higher Education's eight public members: six with the advice and consent of the senate, one recommended by the senate president, and one recommended by the assembly speaker. Also appointed by the governor with the senate's advice and consent is one faculty member from an institution of higher education. Serving ex officio with voting privileges are a representative from the public members of the Higher Education Student Assistance Authority and the chair of the presidents' council, for a total of 11 voting members. The executive director of commission staff, appointed by the commission, is an ex officio nonvoting member. The two student representatives, who are appointed by the governor, were nonvoting members at publication time, but legislation was pending to grant them voting rights.

The commission's primary responsibilities include systemwide planning, research, and advocacy; final decisions on institutional licensure, university status, and mission changes or "excedence"; policy recommendations for higher education initiatives and incentive programs; an annual coordinated (systemwide) budget policy statement; and, upon referral from the New Jersey Presidents' Council, decisions on new academic programs that are unduly costly or duplicative. In addition, the Commission exercises general supervision over the Educational Opportunity Fund (EOF), a state program of both financial aid and academic support for disadvantaged students, and administers several other grant programs.

In exercising its institutional licensure responsibility, the New Jersey Commission on Higher Education ordinarily accepts as sufficient for continuing an institution's license the judgment of the Middle States Association (MSA) with respect to New Jersey college and university accreditation; commission staff accompany the Middle States team on the site visit only in certain circumstances. This practice is especially suitable under restructuring, which has sought to minimize redundant and/or unnecessary state involvement in institutional operations. For non-MSA-accredited New Jersey institutions, the commission staff conduct licensure visits by accompanying either consultants or the appropriate specialized accrediting bodies on site visits. For these (as well as out-of-state) institutions, the commission is advised by the Presidents' Council.

(1) The Presidents' Council: The New Jersey Presidents' Council

consists of the presidents of the state's 31 public institutions, the 14 independent institutions receiving state aid, and four representatives of the 11 other nonpublic degree-granting institutions licensed by the Commission on Higher Education. The Presidents' Council's responsibilities include reviewing and commenting on new academic programs; referring costly/ duplicative new academic programs to the commission; providing research and public information on higher education; advising the commission on planning, and institutional licensure/mission; making recommendations on statewide higher education issues, state aid, and student assistance; and encouraging regional and cooperative programs and transfer articulation agreements. The President's Council's activities are largely guided by a 14-member Executive Board consisting of presidents of five community colleges, three research universities, three state colleges universities, and three nonpublic institutions.

(2)   Institutional Boards: Under state law, a county's board of chosen freeholders appoints eight members of a community college's board of trustees, and the governor appoints two. The county superintendent of schools (voting) and the college president (nonvoting) serve ex-officio. The student body elects from each year's graduating class a nonvoting representative. All trustees of public institutions of higher education serve on a voluntary basis. Trustee boards provide leadership and shape policy for their institutions. Under the restructuring act, the boards are responsible for planning, student tuition and fees, admissions standards, degree requirements, investment of institutional funds, and legal affairs. They also have authority for academic programs, personnel decisions, and capital initiatives.

Each New Jersey county also has a board of school estimate, which consists of the chairperson of the county's board of freeholders, two freeholders appointed by that board, and two members appointed by the college's board of trustees. The board of school estimate determines the overall budget for its community college, including the annual appropriation to the college from county revenues, the amount of which excludes anticipated revenue from other sources, such as state aid and student tuition and fees. The freeholder board collects and appropriates the necessary amount in the same manner as for other county purposes.

(3) Council of County Colleges: A 1967 law established the Council of County Colleges to advise state-level policy makers in matters affecting the community colleges. A 1990 law made the council a trustee-headed nonprofit corporation whose members consist of the trustee board chairs and presidents of the 19 community colleges. Under the same 1994 restructuring act that abolished the New Jersey Board and Department of Higher Education, the council was significantly strengthened. it was given new specific, state-level responsibilities, which include submitting to the state treasurer a statewide budget request for community colleges; the treasurer consults with the council on distributing among the colleges state operating aid and capital appropriations.

FUNDING

Until the 1994 restructuring, the former New Jersey Board of Higher Education held statutory responsibility for a consolidated request for state appropriations for the system. Under restructuring, the Commission on Higher Education annually prepares a coordinated budget policy statement that addresses broad funding issues but does not recommend specific dollar amounts of state appropriations. The Presidents' Council also issues funding policy recommendations each year. The Council of County Colleges submits to the state treasurer a request for state support of the community colleges. The Legislature appropriates a single dollar amount for community college operating aid, $120.2 million in FY 1999.

The state treasurer allocates operating aid to each college in the sector based on a formula recommended by the Council of County Colleges that includes foundation aid for each institution, enrollment funding based on full time equivalent students, and access funding to support the special needs of disadvantaged students. Performance funding is being introduced for FY2000 and will equal one percent of the prior year's state aid, or almost $1 million.

The community colleges receive other operating aid, in the form of state appropriations to cover 50% of the pension costs of community college employees who are eligible for the TIAA-CREF plan; this totaled $18.2 million in FY 1999. In addition, the Council of County Colleges recommends capital construction projects for approval by the Department of Treasury, and the state funds 50% of the annual interest on bonds issued for the approved projects, a total of $21.4 million in FY 1999.

The restructuring act charged the New Jersey Commission on Higher Education with developing recommendations on the funding of higher education in New Jersey. The commission recommended a higher education fiscal policy based on four principles; partnerships of shared responsibility involving students, government, and the institutions; adequate and predictable operating and capital support for each institutional sector; continued commitment by the state to student assistance; and efficient and cost-effective delivery of services by the institutions, which must be accountable for their stewardship of public funds.

Under the recommended funding partnership for community colleges, the state, the county, and students each should provide one-third. In FY 1997 (the most recent year for which data are available), the 33% county share (aggregated across the counties) matched the recommendation; however, the state's 24% was below, and students' 43% share exceeded the recommended share of total revenues sectorwide. The commission recommends that a one-third share for each partner be approached over a seven-year period. The recommended state share applies only to the sector as a whole, because the distribution among the partners vary across the counties and years. Similarly, given the variation of contribution among the counties, it is essential that each maintains its community college funding effort.

In 1997, the Council of County Colleges convened a Committee to Reinvest in New Jersey's Community Colleges, co-chaired by two former state senators who cosponsored the original legislation creating New Jersey's community colleges. The Committee—-comprised of business, government, and education leaders from throughout the state—-was created to lobby the Governor and Legislature to implement the Commission's recommendation for increased state funding to community colleges.

As a result of the committee's statewide grassroots campaign, state aid to community colleges increased by $8 million in FY 1998. In early 1998, Governor Whitman announced an extraordinary, multi-year commitment to increase state aid to community colleges by $12 million per year in each of the four years of her second term.

PROGRAMS AND ENROLLMENTS

With a sectorwide student body topping 121,000, community colleges serve almost four out of every 10 students enrolled for credit at New Jersey colleges and universities, and 44% of the 278,000 undergraduates systemwide. New Jersey community college populations in general include more "nontraditional" students than is true in the other sectors. For example, the average age of a community college student is 27.9 years, compared with an average of 24.2 years for the other collegiate sectors. The part-time attendance rate at community colleges, almost 56%, is the highest of any sector's — by at least 12 percentage points overall, and at least 20 percentage points for undergraduate enrollment. Just under half of all black undergraduates enrolled systemwide attend community colleges.

With nearly 90% of community college students sectorwide attending their home-county colleges, the public two-year institutions serve primarily local populations. Each college offers a broad and diverse curriculum, but cannot offer every course or program that might interest county residents. Students who enroll at community colleges outside their county generally do so to pursue studies not offered at the home campus. In such instances (and in certain other situations), state law permits a system of "chargeback" whereby a student may attend another county's community college at that college's resident tuition rate; under chargeback, the home county reimburses the out-of-county college for its share of operating expenses.

New Jersey community colleges offer more than 479 programs leading to the associate in arts (A.A.), associate in science (A.S.), or associate in applied science (A A S.) degree, as well as more than 300 certificate programs. These colleges account for 90% of all the associate-level degree/certificate programs offered systemwide. The most popular majors are in occupational/technical fields. Six out of every ten formal awards granted by community colleges are in these fields. (Many of these programs prepare graduates for either immediate employment or transfer to a senior institution and further study.) Business and health professions each account for about one-fifth of all graduates. Another one-fifth of degree/certificate recipients graduate with training in engineering/engineering technology or in other occupations, such as protective services. Liberal arts degrees account for a little more than 40% of the graduates.

Although the liberal arts and sciences do not claim the largest share of graduates, such coursework accounts for significant portions of all student credit hours. This reflects in part the general education component of all associate degree programs. Before restructuring, state regulations defined categories of courses and specified the numbers of credits that community colleges had to include as general education in each of the three types of associate degree programs. Since 1994, the colleges have maintained these requirements on a voluntary basis. Accordingly, A.A. degrees usually include at least 45 credits in general education courses (of the minimum total 60 credits required for any associate degree); A.S. degrees, 30 general education credits; and A.A.S. degrees, 20 such credits.

These general education courses along with lecture courses in non-technical occupational fields (such as business), and combined with arts and science-related labs account for more than 60% of student credit hours. Remedial, developmental, and English as a Second Language courses constitute another 20% of the credit hours, and technology and allied health courses, 10%. Adult/General Educational Development courses (as well as noncredit/remedial/ developmental work) generate 7% of the credit hours. These percentages pertain to community college credit hours/enrollments that are eligible for state aid under the formula cited earlier.

Beyond these fundable enrollments, both credit and noncredit, New Jersey's community colleges also offer an extensive array of general interest noncredit courses and other programs that serve workforce and community needs. More than 200,000 individuals sectorwide (annual, unduplicated headcount) participate in such activities, which include customized training programs, continuing education/professional development courses, health and fitness programs, arts and crafts instruction, etc.

As noted above, since the 1994 restructuring, institutional trustee boards have exercised final authority in launching most new academic credit programs after review by the Presidents' Council; only those which are unduly duplicative or unduly expensive or which exceed or change an institution's mission are referred (by the Presidents' Council) to the Commission on Higher Education for action. Before 1994, all but a few independent colleges and universities (those chartered before 1887) were required by law to obtain the former Board of Higher Education's approval before mounting any new degree programs. The former Board's extensive program review process significantly delayed program implementation and was seen by many as too restrictive, and a hindrance to institutional creativity and innovation. It was particularly problematic for the community college sector, where quick response to emerging educational needs is an important part of college missions.

The removal of an unnecessary layer of approval is spurring new county and multicounty programs (both for credit and noncredit). These initiatives respond to needs identified by the business community, service sector, state agencies, and/or other entities. For example, upon request by the New Jersey Food Council, a consortium of seven community colleges created a food industry management option for A.A.S. programs in business; students taking this option at any participating college (others may join the consortium) will receive the same training because the option's curriculum is uniform. Under development at the request of Downtown New Jersey, an entity that promotes economic development in the state's urban areas, is a noncredit uniform curriculum to teach managers how to run successfully a commercial center or business improvement district. Both programs were developed using focus groups of practitioners who identified broad responsibilities and specific tasks of the particular activity. From these, the requisite skills were extrapolated and coursework was designed to provide the appropriate training.

ECONOMIC DEVELOPMENT

A major component of the programs and services offered by community colleges is geared towards economic development; the customized training and continuing education mentioned above are examples. With business and industry outreach centers at all of the 19 community colleges, these colleges also play a major role in small business development. The centers assist local businesses through counseling, seminars on topics of interest to small business owners, and referral services to banks and government agencies. Many New Jersey entrepreneurs are served by the six Small Business Development Centers and two business incubators operated by community colleges.

New Jersey's community colleges are involved in a number of statewide partnerships and projects geared towards economic development. In collaboration with the New Jersey Department of Labor, the colleges play roles in the Self-Employment Assistance (SEA) Program, the Workforce Development Partnership (WDP), and Youth Transitions to Work (YTW) Partnership. For the SEA program, the Council of County Colleges coordinated the design of statewide entrepreneurial training for dislocated workers, and the Network for Occupational Training and Education (NOTE) is administering and delivering most of the training. NOTE is the statewide consortium of community college customized training administrators, all of whom have been connected electronically for over four years. This consortium not only offers statewide training programs but enables community colleges that have expertise in highly specialized kinds of training, such as packaging or commercial glassblowing, to provide that training in other counties. Through NOTE, community colleges have received numerous WDP customized training referrals per year from the Department of Labor. Community colleges became eligible in 1996 to serve as fiscal agencies under the YTW partnership, a state grant program funding educational projects for high school students that include a registered apprenticeship and transition to postsecondary education.

The community colleges also collaborate with the state's Commerce and Economic Growth Commission (CEGC). The Council of County Colleges coordinated the development of the advisory board, draft curriculum, marketing strategy, and delivery mechanism for an Economic Development Academy. Under the auspices of various public and private sector entities, this statewide partnership will provide vital training both for government officials and for economic development professionals. In addition, the Council, on behalf of the colleges, has participated in programs for three industries targeted by CEGC for relocation to or expansion in New Jersey. The new food industry management option (noted above, in the section on programs and enrollments) was an effort to expand New Jersey's already sizable (250,000 employees) wholesale-retail food industry. A related program is an alliance for the South Jersey food production industry, for which a community college is serving as the coordinating agency. Centered at another college is an alliance for the boating and marine industries that has been formed among the Southern New Jersey Partnership for Economic Development, members of the industry, providers of technical assistance, and educational institutions. At a conference on the information technology sector, expected to be a growth leader for New Jersey into the next century, industry representatives identified the need for a multicounty degree or certificate program, along with on-site training and education for participating companies.

All sectors of New Jersey higher education offer training and retraining for disadvantaged and displaced workers, but the community colleges are by far the most active, enrolling more than 27,000 individuals annually. The sector is the hub for a variety of state and federally sponsored programs, including the Workforce Investment Act, the above-mentioned Workforce Development Partnership Program, Work First New Jersey, the state's new welfare-to-work program. These initiatives help individuals, such as displaced homemakers, welfare recipients, disadvantaged youth, and the unemployed (both skilled and unskilled), as well as businesses, meet their needs for occupational training and basic literacy instruction.

ACCOUNTABILITY

Institutional accountability is a natural consequence of institutional autonomy, which was a major objective of the 1994 restructuring of New Jersey's higher education system. In fact, the restructuring act holds public college and university governing boards accountable for effectively managing the institutions, as well as for fulfilling institutional missions and statewide goals. Accordingly, the statute requires trustees to make available to the public annual financial statements and independent financial audits. Also mandated is annual public reporting by each institution of its condition, including, among other aspects, faculty, trustee, and curriculum profiles, as well as status of accreditation and capital projects. The law charges the Commission on Higher Education with establishing the form and general content of such reports. Although not mandated, the Commission includes among its own priorities systemwide reporting on excellence and accountability.

A committee jointly appointed by the Commission and Presidents' Council recommends guiding principles for New Jersey's Excellence and Accountability Reporting System. Annually the Commission adopts a format for institutional reporting and issues a systemwide report. The institutions have reported in every fall since 1995.

The first aggregate, systemwide report appeared in spring 1996. It complemented the individual institutional reports, documenting the system's progress in meeting statewide goals and informing plans for improvement. This initial accountability effort was an overview of the state's higher education system. The second and third reports focussed more intensively on costs and outcomes, respectively, while the next report will explore relationships between the two.

The state's new performance funding system will link a portion of state funding increases to indicators dealing with graduation rates, transfer and articulation, efficiency and effectiveness, and diversified revenues. The state worked with the community college sector regarding the indicators for these institutions.

REFERENCES

New Jersey Commission on Higher Education (1996). *New Jersey's Renewable Resource: A Systemwide Accountability Report.* Trenton, N.J.: Author.

New Jersey Commission on Higher Education (1997). *Higher Education Costs and Revenues: The Second Annual Systemwide Accountability Report.* Trenton, N.J.: Author.

New Jersey Commission on Higher Education (1998). Trenton, N.J.: Author. *Focusing on higher Education Outcomes: The Third Annual Systemwide Accountability Report.*

FOR ADDITIONAL INFORMATION, PLEASE CONTACT:

New Jersey Commission on Higher Education
(state coordinating agency for higher education)
20 West State Street
P. O. Box 542
Trenton, New Jersey 08625
Telephone: (609) 292-4310
Fax: (609) 292-7225
E-mail: rj_che@njche.che.state.nj.us
Website: http://www.state.nj.us/highereducation/
Deputy Executive Director: Dr. Jeanne M. Oswald
New Jersey Council of County Colleges
(statutory organization representing the community colleges)
330 West State Street
Trenton, New Jersey 08618
Telephone: (609) 392-3434
Fax: (609) 292-8158
E-mail: NJCCC@aol.com

NEW MEXICO

Frank J. Renz
Executive Director, New Mexico Association of Community Colleges

OVERVIEW

Community colleges in New Mexico take on many different forms, based primarily on the governing statute under that were established, i.e., university branch campus, community college, vocational-technical institute, constitutional school or educational outreach center. Even though each institution has established its own mission statement, each has the primary mission of bringing postsecondary education opportunities to the communities it serves.

Some institutions focus primarily on transfer education, others on vocational-technical education, but most provide a mix of programs as the basis for their credit offerings. Substantial effort is also placed on providing other programs and services, much of it non-credit, that fulfill a comprehensive mission. These institutions support, in varying degrees, the following: developmental education to include adult basic education and literacy programs; programs with area secondary schools to include tech-prep, concurrent enrollment and school-to-careers; continuing education programs focusing on short-term training and retraining and assistance to small business; and community enhancement to include economic development, cultural enrichment and leadership.

These colleges share several important characteristics that allow them to bring higher education within reach of all New Mexicans: a commitment to academic, financial and geographic accessibility; a commitment to educational equity and student success; and a commitment to teaching excellence.

The community colleges were considered to begin in New Mexico as branch campuses of universities with the passage of the Branch Community College Act in 1957 (even though the state constitution in 1893 established the Military Institute which offers a high school program and the first two years of a transfer education, and in 1909 the New Mexico Spanish-American Normal School, which attained community college status in 1977). Following this, support for "junior"college legislation began to increase, and in 1963, the Junior College Act was passed (amended in

1985 as the Community College Act). Subsequent legislation was passed in 1965, providing for separate institutions whose primary mission was to be vocational and technical training (Technical and Vocational Institute and Area Vocational School acts, which were later amended to include authorization for associate of arts and associate of science degrees). Finally, an additional piece of legislation, the Off-Campus Instructional Act, has assisted in the creation of two educational outreach centers that perform primarily a community college function.

Community college education is currently delivered as follows in New Mexico: 16 colleges serving a comprehensive community college mission (eight of which are university branches); two educational outreach centers; a military institute offering the first two years of a transfer curriculum; a regional university which serves a significant community college mission; and limited associate degree programs among the other research and regional universities around the state.

Due to the varying nature of the community colleges in New Mexico and how they were established, it would be fair to say that these colleges have behaved more like individual entities than as a system. This is changing, however, due to the necessity of collaborating on statewide initiatives and more competition for limited state resources. Today, the colleges work together through the New Mexico Association of Community Colleges (NMACC), established in July 1995.

GOVERNANCE

Public higher education began in New Mexico in 1889, when the Territorial Legislature passed the Rodney Act that set up three institutions of higher learning. The trend of creating institutions continued between 1890 and 1912, in which year New Mexico became a state. The constitution of the state provided for state support of what are now six four-year institutions. A key provision of the constitution was that each institution was to have its own governing board of regents, appointed by the governor. Between 1919 and 1947, efforts were made to reduce the number of institutions and/or to establish a central governing board which would make recommendations (not final decisions) to the legislature. The latter was opted for and resulted in the establishment in 1951 of the New Mexico Board of Educational Finance (changed to the Commission on Higher Education, or CHE, in 1985). This effort did not require a constitutional amendment because local boards of regents would be maintained. This maintenance of autonomy and governance by local boards has had significant implications for higher education policy development in New Mexico.

The CHE is the statewide coordinating agency for all of higher education. Its primary governing authority is upon the approval of college budgets. Otherwise, the CHE assists with statewide planning and policy development as it relates to higher education in New Mexico; exercises program approval authority for graduate programs and associate degree programs at selected institutions; and prioritizes operating budget increases and capital improvement projects for recommendation to the Legislature for all of public higher education in the state. Currently, the CHE is composed of a 15-member Commission (which includes two students, one from a two-year and one from a four-year college) appointed by the governor. There is a staff of 25, which includes an executive director, housed in offices in Santa Fe and Albuquerque.

Another coordinating agency having influence over New Mexico's community colleges is the New Mexico Department of Education, Vocational-Education and Adult Education Division. This is the state-designated lead agency for the administration of the Carl D. Perkins Vocational and Applied Education Act of 1990 and the National Literacy Act of 1991, which are now under revision. This agency has been influential in recognizing the community colleges for their key roles in vocational-technical and adult basic education, primarily through funding allocation decisions.

As mentioned earlier, much of the governance authority over the higher education institutions in New Mexico rests with local boards. The branch community colleges and educational outreach centers have local boards, advisory to their parent university's board of regents which has the ultimate governing authority. Branches have the option of either an elected advisory board or a board composed of a majority of the local board of education in a school district or combined local boards of multiple school districts. Membership ranges from 5 to 20, depending on the local option selected or the district makeup. Responsibilities of this advisory board include: acting in an advisory capacity to the board of regents of the parent institution in all matters relating to the conduct of the branch community college, to include hiring and firing of the chief executive and, in most cases, faculty and staff; approving an annual budget for the branch community college for recommendation to the board of regents; certifying to the board of county commissioners the tax levy for operations; and conducting the election for tax levies and board members, where applicable.

The rest of the community colleges have their own governing boards, mostly elected but some appointed, depending on whether established by the constitution or by statute. Board membership ranges from 5 to 7. The overall responsibilities of these governing boards are as follows: determining financial and educational policies of the college; providing for the management of the college and the execution of the aforementioned policies by selecting a chief executive; hiring and firing other faculty and staff at the recommendation of the chief executive; fixing tuition and fee rates for resident and non-resident students of the district; conferring degrees and other academic credentials; accepting gifts and federal aid on behalf of the college; purchasing, holding, selling and renting property; and authorizing and conducting elections.

No significant changes in the governance structure have occurred over the past 10 years. It is anticipated that discussions will take place over the next few years about combining all or some of the community college governing statutes and about making some of the branch campuses independent of their university parent campus. Along these lines, the 1999 New Mexico Legislature passed legislation that eliminated the Area Vocational School Act and brought colleges established under this statute under the Technical and Vocational Institute Act.

The concept of learning centers, which would broker education from a number of different educational entities, is also being studied and discussed as an alternative to the establishment of new campuses.

FUNDING

The community colleges in New Mexico are funded through a variety of sources, with a two-year I & G (Instruction and General) formula providing the basis for annual operating expenditures. The major source of revenue for community college operations is the state general fund, although there is a local mill levy requirement for all but the constitutionally established colleges. The formula does include components for building renewal and replacement and equipment renewal and replacement (both of which are only partially funded at the present time). The formula does not, however, include provisions for major capital expenditures and acquisitions.

The funding formulas employed by the CHE calculate "Instruction and General" expenditure levels for both two- and four-year institutions.

The nomenclature "Education and General" is common in higher education literature, but in New Mexico, the term "Instruction and General," or "I & G," is used. "I & G" consists of the following institutional functions, with the last four items constituting the General portion of the formula: Instruction, Academic Support, Student Services, Institutional Support, and Plant Operations and Maintenance. Although conceptually the same, there are differences in the two- and four-year formulas.

The sum of these I & G formula calculations generates an expenditure level, not a state appropriation. In order to determine an institution's funding level, certain revenues must be subtracted from this expenditure level, and three transfer amounts must be added. Formula revenue credits include: an assumed level of tuition revenue; 80% of interest earned on previous year's balances; miscellaneous fees at one dollar per formula student credit hour; 50% of previous year's unrestricted federal funds; and local mill levy or land and permanent fund revenue (latter applies to constitutional schools only). Due to the passage of the College District Tax Act, referred to earlier, a minimum mill levy of one for the branches and two for non-branch community colleges was established, and this minimum amount is credited against the formula. All institutions, with voter approval, are authorized to assess up to five mills, with anything over the credited amount being used for enhancement purposes or tuition reductions. Formula fund transfers (additions to expenditures) include: Building Renewal and Replacement (currently only partially funded at 23%); Equipment Renewal and Replacement (currently only partially funded at 41.5%); and the 3% state scholarship program (tuition and fee waivers for 3% of the previous fall headcount at current tuition and fee rates).

A major drawback with the formula in its current form is that it does not fully fund all of the campuses. Five of the colleges receive formula supplements through non-formula adjustments. This situation exists primarily due to the method by which each college was established. The New Mexico State Legislature, with the support of the Commission on Higher Education and New Mexico Association of Community Colleges, is attempting to make formula changes, with the goal that all community colleges are fully funded through a single, more equitable formula. Three significant changes were made recently through legislative action to help bring this about: the 1995 legislature enacted the "College District Tax Act," providing a uniform procedure across the various governing statutes for the authorization, imposition and collection of tax levies for the operation of college districts and the issuance of general obligation and revenue bonds for capital improvements; the 1996 legislature approved the final phase-in for two community colleges that had not been on the funding formula; and the 1997 legislature approved a significant formula revision to the student services portion of the two-year formula. Another significant formula addition, equipment renewal and replacement, was approved for phase-in (at about a third) by the 1995 legislature for both the two- and four-year formulas. The formula level for this component is now at 41.5% of full formula.

The Commission on Higher Education is granted statutory authority to "receive, adjust and approve" postsecondary institution operating budgets prior to submission to the state Department of Finance and Administration. Budget expenditures are approved based on a realistic projection of revenues from tuition and fees, state general fund appropriation, local levy, grants and contracts, and other miscellaneous revenues from both restricted and unrestricted sources. Although these revenue sources vary by institution, at the community colleges the average proportion of revenues by source for 1998-99 is as follows: tuition and fees 13.1%, or $24.1 million); state general fund appropriation (59.6%, or $109.3 million); local levy (25.3%, or $46.4 million), grants and contracts (0.1%, or $0.27 million); and other miscellaneous revenues (1.9%, or $3.4 million). Total revenues available for community colleges in 1996-97 were $183.5 million out of a total of $582.0 million available for all of higher education.

The total share of the state budget for higher education in 1998-99 is 16.37%, whereas ten years ago it was a 16.99% share, fluctuating from year to year between 16% and 18% with a 15-year average of 16.6%. There has been a shift of the state share between the two- and four-year sectors, with the community colleges now receiving 3.66% of the state share (compared to 3% 10 years ago) and the universities receiving 12.71% of the state share (compared to 14.25% 10 years ago). This is reflective of enrollment shifts from the four-year to the two-year sector and recent enhancements to the two-year formula.

Capital building projects are also annually recommended and rank-ordered by the CHE for submittal to the Legislature and governor, with revenues coming from legislatively approved sources such as the state general fund, severance tax bond sales and statewide general obligation bond sales (submitted to the voters only in November of even-numbered years); with limited equipment purchases are also allocated through these sources.

Debt service for capital buildings and equipment is incurred from other sources, primarily through voter-approved local general obligation bonds and revenue bond sales. Local operating reserves or other sources are occasionally made available at an institution for capital purposes.

A Systems Development Fund was funded by the legislature for one year in 1995. This program was exemplary in that it supported model consortium efforts among colleges, schools and other partners for four higher education goals: transfer and articulation, distance education, student retention and academic achievement. Funding has been requested by the CHE over the past three legislative sessions to continue this fund, but no additional money has been approved since the one-time appropriation in 1995.

PROGRAMS AND ENROLLMENT

All of the community colleges in New Mexico are authorized to offer associate degree programs to include the A.A., A.S. and A.A.S. degrees; three of the colleges were originally established primarily as technical schools but expanded into a comprehensive mission in the late 1980s and early 1990s. All also offer certificate programs ranging from less than a year to two years in length. Collectively, there are more than 100 different career training majors offered through these community colleges. A full range of pre-baccalaureate transfer programs is also offered through most of the campuses. On average, the community colleges graduate more than 4,000 individuals each year.

Enrollments at the community colleges in New Mexico have increased exponentially over the past 10 years. Headcount enrollment from the period of 1986 to 1998 has grown from 19,078 to 53,791, or an increase of 182%. FTE during this same time period went from 9,249 to 28,153, or an increase of 204%.

Annualized FTE by instructional cluster for 1997-98 is as follows: Sciences and Office Occupations, 5,793; Business, 2,031; General Academic, 11,383; Fine Arts, 1,198; Health Sciences, 1,698; Developmental, 4,564; and, Trades and Technical, 4,359.

It is estimated that collectively the state's community colleges serve another 85,000 in community services and continuing education non-credit programs. Part of this enrollment is generated from contract training and these numbers alone increased from 5,630 in 1991/92 to 14,584 in 1997/98. Also included are enrollments in ABE, ESL and literacy, which totaled 31,634 for 1997/98. Ninety-six percent of this instruction is delivered through community college-based administrative sites.

Enrollment trends in New Mexico have shifted dramatically from the four-year to the two-year sector. The community colleges housed the majority of the higher education headcount enrollments for the first time in 1994 at 50.5%. Today, the enrollment share for the community colleges is 52%. In addition, the community colleges garner about 70% of the state's local undergraduate enrollment. FTE share has increased less dramatically, given the continuing high number of part-time students, with the community colleges commanding more than 40% of the FTE in 1990 for the first time. Today, the FTE share (the primary driver of the funding formula) for the community colleges is 42.7%.

Another interesting enrollment characteristic, especially given that New Mexico is a minority-majority state, is that the demographic profile of community college students closely mirrors the gender and ethnicity demographics of the state's adult population (according to 1990 Census data). Graduation rates also closely reflect this gender and ethnic distribution.

ECONOMIC DEVELOPMENT

Particularly over the past five years, the community colleges in New Mexico have been making the case in presentations to public bodies, the executive branch and the Legislature for increasing their role in economic and workforce development. Recent efforts have paid off, based on the following indications: the state's school-to-work program is being rolled-out through the 17 community college service areas, with the community college being given the primary role of leading the development of regional partnerships; the state's new welfare-to-work PROGRESS program is contracting with the community colleges and their designated partners, such as the Department of Labor; to do much of the training and support for qualified work activities; and the state's One-Stop program is being orchestrated primarily through the state's labor service centers, but with several housed on community college campuses. In addition, a 1995 statewide survey of business and industry indicated that one in three New Mexico firms typically hires graduates of New Mexico's community colleges.

Community colleges in New Mexico are recognized by leading corporations as major providers of training for high-technology occupations. Corporations annually contribute equipment and expertise to community colleges to support training programs. Intel Corporation, for example, has invested in cutting edge technology for labs to support semiconductor training at several of the community colleges and has provided scholarship assistance for students. The state's national labs, industry and Technology Industries Association (TIA, an organization of 26 high-tech firms in New Mexico), are partnering with the community colleges to develop an industry-validated core technology curriculum for targeted industries.

In 1994/95, more than 160 companies/agencies entered into training partnerships with one or more community colleges. In the past four years, more than 33,000 individuals have participated in one or more programs designed to upgrade the skills of current employees and agency workers. Some of colleges house nationally certified/endorsed training programs or advanced technology centers.

Small businesses, however, (close to 90% of businesses in New Mexico have 50 employees or fewer) are not so able to participate in formal training programs for their employees, usually due to time and cost constraints. To address this need, the state's small business development centers are housed at the community colleges, and they provide business assistance and training at no cost.

A state economic development initiative that has been in existence since 1972, the Development Training Program, is offered to new and expanding businesses in New Mexico. The program subsidizes a minimum of 50% of the salary costs of job trainees, not to exceed 1,040 hours, to meet the objectives of expanding the economic base and providing employment opportunities for New Mexicans. Although these businesses and prospective businesses are not required to partner with the community colleges, some community colleges have been called upon to be the main source of training.

There are few other policies in New Mexico to coordinate efforts and offer incentives focusing on economic and workforce development. This is why the Governor signed an executive order in 1996, creating a state Workforce Development Board, which coordinates all workforce development programs and services in the state directed it to develop a state workforce plan to comply with the National Workforce Investment Act of 1998. The community colleges have representation on this 25-member board. Regional boards are proposed, but not yet formed, and the community colleges have sent a message to the governor about the importance of representation on these boards as well.

ACCOUNTABILITY

As mentioned earlier, the higher education funding formula assists the Commission on Higher Education in determining adequate funding levels for New Mexico public institutions and in determining an equitable distribution of resources among those institutions. Once funds are distributed to the institutions on this basis, each college is accountable to the CHE for its operating budget, and the CHE, in turn, is accountable to the executive and legislative branches. Institutions are also accountable to their local boards for proper handling of their finances. Accountability is also a major component in the accreditation requirements of North Central, the accrediting agency for the region.

An annual report prepared by the CHE, The Condition of Higher Education in New Mexico, summarizes the revenues and expenditures of the state's colleges and universities for public review. Besides the financial summaries, this document contains demographic data about students enrolled; data about tuition and fees paid and financial aid received by these students; and the rates at which students complete degree programs and the fields in which they receive degrees.

In addition, a Program Performance Report is prepared annually by the state Department of Education, Vocational-Technical and Adult Education Division, on secondary and postsecondary performance standards and measures. Included in this report is information about postsecondary program graduates at the community colleges, along with developmental studies completion rates and future success in college-level work.

Because of the national call for increased accountability for higher education and more discussion about it at the state level, the community colleges, through NMACC, have begun to identify institutional effectiveness measures that can be reported collectively to their stakeholders. Among the measures discussed are those connected with: career preparation; transfer success; student satisfaction; graduation rates or other indicators of student progress; financial information; contract training; and school-to-career activities. Ideas are also being borrowed from an AACC publication, Community Colleges—Core Indicators of Effectiveness, and the current requirements of the North Central Accrediting agency. Activities and timelines have already been developed, and the colleges will begin collecting baseline data in fall 1999. This initiative is supported by the Commission on Higher Education and reinforced by 1999 legislation calling for an annual Higher Education Accountability Report and performance-based budgeting by 2004. Finally, somewhat related to accountability, is a law passed by the New Mexico Legislature in 1995, the Higher Education Articulation Act, requiring the establishment of a common 35-hour general education core and 64-hour transfer modules for most pre-baccalaureate-oriented programs. As a result of this law, the colleges are working together to improve course and program articulation which has reduced the number of students having to repeat courses upon transfer.

FOR ADDITIONAL INFORMATION, PLEASE CONTACT:
New Mexico Association of Community Colleges (NMACC)
c/oFrank J. Renz, Ph.D., Executive Director
6401 Richards Avenue
Santa Fe, New Mexico 87505
Telephone: (505) 428-1621
Fax: (505) 428-1469
E-mail: frenz@santa-fe.cc.nm.us

New Mexico Commission on Higher Education
c/oBruce Hamlett, Ph.D., Executive Director
1068 Cerrillos Road
Santa Fe, New Mexico 87501
Telephone: (505) 827-7387
Fax: (505) 827-7392

NEW YORK (SUNY)*

Glenn DuBois
Formerly Director of Community Colleges
State University of New York

OVERVIEW

There are two public systems of higher education in the State of New York: the State University of New York (State University), with its 30 community colleges, and the City University of New York (CUNY), with six community colleges. This article focuses on State University.

The State University of New York is among the world's largest systems of higher education. To understand State University, one must understand its parts: four University Centers, 12 University Colleges (formerly teacher colleges), five Colleges of Technology (previously two-year agricultural and technology colleges), two Health Science Centers, six specialized colleges, five statutory colleges, and 30 locally sponsored community colleges for a total of sixty-four institutions.

Enrollment in State University for Fall, 1994, term was at the fifth highest level in the system's history. Approximately 393,000 (250,000 FTE enrolled in State University. Two hundred thousand students (143,000 FTE) were enrolled in community colleges. Credit-free enrollments for the 1994-1995 academic year should put the total number of students served at State University community colleges in excess of 400,000.

State community colleges are locally governed, comprehensive in nature, offering a full range of programs in associate in arts, associate in science, and associate in applied science.

A few community colleges offer the associate in occupational science—career oriented programs that do not require a liberal arts core.

The colleges are involved in traditional instruction, distance learning, business and community education, JTPA services, Tech-Prep, School-to-Work, and a variety of off-campus instructional programs. Financing is enrollment-driven, with county sponsors, state aid, and student tuition each contributing about a third of the total revenue. All colleges are accredited by the Middle States Association of Colleges and Schools.

*This chapter describes the State University of New York system community colleges only. It does not include any information about the City University of New York community colleges.

Each campus sets its own tuition under a State University cap of $2,500. The average tuition rate for 1995-96 was $2,300—well above the national average, but comparable to community college systems in the Northeast.

STUDENTS

About half of all community college students are enrolled on a part-time basis. Approximately 50% of the full-time students are under the age of 22 and 60% of the part-time students are over the age of 25. More women are enrolled than men. Because so many students are parents, colleges provide childcare services. State University currently gives its community colleges $1.5 million in assistance to help support childcare centers.

Enrollments of minorities are at an all time State University high of 62,000. Since 1976, minority enrollment in State University has increased at these rates: African-American, 81%; Hispanic, 222%, Asian/Pacific Islander, 529%; and American Indian, 12%. Over half (32,000) of the minorities are enrolled in community colleges, representing about 17% of the total community college enrollment. The largest non-white racial group attending community colleges is African-American (9%).

Enrollment patterns at State University community colleges have shifted. Its students are older, more are women, and the population is more racially and ethnically diverse.

As in other states, community college students in New York are taking longer than two years to earn an associate degree. Thirty-six percent of the students will achieve associate degrees after four years of admission, compared to a national norm of 20% (Burke, 1994). Thirty-eight percent of the current students will leave college in their first year of study without a degree; most will transfer to another college.

There has been an overall decline in the percentage of students earning a degree within the traditional time period—from 37.7 percent for the Class of 1977, to 16.3 percent for the Class of 1993. State University studies have indicated that most students drop out of college during their first year of study. However, it should be noted that community colleges enroll a larger proportion of students who are not seeking degrees. Many students attend community colleges to upgrade skills for job advancement rather than to obtain degrees or certificates. When these students do not return to the community college, they are mistakenly included in the attrition data.

Completion rates differ by race and ethnicity for students enrolled in associate degree programs. White (non-Hispanic) and Asian-Pacific Islander students graduate at higher rates than do students from other groups. African-Americans have the lowest degree completion rate after four years of admission at 19%.

The greatest predictor of college success is high school performance. The higher the high school average, the greater chance of graduating college in a more successful and timely manner (Burke, 1994).

More women are attending college than ever before. At some locations, they almost double the enrollment of men. At all locations, they graduate at higher rates than men (41% to 33%).

It is generally true, however, that there is an increase in students requiring additional time to complete an associate degree program. This is also true for baccalaureate students.

Among the graduates, about half will transfer to a four-year college. The college of choice is often a State University state operated institution. State University policy guarantees junior-level status at a state operated four-year institution to all community college graduates of transfer programs (i.e. A.S., A.A. degrees). Many State University colleges also accept graduates of career or occupational programs. Although system wide policy has been established for transfer students, some problems remain. Central administration continues to work toward the goal of a seamless transition from community colleges to state operated four-year institutions.

State University studies indicate that community college transfer students perform as effectively at four-year colleges as the students who began at those institutions.

FACULTY AND STAFF

There are over 13,000 faculty employed at State University community colleges; 4,313 are full-time, with average annual salary of $49,580. The number of part-time faculty has increased from 5,500 in 1982 to 8,806 in 1995. During the same time, the number of full-time faculty increased by only five. In the last ten years, the number of non-faculty positions has increased substantially, from 6,800 to 13,000.

Community college faculty typically teach five classes a semester (15 hours) and spend an additional 36 hours a week on various professional activities such as advising, committee work, class preparation, and research (Burke, 1994).

From 1985 too 1993, the number of female employees at State University's community colleges increased 20% and presently account for 52% of all workers. Female employees have also grown 119% for professional non-teaching positions, and 2% for faculty positions.

During the same time period, minority employment increased 37% and now accounts for approximately 10% of the work force. Minority employees have also grown 130% in professional non-teaching positions, and 45% in faculty positions (Burke, 1994).

HISTORICAL ORIGINS

The history of New York community colleges is relatively brief, since New York was one of the last states to implement a statewide community college system. Chapter 696 of the Laws of 1948 set the course of events that would lead up to the first public comprehensive community college in New York. The legislation authorized the establishment and operation of community colleges:

Either individually or jointly, by counties, cities or intermediate school districts, pursuant

> To the provisions of this article, and providing two-year post-secondary programs pursuant to the regulations prescribed by the State University trustees and receiving financial assistance from the state thereof. (New York State, Education Law, Section 6301.2)

The first community colleges were Orange County Community College and Jamestown Community College (1950) followed by Auburn Community College three years later. Their mission was to provide general and technical education with transfer opportunities to four-year colleges.

Community colleges were organized as units of local governments rather than integral components of state government. The community colleges had to be sponsored by a county, city, school district, or some combination, subject to the approval of State University trustees. Today, a community college is typically sponsored by a county. Five community colleges have two county sponsors.

Community colleges expanded rapidly in New York. By 1960, there were 18 community colleges, responding to the challenge of placing "every high school in the State within commuting distance of a two-year college" (SUNY, 1964, p.xi). By 1967, the community colleges were serving 80,000 students—seven times the number of students being served ten years earlier (SUNY, 1967, p.9). Enrollments and academic programs continued to grow.

The demand for higher education by the tremendous numbers of high school graduates in the late 1960s and early 1970s nearly swamped the community college system. However, the economically disadvantaged were largely absent among student enrolments; they couldn't afford tuition (Martens, 1985). In the early 1970s, less than 10% of enrolled students were minorities. All of that changed with the creation of the Full Opportunity Program of 1970, which guaranteed community college admission to high school graduates and veterans. The incentive to "open the doors" and provide full opportunity was the promise of increased aid. Enrollment hit an all-time high in 1992. Today, State University is one of the largest community college systems in the world.

GOVERNANCE

Twenty-eight community colleges have 10 trustees each: five appointed by the local sponsor (usually one or two counties), four appointed by the governor, and one student representative elected by the student body. Two community college are regional community colleges, with no county sponsor, and each of them is governed by a 14- or 15-member board of trustees.

The community college's board of trustees is the governing body. The board sets policies, appoints personnel, approves curriculum, and adopts budgets, among other duties. State University trustees provide guidelines to the community colleges, approve budgets, presidential appointments, academic curricula, and tuition and fee schedules. The chancellor of the State University carries out the board of trustee policies at the state level, assisted by the director of community colleges and system administration personnel.

State University community colleges are state-aided, not state-operated. The difference is significant. For example, State University trustees appoint the presidents of the state operated colleges, but they approve the community college's presidential appointments. State University has absolute control over tuition and fees at the state-operated units; community colleges set their own rates. Faculty at state-operated colleges are state employees. Community college faculty are employees of the local sponsor, usually a county.

FUNDING

Support for the 1995-1996 fiscal year came from the State of New York (29%), local sponsors (31%), and student tuition (40%). Since 1970, state aid has been allocated according to a specified dollar amount per full-time equivalent student. Counties that export students to a community college pay a charge-back fee to the local sponsor.

The 1996 state aid formula provisions included $1,850 per FTE. In the last three years, community colleges have lost approximately $20 million in categorical state aid. For example, New York gave an extra $212 for every disadvantaged student enrolled in community college, an extra $195 for students enrolled in a technical degree program, and an extra $82 for students enrolled in a business program. All categorical aid has been cut. The State does, however, continue to underwrite some of the costs associated with campus daycare ($1.5 million), rentals ($5 million), and to provide some aid for non-credit remedial courses.

Funding for State University community colleges is essentially an equally shared cost among three sources: the student, the State, and the local sponsor. Recently, however, the student has borne an increasing share, upward of one-third, while the State and the local sponsor each provides something less than that. Half of the local sponsors contribute less than 20%, and some as little as 10%.

Since most students live at home, their overall costs are relatively low. The average annual cost for a full-time community college student in 1993 was $5,695. This included travel, food, and other expenses. In contrasts, the annual cost to attend a state-operated, residential college in 1993 was $9,238.

Over half of all funding goes to support instructional programs at the colleges. Most of the rest is used for support services for students or to maintain the campus.

PROGRAMS

Community colleges see themselves as open-door, "comprehensive" institutions with five particular missions: (1) career education, (2) transfer education, (3) remedial education, (4) community education, and (5) general education. An increasing number of community colleges claim to have an economic development component in their mission—a topic I will discuss later in this paper.

Community colleges offer an extensive curriculum, on an open-admissions basis. There are some restricted programs, particularly in the allied health field, that are only open to students who meet competitive admissions requirements. Generally, most programs are open to all prospective students who graduated from high school or possess a general education equivalency diploma (GED).

The colleges offer traditional classroom instruction, distance learning courses, evening and weekend courses, continuing education programs, and contract courses for businesses and other organizations. Many colleges have off-campus locations where they offer a limited number of courses and programs.

For twenty years, New York community colleges were involved in inmate education programs. Ten colleges provided instruction to approximately 2,000 incarcerated students at numerous prison locations in 1995. Faculty, mostly part-time, taught their classes in the evenings, behind prison walls. Tuition assistance from the state helped finance the cost of inmate education. The executive and legislature cut all tuition assistance for inmates in 1996. Recent research indicated a positive correlation between lower inmate recidivism and college study (Clark, 1991). Inmates who earned an associate degree return to prison at half the rate of inmates with no higher education.

All community colleges in New York are involved in Tech-Prep and School-to-Work programs. Although programs vary, Tech-Prep and School-to-Work programs help secondary level students prepare for an effective transition to college and then work, particularly in a technical vocation. All State University community colleges have developed unique Tech-Prep and School-to-Work programs that typically collaborate with a number of other agencies and groups like chambers of commerce, employers, and BOCES (a public vocational high school).

The transition from school to work is neither smooth nor efficient. Too many high school graduates spend years bouncing from one job to another. In response to this problem, localities, states and the federal government have designed school-to-work programs. Largely because of federal funding, community colleges have played a central role in school-to-work endeavors. In 1995, the State of New York received a five year federal School-to-Work grant with $10 million for the initial year. All community colleges in the state, and their partners (e.g. employers, BOCES, high schools, job service bureaus, parents) will play key roles in designing and implementing school-to-work programs.

ACCOUNTABILITY

As in other states, New York community colleges have been increasingly held accountable by numerous groups, from students and employers to local, state, and federal governments. The first attempt to highlight State University's achievements and shortcomings was led by State University's former provost, Dr. Joseph Burke and articulated in *Performance Indicators (1994)*. Dr. Burke remarked that Performance Indicators is….based on the belief that is the best way to respond to our critics, to ensure system accountability, and to support additional autonomy (p.i.). The report shows State University comparing favorably with other state systems with respect to access, graduation rates, faculty workloads, and the diversity of its work force and students.

Recently, the New York State Department of Education announced plans to issue "report cards" for the state's public and private colleges. A similar initiative was implemented for the state's public elementary schools. This report card, which measured student performance levels in the areas of math and reading in the third and fifth grades, was recently published and caused considerably local attention and generated much press. Discussions are underway concerning the criteria to be used for the higher education report card. Plans are to implement the higher education report card by the end of 1998.

Mandate to Change

In 1995, New York's legislature requested State University to develop a "multi-year, comprehensive, system wide plan to increase cost efficiency." The legislature was particularly interested in:

- Enhancing the application of technology for academic and administrative purposes;
- Increasing learning productivity, including reducing time to program completion;
- Increasing faculty productivity; and
- Enhancing the overall quality of degree offering by strengthening academic specialization.

This charge by the legislature sparked a number of State University initiatives. With respect to community colleges, a task force, primarily composed of community college presidents and trustees, was formed to examine the best model of governance and administration to enhance the effectiveness of community colleges and improve the role of community colleges within State University.

One of the major items the task force addressed was the question of a distinct system for community colleges—separate from State University. The task force examined that option and concluded that community colleges, students, and taxpayers would be better served by having community colleges remain as part of the State University of New York.

The issue then for the task force was to look for ways to make community colleges a more meaningful partner in State University. The task force proposed a revised mission statement to more accurately reflect the role of community colleges in economic development and work force training and the group also developed several recommendations relative to access to higher education, student transfer, and the administration of community colleges. Several recommendations have since become policy including the ability for community colleges to offer tuition discounts to part time students who attend classes at off-campus locations or during off-peak hours.

ECONOMIC DEVELOPMENT

Like other states, New York has become increasingly concerned with economic development. In 1995, State University commissioned a study to determined the economic impact of community colleges. The study concluded that for every dollar in state aid, community colleges returned 5.5 times the aid received from the State. Furthermore, the study claimed that State University's community colleges accounted for the creation of 50,000 jobs (other than people hired to support the colleges). During the year the study was conducted, State University community colleges received $285,049,096 in state aid and had an actual impact of $1,569,894,382—a larger impact than any other economic sector, including agriculture, mining, construction, manufacturing, and retail.

This particular study generated much attention on the role that community colleges play in economic development. It also played a key role in helping to change the perception of legislators and other governmental leaders with respect to economic development and the role of community colleges. Instead of something to be subsidized, more and more legislators are seeing community colleges as a worthwhile investment.

Other Initiatives

In *Learning Productivity* (1993), Dr. Bruce Johnstone, chancellor of

State University from 1988 to 1994, called for State University to look for new ways to become more productive. One of his ideas that has since been realized was to provide college-level learning during the high school years which met the learning expectations of community colleges. Today, more than half of the state's community colleges provide college-level instruction to high school student. Students are graduating high school with college credits. Some students graduate from high school with over 18 credits towards an associate degree.

These are not the only issues that have warranted State University's concern. In recent years, the chancellor has formed task forces to make recommendations regarding statewide problems in higher education. Of these, three are particularly important. They are the task forces on: (1) the under-prepared student, (2) the transition from high school to college, and (3) distance learning.

Task Force: The Under-Prepared Student

The State University task force came to grips with one of the system's most pressing problems: the growing number of students who are seriously under-equipped academically for the rigors of college study. Some of these students come from single parent homes; others have dropped out of high school and subsequently earned a general equivalency diploma (GED); and many have graduated high school with weak academic skills. The problem is extensive. According to the task force report (1995), 94% of all community colleges offered some kind of developmental course; 65% of all students need some kind of remediation in their first semester. The task force claimed that under prepared students can be helped, provided that institutions make a commitment to help them, maintain high standards, and provide necessary supplemental support programs. More specifically, the task force recommended:

- Greater collaboration with secondary schools;
- Rigorous pre-admission assessment testing;
- Appropriate course selection;
- A greater commitment to the under prepared student; and
- An array of supplemental support programs such as first year transition courses, per tutoring centers, computer assisted tutoring, and mentoring programs.

There is little evidence to suggest that developmental education will decline importance in the coming years. More and more students are entering college with weak academic skills. Some taxpayers, however, wonder why they must pay twice for educational preparation. They argue that high schools should be held accountable for preparing students for college rather than supporting remediation programs at community colleges. Removing all support for remediation at the college level will not solve the problem. State University has chosen to work more closely with secondary schools in identifying the skills needed to succeed in college and in developing the appropriate curriculum. Moreover, State University has asked community colleges to strengthen their assessment programs and to enhance their academic support services to assure student success.

Task Force: College Entry-Level Knowledge and Skills

The problem of the underprepared high school graduate is a growing national issue. More and more faculty are voicing concern about the weak academic skills of students. Colleges are responding by implementing supplemental support programs like the educational opportunity program (EOP), tutoring centers, and mentoring programs, and they are also working more closely with secondary schools.

In October 1992, the task force published its findings regarding college transition. Among other things, the task force recommended the development and implementation of a high school senior level college preparatory course to:
- Teach time management skills;
- Develop effective study techniques;
- Introduce students to college level expectations and resources; and
- Serve as the capstone assessment course for graduating students.

Ten high schools in the state have been selected to pilot the course. Teachers across the state are currently being trained to implement the course in their high school's curriculum. The plan is to distribute the course to all high schools by the end of 1997. State University is working very closely with secondary schools in an attempt to strengthen the high school curriculum and make the transition to college more successful.

Task Force: Distance Learning

Distance learning has been around since the early days of the postal service. The term is used to describe numerous situations in which learners and teachers are separated geographically or temporarily. The president's task force on distance learning (1995) was grounded in the assumption that

State University and higher education will undergo significant change related to:

- The introduction of technological innovations;
- The development of new instructional technologies; and
- Changes in the delivery of educational services.

Community colleges, compared to other institutions of higher education, are quickly moving ahead in using technology to improve teaching and enhance learning. Low-tech telecourses have grown considerably in the last few years. More sophisticated technology, such as computer conferencing, has enhanced the relationship and interaction among students and faculty in distance learning programs. Many community colleges have developed two-way interactive telecommunication systems to maximize resources and deliver cost-effective instruction. Libraries are developing on-line reference services for off-campus students.

Adult learners, with employment and child rearing responsibilities, are particularly attracted to distance learning programs. Over half of the state's community colleges are located in rural areas. Many students living in these areas would not have enrolled in college if it weren't for distance learning programs. Today, community colleges are planning to offer full degree programs by distance learning. Tomorrow, students in the eastern part of the state will be able to pursue degrees with institutions in the western part of the state through distance learning. Eventually, students from outside New York, and the country, will pursue State University degrees.

At the same time the president's task force was conducting its investigation, the university senate formed its own group to look at distance learning from the perspective of faculty. The senate's report (1995) joined in the excitement over distance learning and concluded that students in distance learning programs did just as well as students in traditional instructional programs. The group, however, noted that attrition tended to be higher in distance learning programs. This may be attributed to job conflicts, personal problems, or the structure of the distance learning program.

SUMMARY

Since 1995, community colleges have lost approximately $20 million dollars in state tax dollar support. Although community colleges are staged to endure their most difficult period, they remain steadfast in their commitment to provide convenient access to a quality education at the lowest possible cost. In spite of serious fiscal problems, State University's community colleges are a vital part of the system of higher education in the state. They are conveniently located and moderate in cost, giving thousands of people the chance to succeed whether or not they have had a record of prior success.

Students seek community colleges as an opportunity to gain a meaningful career, to obtain the first half of an undergraduate education, to learn new skills for the workplace, or to learn for the pure enjoyment of learning.

With 30 community colleges around the state, students are virtually guaranteed access. Off-campus instructional sites, and distance learning programs have developed many more students attend college.

Pressure to demonstrate efficiency will increase. State legislative emphasis upon accountability will have an impact on many collegiate activities. State University is committed to a process of self-review, reporting on its achievements as well as its shortcomings. Although problems exist, community colleges have been one of New York's greatest success stories. There is, however, much to be done.

Community colleges face the difficult challenge of implementing technological change during a time of unprecedented fiscal restraint. Retention is becoming more of a concern on many community college campuses. Although State University community college attrition rates are lower than the national average, too many students are dropping out as easily as they dropped in. Many more are taking longer periods of time to complete the degree process. Community college leaders will spend considerable effort at identifying ways to help students complete the degree in a more timely manner.

Technology will change the ways teachers and students go about their work and the ways they interact with each other. Soon, every faculty member and student will have a personal computer and a college VAX account. Teachers will interact with their students frequently through electronic mail services. Lectures will be supplemented with multimedia presentations. Textbooks will look like compact disks. More libraries will utilize online, computerized networks. The Internet will become more popular than network television.

Colleges will look for new ways to deliver instruction to an older, more diverse, student body. More students will receive college level instruction at high schools and at their place of employment.

Approximately one-half of today's faculty will retire a little after the year 2000. Tomorrow's faculty will be more diverse, increasingly female, younger, and familiar with instructional technology and courseware.

Economic development will continue to be a priority in New York. Because of their close ties to businesses, community colleges will be key to restoring New York's economy. Many leaders are already convinced that State University community colleges are one of the state's most intelligent investments.

REFERENCES

Bosco, J. (1995). Update: The Economic Impact of SUNY's *Community Colleges on the State of New York. Albany*: State University of New York.

Burke, J. (1994). *Performance Indicators Report*. Albany: State University of New York.

Clark, D. (1991). *Analysis of Return Rates of the Inmate College Program Participants*. Albany: Department of Correctional Services.

Johnstone, B. (1993). *Enhancing the Productivity of Learning: An Imperative for American Higher Education*. Albany: State University of New York.

Martens, F. (1985). *The Historical Development of the Community Colleges of the State University Of New York*. Albany: Office for Community Colleges, State University of New York.

New York State, *Education Law*. Section 6301.2.

State University. (1964). *The Master Plan Revised*. Albany: State University of New York.

State University. (1967). *Progress Report and Interim Revision of the Master Plan for 1964*. Albany: State University of New York.

State University. (1992). Task Force: *College Entry-Level Knowledge and Skills. Albany*: State University of New York.

State University. (1995). Task Force: *The Underprepared Student*. Albany: State University of New York.

State University. (1995). *Distance Learning: The President's Task Force Report*. Albany: StateUniversity of New York.

State University. (1995). *Distance Learning: Interim Report of the University Faculty Senate*. Albany: State University of New York.

State University. (1996). Chancellor's Task Force on *Community Colleges. Albany*: State University of New York.

FOR ADDITIONAL INFORMATION, PLEASE CONTACT:
Director, Community College Education Services
State University of New York
State University Plaza, T-705
Albany, New York 12246
Telephone: (578) 443-5134

NORTH CAROLINA

H. Martin Lancaster
President, North Carolina Community College System

OVERVIEW

The North Carolina Community College System (NCCCS) is the third largest community college system in the country, made up of 59 institutions across the state that serve over 710,000 students (unduplicated headcount). The system's mission is to open the door to opportunity by providing education and training for the workforce, support for economic development and services to communities and individuals.

The NCCCS is the primary agency for the delivery of job training, literacy and adult education in North Carolina. It is committed to providing the state with a well-trained workforce to meet the needs of employers and to help attract new and expanding industry in the state. College transfer programs are available, and the system has made a commitment to provide literacy training for adults which has resulted in a comprehensive collection of training and educational opportunities.

With every North Carolinian within 30 miles of a community college or satellite center, the state's community colleges are accessible as well as affordable. Admission is open to any individual who is at least 18 years of age. Although nearly one-third of all high school seniors will enroll at one of the state's community colleges, the average student in the NCCCS is 29.7 years old in the curriculum program and 37.8 in the extension program. Student ages range from 16 to over 70, tuition is waived for state residents 65 or older. Two-thirds of the students work while attending school.

The community colleges train 95% of the state's firefighters and more than 80% of the state's law enforcement officers, and can boast high scores on many state exams. The passing rate for the community colleges' associate degree nursing and practical nursing students taking licensure exams has consistently been about 94%, higher than that of students from the State's universities.

The North Carolina Community College System was ranked first in workforce preparedness by *Expansion Management* magazine. Top site selection consultants around the country were asked to list state with the best training programs. They cited the fact that North Carolina offers training that "helps companies get results on a consistent basis."

This powerhouse system of today originally developed out of necessity as North Carolina began to shift from an agricultural to an industrial economy. Much like today, people who may have felt they had no need for a four-year baccalaureate education certainly needed something beyond high school.

North Carolina's system of comprehensive community and technical colleges was developed by the North Carolina General Assembly in 1963, when legislators enacted G.S. 115A (later changed to 115D) to bring together an existing network of industrial education centers and a system of public junior colleges. The institutions included six community colleges, 20 industrial education centers and five extension units. At the time, the system was administered by the North Carolina Department of Community Colleges under the North Carolina State Board of Education.

The action, creating the North Carolina Department of Community Colleges, went into effect on July 1, 1963, following the recommendation of the Governor's Commission on Education Beyond the High School, appointed by Governor Terry Sanford. The system got its start with $1 million in its 1963-65, budget with an additional expansion budget in 1964 of $2.5 million.

The statutory mission and purpose of the North Carolina Community College System, as defined in G.S. 115D, is for:

> ". . . the establishment, organization, and administration of a
> system of educational institutions throughout the state offering
> courses of instruction in one or more of the general areas of
> two-year college parallel, technical, vocational and adult edu-
> cation programs. . ."

The law continues:

> "The major purpose of each and every institution operating
> under the provisions of this Chapter shall be and shall continue
> to be the offering of vocational and technical education and
> training, and of basic, high school level, academic education
> needed in order to profit from vocational and technical educa-
> tion, for students who are high school graduates or who are
> beyond the compulsory age limit of the public school system
> and who have left the public schools."

The 1997-98 year was the first year in which the NCCCS used the semester system instead of the quarter system. In addition, it was the first year of implementing a re-engineering of the curriculum programs. A common course library was developed and a comprehensive transfer agreement with the University of North Carolina has been established. Mandated by the Legislature in 1995, the project involved more than 1,200 faculty members from across the state working in teams to write requirements and descriptions for about 3,800 courses. Their work included cutting the 281 program titles by about a third by dropping some dated programs and grouping others into categories.

The system office has had six presidents: I. E. Ready (1963-1970); Ben E. Fountain, Jr. (1971-1978); Larry J. Blake (1979-1982); Robert W. Scott (1983-1994); Lloyd V. Hackley (January 1995-1997); and H. Martin Lancaster (1997 to present). Charles R. Holloman served in an acting capacity from September, 1978 to July, 1979.

The general assembly changed the state-level control of the System in 1979 by creating a provision for a separate State Board of Community Colleges. The board became fully operational in 1981.

GOVERNANCE

The North Carolina State Board of Community Colleges was established by the 1979 North Carolina General Assembly and it assumed governance of the 58 community colleges and the North Carolina Center for Applied Textile Technology in Belmont, N.C., on January 1, 1981. Prior to that date, the System was governed by the North Carolina State Board of Education.

The board has full authority to adopt all policies, regulations and standards it deems necessary to operate the system. The board establishes standards and scales for salaries paid from funds administered by the state board, and for employees exempt from the State Personnel Act.

The State Board requires that all community colleges meet the faculty credential requirements of the Southern Association of Colleges and Schools for all Community College programs. Also, a community college is not allowed to offer a new program without the approval of the state board unless the tuition for the program will fully cover the cost of the program.

The North Carolina Community College System office serves as a resource agency and as an administrative arm of the state board.

The board consists of 20 members: 10 appointed by the governor (four members-at-large and one member from each of the six trustee association regions). Four members-at-large are elected by the North Carolina Senate, and four members-at-large are elected by the North Carolina House of Representatives. The lieutenant governor and state treasurer are ex officio members. A Chair and a vice chair are elected at the July meeting in each odd-numbered year, and they serve two-year terms. Members elect a board chair to serve as the board's leader, spokesperson and presiding officer. The chair is responsible for projecting the public image of the board and for providing positive leadership.

The board's membership should reflect the population of the state in terms of race, age, sex, ethnic origin, economic and social background and the geographical distribution of the state. Members represent business, industry, education and government.

No person may be appointed or elected to more than two consecutive terms of six years on the state board. No member of the general assembly, no officer or employee of the state, and no officer or employee of an institution under the jurisdiction of the state board and no spouse of any of those persons, shall be eligible to serve on the state board. Also, no person who within the prior five years has been an employee of the community college system is eligible to serve on the state board.

The North Carolina State Board of Community Colleges uses a committee structure. It has five committees: Policy, Finance and Capital Needs, Program Services, Legislative and Personnel. The state board chair appoints members and chairs for each committee.

The board meets at least 10 times per year to evaluate the recommendations of the North Carolina Community College System, to set policy for the system and to oversee its operation. The board also meets with the North Carolina State Board of Education (which serves kindergarten through 12th grade) and the board of governors of The University of North Carolina at least once a year to discuss educational matters of mutual interest and to recommend to the general assembly policies appropriate to encourage the improvement of public education at every level of the state.

The North Carolina Community College System, headed by the system president, provides state-level administration and leadership of the community college system under the direction of the state board of community colleges.

The State Board has three major functions: (1) equitable distribution of funds and fiscal accountability, (2) establishing and maintaining state priorities, and (3) educational program approval and accountability.

Through the exercise of its authority in these areas, the board can recommit the System to existing policies or alter the direction of the system through changes in policy.

As part of its administrative function, the system office provides support services for the various program offerings such as nursing, agriculture, and business. The system president's staff assists staff at the colleges by helping to develop and implement curriculums and other programs, and by providing technical assistance in a range of areas. Also, the system office provides other services for the system that would be difficult for an individual institution to initiate, such as statewide data collection.

At the local level, each of the colleges operates under a board of trustees. Each board is composed of a minimum of twelve citizens from the service area in which the college is located. The president or chairman of the executive board of the student body serves as an ex-officio member. Local board members are appointed for staggered four-year terms. Four members each are elected by the local school board and the board of commissioners of the county in which the institution is located. Four members are appointed by the governor.

The board of trustees sets local policy. The local board selects and the State Board must approve selection of each college's president. The president operates the college within state policies and policies adopted by the local trustees. Administrative decisions, such as employment of faculty members, are made by the president. All personnel employed at the colleges are employees of the college and not of the State of North Carolina.

The state board can withdraw or withhold state financial and administrative support from any institution if the required local financial support is not provided, if sufficient state money is not available, if the officials of an institution refuses or is unable to maintain the prescribed standards of administration or instruction, or if the local educational needs for such an institution ceases to exist.

FUNDING

The North Carolina State Board of Community Colleges is responsible for providing funds to meet the financial needs of the institutions as determined by policies and regulations of the state board, according to North Carolina law. The state board has delegated its authority to the local trustees to disburse the funds within the state board's policies and regulations.

The budget items that are part of the state board's responsibility include the plant fund, which covers furniture and equipment for administrative and instructional purposes, library books and other items of capital outlay approved by the state board. Also, the items include current operating expenses, such as general administration costs, instructional services and support services. And it includes additional support for regional institutions, such as matching funds that will be used with local funds.

The state board can accept and reallocate federal funds or aid. Also, state funds appropriated to the North Carolina State Board of Community Colleges for equipment and library books must revert to the General Fund 12 months after the close of the fiscal year for which the money was appropriated.

Funding for the general operations of the colleges comes primarily from four general sources, state tax appropriations, local tax support, student tuition and fees and miscellaneous other sources. State appropriations account for two-thirds of the System-wide funding, with the 1998-99 revenues source listed as follows:

State	75.5%
Local	13.1%
Tuition and Fees	8.4%
Federal	2.3%
Other	0.7%

The colleges vary in their reliance on these revenue sources, primarily because of variations in local support from county governments in the local service areas. County appropriations to the local colleges range from 5% to 20.4%. State appropriations range from 59.2% to 77.5%.

The largest part of the state appropriations are distributed to the colleges based on a formula adopted by the state board. Other money comes from the legislature and federal government for special purposes.

The current funding model is a collection of separate formulas for about 16 program areas that can be broken down as instructional programs, business/industry and other outreach programs and support programs, according to MGT of America, Inc., a Tallahassee, Florida consulting firm that recently studied the funding formula. Money the colleges get from full-time equivalent students cannot be used for utilities or plant maintenance so the colleges must find other money for the expenditures.

The funding formula for the community college instructional program determines the number of personnel units and total amount of operating funds available for instruction at each community college. Allotments are based on the average enrollment of the past two years or the latest year, whichever is greater. Curriculum instruction programs use the average of the fall, winter and spring/projected spring full-time-equivalent students as the enrollment base and the continuing education programs use the average of the spring, summer, fall and winter FTE as their enrollment base for funding. The primary difference in approach is the inclusion of summer FTE for continuing education.

The projected spring FTE for the curriculum instruction programs must be certified by the College president at the end of the 30% reporting date. Adjustments are made to increase or decrease FTE enrollment levels to reflect differences between projected and actual spring FTE enrollment for curriculum instruction. If the general assembly fails to fund FTE at the requested amount, then each college receives a prorated share.

An example of funding for support programs is that the salary for college presidents is based on a statewide salary schedule and includes benefits. Each community college board of trustees has the option of supplementing its president's salary above its statewide allotment.

In another example, the administrative and instructional support, each community college receives both a base allotment and an enrollment-generated allotment. The base allotment is based on the staff needed to serve the first 750 full-time equivalent students and the enrollment allotment generates dollars for each FTE student in excess of the first 750. The administrative and instruction support components include salaries, employee benefits and other costs. The total number of positions generated within the base allotment for each college totals 30 positions.

In addition, the State Board approves budget requests and the allotment of funds to colleges for equipment based upon recommendation by the NCCCS. The distributions to colleges are based on an equipment-full-time-equivalent (EFTE), determined by adding specific category ratios to the FTE for the preceding calendar year and adding the products to obtain a sum for each college. Each college receives a base allotment of $100,000 and colleges with high-cost programs receive an average of the actual expenditures over the past three years with the balance of the appropriation distributed based on the weighted EFTE.

Another example, the library formula, uses the same theory. It uses a library-weighted- full-time-equivalent enrollment count, the current collection is compared to the standard-book entitlement. The allocation includes components for maintenance of the existing collection and expansion.

Current tuition is $20 per credit hour up to 14 hours for spring/fall semesters, with $280 as the maximum tuition charged per semester for in-state students, and up to 9 credit hours for summer session, with a $180/maximum. For out-of state students, the tuition is $163 per credit hour with $2,282 as the maximum tuition for the spring/fall semesters and a $1,467 maximum for the summer session. Tuition is kept low to make sure that people in the community have access to community college services. Also, the colleges increase access through state and federal aid for grants, loans and scholarships. Numerous private companies have established scholarship funds to aid in a student's education.

North Carolina's fiscal year runs from July 1 to June 30.

The North Carolina Community Colleges Foundation, Inc.

The North Carolina Community College System has realized a need to attract support from large companies and corporations whose presence in North Carolina is pervasive and not related to any particular college. The NCCCF was established to provide an avenue to large donors who depend on the community college system for many of their employees. The foundation is not a competitor with local institutional foundations, but rather a resource to be used in increasing local support.

The NCCCF was chartered on September 11, 1986, and was revitalized in February, 1999. The primary mission of the NCCCF is to support the mission of the North Carolina Community College System, to provide an alternative vehicle for contributions to the NCCCS, and to communicate to the public the system's mission and responsiveness to local needs.

PROGRAMS AND ENROLLMENTS

The North Carolina Community College System offers a comprehensive range of educational programs to meet the needs of local communities for employment skills, basic educational skills, job retraining, higher academic education, personal growth and development, and community and economic development.

One area, curriculum programs, offers credit courses leading to certificates, diplomas or associate of applied science degrees. There are more than 1,800 curriculum programs, with more than 200 curriculum curriculum titles. These programs range in length from certificate programs, usually one semester to two years for some diploma programs. The majority of the programs lead to an associate of applied science degree. Programs include business and office skills, nursing and allied health, engineering technologies, transportation technologies and technical industrial occupations. Also, the system offers a significant number of trade and industry programs leading to certificates or diplomas in such areas as construction trades, machine and metalworking occupations and industrial maintenance occupations. Arts and science and general education programs provide academic courses parallel to the first two years of baccalaureate degree programs and are designed for transfer at the junior level into senior colleges or universities.

Developmental education programs are also provided by the colleges. These include, but are not limited to, diagnostic assessment and placement, tutoring, advising, and writing assistance. These courses are non-credit, but do provide the student with courses which prepare them for academic involvement. The course are available for students who need to improve their skills so that they can perform at the level required for college transfer, certificate, diploma and associate degree programs.

Each college offers instruction in basic academic skills and instructional support. Programs include Adult Basic Education (ABE) (K-8 basic literacy skills), Adult High School Diploma (AHS) and General Educational Development (GED) programs (9-12 academic preparation), English as a Second Language (ESL) and Compensatory Education (CED). Students participate in developmental studies courses to prepare them to master collegiate-level course work and study through individualized learning laboratories. The system provides educational opportunities through its major literacy components which consist of 14,197 classes located at work sites, churches, community centers, schools, libraries, sheltered workshops, prisons and the community college campuses.

The associate in general education programs, offered by 35 colleges, are designed for individuals wishing to broaden their education, with emphasis on personal interest, growth and development. The two-year general education program provides college-level courses in English, literature, fine arts, science and mathematics. Though not principally designed for college transfer, they are equivalent to college transfer courses.

Community colleges do offer college transfer programs through the associate in arts, associate in fine arts and associate in science degrees. These are part of the Comprehensive Articulation Agreement (CAA), which addresses the transfer of students between institutions in the NCCCS and the constituent institutions of the University of North Carolina.

Another broad category of programs is continuing education. These non-credit courses may be occupational, academic or avocational in nature. Some are offered as a categorically funded community service. Others are designed to upgrade occupational skills and are funded through enrollment-driven formulas. These courses help the system reach the part of its basic mission that deals with lifelong learning for North Carolinians. Continuing education programs offer numerous opportunities for personal growth. Among these are specific job training and retraining, literacy education and improved use of leisure time.

The Job Training Partnership Act, a federal law enacted in 1982 and amended in 1993, established programs to prepare youth and adults facing serious barriers to employment for participation in the labor force. The job training and support services increase the chances of the eligible individuals obtaining employment and earning higher wages. Individuals who are considered economically disadvantaged, 16 or older, who have certain barriers to employment are usually eligible to participate in a JTPA program. Education and training services include basic skills training, pre-employment skills training, occupational skills training and employment exploration. The services help to decrease welfare dependency, thereby improving the quality of the workforce and enhancing the productivity and competitiveness.

The Carl D. Perkins Vocational and Applied Technology Education Act is designed to make the United States more competitive in the world economy by developing more fully the academic and occupational skills of all segments of the population. This purpose is expected to be achieved through concentrating resources on improving educational programs leading to academic, occupational, training and retraining skill competencies needed to work in a technologically-advanced society.

Correctional education includes classes offered by the North Carolina Community College System to people in facilities operated by the North Carolina Department of Corrections, The Department of Human Resources juvenile training schools, federal prisons and local jails. In 1997-98, 45 community colleges offered instruction to students in North Carolina correctional facilities. Correctional education enrollment totaled 40, 282 in extension (continuing education) and 29,133 in curriculum programs.

Also, the system licenses proprietary schools. Such schools are for-profit businesses which provide education and training. They may be privately owned, a partnership or a corporation. There were 35 licensed schools for the 1997-1998 period.

The North Carolina State Board of Community Colleges is charged with the responsibility for licensing certain proprietary businesses, trade and correspondence schools in North Carolina. This responsibility was transferred from the North Carolina State Board of Education by the General Assembly in 1987.

The North Carolina Center for Applied Textile Technology was established in 1943 as the first vocational school in the state. From the early 1970s, the center was dependent upon the North Carolina Community College System to handle state funds appropriated to the center. Then, in 1990, the state board of community colleges designated the center as a full-fledged, autonomous member of the system.

The center specializes in curriculum and extension instruction designed specifically for the textile industry and is the only school of its kind in North Carolina. Located in Belmont (Gaston County), N.C., the school's campus is nestled within the largest concentration of textile manufacturing plants in the world. Unlike its community college system counterparts, the center's service area is not restricted to Gaston or surrounding counties. The center serves the entire state. Curriculum and continuing education students come from all over North Carolina, other states and foreign countries.

One of the major missions of the community college system is to provide opportunities for the citizens to prepare for new occupational opportunities or to upgrade their knowledge and skills in their current employment. These occupational extension opportunities are provided through single courses or a series of courses specifically designed for an occupation.

The courses can be used for training an individual for employment, upgrading the skills of people presently employed or retraining others for new employment in occupational fields. They are offered to people in all technical or vocational occupations and vary in length according to the complexity of the skill and the need of the employee or employer. Most occupational extension courses are developed and taught on request from a group or an employer. Courses are usually offered at a time and place convenient to the employee and/or employer.

Community service programs are designed to provide courses, seminars and activities that contribute to the community's overall cultural, civic and intellectual growth and assist adults in the development of new skills or the upgrading of existing ones in their academic, avocational and practical skills areas.

For 28 years, the Human Resources Development Program (HRD) has offered pre-employment training, counseling and assistance in placement in jobs or further training for unemployed and underemployed adults in North Carolina. Since 1975, enrollment has totaled 165, 033 students. HRD training focuses on the development of basic workplace skills which are key to employment readiness. The skills include job readiness skills, interpersonal skills and group effectiveness, motivation and goal-setting skills, listening and oral communication skills, problem-solving skills, and assessment of career and employment goals.

In 1997-1998, the system had the following enrollment in its programs:

Full-time equivalent students	137,868 total
Extension	16,998
Curriculum	107,515
Literacy	13,355
Headcount Students (Unduplicated)	748,082 total
Curriculum	211,440
Extension	536,462

ECONOMIC DEVELOPMENT

The North Carolina Community College System is the primary agency for delivery of job training and literacy and adult education in the state. It provides training through a variety of programs designed to help business and industry as well as the citizens of the state.

More than 30 years ago, North Carolina created a new kind of economic development tool: company-specific customized training. It was the first state to recognize that training people for specific jobs in specific companies was a legitimate enterprise for a responsible and responsive government. North Carolina Community College's systems New Industry Training Program is a win-win-win situation that is as relevant to today's complex and sophisticated operations as it was to that first modest program in 1958. The new jobs are a "win" for the community, a skilled and motivated workforce is a "win" for the company, and new skills to meet the challenges of a new job are a "win" for the individual.

Good training has resulted in advantages that have put North Carolina at the top in the nation for new plants in four out of the last five years, sustaining a trend that has made the state a leading manufacturing state. The surprising fact is that no other state has a higher proportion of its workforce employed in manufacturing operations. Other advantages that make the state a hard-to-ignore option are an ideal location within easy reach of the world's major markets and the transportation systems to reach them; equitable and consistent tax policies; some of the nation's lowest construction and operating costs; a public university system that is the envy of the Southeast; and an abundant, bright, and loyal workforce. In short, a dynamic and supportive business climate that makes North Carolina a smart move for employers.

Focused Industrial Training (FIT) is a special training program for North Carolina's traditional industries. Serving primarily manufacturing clients, FIT uses individualized needs assessments and consultations to design and implement targeted, customized training for organizations that need to upgrade workers' skills because of technological or process advances.

The program is designed to serve the special needs of existing North Carolina industry. This program, along with the state's award-winning training program for new businesses, keeps North Carolina's economy strong and healthy by keeping companies strong and healthy.   Since 1981, FIT has trained more than 122,000 people, served 11,000 companies and offered 7,500 different courses.

The North Carolina Community College Small Business Center Network (SBCN) consists of a small business center at each of the state's 58 community colleges. These centers provide a wide variety of seminars and workshops, one-on-one counseling, a library of resources, and referrals as well as other sources of help to owners and operators of small businesses.

The mission of each center is to help the many small businesses within its service area survive, prosper, and contribute to the economic well-being of the community and the state. This service, supported exclusively with state funds, began with eight centers in 1984. Since then, it has grown gradually; the last five colleges joined the network in 1994. Each center receives an annual grant of approximately $61,193.

The In-Plant Training Program enables the colleges to assist manufacturing, service and/or governmental organizations with in service training of their employees. This occupational extension training includes involvement in five areas: industry, business, health, government and agriculture. Training occurs in the facilities or at the site in which an organization normally operates and at the employee's assigned work station. This method of delivering skills training works for companies when it is not feasible to duplicate the training environment in an institutional setting.

In 1996, the North Carolina General Assembly passed the William S. Lee Quality Jobs Act, a package of tax credits aimed at supporting high wage economic development in North Carolina. As part of this act, a Worker Training Tax Credit was passed that requires certification of employers through the North Carolina Community College System.

ACCOUNTABILITY

Educational institutions across the nation are being held accountable for their actions as never before. Federal legislation in the form of the Campus Security and Right to Know Act and Carl Perkins Act regulations have caused colleges to look more closely not just at the process of what they are doing, but also at the end product — the outcomes of their actions. The North Carolina General Assembly, in examining budget requests, is keenly interested in the return on the state's investment in the community colleges. Accrediting agencies, the chief of which is the Southern Association of Colleges and Schools (SACS), have made demonstrated institutional effectiveness a major factor in the accreditation or reaffirmation of a college. The North Carolina State Board of Community Colleges has adopted, as one of four system goals, the goal of Accountability and Standards.

Accountability for the Community College System is shared by the state board, the local boards, state and local administrative staffs and faculty. Each has responsibilities for which it is held accountable. A well-organized and managed system can provide appropriate authority and resources at each level and hold each group appropriately accountable.

The entire process of planning, program review, evaluation of results and the system's publication, Critical Success Factors, make up an essential part of the comprehensive accountability system. Traditionally, accountability has been defined primarily in terms of accountability for funds, but three additional measures indicate how programs are managed.

The measures include Annual Educational Program Audit Summary — Number Audited and Percent of System Instructional Budget Cited for Exceptions; Number and Percent of Programs Reviewed; and Number and

Percent of Eligible Programs Accredited or Reaffirmed.

REFERENCES

Caruthers, J. Kent (1999). *Assessment of the Funding Formula Used by the North Carolina Community College System.* MGT of America, Inc., Raleigh, North Carolina Community College System.

North Carolina State Board of Community Colleges (1998). *Community College Laws of North Carolina.*

North Carolina Statutes, Chapter 115D, Charlottesville, VA: The Michie Company.

Planning & Research (1999). *A Matter of Facts. North Carolina Community College System.* Raleigh, N.C.: North Carolina Community College System: Author

Planning & Research. 1998 Critical Success Factors. *North Carolina Community College System.* Raleigh, N.C.: North Carolina Community College System: Author

Program Services. *Education Guide Catalog 1997-1998.* Raleigh, N.C.: Author

Wiggs, Jon Lee (1989). *The Community College System in North Carolina: A Silver Anniversary History, 1963-1988.* Raleigh, N.C.

FOR ADDITIONAL INFORMATION, PLEASE CONTACT:
North Carolina Community College System
Caswell Building
200 West Jones Street
Raleigh, North Carolina 27603-1379
Telephone: (919) 733-7051
Website http://www.ncccs.cc.nc.us

NORTH DAKOTA

Terrence A. Tollefson
Professor, Department of Educational Leadership and Policy Analysis
East Tennessee State University

OVERVIEW

The North Dakota State School of Science, the state's first two-year college, was established in 1903. (Blom, in Tollefson & Fountain, 1992). the North Dakota Legislative Assembly adopted Senate Bill 209 in 1931, to authorize the establishment of public two-year colleges. Three colleges were created under this act, including Bismarck State College in 1939, the University of North Dakota—Lake Region in 1941, and the University of North Dakota—Williston in 1961. In addition to the North Dakota State School of Science, the other two-year public institution that was established before the state authorizing legislation was enacted was the Bottineau Branch of North Dakota State University, established in 1907 (Dunn & Lindstrom, 1997).

GOVERNANCE

The North Dakota Board of Higher Education, in Bismarck, is the governing and coordinating body for public higher education, including community colleges. (Blom, in Tollefson & Fountain, 1992). The five public community colleges enrolled an estimated 7,000 students in 1998, and five tribal community colleges had about 900 students enrolled (Tollefson & Patton, 1998).

FUNDING

The North Dakota legislature appropriated approximately $25 million in general fund revenues to the public community colleges for 1998-99 fiscal year. (Tollefson & Patton, 1998).

WORKFORCE DEVELOPMENT

The North Dakota community colleges also work closely with and receive federal vocational funds from the North Dakota State Board for Vocational Technical Education (SBVTE). The College Technical Education Subcouncil (CTEC) was established in 1992 to increase cooperation and coordination among secondary and postsecondary institutions, SBVTE and other state agencies concerned with workforce development (Dunn & Lidstrom, 1997). A "major shift" in community college enrollments into workforce development programs is occurring. Although workforce development was not funded by the state in years through fiscal 1998-99, consideration is being given for doing so in this "exploding" area. (Tollefson & Patton, 1998, p. 69).

REFERENCES

Blom, N. S. (1992). North Dakota, in Tollefson & Fountain. *Forty-Nine State Systems*, 1992 Edition, p. 162. Washington, DC: American Association of Community Colleges.

Dunn, E. & Lidstrom, K. (1997, September). The origin, nature and vision of community colleges, in North Dakota, in *Community College Journal of Research and Practice*, 21(6), pp. 591-600.

Tollefson, T. A. & Patton, M. (1998). North Dakota, in *AACC Annual 1998-99*, pp. 69-70. Washington, DC: American Association of Community Colleges.

FOR ADDITIONAL INFORMATION, PLEASE CONTACT:

Office of the Chancellor
North Dakota University System
State Capitol, Tenth Floor
600 East Boulevard Avenue
Bismarck, ND 58505
Telephone: (701) 328-2960

OHIO

Rayma E. Smith
Director of Degree Programs and Undergraduate Issues
Ohio Board of Regents

OVERVIEW

In partnership with local communities, state lawmakers have created a public two-year college system to serve the post-high school educational needs of Ohioans. Geographically dispersed within commuting distance of nearly every Ohioan, the two-year college system includes 15 community colleges, 8 technical colleges, and 30 regional campuses of Universities. All but the university regional campuses are governed by independent boards of trustees whose membership comes from the districts within which the campuses are located.

The core mission of Ohio's public two-year campuses, as mandated by the General Assembly, is to serve the postsecondary education and training needs of citizens through college transfer and career/technical degree programs, workforce training and retraining, and noncredit continuing education courses and programs.

In 1961, on the advice of the Ohio Interim Commission on Education Beyond the High School, the Ohio General Assembly enacted legislation that provided for expansion of postsecondary educational opportunities in several ways: county governments were authorized to create community colleges subject to approval of a new state agency (Ohio Community College Board); school boards were authorized to create technical institutes offering a postsecondary programs in technical education; and counties were authorized to establish university branch districts to help finance facilities for university branch campuses. Following the General Assembly's creation of the Ohio Board of Regents in 1963, authority for approval of the establishment of two-year campuses was subsequently transferred from the Ohio State Department of Education to the regents. By 1971, all of the technical colleges that presently exist in Ohio were chartered; by 1975, seven of the state's community colleges were in place. Since 1986, the Ohio Board of Regents has converted eight technical colleges to comprehensive community colleges.

GOVERNANCE

The Ohio Board of Regents is responsible for the planning and coordination of Ohio's public universities and two-year campuses. Established in 1963, the Board has nine citizen members and two ex-officio nonvoting legislative members. Regents are appointed by the governor for nine-year terms and serve without compensation. Nonvoting ex-officio members are the Chairs of the Education Committees of the Ohio Senate and the Ohio House of Representatives.

A staff of approximately 60 professional and support personnel assists the board in fulfilling its statutory responsibilities. All staff serve under the direction of Chancellor Roderick G.W. Chu, the board's chief administrative officer, who was appointed to the post in January, 1998. The regents, the chancellor, and the chancellor's staff work closely with state officials, the General Assembly, and the leadership of both public and independent colleges and universities in fulfilling their responsibilities.

FUNDING

Funds for the operating support of Ohio's state-assisted two-year campuses are derived primarily from the state instructional subsidy (63.9%) and students (33.5%). Only 2.6% of operating funds are obtained from such other sources as private gifts and grants, endowments, or sales and services.

The state instructional subsidy is distributed by a formula that is driven by programs, enrollments, and physical facilities. The formula included system for protecting an institution from sudden and dramatic enrollment decline and assuring financial stability. Only six campuses (five community colleges and one technical college) have local tax levies for operating support.

The annual in-state student instructional and general fees among the community colleges and technical colleges range from a low of $1,398 (in-district fees for an institution with a local tax levy) to $3,000. Fees for university regional campuses generally are related to those of the universities, with annual regional campuses fees ranging from a low of $2,940 to a high of $3,573 (based on fall 1998 data). Each state-assisted institution is governed by an independent board of trustees, which has the authority to set fee schedules. In recent years, the general assembly has set limits on fee increases.

PROGRAMS

Ohio's two-year campuses offer a variety of two-year programs with the following degree designations: associate of applied science, associate of applied business, associate of technical studies, associate of arts, and associate of science.

ENROLLMENT

Both headcount and full-time-equivalent (FTE) student counts are available for the study of enrollment patterns. The definition of a fall term FTE assumes a 15 credit-hour load, so that FTE is calculated by dividing the total student credit hours by 15. All counts include credit activity only. Noncredit activity such as continuing education is excluded.

In the Fall of 1997, slightly more than 167,000 students were enrolled in Ohio's community colleges, technical colleges, and university branch campuses. Although Ohio's student data base does not distinguish student goals, historical enrollment patterns are depicted in Tables 1 and 2.

Table 1 Headcount Enrollment by Associate Degree Program				
	1997	1990	1985	1980
Business Technologies	32,872	41,808	47,700	44,938
Health Technologies	24,700	25,182	16,866	16,287
Engineering Technologies	16,203	20,439	19,810	20.762
Natural Science Technologies	2,569	2,462	2,043	2,129
Public Service Technologies	12,336	9,812	5,630	7,240
College Transfer	78,949	60,810	43,658	41,317
TOTAL	167,629	160,513	135,707	132,673

Table 2 FTE by Associate Degree Program				
	1997	1990	1985	1980
Business Technologies	16,003	20,912	21,608	22,037
Health Technologies	7,882	8,769	6,905	5,934
Engineering Technologies	6,333	8,050	8,674	9,043
Natural Science Technologies	1,245	1,252	1,079	1,355
Public Service Technologies	4,411	5,458	3,454	3,359
College Transfer	74,789	47,407	35,689	36,019
TOTAL	100,663	91,848	77,409	77,747

Student enrollment in Ohio's two-year colleges has steadily increased over the past five years. Although student enrollments in business, health, and engineering technologies have declined somewhat over this period, there has been significant growth in college transfer programs, attributable primarily to the conversion of eight technical colleges to comprehensive community colleges over the past 12 years.

ECONOMIC DEVELOPMENT

Ohio's public two-year campuses have a solid history of partnering with business, labor, government, and other educational institutions to provide education and training services targeted at building the skills of Ohio's workforce and improving organizational performance. Ohio's public two-year campuses are active partners with Ohio School-to-Work, Ohio One-Stop Employment and Training Centers, Ohio Works First, and Tech Prep as they seek to meet current and future needs for skilled workers.

Since 1986, representatives from Ohio's two-year campuses have been working collaboratively through the EnterpriseOhio Network to expand their collective capability to provide the customized training required by Ohio enterprises. By helping employers develop and sustain a world class workforce, Network campuses are helping to ensure Ohio's long-term economic success. Funds from the Productivity Improvement Challenge Program have supported the capacity building work of the EnterpriseOhio Network, which includes professional development opportunities, demonstration projects, and best practice dissemination.

Through the Legislature's Non-Credit Job Training Appropriation, resources have been made available for the two-year campuses to acquire critical equipment to support training for key economic development projects.

FOR ADDITIONAL INFORMATION, PLEASE CONTACT:
Ohio Board of Regents
30 East Broad Street, 36th Floor
Columbus, OH 43266-5810
Telephone: (614) 466-5810
Fax: (614) 466-5866

OKLAHOMA

Ruth Ann Dreyer
Vice Chancellor for Administration & Board Relations
and
Hans Brisch, Chancellor
Oklahoma State Regents for Higher Education

OVERVIEW

Oklahoma's land-run settlement and late development as the 46th state created a frontier environment that influenced the state's early creation of two-year colleges. The territorial government established the first two-year college in 1901 as a preparatory school (Oklahoma University Preparatory School at Tonkawa, now Northern Oklahoma College). The first Oklahoma legislature meting shortly after statehood in 1908 created three institutions in Wilburton, Warner, and Tshomingo, which later emerged as two-ycar schools. Additional schools were later created in Claremore (1909) and Miami (1919). These early state-supported junior colleges, however, did not serve all areas of the state. To meet local needs elsewhere, 21 public district junior colleges were established during the 1919 to 1939 period as extensions of high schools. Despite several legislative attempts, no provisions were made to provide state funding or to allow school districts to vote extra mills form municipal college support.

A 1941 amendment to the Oklahoma Constitution created The Oklahoma State system of Higher Education headed by the Oklahoma State Regents for Higher Education, a coordinating board of control of institutions. The state-supported two-year colleges became a part of the new state system. Only six of the municipal colleges remained by 1961 due to lack of students and funding. By that time, funding discrepancies for state and municipal colleges had become so severe that state regents' studies recommended municipal junior colleges in Oklahoma either be adequately financed or phased of existence as a part of the higher education structure (Coffelt, 1968). A series of statutory changes from 1967 to 1973 allowed remaining municipal colleges to be brought into the state system. The last municipal college at Sayre was merged with Southwestern Oklahoma State University in 1987. No new state two-year colleges were created between 1919 and 1968, the year when Tulsa Junior College was created. Rogers State College in Claremore was merged with a Tulsa consortium in 1996 and called Rogers University and in 1999 resumed its independent identity and was converted to a four-year university named Rogers State University.

Currently, there are twelve public two-year colleges in Oklahoma that are called "state colleges," "community colleges," or simply a "college."

Two-year Colleges in Oklahoma, 1999
Founding Dates and Locations

Carl Albert State College	1933	1973	Poteau
Connors State College	—	1908	Warner
Eastern Oklahoma State College	—	1908	Wilburton
Murray State College	—	1908	Tishomingo
Northeastern Oklahoma A&M College	—	1919	Miami
Northern Oklahoma College	—	1901	Tonkawa
Oklahoma City Community College	1972	1973	Oklahoma City
Redlands Community College	1938	1973	El Reno
Rose State College	1970	1973	Midwest City
Seminole State College	1931	1973	Seminole
Tulsa Community College	—	1968	Tulsa
Western Oklahoma College	1926	1970	Altus

Two technical branches of Oklahoma State University also have been frequently included with the community college group. Five universities in Oklahoma (Southwestern Oklahoma State University, Cameron University, Oklahoma Panhandle State University, Langston University, and Rogers State University) offer associate degrees.

GOVERNANCE

The Oklahoma State Regents for Higher Education is the coordinating board of control of institutions. Duties of the board include 1) prescribing standards of education, 2) determining functions and courses of study in each institution, 3) granting degrees and other forms of academic recognition, 4) recommending to the Oklahoma State Legislature the budget allocations to each institution, 5) recommending to the legislature proposed fees for all institutions, and 6) allocating to each institution according to its needs and functions.

Governing boards for the two-year colleges are responsible for the supervision, management, and control of the institution. Duties include employing and fixing the compensation and duties of personnel; adopting rules and regulations; entering contracts; purchasing, receiving and disposing of funds; accepting gifts; and acquiring and taking title to property. With two exceptions, the two-year colleges have their own local governing board created by state statute. Connors State College and Northeastern Oklahoma A&M College are governed by the Board of Regents for the Oklahoma A&M Colleges, a constitutional board that also governs two four-year universities and a comprehensive research university. Board size ranges from five to nine members with seven members being the most common. With one exception (an ex-officio State Board of Agriculture position on the A&M Board), all regents governing two-year colleges are appointed by the governor and confirmed by the state senate to serve five- to eight-year terms.

Other than the above-mentioned conversion of Rogers State College from a two-year institution to a four-year university and its associated series of governance changes, there has been no change in governance structure for the two-year colleges in the past decade. Various task force studies, citizen commissions, and even the state regents have made recommendations during the 1990s for changing the governance of two-year colleges. The recommendations have ranged from radical (aligning all institutions under OU and OSU and eliminating local governing boards) to minor (realigning the governance of a particular institution). With the development of OneNet, the state's telecommunication network operated by the state regents in conjunction with the Oklahoma Office of State Finance, most of the board-shuffling proponents are realizing that quality, efficiencies, critical mass, and economies of scale will be achieved by functional mergers and institutional collaborations made possible more by technology and less by reconfiguration of the governance boxes.

FUNDING

Oklahoma two-year colleges are funded primarily from state-appropriated funds and student fees and tuition. For FY 99, primary educational and general budgets of the twelve Oklahoma two-year colleges totaled $179.9 million, with 59% coming from state funds, 20% coming from student fees and tuition, 12% coming from local revenue, and the remainder from other sources. Only three Oklahoma two-year colleges receive local funding: Rose State College, Tulsa Community College, and Oklahoma City Community College. For FY 99, two-year colleges also received $22.5 million in external funds.

Fees and tuition at Oklahoma two-year colleges are below the national average and represent 26.4% of a student's instructional cost.

Since 1988, the state regents have formulated institutional budget needs using a peer funding and a multi-year approach. Two-year institutions around the nation similar to Oklahoma two-year institutions have been identified and used to benchmark funding progress. Oklahoma's three urban colleges have one set of peers and the nine rural colleges have a different set of peers. As a whole, Oklahoma higher education is funding at only 68 cents on the dollar, compared to peer institutions. Factors in the budget formula that influence the institutional budget need and allocation are 1) peer funding parity, 2) funding parity per student for institutions within each tier, 3) number and range of high- and low-cost programs, 4) enrollment mix among high- and low-cost programs, 5) relationship between each actual program cost to the tier standard program cost.

The state does not annually appropriate funds for capital improvements. As of June, 1998, capital funding needs for Oklahoma two-year colleges total $334 million. Approximately 68% of this total is for new construction, and 32% is for modernization and repair. The last capital bond issue was in 1998 and contained $12.6 million for the two-year colleges. Because of the significant capital funding needs and the sporadic and infrequent nature of state capital funding, the state regents created a Section 13 Offset program to meet some of the more pressing capital needs. For FY 99, the state regents allocated $6.8 million in offset funding to 11 of the 12 two-year institutions. Northern Oklahoma College receives Section 13 funds and is not eligible for the offset program.

PROGRAMS AND ENROLLMENTS

Oklahoma two-year colleges have been assigned seven functions by the state regents: 1) to provide general education for all students, 2) to provide education in several basic fields of university-parallel study, 3) to provide one- and two-year programs of technical and occupational education to prepare individuals to enter the labor market, 4) to provide programs of remedial and developmental education, 5) to provide both formal and informal programs of study to serve the community, 6) to carry out programs of institutional research, and 7) to participate in programs of economic development.

Oklahoma's two-year colleges and technical branches offered 717 associate and certificate programs in FY 99: 286 associate of arts and associate of science programs, 264 associate of applied science programs, and 167 certificates.

A total of 93,628 students (unduplicated head count) were enrolled in two-year colleges during 1997-98. This number is down from 98,464 in FY 89, and from a high of 106,993 in FY 93. Oklahoma two-year colleges also enroll superior high school students consistent with state regents' policy. For FY 98, the two-year colleges enrolled 1,616 high school students, which was 71.9% of the high school concurrent enrollment at state institutions. A greater proportion (40.6%) of white students enrolled at two-year colleges in fall 1997 compared to 7.6% of the state's nonresident alien enrollment, 39.1% of the Black enrollment, 40.7% of the Native American enrollment, 35.9% of the Asian enrollment, and 41.7% of the Hispanic enrollment.

During FY 97, state institutions conferred 529 certificates and 6,547 associate degrees. Women earned some 55% of the certificates and 62% of the associate degrees. The top three associate-degree producing institutions were Tulsa Community College with 23.3% of the degrees, Oklahoma City Community College with 10.6 percent, and Rose State College with 9.3%. The most popular programs were in the health professions (20.6% of the degrees), business and management (19.9% of the degrees), and liberal arts and sciences (19.7% of the degrees). Oklahoma private institutions awarded 133 associate degrees and three certificates.

Five of the two-year institutions reported noncredit activity in FY 98 totaling 41,273 participant contacts. The general public and educational institutions were the largest groups served. The vast majority of noncredit participants were involved in education courses. Others were involved in aging courses and in upgrading skills. Workshops and seminars were the primary mode of noncredit delivery.

Remedial education is a key function of Oklahoma two-year colleges. State Regents' policy requires each student with an ACT subject score below 19 to either enroll in a remedial course or undergo secondary institutional assessment. Students scoring below the designated levels on these secondary tests must successfully complete appropriate remedial courses. During the 1997-98 academic year, 35,079 students enrolled in remedial courses. The majority (74.6%) of the remedial students were enrolled at the two-year colleges. Several Oklahoma universities have made arrangements for state two-year colleges to provide remedial education for students enrolled on the university campus. The most notable example is the arrangement between the University of Central Oklahoma in Edmond and Rose State college in Midwest City. Remedial classes in Oklahoma are zero credit, and tuition levels are higher, covering direct costs.

Relationships between state two-year colleges and the state's separate area vocational-technical school system (non-degree granting) have been enhanced. Cooperative agreements, through which courses from the area vo-tech schools count toward an associate of applied science degree, have increased to 257 at 15 two-year institutions involving 107 A.A.S. programs. A $100,000 vo-tech contract with the state regents has resulted in the hiring of a Director of Technical-Occupational Activity who works closely with two-year institutions and area schools on coordination and curricular issues and a system approach to cooperative agreements.

Oklahoma two-year colleges are innovative participants in the electronic delivery of courses and programs, aggressively capitalizing on opportunities possible through OneNet, the statewide telecommunications system. The two-year colleges currently offer 428 electronic courses, which represents 41% of the state's total electronic offerings and 65% of the electronics enrollment. Most of the courses are offered via interactive video and telecourse/videotape, but 62 courses were computer-based Internet offerings. All two-year colleges are a part of Oklahoma's Electronic Campus and offer 72% of its courses. Four two-year colleges participate in the Southern Regional Electronic Campus and offer 72% of its courses. Four two-year colleges participate in the Southern Regional Electronic Campus, with 47 course offerings.

State two-year colleges are also in the vanguard of numerous institutional collaborations and consortiums. For example, four two-year colleges and a university have formed the downtown Oklahoma City consortium, sharing resources and bringing services to the metro area. Four rural institutions in eastern Oklahoma have formed MECCA, a consortium to increase academic offerings in rural areas and to reduce instructional costs.

ECONOMIC DEVLEOPMENT

State leaders in Oklahoma realize that an educated citizenry will yield big dividends for the state. In Oklahoma, a citizen with an associate degree will earn an average of $30,139, compared to $22,626 for anyone with no college experience. In January, 1999, the state regents announced a Brain Gain 2010 initiative, calling for Oklahoma to meet or exceed by 2010 the national average for the proportion of its population age 25 or older holding associate degrees. To meet the goal, Oklahoma will need to add 140,000 associate degree holders. As part of the effort to enhance the state's intellectual capital, the state regents have also announced a "learning site initiative." The initiative is the result of a statewide needs assessment conducted in 1998 by the National Center of Higher Education Management Systems (NCHEMS). The study found that although 93% of the state's population is within 30 miles of an existing higher education institution, 63 of Oklahoma's 77 counties are underserved in one or more ways. A learning site policy adopted by the State Regents in April, 1999, encourages and provides financial incentives for institutions to import courses from other institutions in order to meet area needs and respond to workforce training needs of employers.

For FY 99, the state regents allocated $3.4 million for economic development initiatives that will advance a three-part economic development agenda. Four two-year colleges and a consortium of Oklahoma City area colleges received $916,000 for projects that will provide computer training opportunities; computer-based forensic workforce development for state, national, and international law enforcement, semiconductor and telecommunications technology programs; and workforce development opportunities for the metal fabrication industry. Oklahoma two-year colleges are responding to workforce development challenges with an increasing number of modular, work-responsive offerings. For instance, working together and with representatives of the semi-conductor industry, the colleges are realigning and modernizing curricula to meet industry need.

Under new federal welfare reform laws, all Oklahoma two-year colleges are key participants working with the Department of Human Services and DHS county offices to develop, design, and implement individualized educational training programs. A total of 2,017 recipients have participated in college projects since July 1, 1997, through December 31, 1998. Approximately 632 have been gainfully employed and 703 cases have been closed. A total of $3.2 million was allocated for FY 99 to community colleges for this effort.

ACCOUNTABILITY

Along with quality and efficiency goals of the state regents has come an effort to make higher education more accountable to the public. A four-part systemwide assessment policy was adopted in 1991 that requires that institutions evaluate students at four levels: (1) entry-level to determine academic preparation and course placement; (2) mid-level to determine general education competencies in reading, writing, mathematics, and critical thinking; (3) program outcomes or exit-level to evaluate the outcomes in the student's major; and (4) assessment of student satisfaction to ascertain students' perceptions of their educational experience including support services, academic curriculum, faculty, etc. Institutions are allowed to charge one dollar per credit hour for an assessment fee and are required to make an annual report to the state regents. The reports reflect the evaluation results as well as institutional plans for improvement.

Recognizing that the employability of graduates is one accountability measure, Oklahoma two-year colleges have announced a warranty of assurance to employers that their graduates are competent to perform in the workplace. In 1998, the state regents produced an Annual Employment Outcomes Report, which tracks degree recipients by program into the workforce and yields information about the number and earnings of graduates who stay in Oklahoma to work. Of the 1996-97 graduates from Oklahoma two-year colleges, 90% were employed in Oklahoma jobs.

Graduation rate is also an accountability factor. Only 15% of Oklahoma's 194 cohort of students entering two-year colleges graduated within three years, compared to the 34.5% national average. Freshman dropout rates at Oklahoma two-year colleges are 48.4%, compared to the 47.7% national average. In 1998, the state regents challenged institutions to develop graduation plans for programs. The institutions responded with the two-year colleges presenting plans for numerous programs and assurances that students would graduate in a timely manner.

The ease with which students transfer coursework is a measure of accountability, and the state regents have undertaken several steps to ease the process. An electronic student transcript initiative (SPEEDE) assures record transfer among state system institutions. A faculty transfer curriculum committee has put 4,187 courses on a "guaranteed transfer" list that represents 27 disciplines at all state colleges and universities in Oklahoma.

The extent to which resources are channeled to the classroom and away from "the bureaucracy" is a measure of accountability in which Oklahoma institutions fare well and better than national, regional, and peer average. For FY 99, only one of the three urban two-year colleges exceeded the 13.0% administrative cost cap set by the state regents. None of the rural two-year colleges exceeded its 16.0% administrative cost cap.

REFERENCES

Coffelt, John J. (1968). *The Status and Direction of Oklahoma Higher Education*. Oklahoma City, OK: Oklahoma State Regents for Higher Education: Author

Dreyer, Ruth Ann (1995). *An Exemplary Study of Variables Related to Attitude Toward Property Tax Increases Supporting Community Colleges* (Doctoral dissertation, University of Oklahoma).

National Center for Higher Education Management Systems, *Analysis of Potential Needs for Postsecondary Education Services in Different Regions of Oklahoma*, (1998, October). Denver, CO: Author

Oklahoma State Regents for Higher Education. (1999, January). *Annual Employment Outcomes Report*. Oklahoma City, OK: Author

Oklahoma State Regents for Higher Education. (1999, January 29). *Annual Student Assessment Report*. Oklahoma City, OK: Author

Oklahoma State Regents for Higher Education. (1999, January 29). *Annual Student Remediation Report*. Oklahoma City, OK: Author

Oklahoma State Regents for Higher Education. (1999, January 29). *Brain Gain 2010: Building Oklahoma Through Intellectual Power*. Oklahoma City, OK: Author

Oklahoma State Regents for Higher Education. (1995, May). *Budget Development Presentation*, Oklahoma City, OK: Author

Oklahoma State Regents for Higher Education. (1999). *Educational and General Budgets*, Summary and Analysis, Fiscal Year 1998-99. Oklahoma City, OK: Author

Oklahoma State Regents for Higher Education. (1999, April). *Student Data Report, Oklahoma Higher Education 1997-98*. Oklahoma City, OK: Author

Oklahoma State Regents for Higher Education, *Systemwide Faculty Transfer Curriculum Committee Reports*, January 29, 1999. Oklahoma City, OK: Author

FOR ADDITIONAL INFORMATION, PLEASE CONTACT:
Dr. Hans Brisch, Chancellor
Oklahoma State Regents for Higher Education
500 Education Building
State Capitol Complex
Oklahoma City, Oklahoma 73105-4503
Telephone: (405) 524-9120
Fax: (405) 524-9235
E-mail: hbrisch@osrhe.edu
or
Dr. Ruth Ann Dreyer
Vice Chancellor for Administration & Board Relations
Oklahoma State Regents for Higher Education
500 Education Building
State Capitol Complex
Oklahoma City, Oklahoma 73105-4503
Telephone: (405) 524-9120
Fax: (405) 524-9235
E-mail: rdreyer@osrhe.edu

OREGON

Bret West
Deputy Commissioner
Office of Community College Services
Oregon Department of Community Colleges

OVERVIEW

Oregon is served by 14 community college districts and three community college service districts. Service districts function in areas of the state in which there is insufficient population to support a full district. Each service district is required to contract with a full district for purposes of accreditation (Holland, in Tollefson & Fountain, 1992).

Each Oregon community college is governed by a locally elected board of trustees. Local boards develop and approve operating budgets, set personnel policies, employ faculty and staff, and adopt educational programs. Each community college must comply with state law in matters such as collective bargaining, conducting open meetings, and providing public access to certain records. The state's local budget law sets forth the procedure for developing and publishing a budget; it does not establish spending priorities (Holland, in Tollefson & Fountain, 1995).

The Office of Community College Services (OCCS) coordinates Oregon's community colleges. The commissioner of OCCS, who reports directly to the Oregon State Board of Education, is the chief executive officer of the state board for all community college matters (Holland, in Tollefson & Fountain, 1992).

The 1997 Legislative Assembly moved the Job Training Partnership Act (JTPA) administration to the Office of Community College Services. To recognize the increased scope and responsibilities of the agency, a bill was approved by the 1992 Legislative Assembly that changed the name of the agency to the Department of Community Colleges and Workforce Development (Office of Community College Services, 1998).

In the 1949 the Oregon legislature adopted a law that authorized school districts to establish extension centers to provide college-level courses. Each center was required to operate through a contract with the Oregon State System of Higher Education (now the Oregon University System). Three such school district programs were started, but the one in Bend is the only center still in existence, and it has become Central Oregon Community College (Holland, in Tollefson & Fountain, 1992).

After several unsuccessful attempts in the 1950s, in 1959, the legislature passed a law that authorized the establishment of independent community college districts. Because the state appropriation for district formation was too little, no districts were formed under the 1959 statute (Holland, in Tollefson & Fountain, 1992).

In 1961, the legislature modified the 1959 law to facilitate district formation and appropriated enough money to form new districts. Six districts were established by 1964, and by 1971, there were 13. State appropriations were sufficient to pay over 50% of the cost of direct instruction and over 67% of the money needed for capital projects. Local property tax levies and student tuition provided the remaining funds needed (Holland, in Tollefson & Fountain, 1992).

In the 1960s and 1970s, the legislature appropriated $96 million for community college construction. State support for community college operating budgets gradually declined to approximately 41% of college budgets. Local taxpayers generally approved levy increases to make up for lost state funds. The Oregon community colleges began to have serious budget problems, beginning in 1980. In the early 1980s, Oregon experienced a serious recession. The legislature further reduced its operating support, and some years made mid-year cuts. From 1979 to 1983, state support dropped from 41% to 30%. The recession also interfered with the colleges' attempts to obtain local tax increases (Holland, in Tollefson & Fountain, 1992).

Oregon's community colleges traditionally had been strongly independent until the budget crisis of the 1980s. During that period, they reassessed their previous opposition to a strong state coordinating agency, and, in 1987, the colleges initiated and were successful in obtaining legislative approval of a bill to establish the Office of Community College Services (Holland, in Tollefson & Fountain, 1992). A modification was adopted by the legislature in 1992 that redesignated the agency as the Oregon Department of Community Colleges and Workforce Development (West, 1999)..

Oregon voters approved a property tax limitation measure in 1990. Measure 5 imposed a $5 per $1,000 limit on property tax rates for all education sectors. The measure required state general fund replacement of property tax revenues lost as a result of the new limit. Another property tax limitation, Ballot Measure 47, was passed in 1996, and implementing legislation, Measure 50, was approved by the voters in 1997. Measure 50 required property tax revenues to be rolled back to 1995 levels or cut by 10 percent, whichever reduction was greater. Property tax losses to community colleges were replaced by state funds. The result is that approximately 55% of community college general fund revenues now come from the state (West, 1999).

GOVERNANCE

The Oregon State Board of Education includes seven members who are appointed by the governor with the consent of the Oregon State Senate. The board must include one member from each of Oregon's five Congressional districts and two members at large. Each board member is appointed for a four-year term, with one possible reappointment. Demonstrated misconduct or malfeasance is grounds for removal by the governor. The state board meets once each month. The board meets one day each month as the state board for elementary and secondary education, and another day as the state board for community colleges. The state superintendent of education no longer has any authority over or involvement in community college education. The state board's community college functions include reviewing and approving new educational programs, adopting systems for financial and student accounting, adopting and employing budget allocation formulas, approving facilities construction and acquisition projects, and submitting budget requests to the legislature. In general, the state board is a coordinating board, and local boards govern individual institutions. The Office of Community College Services provides liaison, leadership and support services to the colleges (Office of Community College Services, 1998).

FUNDING

Local property taxes (approximately 24%), state reimbursement (approximately 55%), and student tuition (approximately 21%) are the three main funding sources. The legislature pays for 65% of construction project costs. Local funds make up the other 35% (West, 1999).

The formula for distributing the Community College Support Fund was implemented in 1995-96 and has undergone several revisions since then. The current formula distributes state funds and one-half of local property taxes on a three-year weighted full-time-equivalent (FTE) average from the three most recent academic years (West, 1999).

1998-99 tuition rates for full-time, resident students range from $590 per quarter to $570 per quarter at Oregon community colleges. The average tuition is $543. These figures do not include fees (West, 1999).

PROGRAMS

Oregon's community colleges offer comprehensive college transfer, vocational-technical, adult and continuing education, high school diploma and GED programs. Programs leading to certificates and associate degrees are planned and proposed by local community colleges, based on state board criteria including labor market projections, staffing needs and curriculum standards. After local board approval, proposed new programs are reviewed and approved by the state board (West, 1999).

WORKFORCE DEVELOPMENT

The Oregon community colleges provide numerous programs and services in workforce development, including welfare-to-work programs, small business development centers, and individualized business consulting (West, 1999).

ENROLLMENT

A full-time-equivalent (FTE) student is derived from 510 clock hours. Oregon's community colleges enrolled 85,346 FTE in 1997-98, and enrollments are expected to increase by approximately 4.5% in 1998-99; much of this growth can be attributed to the annexation of Jackson County, the state's sixth most populous county. Total headcount enrollment for 1997-98 was 352, 660 students (West, 1999).

Approximately 39% of the FTE generated in 1997-98 were in lower-division transfer courses. Professional technical enrollments accounted for 31% of the FTE, 20% came from developmental education enrollments, and the balance was in other programs such as self-improvement programs. Developmental education enrollments have been increasingly steady over the last ten years (West, 1999).

REFERENCES

Holland, M. (1992). Oregon, in Tollefson,T.A. & Fountain, B.E. *Forty-Nine StateSystems*, 1992 Edition, pp. 176-178. Washington, DC: American Association of Community Colleges.

Office of Community College Services, (1998, May). *Profile*. Salem, OR: Author.

West, B. (1999). Oregon community colleges. (Unpublished article) Salem, OR: Office of Community College Services.

FOR ADDITIONAL INFORMATION, PLEASE CONTACT:
Deputy Commissioner
Office of Community College Services
255 Capitol St., NE
Salem, OR 97310
Telephone: (503) 378-8648, Ext. 361

PENNSYLVANIA

Leland W. Myers, Executive Director
Pennsylvania Commission for Community Colleges

OVERVIEW

Pennsylvania does not have a community college *system*. The fourteen community colleges and one technical institute, all organized under the Community College Act of 1963, operate as virtually independent, although publicly supported, institutions, responsible mainly to their communities and their "local sponsors."

The Community College Act of 1963 (Act 484, Statutes of 1963) authorized local communities to petition the Pennsylvania State Board of Education to sponsor and establish community colleges. Each college is required to have a local sponsor, which must have taxing authority. In submitting their requests, which must be accompanied by a feasibility study and a plan for implementation, local sponsors are required to commit and demonstrate that they will provide for two-thirds of the operating cost of the college. Student tuition, equal to no more than one-third of the operating costs, is counted as part of the local sponsor's contribution, as are federal and other specialized funds.

Nine of the colleges and the technical institute are sponsored by their respective counties. Five are sponsored by consortia of local school districts, ranging from 11 to 22 in number of members. Local sponsors either elect or appoint the 15 members of the board of trustees of their community colleges. Trustees are responsible only to their local appointing authorities, with little or no policy direction or administration from the state level, except through annual audits conducted by the state comptroller's office in cooperation with the Pennsylvania State Department of Education.

Only 65 of the 501 school districts in Pennsylvania participate as sponsors of community colleges, together with only 11 of 67 counties, and the city-county of Philadelphia.

GOVERNANCE

Each community college in Pennsylvania has a local sponsor, which may be either a city (as in the case of Philadelphia), a county, an individual school district or a consortium of school districts. The key to sponsorship is that the sponsor(s) must have taxing authority; community college boards of trustees were not granted such power, because their members are not chosen by the general electorate. Local sponsors — school directors (boards), city councils, or boards of county commissioners – elect or appoint the 15 members of their respective college governing boards of trustees for renewable terms of six years.

Sponsors must approve the annual budgets of the colleges, although the state department of education exercises a limited amount of control over the colleges through the allocation of state funds according to a statutory formula, and through extensive post-audit procedures. Where a community college is sponsored by a consortium of school districts, a majority of the members of the consortium must approve the annual budget.

The state board of education must authorize new colleges or branch campuses and the addition or withdrawal of local sponsors, and has the responsibility for adopting policies, standards and regulations necessary to implement the Community College Act of 1963. These powers include establishing minimum requirements for physical facilities and equipment, curriculum, faculty, standards and other professional requirements, qualifications for admission and advancement of students, requirements for satisfactory completion of two-year programs, degrees, and the diplomas or certificates to be awarded, and means of financing the community college (Pennsylvania School Code, Sec. 1902-A).

The Pennsylvania Secretary of Education recommends the amount of the annual budget request for the colleges, based on a statutory formula and the colleges' enrollment projections. The department receives the legislative appropriation after approval by the governor, and the secretary authorizes quarterly payments to the colleges. Through the state comptroller's office, the department performs annual financial audits of the colleges to assure compliance with accounting and operating regulations. The secretary of education may issue policy guidelines and letters without consultation or approval by the state board of education. In practice, the secretary or staff members of the department of education generally consult with the colleges before issuing policy guidelines or letters.

FUNDING

The community colleges are funded from three main sources: local sponsors, the Commonwealth of Pennsylvania, and student tuition and fees. In 1997-98, preliminary data from the Commission for Community

Colleges show that total unrestricted operating revenues amounted to just over $400 million. Of this, approximately $88 million, or 22.4%, came from local sponsors. The Commonwealth of Pennsylvania, through a reimbursement formula enacted into statutes, contributed approximately $132 million, or 33.6%. Revenues from student tuition and fees amounted to more than $165 million, or just over 41%. In addition, the colleges received just over $10 million from other sources.

The Community College Act obligated local sponsors to pay two-thirds of the net operating costs, and the state to pay one-third. That act was quickly amended to allow student tuition, up to one-third of costs, to offset local sponsors' contributions, thus in practice reducing local sponsors' obligation to one-third. In addition, the act called for the state to pay one-half of all capital costs (including long-term leases, purchase of land and buildings, and construction and initial equipment of facilities).

In 1974, the legislature enacted a program of "stipends" of $300 for each full-time- equivalent student (FTES) enrolled in technical and occupational programs, designed to encourage the colleges to offer such programs to enhance the state's vocational education efforts. The program was enlarged later to provide variable stipends for three different categories: advanced technology, statewide programs, and all others. Today's reimbursement rates are: advanced technology, $1460 per FTEs; statewide programs, $1,360 per FTES; and all others, $860 per FTES. Each program classified in the "advanced technology" category must be reviewed at least once every five years.

Variable stipend funding amounts to about 18.5% of the colleges' total state operating reimbursement, and encompasses about 900 programs. Any changes in programs eligible for the stipend must be approved annually by a committee made up of four community college representatives and four representatives from the department of education. The Executive Director, Commission for Community Colleges, serves as a nonvoting ex-officio member of the committee.

The colleges receive the state portion of their funding on a reimbursed basis per FTES, determined according to a formula contained in the Community College Act, and amended periodically by the Pennsylvania General Assembly. The final determination and a financial adjustment are made following an audit, which often takes two or more years to complete. At one time in the early 1990s, the auditing process was as much as eight years behind schedule for some colleges.

Until 1993, the law called for each college to receive funding from the state equal to one-third of its net operating costs, or a fixed amount per FTES, whichever was less. In all but one or two cases, the colleges normally received the fixed amount per FTES, since it always was set by the legislature at a number that was less than the equivalent of one-third of operating costs. In the colleges that received one-third because of lower operating costs, the actual amount received per FTES was less than that received by the other colleges.

In 1993, upon the recommendation of the Pennsylvania Department of Education, the legislature enacted a variation on the formula, theoretically designed to provide more state funding for colleges whose local sponsors were relatively poorer than the others. The proportion of state funding is determined by the total taxable personal income of the local sponsors, and could range between one-third of net operating costs (for the relatively "wealthiest" sponsors) and one-half (for the relatively poorest sponsors). This formula adversely affects small, rapidly-growing institutions, and those operated at lower cost, by limiting their state funding to an amount less than the fixed amount per FTES received by the other colleges. The wording of the new law is similar to the earlier provision that a college would receive the lesser of the two amounts.

One college, for example, spent more than $600,000 beyond its initial budget in 1998-99 in order to avoid losing $300,000 from the amount "earned" through its enrollment count. Two others, new and fast growing, annually have lost funds because of the "whichever is less" clause in the law. The Commission for Community Colleges has requested that the "ceiling" be repealed, and various studies of community college finance in the past three years also have recommended its deletion, but the legislature has not yet acted.

Except for Montgomery County Community College, which is funded locally by the County of Montgomery, and Harrisburg Area Community College, funded by a consortium of 22 school districts, local funding has never reached the statutory target of one-third of the colleges' operating costs. In 1997-98, the statewide average was approximately 22.4%, ranging from a low of 10.1% to a high of 33.1%; the statewide average low point was reached in 1993, when local sponsors provided only 16.9% of the colleges' revenue. The college with the lowest reported local revenue (Beaver) also reported the highest proportion of tuition revenue (51.5%).

After nearly a year of study, the Pennsylvania State Board of Education recommended in 1996 that a state community college coordinating board be created. Its purpose would be to revise what was called in testimony "a dysfunctional formula" for funding the colleges, and to give the colleges a voice in the preparation of the annual governor's proposed budget. The board would then continue to oversee the state's support of the colleges. Legislation to carry out the board's recommendation was introduced in both houses of the Pennsylvania General Assembly in 1997, but died with the sine die adjournment of the body in November, 1998. Legislation has been introduced again in 1999 in both houses, with the support of the Community College Commission, and with opposition from two of the 15 colleges (Montgomery and Harrisburg).

Revenue from student tuition, which is limited to the equivalent of not more than one-third of net operating costs, nevertheless in 1997-98 amounted to a statewide average of 41.6% of unrestricted operating revenues. The range was from 29.4% to 51.5%. The one-third limitation applies only to students from sponsoring areas; students from "non-sponsoring" areas are required by law to pay double tuition, although their areas may provide "in-kind" assistance, thus reducing the actual amount of tuition paid by the students.

Harrisburg Area Community College, whose 22 sponsors by contract pay an amount equal to tuition for each of their students attending the college, reported tuition revenue at 49.1% of total unrestricted revenues for 1997-98. The college said that actual local funding for 1997-98 would amount to only 15.2% of its total unrestricted revenues. Many community colleges in recent years have begun to reach out to recruit students from nonsponsored areas, and even to establish branch campuses, because of the added revenue possible.

PROGRAMS AND ENROLLMENTS

Among the 15 institutions organized under the Community College Act, the two newest are nontraditional "colleges without walls." Northwest Pennsylvania Technical Institute, with three counties as local sponsors, assists employers in its area of the state by helping them determine their needs, then finding another institution that can help meet those needs. Accredited by the Council on Occupational Education and currently a pre-candidate for accreditation by the Middle States Association of Schools and Colleges, the institute maintains no classrooms or other space on its own, except for administrative headquarters in Erie.

Cambria County Area Community College (CCACC) began life in 1994 in a state-owned vocational rehabilitation center, utilizing cooperative arrangements with a private school and an area vocational school for the use of classroom space, tied together with electronic technology. Today, because of community demand, CCACC has received approval from the department of education to lease four other sites in its area. Cambria also is a candidate for Middle States accreditation.

Each community college is authorized to establish its own programs, without approval from a state agency, so long as the program approval process meets regulations and audit policies set by the department of education for both credit and noncredit courses and programs. Because of the structure of the state funding formula for the colleges, each institution is free to develop primarily in response to its community. Consequently, some colleges have retained their emphasis on academic and transfer programs, while others have taken advantage of added revenues from the variable stipend program and emphasized technical and occupational programming.

While the 1963 Community College Act stipulated that the colleges were to be primarily vocational and technical in nature, an amendment very quickly changed that provision to allow each college to meet the educational needs of its community, whatever those may be. As a result, the ratio of "academic" to "vocational/technical" credit enrollments rose to 70% by the early 1970s. By 1975-76, academic enrollments had declined slightly, and enrollments were almost evenly divided, with approximately 55% in academic pursuits. In1996-97, academic enrollment statewide stood at 50.4% of all students, including those enrolled in noncredit courses and programs, many of which were technical or occupational in nature.

Community colleges today maintain literally scores of articulation agreements with other higher education institutions, both public and private, within Pennsylvania and outside the state. Some are limited to a single program, while other agreements allow students to transfer to third-year status, provided they have attained associate degrees.

After nearly a decade of negotiations among the faculties of the community colleges and the four-year state universities, the Board of Governors of the State System of Higher Education early in 1998 created an "Academic Passport," guaranteeing community college students acceptance of their degrees and their general education credits. The state legislature has enacted a resolution calling on all publicly funded higher education institutions to establish a statewide system of articulation, considering such factors as a common course indexing system, as well as "core-to-core" and "program-to-program" articulation. Work is in progress to meet the legislature's concerns.

Articulation agreements have led to a significant new era of cooperation between the community colleges and the public and private four-year colleges and universities of the Commonwealth of Pennsylvania. Several community colleges have reached agreement with four-year institutions either to teach one or more lower division courses at the senior institution, or for the senior institution to offer selected third- and fourth-year courses and baccalaureate programs on the campuses of the community colleges.

ECONOMIC DEVELOPMENT

Over the past two decades, most of the community colleges in Pennsylvania have established business and industry assistance centers and other activities designed to help employers determine their needs for training and employment, several using the relatively new "Work Keys" program. The scope and variety of these activities on- and off-campus, as well as at business sites, rival those of the regular academic and occupational programs on campus.

The Pennsylvania Commission for Community Colleges annually conducts a survey to determine the number of contracts held by the colleges for education and training of employees. In 1997-98, the colleges maintained nearly 1,300 contracts, assisting more than 45,000 employees. That number has grown from a little more than 600 contracts in 1995, the first year of the Commission's survey. Additionally, several colleges held numerous contracts for consulting or other services.

Contractors include major multi-national corporations, banks, hospitals, state and local government agencies, professional corporations, "mom-and-pop" businesses, and non-profit organizations. Programs range from English as a second language, general education and supervisory leadership, to hazardous waste handler certification, entreprencurial education and business incubator activities. One college, Butler, offers a program in metrology, which has attracted enrollments from foreign nations, as has a program in plastics technology at Northampton Community College.

The 1998-99 state budget also contained a $2 million appropriation for "business partnership challenge grants," which matched state funds to sums pledged by local businesses for education and training. While funds for the program were authorized in April of 1998, it was not until April of 1999 that the first funds were awarded by the Pennsylvania Department of Education. The $2 million offered by the state was reported by the department to leverage more than $8 million in private funding from business and industry.

In addition to the "partnership" program, the legislature appropriated $9 million in the 1998-99 state budget at the request of the governor for a "guaranteed free training program." Administered by the Pennsylvania Department of Community and Economic Development, grants are for the use of businesses which meet such criteria as hiring 12 or more new employees in a year, at average wages exceeding 150% of the minimum wage, and keeping them employed for six months or more. The community colleges and the state university (SSHE) system developed a unique partnership, now dubbed "WEDnetPA," for the purpose of providing the widest possible geographic and programmatic coverage. The first grants under that partnership, which also includes the Pennsylvania College of Technology (PCT), also were announced in April, 1999. (Until 1988, PCT was named the Williamsport Area Community College, but is solely-owned affiliate of the Pennsylvania State University.)

Despite their long-time activities in education and training for business and industry, the community colleges of Pennsylvania have not been made an integral part of the state's workforce development effort, relegated instead to the role of "provider," subject to the policies of local workforce investment boards (WIBs), which are organized under a Human Resources Investment Council established by a governor's executive order in 1997.

The same is true of the colleges' status with the school-to-work and welfare-to-work programs.

ACCOUNTABILITY

Community colleges in Pennsylvania are uniquely accountable to their local sponsors, whether county boards of commissioners, boards of school directors, or city councils. These bodies, as local sponsors, appoint or elect the members of the colleges' boards of trustees, and have the power not to re-appoint. Even more immediate accountability occurs because of the fact that college budgets annually must meet the approval of their local sponsors. There have been situations in recent years in which local sponsors have threatened not to approve, and have caused college presidents to consider issuing orders to close the college's registration process, to suspend classes, and in fact to close the colleges. The anomaly is that while a college may be in negotiation with its teachers' union over next year's salaries and working conditions, a sponsoring school district may be in negotiation with its union over the same issues at the same time, leading to an apparent conflict of interest. No legal actions ever have been taken to clarify the situation.

In addition to their relationships with their local sponsors, the colleges also are accountable to the state department of education through the office of the state comptroller. These two offices work together, through the use of regulations, rules, policy guidelines and policy letters, the latter two of which may be issued by the secretary of education without consultation or approval by the state board of education. In practice, the secretary or staff members of the Pennsylvania Department of Education may consult with the colleges before issuing policy guidelines or letters.

Because the Commonwealth of Pennsylvania by law pays half the colleges' capital costs, the department of education must also approve all long-term leases, as well as expenditures for purchase of land, buildings and other facilities, and for construction.

REFERENCES

Fountain, B. E., and Tollefson, T. A. (1989). *Community Colleges in the United States: Forty-Nine State Systems*. Washington, DC: American Association of Community and Junior Colleges.

House Subcommittee on Higher Education, Pennsylvania House of Representatives (1998, January). *A Report on Pennsylvania's Community Colleges*. Harrisburg, PA: Author.

Myers, Leland W. (1999, April-May) Pennsylvania community colleges: Troubled past; Bright future?" *Community College Journal of Research and Practice*, 23(3), pp. 283-304.

Overholt, Maury (1987). *Twenty-Year Overview of Financial Statistics of Community Colleges*. Harrisburg, PA: Commission for Community Colleges.

Pennsylvania Commission for Community Colleges (1998). *Statewide Database Task Force Report*. Harrisburg PA: Author.

FOR ADDITIONAL INFORMATION, PLEASE CONTACT:
Pennsylvania Commission for Community Colleges
800 North Third Street, Suite 405
Harrisburg, PA 17102
Telephone: (717) 232-7584
Fax: (717) 233-4723
or
Pennsylvania Department of Education
Harristown Building
333 Market Street
Harrisburg, PA 17126
Telephone: (717) 783-6788

RHODE ISLAND

Edward J. Liston
President, Community College of Rhode Island

OVERVIEW

In January of 1960, the Rhode Island General Assembly established the Rhode Island Junior College state system. The legislation closely followed the recommendations of the Commission to Study Higher Education, which called for the establishment of a statewide system of junior college campuses with facilities in the areas of Pawtuxet Valley, Blackstone Valley, and mount Hope. In March of 1964, the Board of Trustees of State Colleges appointed Dr. William F. Flanagan as the first president of Rhode Island Junior College. The college began instruction in temporary facilities in Providence on September 24, 1964. The college had planned to admit 200 students initially but a surge of applications was used to persuade Governor John Chafee to authorize increasing the enrollment to 325 students.

In October of 1964, Royal W. Knight gave the college 80 acres of land, along with several historic buildings. This became the Knight Campus. Additional adjacent land was acquired to increase the campus size to 205 acres. The Knight Campus opened with an enrollment of nearly 3,000 students in 1972. All facilities here are housed under one roof, in a futuristic megastructure that encourages social, educational, and cultural exchanges among the entire student body.

In June, 1969, a master plan was unveiled for the Blackstone Valley campus of Rhode Island Junior college. The plan updated the overall projections for full development of the Rhode Island Junior College state system and developed basic design criteria for the second campus, eventually named the Flanagan Campus, in honor of the college's first president. Rhode Island voters in 1970 authorized a $12.25 million bond issue for construction of the Flanagan Campus and for preliminary planning of a Newport-Mount Hope campus. Construction began on the Flanagan Campus in Lincoln in the summer of 1974. This 300-acre campus opened its doors in September, 1976, with an enrollment of 1,700. Like the Warwick facility, the design of the Flanagan campus encourages interaction among all students. One large building, made up of three connecting modules, totals nearly 7.5 acres of floor space.

The college's second president, Edward J. Liston, took office on April 1, 1979. Under his leadership, the college continued to expand, offering credit and noncredit courses at satellite locations in high schools across the state.

The Rhode Island Board of Regents for Education in June of 1980 approved a change in the name of the college from Rhode Island Junior College to the Community College of Rhode Island, to reflect the true mission of the institution—to be a college that is community-based, responsive to community needs, broad in purpose, and oriented to public service.

During the 1980s, CCRI established strong partnerships with both secondary schools and the business community. These led to the establishment of the Cooperative Education and Tech Prep programs and the Center for Business and Industrial Training. At the same time, the college expanded the scope of its program offerings, moving into new health fields such as dental hygiene and physical therapy.

In the spring of 1990, CCRI reestablished its roots in the inner city, when it acquired a building in Providence, then opened its third campus in September. Nearly 650 students enrolled for college credit during its first semester of operation, with an additional 150 participating in the General Equivalency Diploma (GED) preparation and testing program.

CCRI was established to provide all Rhode Islanders with access to higher education. The system maintains an open-door admissions policy and relatively low tuition to ensure accessibility. Today, approximately 15,000 students attend classes at three main campuses and five satellite facilities across the state. Those pursuing an education at CCRI have the opportunity to select from over 50 programs of study. Students choose CCRI for a variety of reasons, including low cost, convenient location, and flexible scheduling options. Some enroll with the intention of eventually transferring into baccalaureate degree programs, whereas others select programs of study that prepare them to enter directly into the workforce.

In addition to serving students enrolled in college credit programs, during the last year CCRI enrolled more than 15,000 students in noncredit programs offered through the Office of Community Services. These programs range from state-mandated motorcycle safety courses to GED preparation and testing, from vocational training for adults to a variety of individual courses for personal enrichment and enjoyment.

CCRI's high school partnership program has become a national model. The Tech-Prep associate degree program was initiated in 1987 to provide high school students who are not enrolled in college preparatory courses with an alternative to the ineffective general education track. Students enroll in the program in the 11th grade, taking core courses such as principles of technology, applied communications, and mathematics for technology. Upon successful completion of the high school portion of the program, students are guaranteed admission to specific technical programs at CCRI. The program started with an enrollment of 105 students in six high schools. Today over 1,400 students from 29 high schools are enrolled. In addition, more than 250 are credited at CCRI in the second phase of the program.

Last year, nearly 2,000 employees of Rhode Island companies participated in special programs offered through the CCRI Center for Business and Industrial Training. The center assists local businesses, industries, and community organizations in developing and enhancing their workforce through customized training offered either on-site or in college facilities.

CCRI also interacts with the business community through the cooperative Education program, which offers students enrolled in most program opportunities to find employment in their fields of study while attending college. As many as 200 employers and 400 students have participated in the program annually.

MISSION

The CCRI Mission Statement, adopted by the Rhode Island Board of Governors for Higher Education in 1981, is as follows:

Mission I: CCRI will provide an ambitious array of postsecondary occupational programs and courses designed to prepare students for, and enhance their competence in, paraprofessional and technical jobs in business and industry beyond what might be achieved in high school.

Mission II: CCRI will offer programs and courses designed for students who wish to transfer their credits to other institutions of higher education, and will work closely with other Rhode Island institutions to develop and improve articulation and transfer programs.

Mission III: CCRI will give special attention to the quality of its offerings and the effectiveness of its instruction.

Mission IV: CCRI will provide such student services as may be necessary to a student's academic progress and as are feasible

Mission V: CCRI will provide adult residents of Rhode Island with open access to postsecondary education.

Mission VI: CCRI will make its facilities available to community groups and the public in general at as low a cost as possible.

Mission VII: CCRI will sponsor a wide range of non-profit forums, workshops, seminars, courses, lectures, exhibitions, concerts, shows, and tours.

Mission VIII: CCRI will assist community organizations, local businesses and industries, and appropriate state and municipal government agencies to develop and enhance their own educational programs, and will work with these groups to further the state's economic development objectives

Mission IX: Where feasible, CCRI should involve community representatives in establishing and evaluating its programs and activities.

GOVERNANCE

In accordance with the Education Act of 1981, Title 16, Chapter 59 of the General Laws of Rhode Island, the Rhode Island Board of Governors for Higher Education is vested with the legal authority for the three public institutions of higher education in the state. The board of governors has the responsibility of "formulating broad policy to implement the goals and objectives established and adopted by the board of governors." The Rhode Island Commissioner of Higher Education and the staff of the Office of Higher Education assist the board in discharging its responsibilities. Each college president is responsible for the administration and operation of his/her individual institution.

The board of governors consists of 13 members, of whom 10 are public, appointed by the governor with the consent of the senate. These 10 serve for three-year terms, appointed at staggered intervals. The remaining three members are the chairperson of the Board of Regents for Elementary/Secondary Education, the chairperson of the Senate Finance Committee (or designee), and the chairperson of the House Finance Committee (or designee).

The board of governors establishes and reviews institutional policies related to programs, services, and financial matters. Duties and responsibilities include the adoption and submittal of the budget; the allocation of appropriations; the adoption of standard accounting procedures the approval of tables of organization; the creation, abolishment, and consolidation of departments, divisions, programs, and courses of study; and the acquisition, holding disposition, and general management of property.

The meetings of the board of governors are the primary means by which the board establishes and maintains productive channels of communication with the community college and other higher education institutions. At each of the meetings, the president reports on the operations of the institution. Inter-institutional meetings and forums are arranged under the auspices of the board to explore topics of mutual interest, such as articulation and transfer issues, common problems associated with ESL students, and other system-related issues.

CCRI operates a multicampus community college with one administration. The president, vice president for academic affairs, vice president for business affairs, and vice president for student affairs oversee operations at all sites. The president is assisted by an executive staff consisting of the assistant to the president/public relations director, director of development, director of institutional research and planning, and the director of affirmative action and minority affairs, who also serves as director of the Providence Campus.

Included in the governance system at CCRI are four collective bargaining units representing faculty, professional staff, classified staff, and campus nurses. The Rhode Island Commissioner of Higher Education and that office's legal counsel are also engaged in the collective bargaining process. There is one other group of employees at the college who have no collective bargaining arrangements and work at the pleasure of the board of governors.

PROGRAMS AND ENROLLMENTS

The student body, with an enrollment of approximately 15,000, is diverse in age, culture, and experience. Women comprise 62%, 68% are part-time, 16% come from ethnic minority groups, and over 53% are 25 years of age or older. In the fall of 1997, students under 20 accounted for 19% of the enrollment. Of these, 72% were full-time students.

Students who are successful in completing programs of studies at CCRI achieve their education or career goals by transferring to four-year colleges or universities, obtaining employment in their chosen fields, or by a combination of work and continued study. The college's Office of Cooperative Education and Career Placement conducts follow-up surveys of each graduating class. According to the most recently published survey, 86% of the 1997 graduates were employed (54.4% full-time) and 39.5% are continuing their education (28.5% full-time). Although a number of students continue to move directly into Rhode Island's workforce after earning an associate degree, more and more are attending CRI to complete the first two years of a baccalaureate education. For these students, transfer of college credit from CCRI to four-year colleges and universities is critical.

A formal articulation and transfer agreement, established by the board of governors and updated on an annual basis, exists among the three public institutions in Rhode Island. In addition, CCRI has been aggressive in developing transfer agreements with both public and private colleges throughout the state and region. The most recent effort has focused on encouraging the receiving institutions to agree to a dual acceptance program.

Volunteerism, currently receiving increased attention on campuses across the country as a result of President Clinton's national service initiative, is becoming increasingly visible on CCRI campuses. CCRI hosts two volunteer fairs a year and works with other colleges in the state through the Rhode Island Campus Compact to promote and expand community service opportunities.

The CCRI Office of Community Services provides workshops, seminars, conferences, non-credit courses, and special programs for Rhode Island residents. CCRI has the largest high school equivalency preparation and testing program in the state, serving approximately 50% of the total state graduates. The Small Business Development Center, which targets businesses owned by minorities, offers training seminars and free consultant services. Projects SPHERE and REACH provide services to single parents and homemakers. Vocational Training for Adults helps the unemployed and underemployed find new career paths. Traffic safety-related programs offered through CCRI include the state-mandated motorcycle safety program, school bus driver training, defensive driving, and driving-while-intoxicated programs.

Other programs include summer youth employment and training; continuing education for real estate personnel and dental assistants; contractual testing for teachers, police, and firefighters; asbestos abatement training; lead-based paint removal techniques; and training and testing of commercial truck drivers.

CCRI encourages community organizations to use campus facilities for conferences, seminars, athletic events, cultural performances, and public hearings. Over 400 agencies per year use college facilities for meetings, public events and activities.

FUNDING

Because the mission of the college is to provide citizens of Rhode Island with access to education, CCRI has attempted to maintain tuition and fees at a modest level. This has meant trying to keep increases in line with changes in the Consumer Price Index (CPI). However, increases have exceeded CPI from 1987 to 1995. Tuition and fees have since remained at approximately 1995 levels, $873 for in-state residents and $2,38 for out-of-state residents. In-state part-time students pay $73 per credit; out-of-state part-time students $217, plus applicable fees.

CCRI received over $4.8 million in third-party funding to provide training and student support services in 47 projects for fiscal 1998-99. The college receives 34% of its third-party funding directly from federal sources; 58% from state sources that indirectly distribute federal monies from the U.S. Department of Labor's Job Training partnership Act (JTPA), the U.S. Department of Education's Perkins Act, and the U.S. Department of Health and Services Welfare Reform Act (JOBS); and 8% from private-sector trade associations and/or private foundations.

The state appropriation for the current fiscal year is $34,363,530. The total unrestricted budget is $54,389,894.

CCRI is well positioned to benefit from the new state administration's announced intention to embrace a regional approach to economic development. The college already works closely with local chambers of commerce and economic development entities and stands poised to emerge as the training arm of regional economic development programs. A similar situation exists with respect to President Clinton's support of school-to-work initiatives. CCRI's Tech-Prep and Cooperative Education programs, together with other grant-funded projects, collectively demonstrate a strong school-to-work effort, making the college a likely recipient of additional funding for expanded programs.

As CCRI moves into its fourth decade of providing educational opportunities for Rhode Island residents, it will focus on strengthening both school-to-work career programs and transfer initiatives that encourage high school students to consider CCRI for the first two years of a baccalaureate degree. This would include continuing to aggressively seek articulation and dual acceptance agreements with four-year colleges and universities.

The college also will focus on telecommunications and how it can position itself to make maximum use of the emerging technologies to ensure that CCRI is on-line and state-of-the-art in years to come. Goals for improved use of technology range from expanding access to the Internet to automating the college application system.

The college also will focus on telecommunications and how it can position itself to make maximum use of the emerging technologies to ensure that CCRI is on-line and state-of-the-art in years to come. Goals for improved use of technology range from expanding access to the Internet to automating the college application system. A college telecommunications committee and a board of governors subcommittee on telecommunications are reviewing the current state of technology on campus with an eye to developing plans to be implemented as resources become available.

Despite concerns about budget and finances, which are shared with colleges across the country, CCRI will continue to move forward where necessary and remain flexible and responsive to community needs.

FOR ADDITIONAL INFORMATION, PLEASE CONTACT:
Edward J. Liston, President
Community College of Rhode Island
400 East Avenue
Warwick, RI 02886
Telephone: (401) 825-218
Fax: (401) 825-2365
E-mail: eliston@ccri.cc.ri.us

SOUTH CAROLINA

James L. Hudgins
Executive Director
South Carolina State Board for Technical and Comprehensive Education

OVERVIEW

Established in 1961, the South Carolina Technical Education System is a system of 16 two-year postsecondary technical colleges and a specialized industry training program called Special Schools. This system has the statutory mission of supporting South Carolina's economic development through the provision of technical and occupational training programs and support services. The Technical Education System employs approximately 3,900 full-time employees and operates with an annual budget in excess of $300 million. More than 900 programs are offered to students throughout the system. In 1997, the colleges and the Special Schools training program enrolled more than 200,000 students and trainees. The colleges enrolled more than 80,000 students in credit programs and more than 114,000 in non-credit occupational advancement programs.

Mandated by legislation to maintain "open admissions policies" and "establish and maintain low tuition and fees," the Technical Education System is the vehicle for educational access in South Carolina

In the late 1950s and early 1960s, South Carolina faced a serious problem. Young people were leaving the state, where agriculture was the economic base, to take jobs in other states where industry was growing. The state had no mechanism in place to offer training services to its citizens or to help draw industry into the state. In 1961, a joint legislative study committee was formed to study this problem. The study and subsequent recommendations made by this committee resulted in one of the most significant pieces of legislation in South Carolina's history.

The specific recommendations regarding technical training (outside the existing high school program) fell into two main categories:

1. An intensive program to provide immediate training for established industries and for particular industries; and
2. A technical training program to train high school graduates for initial employment as technicians in industry and to offer trade extension courses for people desiring employment in industry and to

those already employed who want to improve their ills.

The 1961 General Assembly, guided by this committee's recommendation, enacted legislation which authorized the establishment of the South Carolina Advisory Committee for Technical Training. This act provided for an eight-member committee, appointed by the governor and representative of each of the state's congressional districts.

One of the advisory committee's first actions was to appoint a coordinator of technical and industrial training and move immediately to implement the industry training program (now called Special Schools) which was mandated by the authorizing legislation.

Once the Special Schools program was underway, attention turned to the establishment of the companion program of permanent technical education institutions. The main goal in planning the system was simple and pragmatic — to make a suitable training program available to any adult South Carolinian who wanted to obtain a marketable skill.

Historical Timeline

Sept. 20, 1961   The first region of the state to apply for a center was Greenville County. Within a year, Greenville Technical Education Center was built and opened its doors to the first students.

Spring of 1962   Applications were approved for centers in Spartanburg, Richland and Sumter counties, and for the tri-county area of Anderson, Oconee and Pickens.

Fall of 1963   All four of these centers were training students in newly opened facilities. Florence-Darlington, Berkeley-Charleston-Dorchester and York Technical Education Centers opened their doors.

1966   Horry-Marion-Georgetown and Piedmont Technical Education Centers opened their doors.

1968   Orangeburg-Calhoun Tech and Chesterfield-Marlboro Tech had opened.

1969   The General Assembly transferred the administration of the state's three area trade schools to the Technical Education System.

1969   The Williamsburg Regional Manpower Training Center

	opened in Kingstree.
1971	The 1971 General Assembly had directed the South Carolina Commission on Higher Education to conduct a joint study on a proposal to establish a system of community colleges within South Carolina.
1972	The report resulting from the study led to the passage of Act 1268 by the 1972 General Assembly. Act 1268 established the State Board for Technical and Comprehensive Education (State Tech Board). The act authorized, at local option and with State Tech Board and Commission on Higher Education approval, the addition of first and second-year college parallel curricula to the technical education centers. Act 1268 represented the General Assembly's response to the state's need for an economic offering of lower- division college courses at a moderate cost to the student and within commuting distance. Act 1268 resulted in all colleges within the South Carolina Technical Education System receiving State Tech Board and Commission on Higher Education approval to offer the associate in arts and the associate in science degrees.
1972	Aiken Tech opened its permanent facilities.
1973	Trade schools located at Beaufort, Denmark and West Columbia officially became technical education centers.
June 1976	The General Assembly passed Act 654. Act 654 was especially important in that it expressly provided for the technical education centers' Area Commissions to continue. It also delegated the primary responsibility of local governance and supervision of institutions to the Area Commissions.
1979	All sixteen technical education centers had been officially recognized as technical colleges.

GOVERNANCE

The South Carolina Technical Education System is governed by a 12-member board, appointed by the governor, one from each congressional district, with the advice and consent of the legislative delegations of the congressional districts involved. Four members are appointed at large — one of whom must be experienced in policy development for secondary vocational education and adult basic and adult vocational education, and one of whom must be experienced in policy development for federal job training programs. The state superintendent of education and the director of the State Department of Commerce serve as ex-officio members. The South Carolina State Board for Technical and Comprehensive Education is responsible for the state-level development, implementation and coordination of post-high school occupational, vocational and technical training and education.

Board officers include a chairman, vice chairman and any other officers deemed necessary to fulfill their responsibilities. Officers are elected annually to serve a one-year term, (effective July).

1. The chairman appoints a nominating committee of at least three board members 30 days prior to the election who shall recommend a slate of officers for consideration by the board. Additional nominations may be received from the board members. All members are eligible to be officers of the board.

In addition, each college is governed locally by an Area Commission, each of which is legislated to: adopt rules and regulations for the expenditure of funds; acquire real and personal property for the construction and equipping of institutions; employ the institutional chief administrative officer and personnel; exercise the right of eminent domain in the geographical area served; apply for, receive and expend monies from state, local and federal agencies; maintain accounts of receipts and expenditures in accordance with uniform bodies and the State Tech Board; and award certificates, diplomas and associate degrees.

FINANCE

Fiscal year 1995-96

Current Unrestricted Funds

	Amount	Percentage
State Appropriations	$149,144,847	55.5%
Federal Funds	686,962	3%
Student Fees	64,084,917	23..9%
County Appropriations	26,027,546	9.7%
Auxiliary Enterprises	22,613.755	8.4%

Other Sources	6,025,924	2.2%

Total Unrestricted	$268,583,951	

Current Restricted Source of Funds

Federal

Job Training Partnership	$7,698,264	12.1%
Other Federal Grants	15,207,096	24.0%
Student Financial Aid	34,093,682	53.8%
State	3,932,580	6.2%
Other	2,446,828	3.9%

Total Restricted	$63,378,450	

During a period when technical college enrollments have risen by more than 50 percent systemwide, appropriations have not proportionally supported enrollment growth. The following graph shows the enrollment of the system versus the percentage of funding since 1989.

FUNDING

South Carolina is in the midst of major funding reform. In 1996 the state legislature passed Act 359, which says that by the year 2000, all of higher education in South Carolina will be funded based 100 percent on performance. Until 1997-98, funding for South Carolina's colleges and universities was based solely on a formula using full-time equivalency figures, which meant that funding was enrollment driven.

The new funding model includes a performance rating process that bases performance evaluation on individual institutional goals (benchmarks). The model includes funding methods that also allocate dollars to institutions based on their respective performance rating, as well as their financial need, which is determined using national figures. During 1997-98, the first year of implementation, $4.6 million of state appropriations for higher education was based on the performance of institutions on 14 of the 37 measures outlined in the legislation. State appropriations of $250 million were bases on 21 of the 37 measures for the second year. By academic year 1999-2000, when this new funding model will be fully implemented, 100 percent of state funding for higher education will be based on 37 performance indicators (see Accountability) and the old enrollment-driven funding system will end. This new performance-based funding methodology is setting a precedent as no other state has attempted to base 100 percent of higher education funding on performance alone.

Tuition And Fees

Technical colleges are required by law to maintain moderate tuition costs. The State Tech Board establishes a minimum and maximum instructional fee for all approved technical education programs. The Area Commission for each institution sets the individual college fees within the established range. The Area Commission may also assess plant and capital fees per semester to offset plant funding deficiencies and funding of approved capital improvement plans, respectively. Assessment of plant and capital fees requires approval by the State Tech Board.

The average full-time tuition cost per semester is $507.28, including plant and capital fees.

PROGRAMS AND ENROLLMENTS

The 16 technical colleges in South Carolina offer a wide range of post-secondary programs at the associate degree, diploma and certificate levels. More than 900 programs are offered to students throughout the Technical Education System (328 associate degree, 133 diploma and 526 certificate programs). The associate degree, diploma and certificate programs are grouped in the following discipline and technology clusters:

Agriculture
Arts and Science
Business
Computer Technology
Engineering Technology
Health Science
Industrial Technology
Occupational Technology
Public Service

Program levels are designated by the following ranges of semester credit hours:

Associate Degree Programs   60-84 semester credit hours
Diploma Programs   40-52 semester credit hours
Certificate Programs   8-40 semester credit hours

Cluster	Annualized Headcount	Annualized FTE (Full Time Equivalent)
Agriculture	611	424
Arts and Science	16,302	8,779
Business	12,008	6,506
Computer	5,674	3,029
Engineering Technology	4,781	2,658
Health Science	14,214	8,437
Industrial Technology	6,119	3,644
Occupational Technology	855	494
Public Service	6,092	3,392
Undetermined/Other	16,484	3,574
Total	83,090	40,955

Degrees Awarded Systemwide – FY 1997:

4,944 associate degrees

1,275 diplomas

2,634 certificates

Graduates

Numbers of technical college graduates by cluster were highest in the health sciences (2,234graduates), business (1,652 graduates), industrial technology (1,560 graduates) and public service (951 graduates).

ENROLLMENT FIGURES

For fall, 1997, the Technical Education System enrolled 57,621 students in credit programs. This represented 40,954 full-time equivalent students. Fifty-six percent were part-time students, with 42.7% full-time. In addition to the credit programs offered at the colleges, there were 127,318 students enrolled in continuing education courses during FY 1997.

By racial composition in fall 1997, 68% were white non-Hispanic, 28% black, 2% Asian or Hispanic, and 2% other. Men represented 39.7% of the system's total enrollment, while women still made up the majority with 60.3%.

ECONOMIC DEVELOPMENT

The South Carolina Technical Education System was founded in 1961 to support economic development in the state. The system has been recognized as having one of the premiere industry training programs in the United States. This industry training program, called Special Schools, provides customized training programs for new and expanding industry at little or no cost to those companies. South Carolina has seen significant growth in recent years in its manufacturing base, and Special Schools (as part of the South Carolina Technical Education System) is a tool often used to help bring this industry into the state.

The services Special Schools offers a company are comprehensive and go beyond just "worker training." The services provided include curriculum development, providing and training instructors, preparing the training site and recruiting/screening applicants for the training program. Pre-employment training, structured post-employment training or a combination of the two are provided to the company.

Special Schools, using only state dollars (no federal monies), provides comprehensive training services to the company. Special Schools training programs are totally customized and are driven by the needs of the company. Everything is built around the start-up date of the company.

Last year, approximately 8,666 individuals completed training through Special Schools in 171 companies. The S.C. State Board for Technical and Comprehensive Education manages the Special Schools program, but provides regional and local managers to work with individual companies to tailor the training they need to start up their operation "in the black." Since Special Schools began, almost 200,000 people have been trained for new jobs in more than 1500 companies.

About half the training done through Special Schools is for existing companies that are expanding their operations in South Carolina. As long as a company is creating new jobs on a level that is cost-productive, those employees can be trained through Special Schools. The Technical Education System has been working with some companies for a number of years because they continue to expand their operations and create additional jobs.

South Carolina companies benefit from having training coordinated in a cooperative manner between the Special Schools program and the state's technical colleges. The technical colleges get involved early with the new company and, at the conclusion of Special Schools training, are prepared to offer on-going training through the continuing education operations. Special Schools will provide all training materials developed for the company to the local technical college. Through the Technical Education System, a company is never without the resources to train its employees. The technical colleges play a vital role in providing higher levels of learning to the industries in South Carolina.

It is through a strong partnership between Special Schools and the state's technical colleges that the South Carolina Technical Education System is able to offer companies the start up and ongoing training they need to be successful.

ACCOUNTABILITY

With the advent of performance funding, South Carolina's technical colleges are experiencing a renewed emphasis on accountability measures. In the new performance funding legislation, Act 359, colleges will be measured on 37 separate indicators, which have been grouped into the following nine broad categories:

1. mission focus;
2. quality of faculty;
3. instructional quality;
4. institutional cooperation and collaboration;
5. administrative efficiency;
6. entrance requirements;
7. graduates' achievements;
8 user-friendliness of institution; and
9. research funding.

Some of the 37 indicators proposed in the new legislation don't apply to the South Carolina Technical Education System, as its mission varies significantly from the other sectors of higher education within the state (an example would be SAT and ACT scores of the student body). Act 359 outlines specifically the mission of each higher education sector, with technical education having the mission "…to provide postsecondary vocational, technical and occupational diploma programs leading directly to employment and associate degree programs which enable students to gain access to other postsecondary education programs."

The premise of the performance funding initiative is to encourage institutions of higher education, including the two-year technical colleges, to strive for higher goals and obtain a higher level of success. By the year 2000, 100 percent of the funding for higher education will be based on how well institutions perform on the list of indicators developed by the legislature.

FOR ADDITIONAL INFORMATION, PLEASE CONTACT:
Dr. James L. Hudgins
Executive Director
South Carolina State Board for Technical and Comprehensive Education
111 Executive Center Dr.
Columbia, SC 29210
Telephone: (803) 737-7782
Fax: (803) 737-7781

SOUTH DAKOTA

Patrick Keating
State Director, Division of Workforce and Career Preparation
South Dakota Department of Education and Cultural Affairs

OVERVIEW

The postsecondary technical institute system started in 1961, when the South Dakota legislature approved the concept of local school districts' beginning postsecondary vocational-technical programs. Six districts opted to do so and, presently, four school districts still exercise local day-to-day governance authority over their respective technical institutes.

POSTSECONDARY TECHNICAL INSTITUTES' STATE VISION AND MISSION

The vision statement is:
- To promote educational excellence and innovation to meet the emerging technologies of the 21st century and to assist South Dakota to become a leader in economic development in the global market place.

The mission of the technical institutes is to:
- Provide high-wage, high-tech programs to meet economic and student needs;
- Provide necessary staff development for changing, emerging and new technology;
- Provide a seamless transition between all levels of education and work for students;
- Provide program/training that meets industry standards;
- Provide work-based learning for specialized training;
- Develop long-range plans for repair, maintenance and new buildings;
- Improve the image of postsecondary technical education; and
- Maintain long-range financial stability.

GOVERNANCE

The South Dakota Board of Education (SDBE) is the state-level governing board. The board is appointed for four years by the governor. The president of the board is elected for a one-year term by board members.

The SDBE governance includes:

1) approval of the allocation of funds from the legislature to each technical institute;
2) approval of all new programs;
3) approval of all continuing programs on three-year cycles;
4) bonding authority for buildings at the technical institutes; and
5) approve the percentage of Perkins federal funds allocated at the secondary and postsecondary levels.

The governing board of education at each school district is responsible for overall budget, maintenance, daily operations and personnel decisions of the technical institute. The director of each institute serves as the CEO/president of the institute under the superintendent of each school district.

The Department of Education and Cultural Affairs (DECA) oversees SDBE policy on credentialing of instructors; financial management of the state and federal allocations; and program development, approval, retention and elimination.

The Division of Workforce and Career Preparation (DWCP) in DECA is responsible for carrying out the SDBE policy for DECA.

In 1995, the South Dakota Governor, William J. Janklow, instituted the Council of Technical Institutes (CTI). It is comprised of the local education agency superintendents, the director of each technical institute and the director of DWCP. The council makes recommendations to the SDBE on program development, retention and elimination; budget and formula distribution; building development; and the development of a statewide plan for the institutes.

The proposed statewide plan is to enhance the image of postsecondary technical education as a statewide delivery system and to develop high-tech, high-wage programs to meet state economic development needs.

FUNDING

The postsecondary technical institutes are funded from tuition and fees, federal funds, state funds and other funds totaling $28,126,736. In 1998, the funding total by category on a statewide basis was:

Tuition/Fees:	$9,138,999
Federal Funds:	$2,356,677
State Funds:	$14,093,377

Other Funds: $2,537,683
Explanations for Revenue Budget:

Tuition/Fees—Revenue collected from students that are enrolled in credit-bearing courses.

Federal Funds—The Carl D. Perkins Vocational and Applied Technology Education Act provides federal funds to improve technical education. Federal funds help support the following types of activities at the technical institutes:

1) Supplementary services designed to meet the needs of special population students;
2) Upgrading of curriculum;
3) Purchase of equipment;
4) Staff development;
5) New program development; and
6) Guidance and counseling

Federal funds account for approximately 8% of the total revenue received by the technical institutes. Federal funds cannot supplant local or state funds. Federal funds are distributed to the technical institutes based on the number of Pell grants and Bureau of Indian Affairs grants issued at each institution.

State Funds—State-appropriated funds are used to support instructional costs, and operation and maintenance of facilities. State funds account for approximately 49% of the total revenue received by the technical institutes. State funds may be set aside for bonding, maintenance and repair, day care facilities, and business and industry training. The remaining funds are distributed using a formula that includes per-student program wage factor and the number of full-time equivalent (FTE) students.

Other Funds—Revenue the technical institutes receive from a variety of areas labeled "Other Funds". Examples of other funds are: farm operations, donations and contributions, automobile services, and cosmetology services.

The state allocation is a performance-based formula system. The formula is based on three components per program:

1) Wages that include a minimal wage that must be earned based on the length of program with a factor up to 35% of the minimum wage set for a program, so a program could get from a 1.0 to 1.35 multiplier for determining reimbursement.

2) The number of completers from a program based on the state standard that 80% of FTE students in the program will complete this program. A completer is one who obtains a degree, diploma or certificate from the program.
3) Cost reimbursement of programs is based on state economic development factors. A program is designated as a basic program ($1,500 per completer), a support program ($2,500 per completer) or an economically-targeted program ($3,500 per completer), adjusted for the length of the program.

The above three factors are used as multipliers to determine how much each program will be reimbursed from the state-allocated money. This is not designed as a budget-need formula, only on how the state allocation will be distributed.

PROGRAMS AND ENROLLMENTS

The South Dakota technical institutes presently offer A.A.S. degrees, diplomas or certificates. Eighty percent of the two-year programs offer A.A.S. degrees. The curriculum for A.A.S. degree programs must provide not less than 20% of the credit hours in general education and not less than 70% of the credit hours in technical education. Almost every program is 72 credits in length. Diploma programs vary in their general education requirements, based on industry and program review recommendations.

Transferability of program credits to four-year colleges or universities is based on individual articulation agreements. Each institute is accredited by the North Central Association of Colleges and Schools..

Presently, the technical institutes have 9 agriculture, 19 business, 3 marketing, 43 trade and industry and 21 health occupation programs.

Each institute provides Adult Basic Education/GED programs as a separate component through the local school district.

The Division of Workforce and Career Preparation reviews all programs on a three-year cycle with a "Program Improvement Process". In this process, many standards for good programs are reviewed by a team comprised of industry and teaching representatives. Programs must demonstrate the ability to keep up with industry standards, provide teacher in-service and professional growth, develop and upgrade curriculum, develop plans for technology upgrades and provide proof of placement of completers meeting state standards for placement and wages for continued state funding. Criteria for many of these standards are set by members of the industry review team.

Customized Business and Industry training (BIT) offers non-credit-bearing courses for upgrading skills. Over 11,100 individuals took advantage of such training in 1998.

The Division of Workforce and Career Preparation (DWCP) provides statewide leadership and monitors the utilization of state funds used to provide training and periodically audits the use of funds. Each BIT program undergoes a formal review within each of the postsecondary institutes to assure quality of training provided, responsiveness of training to needs of the community, compliance with federal and state rules affecting the training offerings, availability of offerings to "special populations" and assures non-discrimination.

The postsecondary institutes employ and supervise the program coordinator and staff. They provide leadership in the structuring and provision of the Business and Industry Training program. This includes ensuring that the training provided is consistent with the quality standards set by industry and that all training activities offered are responsive to needs established by the local communities in which the training is requested. While each institute provides training space on campus, mobile units are also used to supply training to numerous communities.

ECONOMIC DEVELOPMENT

The technical institute directors, the director of the Division of Workforce and Career Preparation, and the Commissioner, Governor's Office of Economic Development (GOED) meet to develop potential new programs based on economic target areas, develop local training programs that can receive state funding for employers, develop funding resources for upgrading technology in programs and meet with local economic developers to describe services available for present employers and prospective employers.

Such a program has led to over $8 million from the governor's office for upgrading and supplying technology to the institutes over the past four years. Approximately $4 million has been made available to employers for specialized training that meets wage requirements.

FOR ADDITIONAL INFORMATION, PLEASE CONTACT:
Patrick Keating
State Director
Division of Workforce and Career Preparation
Department of Education and Cultural Affairs
700 Governors Drive
Pierre, South Dakota 57501-2291
Telephone: (605) 773-3247
Fax: (605) 773-4236

TENNESSEE

Lynda Phillips-Madson
Associate Vice Chancellor for Academic Affairs,
Tennessee Board of Regents
and
George Malo
Assistant Vice Chancellor for Research and Assessment,
Tennessee Board of Regents

OVERVIEW

The State University and Community College System of Tennessee was established by the Tennessee General Assembly in 1972. Upon its founding, the system included six universities and 10 community colleges. Effective in July, 1983, the Tennessee General Assembly transferred the governance of four state technical institutes and 26 state technology centers from the Tennessee Board of Education to the Tennessee Board of Regents (TBR). "Tennessee Technology Centers" were formerly known as "Tennessee Area Vocational-Technical Schools."

At this time, the Tennessee Board of Regents is among the largest systems of post-secondary education in the nation. The Tennessee system currently governs 46 institutions—six universities, 12 community colleges, two technical institutes, and 26 technology centers—that offer programs in 90 of our state's 92 counties. The regents system currently enrolls more than 181,000 students.

The Tennessee Board of Regents community colleges and technical institutes are as follows:

Chattanooga State Technical Community College (Chattanooga);
Cleveland State Community College (Cleveland);
Columbia State Community College (Columbia);
Dyersburg State Community College (Dyersburg);
Jackson State Community College (Jackson);
Motlow State Community College (Tullahoma);
Nashville State Technical Institute (Nashville);
Northeast State Community College (Blountville);
Pellissippi State Technical Community College (Knoxville);
Roane State Community College (Harriman);

Shelby State Community College (Memphis);
State Technical Institute at Memphis (Memphis);
Volunteer State Community College (Gallatin); and
Walters State Community College (Morristown);

Usually considered to be the impetus in Tennessee behind the movement to establish community colleges, *Public Higher Education in Tennessee* was a study initiated in 1955 by the Legislative Council of the Tennessee General Assembly. Responsibility to establish a statewide network of "regional-type institutions of higher learning" was assigned to the Tennessee State Board of Education. (Rhoda, 1979, pp. xix-xx). The plan whereby community colleges in Tennessee would be established located the "regional institutions of higher learning" near cities and towns "where industry and business were already located and in select rural areas to which the state hoped to lure new industry." (Consacro & Rhoda, 1996, p. 577).

GOVERNANCE

The State University and Community College System of Tennessee is governed by the Tennessee Board of Regents (TBR). The board is by law responsible for the establishment, management, and coordination of each of the institutions it holds in trust. Through its professional staff, the Board of Regents of Tennessee provides centralized services and sets procedures for its member institutions.

The Board of Regents of Tennessee consists of 18 members, including four ex-officio members, 12 lay-public members, one faculty member, and a student regent. The ex-officio members include the governor of the state, the commissioner of education, the commissioner of agriculture, and the executive director of the Tennessee Higher Education Commission, who is a non-voting member. The governor, subject to confirmation by the state senate, appoints the public members of the board. One public member is appointed from each of the congressional districts of the state. Three public members are appointed "at-large," one from each of three "grand divisions" of the state. The governor appoints the faculty member for a one-year term. The student regent serves a one-year term, after nomination by campus presidents and appointment by the governor. The term of service for public members appointed to the Tennessee Board of Regents is six years.

The current chief executive officer of the regents system is Chancellor

Charles E. Smith, who acts on behalf of the board, with delegated responsibility for management of system campuses. Campus presidents report to the board of regents through the chancellor.

FUNDING

The Tennessee Board of Regents Committee on Finance and Business Operations consists of directors who are not officers of any university. This committee oversees the financial reporting process of the system. The campus business offices and internal audit staff meet on a quarterly basis with the board staff to discuss financial reporting and internal control issues.

During 1998-99, the system's current fund revenues exceeded one billion dollars. Out of this $1.195 billion budget for the system, the community colleges and technical institutes budgets accounted for $347.6 million in unrestricted and restricted revenues.

Through legislative appropriations, the state provides the most significant amount of general fund support to the regents system of higher education. The unrestricted state appropriations budgeted for 1998-99 totaled $543.6 million. Of this amount, the community colleges and technical institutes were to receive $172.6 million. During the 1997-98 year, state appropriations accounted for 45.4% of total system revenues.

The second largest source of current funding support to the regents institutions was student tuition and fees, which totaled $251.1 million during 1997-98. During 1998-99, the income from student tuition and fees was budgeted at $292.9 million. Of this amount, the community colleges and technical institutes were expected to collect $172.6 million in student tuition and fees. A full-time student taking 12 credit hours or more attending a community college or technical institute during 1998-99 paid $565 a semester in in-state tuition (maintenance fees). This amount was a 4% increase over the previous year. In addition, each full-time community college and technical institute student paid $50 a semester in technology access fees. Other fees, including student activity and student government fees, varied by institution.

The third largest source of general current funding was gifts, grants, and contracts. During the 1997-98, these funds totaled $218.9 million for the system. Grants and contracts received from federal agencies totaled $153.5 million.

PROGRAMS AND ENROLLMENTS

Programming offered at each two-year institution are to reflect the local needs and character of the community in which it is located. If the local college cannot provide the needed programs, other institutions can be requested to do so. The two-year institutions have multiple sites that provide degree programs for students who plan to transfer to upper-division colleges and universities, degree and non-degree programs in business, industry and government for students who do not plan to transfer, and public service and continuing education programs to promote marketable skills and personal growth of individuals.

Students planning to transfer to baccalaureate programs may earn associate of arts (A.A.) degrees or associate of science (A.S.) degrees. A student in an associate-degree program selects a university-parallel major as the transfer program within which an area of emphasis such as art, English, mathematics, pre-medical, etc. is selected. A general studies area of emphasis also provides students the opportunity to complete general education requirements before advancing to specialized areas.

The associate of applied science (A.A.S.) degrees are awarded to students who do not plan to transfer to four-year institutions and are designed to prepare students for immediate employment in specialized areas. The A.A.S. degree normally requires a minimum of 60 semester credit hours, including at least 36 hours in a specialty field.

Programs leading to technical certificates or certificates of credit are designed to respond to the needs of business and industry or to provide a short-term program in a concentrated area to develop specific career skills. In addition, special credit courses or groups of courses are also provided to meet specific education objectives. These courses prepare students to become certified in various occupations such as emergency medical technicians, or are designed to satisfy apprenticeships or business needs. The colleges also provide remedial/developmental coursework for students who are found to be deficient in basic academic requirements or who wish to improve upon skills that have been lost due to time away from academic study.

The fall, 1998, headcount enrollment of the community colleges and technical institutes under the Tennessee Board of Regents was 75,964 students. Although this figure represented a 1.4% drop over the previous year, the enrollments at the two-year institutions have grown by over 48% during the past ten years. The full-time-equivalency (FTE) enrollment (defined as one student taking 15 credit hours) was 46,635 during the Fall of 1998. The FTE enrollment has grown by over 54% during the past ten years.

Part-time students accounted for 56.8% of the community college and technical institute enrollment during 1998-99. These institutions are serving non-traditional students, as the average age of students attending Tennessee's community colleges and technical institutes is 27.6 years old. Over 59% of the students are women and close to 16% of the students are African-American. Ninety-seven percent of the students attending Tennessee Board of Regents two-year institutions are residents of Tennessee.

An estimated 6,700 students received credentials from two-year institutions during 1997-98. Of this number, over 1,300 students received certificates and 5,400 received associate degrees.

Thirty-four percent of students attending two-year public institutions in Tennessee receive some type of financial aid. During 1997-98, over 37,800 students received financial aid totaling $70.6 million.

WORKFORCE DEVELOPMENT

Workforce development is an educational process that enables Tennessee residents to obtain the technical skills and professional training necessary to compete in today's highly competitive job market. Workforce development provides quality career opportunities for individuals, a skilled workforce for business and industry, and many economic benefits for the state and its citizens.

Tennessee Board of Regents' formal workforce development efforts are centered around occupationally-related education and training conducted at Tennessee's 12 community colleges, two technical institutes, and 26 technology centers. The Tennessee Board of Regents and the State Department of Education participate in the national technical preparation initiative by providing programs specifically designed to prepare students for a postsecondary degree, certificate, or apprenticeship leading to employment in related career fields. Fourteen technical preparation consortia, located at the two-year institutions, serve students across Tennessee. Articulation agreements between TBR institutions and K-12 schools provide students with the opportunity to receive postsecondary course credit for skills learned in high school.

In addition to formalized classroom training, TBR institutions provide customized training to firms and industries through special industry training contracts. Currently, Tennessee's technology centers and two-year institutions are the primary deliverers of skilled occupational training in the state. These TBR institutions provide job training and retraining for more than 100,000 new labor market entrants and incumbent workers annually. Tennessee employers frequently turn to Tennessee technology centers to meet their needs for technical training, workplace literacy, and managing technological change in the workplace. In 1998, approximately 11,000 workers obtained customized training through contracts between employers and technology centers. Two-year institutions provided customized training to approximately 5,000 workers through contracts with employers.

Customized training or need-centered training provides access to resources that can be mobilized where and when an employer requires them. Need-centered training is developed in cooperation with business and industry. Need-centered training ensures:

- Business and industry define minimum quality standards;
- Business and industry help design the curriculum;
- Business and industry are assured of lower cost of training and recruiting; and
- Business and industry are assured of a skilled, professionally trained workforce.

ACCOUNTABILITY

The Tennessee Board of Regents and the institutions under its governance are committed to providing a quality postsecondary education to the citizens of the state of Tennessee. The board also strives to ensure access to its institutions through diversity in programming, reasonable costs, and a geographic presence for those wishing to further their education. Through many outreach and research programs, the system also provides public service to the various communities of Tennessee.

The Tennessee Board of Regents has always believed that it should be accountable to the public and the students being served. The board has continually evaluated its offerings and activities throughout the years to ensure that the best public education and services are provided. The results of these evaluations also provide information on how well the system has met the needs of Tennesseans and what adjustments are needed in an ever-changing society. Besides reporting to various legislative oversight committees, the board of regents addresses accountability in a more visible manner through: a first of its kind report card to the public, performance funding standards, and an Agenda 2000 document that states the board's commitment to the people of Tennessee.

The annual report card is intended to act as a vehicle for the board of regents system to provide information on various indicators of accountability. The indicators address outcome measures rather than inputs. While the report card also indicates areas upon which improvements can be made, it does show that public higher education in Tennessee has value and has provided a profitable return to the state. The report card is organized around four major categories of accountability. The major categories include Student Learning, Academic Programs, Faculty Productivity, and Financial Accountability. Under each category are various indicators of measurement that, taken together, provide a status of the major category. Examples of indicators under student learning are passing rates for licensure field, percent of students placed in jobs, student and alumni satisfaction, and graduation rates. Program accreditation status is an indicator under academic programs, and faculty workload can be found under faculty productivity. Examples under financial accountability include expenditures by functional area, staffing patterns, private giving, and financial aid.

The institutions of the board also are held accountable through performance funding standards. Under the performance funding program, institutions can earn up to 5.45% over their operating budgets. The incentive funding is used to improve the quality of an institution's program and services and has resulted in substantive improvements in academic programs. The program measures each institution on a set of quantitative outcomes-based standards. (THEC, 1998)

The Tennessee Board of Regents has also published its Agenda 2000: The Board of Regents Commitment to the People of Tennessee. This 17-page document provides a statement through various agenda items to confirm and secure the board's role as a primary contributor to the state's effort to expand the educational levels of its citizens and to improve the quality of life. The Agenda sets forth priorities designed to prepare the Tennessee Board of Regents to function relevantly and efficiently in the 21st century. The Agenda provides a sense of direction to build effective partnerships with communities, business and industry, and the public schools.

REFERENCES

Consacro, D. P., & Rhoda, R. G. (1996, November-December). Community Colleges in Tennessee. *Community College Journal of Research and Practice*, 20(6), pp. 575-584.

Rhoda, Richard G. (1979). Introduction. In Nicks, R. S. (Ed.), *Community Colleges of Tennessee: The Founding and Early Years*. Memphis, TN: Memphis State University Press.

Tennessee Higher Education Commission (1998). *Performance Funding Standards*, 1997-98 to 2001-02. THEC Publication, Nashville, TN: Author

FOR ADDITIONAL INFORMATION, PLEASE CONTACT:

Tennessee Board of Regents
Office of Academic Affairs
1415 Murfreesboro Road, Suite 350
Nashville, TN 37217
Telephone: (615) 366-4400
Fax: (615)366-4464
Website: WWW.TBR.STATE.TN.US
E-mail: lpmadson@tbr.state.tn.us
　　　　gmalo@tbr.state.tn.us

TEXAS

Glenda O. Barron, Assistant Commissioner and
Lynette Heckmann, Assistant to the Assistant Commissioner
Community and Technical Colleges Division
Texas Higher Education Coordinating Board

OVERVIEW

Texas has 50 community college districts with 74 campuses, three technical colleges, and three public lower-division institutions. In 1985, the Community and Technical Colleges Division of the Texas Higher Education Coordinating Board was established to provide coordination of the community colleges. Local boards of trustees and regents govern the institutions and are responsible for all administrative functions; however, they operate within the policies and guidelines set by the coordinating board.

Each community college governing board has from seven to nine members who are elected by voters within the college district. The Board of Regents for the Texas State Technical College System is comprised of nine members who are appointed by the governor.

The three public lower-division institutions are components of the Texas State University System. The nine members of the Board of Regents for the Texas State University System are appointed by the governor.

MISSION AND GOALS OF SYSTEM

The Texas Education Code in Section 130.003(e), states that the purpose of each Texas public community college is to provide:

(1) Technical programs up to two years in length leading to associate degrees or certificates;

(2) Vocational programs leading directly to employment in semi-skilled and skilled occupations;

(3) Freshman and sophomore courses in arts and sciences;

(4) Continuing adult education programs for occupational or cultural upgrading;

(5) Compensatory education programs designed to fulfill the commitment of an admissions policy allowing the enrollment of disadvantaged students;

(6) A continuing program of counseling and guidance designed to assist students in achieving their individual educational goals;

(7) Workforce development programs designed to meet local and statewide needs;

(8) Adult literacy and other basic skills programs for adults; and

(9) Such other purposes as may be prescribed by the Texas Higher Education Coordinating Board or local governing boards in the best interest of postsecondary education in Texas.

Texas Education Code Section 135.01(b) requires the Texas State Technical College System to serve the state by offering occupationally oriented programs with supporting academic course work, emphasizing highly specialized advanced and emerging technical and vocational areas for certificates or associate degrees. In addition, the TSTC System is directed to serve the state in the area of economic development. The system's economic development efforts to improve the competitiveness of Texas business and industry include exemplary centers of excellence in technical program clusters on the system's campuses and support of educational research commercialization initiatives.

BACKGROUND

The Texas legislature adopted the first public junior college law in 1929. Most of the first institutions were initiated as extensions of public high schools to grade levels 13 and 14. The superintendent of schools in each district acted as the junior college president, and the highest college administrator held the title of dean. (Campbell & Thompson, in Tollefson & Fountain, 1992).

The 1949 Texas Legislature established the Legislative Council to study and make recommendations on "the junior college issue." The council recommended, and the legislature approved, that the Texas State Board of Education be assigned the responsibility of exercising state-level oversight over public junior colleges. In 1965, the Texas Legislature enacted House Bill 1, which established the Coordinating Board and transferred "general control" over the community colleges to the new coordinating board, Texas College and University System, but left state-level administration of vocational and technical programs under the authority of the Texas State Board of Education and its staff in the Texas Education Agency (Campbell & Thompson, in Tollefson & Fountain, 1992).

The Texas Legislature adopted a law in 1975 that authorized the state board of education to delegate, through a contract, to the coordinating board to provide state-level administration of vocational and technical education in public colleges and universities. Community colleges success-fully resisted this transfer of authority to the coordinating board for about 10 years. Consequently, the Texas Legislature transferred state-level authority over community college vocational and technical education to the coordinating board. At the same time the legislature transferred state-level oversight over Texas State Technical College System from the state board of education to the coordinating board. That new coordinating board authority over TSTC included approval of degree programs and facilities acquisition and construction (Campbell & Thompson, in Tollefson & Fountain, 1992).

The Select Committee on Higher Education recommended, and in 1987 the legislature adopted, a law requiring the development and implementa-tion of a program to test the basic skills of all incoming freshman stu-dents at all Texas public colleges and universities. The new law also changed the name of the coordinating board to the Texas Higher Education Coordinating Board, authorized the coordinating board to restrict univer-sity enrollments, established four major research programs under the administration of the coordinating board, and changed the board to estab-lish a statewide telecommunications network (Campbell & Thompson in Tollefson & Fountain, 1992). The Texas Legislature adopted legislation charging the coordinating board, in collaboration with other entities, to develop:

A comprehensive five-year master plan for higher education;

Funding formulas and summary and analysis of institutional appropria-tions requests to provide a statewide view of funding needs; and

Policies on transferability of lower division courses among institutions of higher education.

In 1993, the Texas Legislature passed legislation that added workforce development programs designed to meet state and local needs and adult lit-eracy and other basic skills programs to the statutory purposes of the pub-lic junior and community colleges.

The 74th Texas Legislature in 1995 passed two items of particular importance to community colleges. The first permits high school students to attend college classes at local community colleges and receive both high school and college credit. In addition, the community colleges' boards of trustees are allowed to waive tuition and fees for high school students while providing a means for state funding to flow to both the high school and the community college.

The second piece of legislation established non-overlapping service areas for most of the 50 community college districts. It specified the counties and/or school districts served by each community college district. However, it did not establish pre-eminence or any special status for the community college serving the district vis-a-vis other institutions of higher education within the district. There are a few areas of the state that were not designated as service within the area of any particular community college district. Service to these non-designated areas would continue under coordinating board rules and guidelines.

In 1997, the 75th Texas Legislature enacted legislation directing each community college to prepare an annual performance report. The report is to include the rate at which students have completed attempted courses, the number and types of degrees and certificates awarded, the percentage of graduates who have passed licensing exams related to their degrees or certificates, the number of students or graduates who have transferred to or been admitted to public universities, TASP Test passing rates, the percentage of students who are academically disadvantaged, the number of students who are economically disadvantaged, the racial and ethnic composition of the student body, and the percentage of student contact hours taught by full-time faculty. This is the first performance-based accountability reporting required of Texas community colleges.

GOVERNANCE

In 1965, when the legislature established the Texas Higher Education Coordinating Board, the new board was given the assignment of achieving "excellence for college education" for all Texans. The legislature also directed the board to assure efficient and effective use of all resources, elimination of unnecessary duplication of effort regarding programs, buildings and equipment, and the provision of adequate resources to fulfill the goals of postsecondary education.

The governor appoints the 18 at-large members of the coordinating board, upon the advice and consent of the state senate, for six-year terms. The governor also appoints the chair and vice chair of the board. No state coordinating board member may be a community college board member or be employed in education. The coordinating board is mandated to meet in Austin in January, April, July and October, and the chair may call additional meetings as needed. Board members provide their services without pay, but they may be reimbursed for board-related activities approved by the chair. The coordinating board's responsibilities include statewide coordination of all higher education and the provision of recommendations to the governor and legislature about higher education needs, but local boards of trustees and presidents have retained their historical responsibilities and authority for individual college policymaking, planning, development and administration of community college operations (Campbell & Thompson, in Tollefson & Fountain, 1992).

Texas has 35 public universities, three lower division institutions, 50 community college districts with 74 campuses, three technical colleges, and eight public health-related institutions. In addition, Texas has 37 independent senior colleges, three independent junior colleges, and one independent medical school.

An election to establish a new community college district may be authorized by the coordinating board when specified criteria have been fulfilled and the board deems it appropriate. In such a case, district voters approve the establishment of the district, elect trustees, and set taxation and bonding policies. The trustees of the new district are elected at the same times when the elections to establish them are held. (Campbell & Thompson, in Tollefson & Fountain, 1992).

Since the establishment of the coordinating board in 1965, the legislature has delegated additional functions to the board. State department divisions of administration, community and technical colleges, finance, campus planning and research, educational partnerships, student services, and universities and health-related institutions help the coordinating board fulfill its responsibilities.

The commissioner's office oversees the offices of planning, access and equity, governmental relations and public information, internal auditing and general and general counsel. The assistant commissioner for community and technical colleges supervises 38 professional, technical, and support staff members who provide statewide coordination and assistance to the community colleges. This office also provides information and advise on accountability in all areas of public community and technical college operations as well as the three lower division institutions. The division is also responsible for the oversight of degree-granting proprietary institutions, which currently number 39.

For the fiscal year ending August 31, 1997, the coordinating board employed 275 staff members in Austin. The coordinating board has no branch offices.

FUNDING

Local property taxes, state appropriations, student tuition and fees, and the federal government are the four primary funding sources. Local tax support of college operating costs range significantly from one college district to another.

For the fiscal year ending August 31, 1998, 17.9% of current fund revenue came from local property taxes, 37.9% from state appropriations, 19.9% from student tuition and fees, 14.4% from federal grants, and 9.9% from other sources. In 1941, the legislature appropriated a total of $325,000, or an average of about $50 for each of 6,500 full-time student equivalents (FTSE) (Campbell & Thompson, in Tollefson & Fountain, 1992). State appropriations for public community colleges have increased dramatically since 1941, due to more colleges, very significant growth in enrollments, and increased support from the state legislature.

Legislative appropriations exclusive of fringe benefits for fiscal year 1998 totaled $683,376,495. The number of college districts increased from 22 in 1941 to 50 in 1998.

The coordinating board and its staff have developed statewide funding formulas to support portions of educational and general (E&G) operations. Local taxes also supplement state appropriations for E&G expenditures as well as paying all the costs of physical plant operations and maintenance. The formula dollar amounts are revised by the coordinating board each year, based upon an annual study of community college expenditures that is conducted collaboratively with an advisory committee selected by the community colleges. Statewide median costs per contact hour for each of the program areas are used to determine the recommended formula rates. To receive funding in the formulas, all programs must be approved by the coordinating board. the formulas provide the basis for college budget requests. They do not generate community college entitlements to state appropriations, but they are used to allocate the amount of money that the legislature does appropriate. State appropriations are disbursed to community colleges after coordinating board receipt of actual enrollments and contact hours, and reimbursements are restricted to base-year enrollment and appropriation figures (Campbell & Thompson, in Tollefson & Fountain, 1992).

For 1997-1998, a full-time (taking 15 semester credit hours or more) resident student at a Texas public community college paid between $235 and $828 in tuition and fees per semester. A full-time nonresident student paid between $398 and $4,214.

PROGRAMS

Assessment

Since 1989, each student taking courses at a Texas public institution has been required to take the Texas Academic Skills Program (TASP) Test before completing nine hours of college-level coursework. Students who do not achieve passing scores on any or all sections of the test (reading, writing, mathematics) must be enrolled in remedial courses to help them develop the necessary skills. Until all sections of the TASP Test are passed, no student may take upper-division courses or receive an associate degree.

Legislative changes to the TASP statute that were implemented in the fall of 1998 have required that students be assessed before initial enrollment so that those students needing additional assistance can begin their developmental coursework in their first semester. The Board has been given the authority to identify alternative tests to the TASP Test that can be used for initial assessment. In addition, state funding to community and technical colleges is now limited to 27 hours of developmental coursework per student. Universities are limited to 18 semester credit hours of funding for each student.

Program Approval Process

Technical and vocational education programs in Texas community and technical colleges are approved through a process determined by their nature and format. Prior to their implementation, programs receiving state funds must be approved by the local governing board and then by the coordinating board. Once received by the board, each proposed new technical program is assigned to an appropriate staff member for initial review. A peer discipline expert is asked to serve as a field reader of the proposal and participates in the formal review. At a formal new program review, individuals from the requesting institution come to the board offices (or through video telecommunications) to present the proposed program through a discussion of the following issues: (1) demonstrated local need (regional and state need also considered), (2) availability of employment opportunities for graduates, (3) a satisfactory and ongoing number of persons for the applicant pool, (4) the institution's fiscal and physical ability to support the program, (5) availability of adequately prepared faculty, and (6) necessary equipment for program implementation. Following the review, a recommendation is made to the commissioner regarding approval.

Certificate and applied associate degree programs in vocational and technical areas are approved by the commissioner of higher education upon recommendation of the new program review committee. If the commissioner does not approve a particular program or another institution objects to a program, the program is submitted to the coordinating board for action.

Types

Community colleges offer associate degree programs designed to allow transfer to senior colleges and universities, technical and vocational education programs at the certificate and associate in applied science degree levels, and adult basic education programs that allow students to earn high school equivalency status. Adult and continuing education courses, which are usually short-term and intensive, provide for initial entry into certain work situations as well as for retraining and upgrading for persons already employed. Tech-Prep programs are available in conjunction with secondary institutions. Linkages with other community resources, such as business and industry, job training centers, and other agencies, are supported and encouraged. Texas guidelines require that where state or national accreditation is appropriate and/or required, technical and vocational education programs in these areas will be developed in compliance with the minimum standards established by those accrediting bodies.

Degree Requirements

In addition to satisfactory completion of the core curriculum in a technical or vocational education program, a minimum of 15 hours in required general education courses must be included in the requirements for an applied associate degree.

FALL 1998
HEADCOUNT ENROLLMENT AND NUMBER OF INSTITUTIONS

Institutions Under Board Authority	1998 Preliminary Fall Headcount	Number of Institutions
Public Community/Junior Colleges	416,412	74 Institutions (50 Districts)
Public Technical College System	8,772	3 Institutions
Public Lower Division Institutions - Lamar Institutions	6,072	3 Institutions
Proprietary Institutions	9,500 (est)	39 Institutions
Subtotal — Lower Level	440,756	

The largest community college district, Dallas County Community College District, enrolled 48,125 students in fall 1998. The smallest enrollment was 769 at Clarendon College.

REFERENCES

Campbell, D. F. & Thompson, L. W., Jr., in Tollefson,T. A. & Fountain, B. E. (1992) *Forty-nine State Systems, 1992 Edition.* Washington, DC: American Association of Community Colleges.

FOR ADDITIONAL INFORMATION, PLEASE CONTACT:
Dr. Glenda O. Barron
Assistant Commissioner for Community and Technical Colleges
Texas Higher Education Coordinating Board
P O Box 12788
Austin, Texas 78711
Telephone: (512) 483-6250
Fax: (512) 483-6444
E-mail: barronga@thecb.state.tx.us

UTAH

William G. Ingram
Senior Vice President and Chief Instructional Officer
Durham Technical Community College

GOVERNANCE

Public two-year institutions in Utah are part of the Utah System of Higher Education. This system includes four comprehensive community colleges among a total of nine public colleges and universities. The system is governed by the Utah State Board of Regents. Each institution in the system also has a board of trustees that maintains authority over certain aspects of institutional operation (Utah State Board of Regents, 1998).

FUNDING

In 1997-98, the state appropriation to public two-year institutions in Utah was approximately $110.3 million, which represented a seven-percent increase over the previous academic year. This figure also represented 22% of the total state expenditure on higher education. In 1996-97, individual Utah community colleges received between 37 % and 52 % of their total operating budgets from the state. Average 1996-97 tuition and fees to Utah's four public community colleges was $1,757 (Schmidt, 1998).

PROGRAMS AND ENROLLMENTS

All four public two-year institutions in Utah offer comprehensive programs that include general studies and the liberal arts as well as technical programs. Institutions award the associate in arts (A.A.), associate in science (A.S.), and associate in applied science (A.S.S.) degrees, and they offer a variety of diploma and certificate programs. Utah Valley State College consists of independent lower and upper divisions. The lower division provides a comprehensive community college program while the upper division offers several baccalaureate degrees (Utah State Board of Regents).

In 1997-98, enrollments in Utah's four community colleges totaled 32,190 students, which represented 35% of the total enrollment in all public higher education institutions in the state. That figure also represented an increase of 123% over enrollments in 1987-88, when community college enrollments accounted for approximately one-quarter of the total public higher education enrollments in Utah (Utah Board of Regents, 1998).

REFERENCES

Schmidt, P., (1998, November 27) State spending on higher education rises 6.7% in 1998-99 to a total of $52.8-billion, *Chronicle of Higher Education*, 45(13), pp. A26-A28.

Utah State Board of Regents, (1998, May 17). www.utahsbr.edu Salt Lake City, UT: Author

FOR ADDITIONAL INFORMATION, PLEASE CONTACT:
Utah System of Higher Education
3 Triad Center, Suite 550
355 West North Temple
Salt Lake City, Utah 84180-1205
Telephone: 801-321-7123
Internet: www.utahsbr.edu

VERMONT

David Buchdahl
Academic Dean
Community College of Vermont

OVERVIEW

The Community College of Vermont (CCV) is a state-supported two-year, open admissions college. It is also a complex learning organization, dedicated to improving teaching and learning for students, instructors, and staff, and for the employees of other organizations to whom CCV provides training and education in a variety of formats. It has no full-time faculty; it owns no property, and last year it served nearly 7800 different students in regular classroom instruction, and an estimated additional 1000 individuals through work-place programs. CCV has twelve site locations around the state. It is Vermont's only community college, but it is part of a broader Vermont Sate College System that includes three separate four-year, campus-based colleges and a two-year technical college. The five colleges in the system serve about 10,000 students or about 7500 full-time-equivalent (FTE) students. The ratio of instate to out-of state students is very different for CCV than for the rest of the colleges. On average, about 60% of the students on the four "campus-colleges" are from Vermont, while approximately 98% of CCV students are Vermont residents. Thus CCV serves nearly 80% of the students in the system, just about one-third of all FTEs and about 45% of in-state FTEs. These numbers are meaningful in the context of Vermont, a small rural state with a population of less than 600,000. About one-fourth the population are concentrated in the city of Burlington and surrounding Chittenden County, which boast IBM's largest chip manufacturing plant (located just outside Burlington in Essex Junction) and the University of Vermont (in Burlington). CCV's Burlington site, opened in 1983, now serves about 27% of all CCV students.

When CCV was created in 1970, its mission was to deliver quality, affordable post-secondary education in local Vermont communities and in innovative and flexible ways. While much else has changed at CCV in the past thirty years, CCV's basic mission has not. The focus is still on access and affordability, with a special emphasis placed on serving those individuals who would otherwise have limited opportunities for higher education because of geographical isolation, lack of academic preparation, or other constraining factors. CCV's student population also includes a growing number of recent immigrants, a small but notable population, particularly in Chittenden County.

At the outset, CCV depended entirely on part-time instructors who were hired to teach on a semester-by-semester basis. Academic coordinators worked out of small rented offices, hired instructors, advised students, and used high school classrooms and church meeting halls to deliver courses and programs. In thirty years, the facilities have expanded to include classrooms, computer labs, small science labs, virtual library resource rooms, and student lounges; but all college facilities are still rented and more significantly, 100% of CCV courses are taught by part-time instructors, who are still hired on a semester-by-semester basis by academic coordinators, the college's full-time academic staff.

In December, 1970, the college offered its first ten courses in Washington County in Central Vermont. In September of 2000, CCV will run about 750 courses throughout the state, of which almost 30% will be in CCV's Burlington center. Other CCV sites are located in Bennington, Brattleboro, Middlebury, Montpelier, Morrisville, Newport, Rutland, St. Albans, St. Johnsbury, Springfield, and White River Junction. Central administrative offices are housed in the "State Buildings Complex" in Waterbury, right next door to the administrative offices for the Vermont State Colleges system.

The college employs over 500 part-time instructors each semester and a full-time administrative staff of 125, including around 40 academic coordinators. Coordinators plan the semester schedule for particular sites, hire instructors and advise students. Instructors and coordinators serve on academic committees which function somewhat like traditional departments in terms of evaluating and improving the curriculum and the teaching and learning process.

GOVERNANCE

The Community College of Vermont is one of five public colleges in the Vermont State Colleges System. The system consists of three four-year colleges—Castleton State College, Johnson State College, and Lyndon State College—offering liberal arts and professional programs; a two-year technical college—Vermont Technical College; and CCV. The Vermont State Colleges is a public, non-profit corporation created by the

Vermont legislature in 1961 and governed by a board of trustees. The VSC board has 15 members, including the governor, ex-officio. Half the board members are gubernatorial appointees; four members are elected by the legislature. All serve staggered six-year terms. No explicit qualifications for appointment exist. The full board meets eight times a year and has standing committees that meet separately the week before each full board meeting.

CCV is governed by the chancellor of the Vermont State Colleges and its board of trustees. The president is CCV's chief executive officer, operating within the policies and procedures of the VSC Board of Trustees. The President has final decision-making authority concerning the internal affairs of the college.

Internally, the college has two governing boards. The President's Council proposes, discusses, advises and recommends institutional policies and procedures to the president. The Academic Review Board approves new courses and programs, and carries out continuing review and evaluation of academic programs and the teaching and learning process. New academic programs, however, including certificates and degree concentrations are reviewed by the five chief academic officers of the Vermont State Colleges, then the five presidents and the chancellor of the system before they are finally approved by a vote of the VSC Board of Trustees.

PROGRAMS AND ENROLLMENT

In the Spring of 1999 semester, CCV enrolled over 4,600 students, or almost 2,400 FTE, making it the second largest college in Vermont, second only to the University of Vermont. About 12% of these students are full-time. Four years ago, CCV piloted two on-line, web-based courses. In Fall 2000, the college will offer 30 courses, with an expected enrollment of 20 students per course. Most on-line students are supplementing regular CCV classes with an on-line course, but some students enrolled at CCV for the first time because of the opportunity for on-line learning. Courses offered on-line range from business law to statistics to a history of the holocaust. The average class size for on-ground courses is 12.5 students. The small class-size average permits CCV to offer classes in its many locations, and to address the needs of individual students who may be ill-prepared for success in post-secondary education. Nearly 30% of the students who begin at CCV require a full year of basic math/algebra and basic writing before they are permitted to enroll in college-level courses. Just over two-thirds of CCV students are enrolled for an associate degree, and 71% are women. The median age is 34. As in most community colleges, students enroll for a wide variety of reasons—earning an associate degree, transferring to a four-year college, enhancing job skills, or simply pursuing a personal interest.

Degree Programs.

CCV offers a two-year associate degree with the following concentrations available throughout the state:

Accounting	Early Childhood Education
Business	Financial Services
Business Computer Applications	Human Services
Computer Management Systems	Office Management
Corrections/Criminal Justice	Secretarial Studies
Technical Studies	Liberal Studies

In addition, CCV offers certificates in some of these areas and has developed a 30-credit certificate for a lab assistant. In 1999, CCV awarded degrees to 386 students, the largest graduating class ever. One hundred fifty-five of these degrees were in the concentration area of liberal studies.

General education requirements for the associate degree are organized by areas of competence, which include: communication; human inquiry; and math, science, and technical applications.

In addition, the college offers an associate of applied science (A.A.S.) degrees in manufacturing systems and facilities maintenance. The A.A.S. program is offered in certain locations where the college maintains cooperative arrangements with area vocational centers and employers. It was originally designed for employees at the IBM plant in Chittenden County. Students can also design their own concentrations and have them approved by the Academic Review Board.

Seminar in Educational Inquiry

Every student who wants to earn the associate degree is required to take a three-credit capstone course called Seminar in Educational Inquiry. This course allows graduating students the opportunity to reflect on what they have learned and to develop advanced critical thinking skills within a context of cross-curricular studies. Reading and discussion promote reflection and writing on one's education and the future. Students also develop a research or creative project on a topic or question of personal significance. Together, the seminar and the project serve as vehicles for the assessment of graduates' writing, research and communication ability. Equally important, students become more aware of themselves as learners and the relations among education, learning, personal development and identity.

Teaching for Development

For many years, CCV has placed a strong emphasis on teaching for personal development and the role that education can play in transforming lives. Many students begin CCV with a course entitled "Dimensions of Learning", designed by CCV in 1981 to build confidence, academic skills, and motivation among adults who are new to college, who may have been out of school for a long time, or who may not have met with great success in earlier academic experiences. The semester-long humanities course has a strong liberal arts focus, and provides students with extensive support, while they hone their critical thinking and study skills. In addition to boosting students' self-esteem and confidence in their academic potential, it also serves to build momentum and enthusiasm for further higher education. Since its inception, the course has become so popular that CCV now typically offers more than 25 sections of "Dimension of Learning" throughout Vermont each semester. What makes Dimensions of Learning so exciting and successful is its combination of engagement with serious intellectual issues and texts— e.g. the Holocaust, gender inequality, the allegory of the cave in Plato's Republic—with careful attention to academic skill building.

More generally, CCV stresses teaching for development across the curriculum and offers an orientation session and continuing workshops for all instructors which emphasize the importance of engagement, active learning, and throughout in all aspects of the teaching and learning process. A few years ago, we borrowed from Arthur Chickering and Zelda Gamson's "Eight Principles of Good Practice" and revised them into CCV's "Principles of Good Teaching and Learning". The Principles are now distributed to all instructors and serve as a foundation for our extensive instructional development activities. Along side of CCV programs, these principles describe the heart of CCV's academic mission., which is empowering learners, particularly those who, without CCV, would lack access to post-secondary education:

CCV Principles of Good Teaching and Learning

The best teaching and learning occurs when:

- The classroom climate is one of mutual respect among all participants. It is a primary responsibility of CCV instructors to foster and exhibit respect for all students in the classroom, to hear every student's voice, especially those who have been silenced in previous educational settings. Respect involves a recognition of different points of view, different values, different styles of learning, different talents, and different kinds of intelligence.

- <u>Students are motivated</u>. The stronger the desire to learn something, the more learning will occur. Instructors who display genuine passion for their subject matter and communicate high standards can generate a similar enthusiasm among students. Love of learning is the strongest motivation we can provide for our students.

- <u>The learning environment in the classroom is treated as a holistic, dynamic system designed to accommodate different ways of learning and knowing:</u> Instructional methods should promote a cycle of learning that includes opportunities or direct hands-on experience; for reflection through reading, writing, and discussion; or students to derive personal meaning or make connections to their daily lives; and for discovering direct applications for the learning. The deepest learning states often occur when the whole brain is engaged, when analytical left-brain processes are accompanied by a range of right-brain understandings.

- <u>Content is presented with the "big picture" first as a context for the specific, differentiated information of the subject</u>. The most meaningful learning generally occurs when students have a context for the specific content they are trying to learn. This content—information/material/activities—should be connected either to broader foundational concepts or to students' personal experiences. Learning that lacks a contextual framework tends to be superficial and of short duration.

- The class encourages dialogue and collaboration among students as well as between students and the instructor. Dialogue among classroom participants allows or the integration of new knowledge with what students already know, which in turn generates further understandings and fresh insights. Interactions among students and teachers can be the most effective triggers of meaningful learning.

- The class provides opportunities for direct experience and active application of course content. Students generally learn things best if they experience them first hand or apply them directly to solve a problem. Providing students with opportunities to teach others what they are learning is one of the most effective ways to accomplish this kind of applied learning in the classroom.

- <u>Student development and transformation becomes an intentional goal of the teaching and learning process</u>. Student development involves positive changes in students frames of reference and their ability to think critically and abstractly. This transformation is most likely to occur in an environment that includes safety and trust and provides occasional experiences of cognitive dissonance or disequilibration (i.e. experiences which lead students to question their own taken-for-granted beliefs and frames of reference.)
- <u>Assessment is an ongoing process that provides prompt feedback to students about their learning</u>. Assessment is most effective when there is the least anxiety and the maximum potential to learn from the assessment procedure. Hence, assessment should be perceived by students as a natural and on-going part of the cycle of learning.

Assessment of Prior Learning

CCV also offers an "Assessment of Prior Learning" (APL) program through the Vermont State Colleges' Office of External Programs. In this course, students may assess learning acquired through work or other non-college experiences for college credit. Students are guided through the process of describing and documenting their experiential learning in a portfolio. This document is then reviewed for credit by an Advanced Standing Committee composed of appropriate faculty and professionals. The credit awarded through the Office of External Programs may be transferred to CCV, the other Vermont State Colleges, and many other institutions. Currently, more than 25% of CCV graduates use the assessment program as an integral component of their degree.

Articulation/Transfer

CCV has been active in developing articulation agreements for both entering and exiting students. CCV has developed formal articulation agreements with programs in high schools and technical centers that allow students to earn six to nine college credits for courses completed in high school if they enroll in CCV degree programs and complete at least six credits of CCV courses. These articulation agreements exist in business, accounting and certain areas of technical studies.

CCV also has transfer agreements with many public and private colleges in Vermont, inside and out of the Vermont State College system. In the fall of 1998, the presidents of Community College of Vermont and University of Vermont signed the first extensive transfer agreement between these two schools. The agreement provides each student who completes a two-year CCV degree with at least a 2.5 grade-point average to enter as third-year students in UVM's College of Arts and Sciences. Depending on the major, a student can expect to complete a four-year degree with just 60 additional credits from UVM. CCV is very committed to its role of providing the first two years of a four-year liberal arts degree. Students leaving CCV transfer to many four-year schools throughout Vermont and New England, including a handful each year who are accepted into the Ada Comstock program for non-traditional students at Smith College in Northhampton, MA.

Workforce Education and Partnerships

CCV is committed to providing education and training to the incumbent work-force not only through regular course offerings, but also by customized arrangements made directly with employers. This can include short-term non-credit training (a computer applications delivered to State Department of health employees, for example, or a Frontline Supervision workshop for Ben and Jerry's) as well as degree and certificate programs developed for particular employers, e.g. an Essential Workplace Skills certificate for B.F. Goodrich employees in Vergennes. CCV is particularly interested in forming longer-term partnerships with businesses who want to develop themselves as "learning organizations" devoted to continuous improvement and life-long learning for all employees. CCV can become an important on-going supplier of courses for these companies. While businesses are always faced with immediate short-term training needs, CCV believes that its most valuable contribution as an educational partner will be in providing longer-term educational frameworks for learning organizations.

CCV has contracted with Vermont's Department of Social Welfare (DSW) to provide educational support for eligible welfare recipients who are enrolled in DSW's Reach-Up program. In five of the college's site offices, CCV academic coordinators now serve as contracted Reach-Up Case Managers. CCV Reach-Up case managers assist students in getting ready for work through classes, workshops, and training programs that address life skills, job-readiness, and occupational training.

FUNDING

By statute, the Vermont State Colleges System receives financial support from the state of Vermont. On average, the appropriation provided by the Vermont General Assembly is approximately 26% of the Vermont State College's operating budgets, but there is no funding formula that distributes the lump-sum appropriation from the legislature in any equitable way among five colleges. Instead, the annual appropriation for each college is negotiated between presidents and the chancellor, with minimal input from the board of trustees and none from the legislature. The long-term result is that the proportion of the general operating budgets filled by state-appropriated dollars varies significantly among the five colleges, from around 50% at the two-year technical college down to about 14% at CCV for FY2000.

For FY2000, CCV will receive $1.47 million out of a total state appropriation that is about $17.7 for all the five colleges, the chancellor's office, and a Vermont Interactive Television system. In addition, there is a capital budget of $3.2 million. The $1.47 state appropriation helps support CCV's general operating budget of $10 million dollars. CCV's total annual budget for FY2000 is $14.8 million, which includes about $4.3 million in restricted funds (Title IV financial aid, Trio and Perkins grants and gifts and restricted funds) and another $.5 million in a designated fund for workforce education and training.

The relative decline in appropriation as a share of the college budget has been dramatic at CCV over the past decade, from 40% in 1990 to the current 14%. As the college's state appropriations have decreased relatively in recent years, tuition has increased proportionately, more than 50% since FY2000. In 1999-2000, tuition for in-state students will be $108 per credit, making CCV one of the most expensive community colleges in the nation. Students living in states that border Vermont qualify for a New England Board of Higher Education rate, which is 150% of in-state tuition. But what frequently occurs is an out-migration, as Vermont students discover that they can attend community and technical colleges in Massachusetts, New York and New Hampshire for less than the cost of in-state tuition at CCV. In 1998, the state established a commission to study the funding for higher education which examined the conditions and issues surrounding funding of the Vermont State Colleges, the University of Vermont, and the Vermont Student Assistance Corporation. While the 1999 legislature did make some increases to higher education for the FY2000,

Vermont is still ranked near the bottom of all 50 states in per capita state funding for higher education. For some years, CCV has been trying to secure a significantly larger share of the state appropriation but with little success to date.

ACCOUNTABILITY

Given the small state appropriation to the Vermont State College System, and the even slimmer portion extended to Community College of Vermont, it is sensible that there is essentially no accountability to the legislature. The accountability to the chancellor's office and the board of trustees, on the other hand, is sometimes perceived as more than it should be given current funding realities. These and related issues are being addressed by a systemwide strategic planning process that is investigating alternatives to the current pattern of governance and funding.

The absence of state accountability may not continue for long. The Vermont state legislature is taking an active role at the K-12 level in mandating assessment of student learning outcomes and performance reports, and these efforts may eventually be extended to the post-secondary level. In the meantime, mandated accountability is limited to Trio- and Perkins-funded programs, which will drive assessment in particular directions for the next several years. As part of Perkins funds requirements, CCV will report learning outcomes in selected academic and vocational/technical skills for students enrolled selected vocational and technical programs. Beyond mandates, however, CCV is fundamentally committed to report results to instructors and students as a means of improving the teaching and learning process. Are students learning what the CCV curriculum is designed teach? Are they becoming empowered learners? How do we know, and how do we inform our self as an organization about classroom results, from English composition to programming in C+, from a course in U.S. history to a course in small business management. Are students prepared for the workplace, as day-care providers or office accountants? Are they prepared to transfer into a program at another state college or the University of Vermont? This is the accountability that guides CCV most clearly as we think about improving the teaching and learning process in the ways that matter most.

FOR ADDITIONAL INFORMATION, PLEASE CONTACT:
Barbara Murphy, President
Community College of Vermont
P.O. Box 120
Waterbury, VT 05676-0120
Telephone: (802) 241-3535
In Vermont: 1-800-CCV-6686
   Fax: (802) 241-3526

VIRGINIA

Joy S. Graham
Assistant Chancellor for Public Affairs

OVERVIEW

Founded in 1966, the Virginia Community College System is comprised of 23 comprehensive community colleges located on 38 campuses throughout the Commonwealth of Virginia. As comprehensive community colleges, the primary mission includes associate in arts and sciences degrees designed to transfer to public and private senior institutions, associate in applied science degrees designed to lead directly to work, certificate and diploma programs, developmental education, continuing education including workforce development, and community services programs.

Mission

Thomas Jefferson, in his Notes on the State of Virginia, 1781, wrote, "The general objectives of this law are to provide an education adapted to the years, to the capacity, and the condition of every one, and directed to their freedom and happiness."

The Virginia Community College System functions within the educational community to assure that all individuals in the diverse regions of the Commonwealth of Virginia are given a continuing opportunity for the development and extension of their skills and knowledge through quality programs and services that are financially and geographically accessible.

Through the 23 comprehensive community colleges, the VCCS provides leadership in determining and addressing both the needs of individuals and the economic needs of the regions the colleges serve.

Occupational/technical education, transfer programs, developmental studies, continuing education, training for business and industry and community services are the primary avenues through which the mission is fulfilled. In order to assure that all students have an equal opportunity to succeed, each college provides a comprehensive program of student development services.

Goals

The purposes of the financially accessible, high quality, comprehensive educational programs and services of the VCCS are to support the economic development of the Commonwealth and to meet the educational needs of her citizens.

The program goals are:

To offer associate degree programs to prepare individuals for careers as workers in occupational and technical fields;

To offer associate degree programs to prepare individuals for transfer, as juniors, to baccalaureate degree programs in senior institutions of higher education;

To offer diploma and certificate programs to prepare individuals for careers as technicians, skilled and semi-skilled workers;

To offer developmental programs to prepare individuals for the academic rigors of the regular instructional programs of the college;

To offer student development services which assist individuals with decisions regarding occupational, educational, and personal goals;

To offer workforce training programs where specific employment opportunities are available in new, expanding, or existing businesses, industries, and governmental agencies;

To offer continuing education programs to provide educational opportunities for individuals who wish to continue and expand their learning experiences. Such programs include credit and non-credit courses, seminars and workshops; and

To offer community services to provide cultural and educational opportunities which are in addition to other programs of the college.

History

In the early 1960's, opportunities for education beyond high schools were limited, especially in the areas of a two-year education. Virginia was unable to meet the increasing demand for skilled technicians who were a special need of industries that were moving into the state. An awareness of new postsecondary educational needs in Virginia were also blossoming in the minds of leaders in state government.

In 1962, the first year of Governor Albertis S. Harrison's term, the General Assembly established the Commission of Vocational and Technical Education. Chaired by D. French Slaughter, the commission came to be known as the Slaughter Commission. In response to the Commission's call for increasing vocational educational opportunities in the state, the Department of Technical Education was established in 1964 to develop and administer area vocational and technical schools (Slaughter, 1963, pp. 1-3).

Also in 1964, the Higher Education Study Commission, chaired by Lloyd C. Bird, and thus known as the Bird Commission, was appointed to examine issues related to increased educational opportunities. One of its priorities was to identify postsecondary institutions that would "fill the most significant gap in Virginia's present provision of higher education" (Russell, 1965, p. 6).

Mills E. Godwin, Jr., Lieutenant Governor under Governor Harrison, was elected Governor in 1965. His first major policy address to the General Assembly in early 1966 outlined his plan for extending the base of higher education in the State: development of the state-wide system of community colleges. In that historic address to the combined houses of the legislature, Governor Godwin stated, "If we look at the number of potential students, and if we also look at the relative costs involved, the implication is clear that a community college system is the quickest, and most efficient, the most economical, in fact, virtually the only way was the future demands of our young people can be met." These recommendations became the basis of the community college legislation which was passed by the General Assembly in 1966.

The 1966 session has been called a "Momentous Legislative Session." Not only was the comprehensive community college system created, but the first state sales tax was enacted in order to pay for it.

A state board was appointed and local boards were established to act in an advisory capacity to the State Board. Technical schools and university extensions and branches which existed in 1966 came together with new colleges to form the system that exists today.

By the fall of 1966, two colleges in the community college system were operational. Northern Virginia Community College and Virginia Western Community College in Roanoke, Virginia, had a combined enrollment of 3,578 students. By the fall on 1970, a total of 27,840 students were enrolled in sixteen community colleges. And, as the doors opened on the 1972-73 academic year, the remaining seven community colleges have also been established, completing the 23 community colleges envisioned in the early master plan for the state-wide system of community colleges in 1966.

GOVERNANCE

The Commonwealth of Virginia has invested the governance of the state system of community colleges in the State Board of Community Colleges, a fifteen member board appointed by the Governor and confirmed by the Virginia General Assembly. Members are appointed for four-year terms and may be re-appointed for a second four-year term. The State Board has responsibility for governing the VCCS, including all 23 community colleges that comprise the System. It is responsible for the establishment, control, administration, and supervision of all community colleges in the Commonwealth of Virginia.

The state board hires the chancellor of the Virginia Community College System, who is the chief executive officer of the System. The community college presidents are responsible to the chancellor for the operation of the community colleges and are responsible to the local college board for those areas in which the college board has been empowered to act and which are assigned to the president by the college board.

Each community college has a local advisory board with members appointed by the local governments that make up the college's service region. Each county and city government located within the college service area appoints members to the local board based on the size of their population. They are advisory in nature with powers delegated to them by the state board. A minimum of nine persons shall be appointed to the local college board with at least one person from each political subdivision sponsoring the college.

The state board members are appointed from the state at-large. Officers, employees, or members of a governing board of any public institution of higher education, or any members of the State Board of Education, or any members of the Virginia General Assembly are not eligible for appointment (Code, 1997, pp. 421-428).

A chair and vice chair are elected at the May meeting of the board by its membership to take office July 1 for a period of one year. The board has committees established in the areas of budget and finance, facilities, audit, academic programs, personnel and an executive committee. The committees meet prior to each state board meeting and other times as deemed necessary by the committee chairman. The state board meets at least as often as every other month and regularly meets in September, November (in conjunction with a System-wide annual meeting), January, March and May. The board meets in July on call of the chairman.

The Virginia Community College System is designated by the legislature as one institution of higher education and the state governing board is vested with the same authority and powers as the boards of visitors of the other state-supported institutions of higher education in Virginia. As is true with all higher education governing boards, it is subject to the coordinating powers of the State Council of Higher Education for Virginia.

The administrative staff members reporting to the chancellor include the vice chancellor of finance and administration, the vice chancellor of academic and student affairs, the vice chancellor of instructional technology, the assistant chancellor of public affairs, and the assistant to the chancellor for policy. The auditor reports directly to the State Board for Community Colleges.

FUNDING

Virginia community colleges receive funding from two major sources: state appropriations and student tuition and fees. In 1997-98, state appropriations comprised 57.9% of the VCCS budget, with 31% coming from tuition and fees, 7.3% from federal, state, private, and local grants, 3.4% from auxiliary enterprises, and .4% from other sources. In total dollars, the VCCS operates with a budget of $404,072,562. An additional $32 million was appropriated for capital outlay expenditures (Annual Report, 1998, p. 21).

The process begins with the State Board for Community Colleges submitting its request to the Governor through the Secretary of Education, with copies to the State Council of Higher Education for Virginia and the Virginia Department of Planning and Budget. The State Council of Higher Education submits recommendations on higher education budget requests to the governor. Prior to the legislative session, the governor proposes a state budget. During the legislative session, institutions of higher education, including the Virginia Community College System, have delegates and senators submit amendments to the budget for supplemental funds for specific programs or projects. At this point, recommendations of the state council are again considered.

The house and senate pass their respective budgets, each including some amendments for community colleges. A final budget is submitted to the house and senate after a committee of conference from each House has agreed on a final version. The legislature passes the budget just prior to adjourning. The governor has the option of signing the budget bill or vetoing sections of the budget before the legislature comes back into session 60 days after adjournment for a reconvened session. The legislature then has the final say: approve the budget with the governor's amendments or override his veto. Once the reconvened session is adjourned, the budget is signed and becomes law.

All state appropriations for community colleges are given to the system for distribution to the 23 community colleges. Based on a formula approved by the state board and the council of presidents, funds are appropriated to the colleges based on enrollment, special programs, and other considerations.

After more than five years of rapidly escalating tuition costs, the governor and the legislature froze tuition rates and provided general funds to accommodate the lack of tuition revenue. For the 1997-98 academic year (as was the case for the past four years), tuition for in-state students was $46.65 per credit hour and for out-of-state students was $160.00 per credit hour. Tuition is based on the number of credits taken per semester, with no maximum rate for full-time students.

Although tuition costs had not increased, there was still concern that high tuition rates were limiting access to higher education for too many Virginians. Therefore, in the 1999 Virginia General Assembly, the governor proposed a twenty percent roll-back in tuition costs at both community colleges and public colleges and universities. State funds have been appropriated to accommodate the lower tuition costs. For a community college student, tuition for 1999-2000 will be reduced to $37.12 per credit hour. Out-of-state students will pay $164.82 per credit hour, a 2.8% increase.

Colleges will still charge a $1.50 per credit hour technology fee that each institution uses to upgrade its infrastructure and purchase new hardware and software to keep current in the use of technology in the classroom and for alternative delivery of courses and programs. They may also charge fees for student activities and parking, if the state board has approved the fees. Tuition for noncredit courses varies, depending on the length and type of course.

PROGRAMS AND ENROLLMENTS

All 23 community colleges are comprehensive colleges, providing both occupational/technical programs leading directly to work and transfer programs enabling students to enter senior institutions as juniors to complete work on their baccalaureate degrees. They also provide services to serve the needs of individuals and the communities they serve. These services include student development services, developmental education programs, work force training and retraining, and continuing education courses.

The Virginia Community College System is also responsible for apprenticeship-related instruction for all apprentices approved through the State Department of Labor and Industry. Related instruction classes are structured to meet the needs of business and industry in the employment of apprentices.

Curricular offerings in the VCCS are found in the VCCS Curriculum Guide and are used by all Virginia's community colleges to assure smooth transfer between and among the community colleges and senior institutions in Virginia.

There are ten clusters for degree programs; three provide for the college transfer program and seven cover all programs in the occupational/technical curriculum. The three transfer degree clusters are the associate in arts, the associate in science, and the associate in arts and science. The seven occupational/technical clusters are the associate in applied arts, agricultural and natural resources technology, arts and design technology, business technology, engineering and industrial technology, health technology, and public service technology.

A new associate in applied science degree in technical studies has been approved by the state board and is awaiting approval by the Virginia State Council of Higher Education. This new degree program was developed in cooperation with business leaders and community colleges to address the need to blend multiple technical skill sets with critical thinking and interpersonal skills to graduate well-rounded workers. It is designed to provide a broad foundation of general education and technological knowledge, along with a concentration in a technical field identified by industry needs, that will prepare the student to enter or advance in technical fields upon graduation. An experiential learning component is an integral part of the degree program.

Associate degree programs are planned programs of study composed of a range of 60 - 63 semester hours for transfer programs and 65-69 semester hours for associate degrees in occupational/technical programs at the 100 and 200 course levels. All associate degree programs must be approved by the Virginia State Board for Community Colleges and the State Council of Higher Education. Each associate degree curriculum must include general education components consisting of coursework in communications, arts and humanities, social sciences, mathematics and science.

In addition to associate degree programs, the community colleges in Virginia offer diploma, certificate, and career studies certificate programs. Developed in response to local needs identified by local curriculum advisory committees, each community college develops its own diploma and certificate programs with approval by the chancellor.

ᐟ Diploma programs have a two-year curriculum with a major in an occupational area designed to meet the curricular and institutional objectives. A certificate program is a one-year program with 30 semester credit hours in an occupational area. A career studies certificate program is less than one year in length in an occupational area.

The Virginia Community College System served 74,295 full-time equivalent students in credit courses in 1997-98. In annualized unduplicated headcount, 215,709 students enrolled in Virginia's community colleges in 1997-98 (Annual Report, 1998, p. 20). An additional 70,400 students enrolled in non-credit courses. Over 900 businesses, industries, and governmental agencies in Virginia also contracted with community colleges to provide work force training or retraining.

The average age of students enrolled in Virginia's community colleges is 29. Gender make-up is 59% female and 41% male ; racial make-up is 74.4% Caucasian, 15.3% African-American, 5.4% Oriental, 2.9% Hispanic, .4% Native American, and 1.6% in other categories. Transfer program students account for 32.4% of Virginia's community college enrollment, with 32.7% in occupational/technical programs and 35% unclassified. Over 95% of the student body are classified as in-state students and 72.7% are enrolled part-time. Forty-three percent of all students enrolled in higher education in Virginia in fall 1998 attended one of Virginia's community colleges.

The Virginia Community College System joined with Old Dominion University and Virginia Tech to initiate a state-wide high speed, two-way audio and video network. This network, called NET.WORK.VIRGINIA, has linked all 38 campuses of the VCCS enabling them to offer courses originating at one site to another or to multiple sites around the Commonwealth of Virginia. In 1997-98, over 16,289 students enrolled in distance education courses, which is 7.6 percent of total VCCS student population. More than 1,000 distance education courses were offered in 1997-98, a numbers that is rapidly increasing in the current academic year.

ECONOMIC DEVELOPMENT

When Virginia businesses seek training assistance, more than two-thirds contact their local community college, according to a survey of more than 6000 businesses conducted in 1995 by the Virginia State Chamber of

Commerce, the Virginia Manufacturers Association and the Commonwealth of Virginia. The VCCS launched a statewide workforce training initiative called VIRGINIA WORKS which provides a core of workforce services at each of the 38 community college campuses. VIRGINIA WORKS attempts to improve the economic competitiveness of Virginia by strengthening the existing framework for workforce training and services.

Goals of VIRGINIA WORKS include creating classrooms of the future by maintaining and providing a comprehensive up-to-date curriculum of occupational/technical programs in current and emerging professions and technologies and establishing Workforce Development Centers on community college campuses. These Centers will provide a full array of employment and training services localized to meet business and industry needs in the College service area. Another goal is the establishment of lead "Institutes of Workforce Excellence to serve a unique need of a region act as the host provider of specialized statewide training and curriculum development needs. Institutes in semiconductor manufacturing, advanced manufacturing technology and information technology have been created to provide such specialized services.

The Virginia General Assembly established the Community College Incentive Scholarship Program and Fund to provide tuition and fees to second-year, full-time community college students in designated technical training programs that address Virginia's workforce training needs (Code, Vol. 5, pp. 425-426). These students must have a B average or better in order to qualify. The program, which will begin awarding scholarships in July, 2000, will be administered by the Virginia State Board for Community Colleges. The state board, in consultation with the Virginia Economic Development Partnership and the Virginia Workforce Council, will determine the training programs that address these workforce development needs.

Virginia's community colleges have worked closely with business and industry in workforce training since their beginning in 1966, but until 1998 there was no state funding appropriated for noncredit courses that address these needs. Although the issue of funding noncredit instruction had been raised many times over the years, the perception that noncredit courses were avocational in nature and devoted to leisure activities and hobbies, prevented the legislature from funding them. A bill to establish a joint legislative subcommittee to study noncredit education for workforce training in Virginia passed the legislature in the 1997 session. The subcommittee was comprised of members of the Senate and House of Delegates and five business leaders. Ex-officio members included the chancellor of the VCCS, the secretary of Commerce and Trade and Education, the president of the Center for Innovative Technology , the president of the Virginia State Chamber of Commerce and the director of the State Council of Higher Education for Virginia.

The joint subcommittee developed a process for identifying courses and programs in highest demand by business and industry, for assessing the future demand and appropriate public policy for noncredit and workforce training programs, and recommended am appropriate share of the costs of such programs to be borne by the Commonwealth. These recommendations were submitted to the 1998 general assembly along with a package of legislative and budgetary initiatives (House Document No. 85, 1998). A Statewide Workforce Training Council, staffed by the Virginia Community College System, was created and state monies were appropriated to begin funding noncredit workforce training. Funds to employ Coordinators of Workforce Training at fourteen community colleges and to create five Workforce Development Centers were also appropriated.

At the request of the council, legislation was introduced in the 1999 session of the Virginia General Assembly that broadened the scope of the Council to include the new Workforce Investment Act passed by Congress in 1998. This legislation passed the General Assembly and is awaiting the Governor's signature (House Bill 2558/Senate Bill 1257, 1999). The Virginia Community College System will continue to staff the newly created Virginia Workforce Council sharing those responsibilities with the Virginia Employment Commission. Also during the recently concluded 1999 legislative session, funds were appropriated to eight additional workforce training coordinators and to expand the funding base for noncredit workforce training. In January, 1999, a Worker Retraining Tax Credit went into effect allowing employers a tax credit equal to thirty percent of all expenditures paid or incurred by the employer for eligible worker training at a Virginia community college (Code, section 58,1, pp. 124-125).

ACCOUNTABILITY

Beginning in 1994, public institutions of higher education in Virginia were mandated by the Virginia General Assembly to restructure in order to improve efficiencies of internal operations and instructional programs and propose better ways to meet the educational and training needs of the commonwealth's citizens and employers. The legislature wanted a restructuring plan with yearly updates to be submitted to the State Council of Higher Education for Virginia which state how faculty are deployed, how administrative and instructional costs would be minimized, and how additional enrollments would be accommodated with limited resources.

In its initial restructuring plan, the VCCS committed to review course offerings in order to reduce redundancy and minimize duplication, scrutinize the costs and effectiveness of developmental courses, reduce the number of credits required to graduate, increase the graduation rate of students in associate degree programs, revamp technology programs to ensure students have exceptional skills and knowledge of prevailing industry practice and are trained on state-of-the-art equipment, work with senior institutions to fully implement the State Policy on Transfer, and to sponsor a major faculty development program to offer faculty continual opportunities for keeping up-to-date with their professional field and becoming adept at using new instructional technologies.

Since that initial plan was submitted, more than 90 courses were deleted from the Master Course File and over 600 courses were reviewed and revised. The State Board approved reduced ranges for all associate degrees in July, 1995. Approximately 350 of 400 degrees were shortened as a result of this extensive study. The VCCS Faculty Development Program was launched and continues to offer extensive faculty development opportunities: well over 5,000 faculty and staff have participated in discipline peer meetings, numerous research grants have been awarded to faculty, and over 30 teleconferences have been held. Individual Development Plans are implemented at each college and the program was expanded to include classified staff professional development opportunities. The VCCS Professional Development Program has received national recognition and numerous awards.

Each year new initiatives are added to the restructuring plan and status reports are submitted that identify which initiatives are completed and which are on-going.

The State Council of Higher Education for Virginia, the coordinating body for higher education, also requires ongoing student outcomes assessment to ensure continuous and timely resolution of problems related to student learning and program improvement. Each year a special focus area is identified for college attention and Systemwide analysis. In Fall, 1995, colleges reported on general education, majors, off-campus, distance learning, and dual credit instruction. In the fall of 1996, colleges reported on assessment of developmental studies and transfer student progress.

Perhaps the most significant accountability issue is the initiation of performance measures mandated by the Virginia Department of Planning and Budget. All state agencies, including public institutions of higher education, were required to incorporate a set of performance measures with their budget submissions beginning with the 1996-98 biennium. The Performance Budgeting process calls for establishment of baseline data and the setting of a target for each measure. The six core performance measures for the Virginia Community College are: 1) graduation rates; 2) progression and retention; 3) transfer rates; 4) dollars expended on instruction as the percent of total E&G expenditures; 5) management standards; and 6) faculty productivity. Other areas that are measured include the percent of graduates who are employed in program-related work or pursuing further study, students who identify their program as having contributed significantly to their functioning as workers and citizens, and classroom utilization rates.

Although institutions continue to update performance measures and report progress, there has not yet been a clear relationship between them and the institutional base budget. In 1998, the legislature formed a Joint Subcommittee on Higher Education Funding Policies to examine past and current funding policies and recommend new policies more appropriate to the needs of higher education in the years ahead. This two-year study will make its recommendations to the 2000 Virginia General Assembly. The Governor also established the "Blue Ribbon Commission to Evaluate the Needs and Goals of Higher Education in Virginia in the 21st Century." This Commission, comprised of legislators, educators, Board members and citizen members, is also expected to make its recommendations to the Governor and the legislature prior to the 2000 general assembly session.

REFERENCES

Acts and joint resolutions of the general assembly of the Commonwealth of Virginia (1966). Richmond: Commonwealth of Virginia, Department of Purchases and Supply.

Appropriations act. Chapter 464. (1998, April 14): Richmond: Commonwealth of Virginia, Office of Purchases and Supply.

Code of Virginia. Chapter 16. (1997). State board for community colleges and community college system. Richmond: Commonwealth of Virginia, pp. 421-428.

Code of Virginia, §58.1-439.6 (1998). Worker retraining tax credit. Richmond: Commonwealth of Virginia, pp. 124-125.

Godwin, M. E., Jr., (1966). *Address to the General Assembly from the Governor*. Journal of the Senate, Feb. 3, Senate of Virginia: Richmond, VA.

House Document No. 85. (1998). Report of the joint subcommittee to study noncredit education for workforce training in Virginia. Richmond, VA: Commonwealth of Virginia.

Jefferson, T. (1955). *Notes on the State of Virginia, 1781*. The Institute of Early American History & Culture. Williamsburg, Virginia: University of North Carolina Press.

Russell, J. D. (1965). *Report of the Higher Education Study Commission*. Richmond: State Council of Higher Education for Virginia.

Slaughter, F., (1963). *Vocational and Technical Education in Virginia: Present and Future Needs. A Report Of The Commission On Vocational Education To The Governor And The General Assembly Of Virginia*. House Document No. 9, Richmond: Commonwealth of Virginia, Department of Purchases and Supply.

Virginia Community College System (1998). Connect to Your Future: *The Virginia Community College System 1997-98* Annual Report. Richmond: Commonwealth of Virginia.

FOR ADDITIONAL INFORMATION, PLEASE CONTACT:

Dr. Arnold R. Oliver
Chancellor
Virginia Community College System
101 N. 14th Street
Richmond, Virginia 2321
Telephone: (804) 786-6408
Fax: (804) 786-3786
E-Mail: aoliva@vccs.cc.va.us

WASHINGTON

Terrence A. Tollefson
Professor, Department of Educational Leadership and Policy Analysis
East Tennessee State University
and
William G. Ingram
Senior Vice President and Chief Instructional Officer
Durham Technical Community College

OVERVIEW

Public junior college education in the state of Washington began in 1915, when Everett High School's principal, A. C. Roberts, added one year of post-high school education. Forty-two students enrolled in that first year, and 13 of them completed a full academic year of course work. The postsecondary education was tuition-free until 1923, when the school board decided to charge five dollars per month. No students enrolled and Washington's first venture into junior college education ended (Crawfurd, 1959; and Rulifson, 1967; cited in Terrey, 1997). Four junior colleges were in operation in Washington by 1930, which were established as follows: Centralia, 1925; Mount Vernon, in 1926; Yakima, in 1929; and Grays Harbor in Aberdeen, in 1930. All were established with the support of Dean Friederick Bolton, of the University of Washington (Terrey, 1997).

After two conflicting attorney general's opinions in 1926 about the legality of using public tax funds to support junior college education without authorizing legislation, such a bill was enacted by the legislature and vetoed by the governor in 1929. Four additional junior colleges were established in the 1930s. It was not until 1941, however, that legislation to provide funding to public junior colleges was finally passed. In 1945, a law was enacted that permitted junior colleges to join local school districts, and in 1946 all nine junior colleges petitioned the Washington State Board of Education to join the school districts in which they were located. The 1946 Strayer Report identified a total of at least 16 locations deemed appropriate for junior college sites, and in 1961 the state legislature eliminated all numerical and geographic restrictions on establishing two-year colleges, which by then were called "community colleges. Twelve new community colleges were established in the 1960s (Terrey, 1997).

In 1991, the Washington state legislature shifted the coordinating authority over five existing postsecondary vocational technical institutes from local school districts to the newly redesignated Washington State Board for Community and Technical Colleges. Those institutions had been established as follows: Bates, in Tacoma, in 1940; Renton, in 1942; Clover Park, in 1942; Lake Washington, in 1949; and Bellingham, in 1957. Cascadia Community College, near Seattle, was established by the state legislature in 1994, which was the first new community college in Washington in nearly a quarter of a century (Terrey, 1997).

GOVERNANCE

The Community College Act of 1967 established the basic governing structure for the Washington community colleges. This act divided the state into 22 districts, several of which were later subdivided, for a new total of 30 districts. Each district has a five-member board of trustees, with each member serving a five-year term. Board members are appointed by the governor, with the consent of the state senate. The state board initially included seven members, one from each congressional district, who were appointed for four-year terms by the governor, with the consent of the senate. With the addition of two new Congressional districts, the state board now has nine members (Terrey, 1997). The 1967 legislature statement of purpose is as follows:

The purpose of this act is to provide for the dramatically increasing number of students requiring high standards of education either as a part of the continuing higher education program or for occupational training by creating a new, independent system of community colleges (Terrey, 1997, p. 185).

FUNDING

State appropriations for Washington community colleges increased from $382 million in fiscal year 1997 to $409.5 in FY 1998 and to $421.6 million in FY 1999 (Tollefson & Patton, 1998).

The Washington State Board for Community and Technical Colleges has a "Performance Funding Allocation" of $2.05 million for the statewide system, or approximately one-half of one percent of the state appropriation for community college operations. Performance funding is allocated for achieving target levels of improvement in each of four "performance indicators": workforce training, transfer, student efficiency, and core course completion (Washington State Board of Community and Technical Colleges, 1999).

PROGRAMS AND ENROLLMENTS

The Washington community and technical colleges all are open-admissions institutions with comprehensive missions that include providing degree programs in college-transfer and occupational areas, as well as literacy and developmental training (Terrey, 1997). Approximately 185,000 headcount students enrolled in the fall of 1997 (Tollefson & Patton, 1998) and a record total of over 440,000 students in 1997-98, for an annual FTE of nearly 117,500 (Link & Hale, 1998).

WORKFORCE DEVELOPMENT

In 1991, the state legislature amended the Community College Act of 1967 as part of the Workforce Training and Education Act (Link & Hale, 1998). As described earlier, the revised Community and Technical College Act of 1991 redesignated the five vocational-technical institutes as "technical colleges" and transferred them into the community and technical college system (Terrey, 1997; Link & Hale, 1998). In late 1997, the state allocated an additional $70 million to the Washington community and technical colleges for workforce training (Hale, 1997, personal communication).

REFERENCES

Link, A. & Hale, E. (1998, November). *Washington Community and Technical Colleges Academic Year Report, 1997-98*. Olympic, WA: Washington State Board for Community and Technical Colleges.

Terrey, J. N. (1997, March). Washington community colleges: History and development. *Community College Journal of Research and Practice*, 21(2), pp. 185-201.

Tollefson, T. A. & Patton, M. (1998)Washington, in *AACC Annual* 1997-98, pp. 85-86. Washington, DC: American Association of Community Colleges.

Washington State Board for Community and Technical Colleges (1999, May 17). Washington community and technical college 1998-99 performance funding allocation - $2.05 million assigned to demonstrated performance.www.sbtc.ctc.edu

FOR ADDITIONAL INFORMATION, PLEASE CONTACT:

Office of the Executive Director
Washington State Board for Community and Technical Colleges

319 Seventh Avenue
P. O. Box 42495
Olympia, WA 98504-2495
Telephone: (360) 753-2000

WEST VIRGINIA

James L. Skidmore
Vice Chancellor for Community and Technical College Education
State College and University Systems of West Virginia

OVERVIEW

The community college system in West Virginia is governed by the State College System Board of Directors and the University Systems Board of Trustees. The community and technical college system includes two free-standing community colleges, six community and technical college components of four-year institutions, the community and technical college of Marshall University, and two two-year branches of West Virginia University (Call, in Tollefson & Fountain, 1992).

The community and technical college system in West Virginia provides access to affordable, quality education. Both transfer programs and career-technical training programs are provided, as well as credit and noncredit continuing education, business and industry training in basic skills, and workshops and seminars to meet cultural, civic, and personal interests. (Call, in Tollefson & Fountain, 1992).

What is now West Virginia University, a land-grant university, was established as a two-year institution in 1885 in Montgomery, West Virginia, and another campus was established in Keyser, West Virginia, in 1901. College-transfer programs were emphasized at both campuses. The Montgomery campus has become a campus of WVU, and the Keyser branch is still a two-year branch of WVU (Call, in Tollefson & Fountain, 1992).

In 1961, the legislature authorized the establishment of two-year branch campuses offering transfer, vocational-technical, and adult education programs. Four 4-year branch campuses were established as a result of this legislation. Transfer programs were the primary offerings at the branch colleges. Additional legislation was enacted that charged the West Virginia Board of Regents to develop a plan for a comprehensive community college system. The law also authorized the board of regents to convert branch campuses to community colleges. In 1971, three branch campuses were converted into one single-campus community college and one community college with two campuses. Another two-year campus was established in 1972 from a branch campus of a four-year college, for a total of three community colleges in the West Virginia Board of Regents system (Call, in Tollefson & Fountain, 1992).

The West Virginia Board of Regents, in collaboration with the senior institutions, established community college components within each of seven four-year institutions. The community college components provided terminal two-year programs (Call, in Tollefson & Fountain, 1992). During the 1999 legislative session, Eastern West Virginia Community and Technical College was created to serve the eastern region of West Virginia. This will be the first community and technical college in West Virginia to be established that was not a conversion from a established branch campus (Skidmore, 1999).

GOVERNANCE

There are two state-level boards that govern the community and technical colleges, the State College System Board of Directors, and the University Systems Board of Trustees. Each board includes 17 members, 12 of whom are appointed by the governor, whereas five members are ex-officio. The ex-officio members represent faculty, students, and classified employees in the two systems. The chancellors of the respective systems and the state superintendent of schools are also ex-officio members. Each appointed member serves a six-year term. A president, vice president, and secretary are elected for one-year terms by the board members (Skidmore, 1999).

The boards govern and coordinate the two higher education systems. They are directed to "prescribe and allocate among the state colleges and universities specific functions of responsibilities to meet the higher education needs of the state and avoid unnecessary duplication." Preparing master plans for public higher education, supervising the budget process, establishing data management systems and, reviewing academic programs at least every five years, employing a uniform system of personnel classification, evaluating presidents, and submitting an annual report to the Joint Committee on Government and Finance are specific responsibilities of the two boards. Each local institution in the system has a board of advisors that works closely with the president of the institution (Skidmore, 1999).

The West Virginia State Department of Education has no authority over the community and technical colleges. It does, however, supervise vocational-technical schools in the state, which offer both secondary and post-secondary programs. Vocational-technical schools are not authorized to award college credit or associate degrees, but do confer diplomas and certificates (Call, in Tollefson & Fountain, 1992).

FUNDING

State-appropriated funds, federal funds, and tuition comprise the three primary funding sources. Funding is based on full-time-equated (FTE) students, a factor in the resource-allocation model. The board also establishes priorities for funding. (Call, in Tollefson & Fountain, 1992).

Tuition and fees for an in-state student range from $1,210 per year at the freestanding community and technical colleges to $2,518 at each community and technical college component within a senior institution. For the first time in the history of the community and technical college system, the legislature in 1999 allocated separate funding to support workforce development initiatives at the community and technical colleges (Skidmore, 1999).

PROGRAMS AND ENROLLMENT

The two governing boards review and approve all new programs. The Academic Affairs Advisory Committee makes recommendations to the board and then the board votes on approval or disapproval. Legislation was passed during the 1999 legislative session that permits free-standing community and technical colleges to implement occupational programs without board approval, but which requires a post-audit review of each new program after being in existence for three years (Skidmore, 1999).

Headcount enrollment is the total number of students enrolled at a given institution. Full-time equivalence is one FTE per 15 credit hours. There has been significant growth in the career-technical programs (198%) since the community college system was developed. The largest increases have come in business programs, public service programs, and technology. The FTE enrollment for community and technical colleges was 13,405 in the fall of 1998 (Skidmore, 1999).

The community and technical colleges provide delivery of A.A. and A.S. transfer programs and A.S. and A.A.S. occupational programs that prepare individuals to enter the workforce upon completion. The system has a strong component of 2+2 programs, particularly in the community and technical colleges within four-year institutions (Skidmore, 1999).

REFERENCES

Call, D. M. (1992). West Virginia, in Tollefson,T. A. & Fountain, B. E. *Forty-Nine StateSystems, 1992 Edition*, pp. 233-235. Washington, DC: American Association of Community Colleges.

Skidmore, J. L. (1999). West Virginia community and technical colleges. (Unpublished article). Charleston, WV: State College and University Systems of West Virginia.

FOR ADDITIONAL INFORMATION, PLEASE CONTACT:
Vice Chancellor for Community and Technical Colleges
State College and University Systems of West Virginia
1018 Kanawha Boulevard East
Suite 700
Charleston, West Virginia 25301
Telephone: (304) 558-0265

WISCONSIN

Edward Chin
State Director and Executive Officer
The Wisconsin Technical College System Board

OVERVIEW

The Wisconsin Technical College System (WTCS), with sixteen districts, serves over 430,000 students annually. In 1997-98, one out of every nine adults in the State of Wisconsin enrolled in at least one class at a Wisconsin technical college. The WTCS has 46 campuses and more than 1,000 outreach centers located throughout the state within commuting distance of nearly all of the state's population. In addition, with the increased use of distance education technology, the WTCS provides access to selected programs across district lines, offers a complete associate of arts degree over broadcast television in southeastern Wisconsin, and has begun to offer selected occupationally related instruction over the Internet.

The WTCS provides (i) occupational education below the baccalaureate level, including associate degrees, (ii) training of apprentices, and (iii) adult education below the professional level. The WTCS seeks to promote full participation in our complex society through:

- Increasing employability skills of new labor market entrants, reentrants, and incumbents;
- Fostering economic development;
- Providing educational opportunities to high schools age students and facilitating their transition to postsecondary education; and
- Facilitating collegiate transfer;
- Providing opportunities for community services and pursuit of avocational interests;
- Providing opportunities for adult basic education; and
- Addressing barriers to full participation in the workforce.

The origins of the WTCS lie in legislation passed in 1911 to provide (i) continuation schools for boys and girls, ages 14 to 16 who had left high school without a diploma, (ii) trade schools, (iii) evening schools for adults, and (iv) schools to provide related instruction for apprentices. The 1911 legislation fixed, in large measure, the broad structural framework for the provision of vocational education and training that persists in Wisconsin today: (i) local control exercised through boards appointed at the local level with responsibility for overseeing industrial education; (ii) the provision of separate taxing authority which resides solely with the local boards of industrial education; (iii) an attempt to encourage coordination between these boards of industrial education and local school boards; (iv) a state board appointed by the governor, with ex officio representation by heads of related agencies, and charged with allocating state aid to local boards; and (v) a provision to balance power both on the local and state boards between management and workers through positions designated for equal numbers of employers and employees.

Over the years, the state's the economy has evolved and the skills demanded of workers have increased in complexity. The organization and scope of the WTCS have also evolved within its original broad structural framework of shared state and local responsibility and financing of technical and adult education. In legislation enacted in 1965, lawmakers, the governor, and other state policy makers explicitly rejected the creation of a state community college system. Instead, policy makers created a statewide system of vocational, technical, and adult education districts. In 1993, the name of the system was changed to the Wisconsin Technical College System to reflect the evolution of district technical institutes into degree-granting technical colleges.

Although three WTCS districts provide limited liberal arts collegiate transfer programs, occupationally related technical education remains the primary focus of the WTCS. A separate system of two-year University of Wisconsin centers has primary responsibility in the state for liberal arts collegiate transfer programs. Over the last eight years, however, state policy makers have recognized the increasing need to provide opportunities for technical college students to continue their education in a baccalaureate setting. As a result, the WTCS has fostered the development of program articulation agreements between technical colleges and four-year institutions. The WTCS also has worked with the University of Wisconsin System Board of Regents to changed the transfer policies of the UW System to accept WTCS credits from occupational as well as liberal arts programs.

GOVERNANCE

The WTCS operates under a model of shared governance in which responsibility for the operation of the WTCS is shared by a state board and sixteen district boards. The Wisconsin Technical College System Board is the state agency statutorily responsible for the initiation, development, maintenance, and supervision of programs with specific occupational orientations below the baccalaureate level, including associate degrees, training of apprentices, and adult education below the professional level. In addition, the state board is charged with determining the organization, plans, scope, and development of technical colleges in Wisconsin.

The state board consists of 13 non-salaried members. Nine public members are appointed directly by the governor for six-year, staggered terms: one employer of labor, one employee who does not have employing or discharging power, one person whose principal occupation is farming and who is actually engaged in the operation of farms, and six additional at-large members. The governor also appoints a student member who is enrolled at least half-time and in good academic standing at a technical college for a two-year term. Three persons or their designees serve in an ex officio capacity: the state superintendent of public instruction, the secretary of the Wisconsin Department of Workforce Development, and the president of the University of Wisconsin Board of Regents. State board members elect a president, vice president, and a secretary. The president appoints two additional members of the board to serve with the elected officers as the board's executive committee. The state board meets approximately nine times a year, rotating its meetings between the state office in Madison and the college campuses around the state.

The operations of the state board are carried out by a staff headed by a state director who is appointed by and serves at the pleasure of the board. The state director is the executive officer of the WTCS and is responsible for all administrative and supervisory matter, including the development, implementation, and evaluation of all program plans. The state board staff carries out the board's policies and assures conformity to state and federal laws and regulations. Major state board staff responsibilities are divided between two divisions. The Division of Finance, Planning, and Policy is responsible for budget preparation, policy development, systemwide facilities development, government relations, research and long-range planning, and the provision of support staff services such as data processing, personnel, and labor market analysis. This division also is responsible for oversight of district budgets, enrollments, and policies. The Division of Program and Economic Development is responsible for program definition, approval, evaluation, and review and for educational programs and services for persons with special needs. This division provides professional development for district faculty, staff, and administrators, monitors district program activities for accountability and program improvement, and coordinates system offerings with other educational systems. This division also is responsible for district personnel certification, student financial aid, federal and state projects for targeted populations, adult and continuing education outreach, and school-to-work initiatives.

The state's technical college districts are governed by district boards appointed by local elected officials. Depending on the way in which the district was created, the local board may be appointed either by the county board chairpersons of the counties which constitute the district or by the presidents of the school boards within the district. Each district board is composed of nine members who are residents of the district, including two employers, two employees, three additional members, a school district administrator, and one elected official who holds a state or local office. District board members serve staggered three-year terms. Each district board is empowered to operate the district schools established by it. Typically, each district operates a single college with multiple campuses. One district, Wisconsin Indianhead Technical College District, which covers the sparsely populated northwestern one-third of the state, operates four separate colleges.

The operation of each district board is carried out by district staff, headed by a district administrator/president appointed by the district board. The district administrator is the chief executive officer of the district and president of its college or colleges. Local district staffing patterns are governed by the technical college districts and differ by district so as to reflect differences in the complexity and size of the districts and district board preferences. District administrators are typically assisted by a staff of vice presidents overseeing major functional areas such as instructional services, student services, administrative services, and business and industry outreach, as well as campus deans or administrators for each branch campus.

FUNDING

Funding for the WTCS comes from four primary sources: local, state, federal, and student fees (tuition and materials fees). Other sources of revenue include income from contract training and technical assistance and from miscellaneous activities. Projected operating expenses for the WTCS for 1998-99 total about $620,000,000 statewide. Additional expenses not directly attributable to operations are expected to result in an overall WTCS budget totaling nearly $915,000,000. These additional expenses include an estimated $97,000,000 for capital expenditures and an estimated $63,000,000 for debt service.

In 1998-99, local property tax levies are expected to fund approximately 53% of the operating costs of the WTCS statewide. District boards are empowered to levy a tax, not exceeding 1.5 mills on the full value of the taxable property of the district, for the purpose of making capital improvements, acquiring equipment, and operating and maintaining the schools of the district. The mill limitation is not applicable to taxes levied for the purpose of paying principal and interest on bonds or notes. The district board also may borrow money and levy property taxes to be used for the purchase or construction of buildings, for additions, enlargements, and improvements to buildings, and for the acquisition of sites and equipment.

In 1998-99, state aid is expected to fund approximately 21% of the operating costs of the WTCS statewide. The state does not aid avocational courses, but does aid debt service. The state aid formula is based on each district's proportion of the total statewide aidable cost modified by an equalization factor that considers a district's property value and full-time equivalent students served.

In 1998-99, federal funds are expected to fund nearly 5% of the operating costs of the WTCS statewide. The WTCS used these federal funds to stimulate new program development, operate activities to meet the needs of special populations, and provide a small amount of campus-based student financial aid. Federal funding for the WTCS comes primarily from the Carl D. Perkins Vocational and Applied Technology Education Act, the Adult Education Act, and the Job Training Partnership Act. Additional federal funding for WTCS operations in the form of federal students aid is included under the next section on tuition revenue from students.

In 1998-99, program fees (tuition), materials fees, and other student fees are expected to fund about 16% of the operating costs of the WTCS statewide. Reflecting their origins as continuation schools, adult vocational school courses originally were free of charge in Wisconsin. In 1975, student tuition was charged for the first time. There are still no fees for students enrolled in adult high school, adult basic education, or English as a Second Language instruction. Persons 62 and older are also exempt from program fees for vocational-adult courses. By statute, the state board is required to set uniform program fees for the system as a whole for liberal arts collegiate transfer, postsecondary, and vocational-adult programs. For the collegiate transfer program, the state board must set tuition or program fees to cover not less than 31% of the statewide average operational costs of liberal arts programs in the districts. For postsecondary and vocational-adult programs, the state board must set tuition or program fees to cover no less than 14% of the combined estimated statewide operational costs of postsecondary and vocational-adult programs. The state board is required to set tuition for students who are not residents of the state or subject to a reciprocity agreement with another state at a level based on 100% of the statewide cost per full-time equivalent student for operating the programs in which they are enrolled. For 1998-99, resident tuition for collegiate transfer programs is $76.35 per credit, non-resident tuition is $258.60 per credit; for postsecondary and vocational-adult programs, in-state tuition is $57.00 per credit, non-resident tuition is $440.90 per credit.

Income from contracts, fund balances brought forward, and other miscellaneous sources of funds are expected to fund about 6% of the statewide operating costs of the WTCS in 1998-99.

Increased demand on financial resources and rapid developments in technology have served as catalysts for new cooperative ventures among technical college districts. Districts have been cooperating on projects for many years, but the number of joint efforts recently has escalated significantly as public pressure control costs have increased. These cooperative efforts fall in two categories: (i) projects impacting programs and students and (ii) joint purchasing.

All districts, for instance, have cooperated by funding a coordinated statewide marketing effort promoting the many benefits of the Technical Colleges for students, employers, and the public. Additional examples of cooperative programmatic efforts include:

- WTCS districts working together to invest in telecommunication technology such as regional fiber optic networks and other similar technologies to create opportunities for sharing courses and programs among districts and with University of Wisconsin campuses and K-12 schools. Such networks also facilitate opportunities for joint staff development efforts, reduced travel costs, and consolidated telecommunication bandwidth for voice, data, and video.
- Development and implementation of a uniform enrollment appli-

cation form and fee statewide for use by all districts, which began with fall 1996 students. This assisted in reducing barriers to students in obtaining access to programs in any district.

- Joint development of an institutional effectiveness model for use by the districts. Districts are continuing to work cooperatively on developing specific action steps needed to collect data, analyze effectiveness measures, and incorporate results in on-going assessment and continuous improvement processes.
- Shared use of a computerized Student Employment Information System (SEIS) developed by MATC-Milwaukee. This software can list employer openings; track students; generate reports and mailings to students; and permit access by both faculty and students.

Efforts to coordinate joint purchasing have yielded both short- and long-term savings for WTCS districts. Immediate financial savings occur through leveraging of the marketplace; longer-term savings arise because districts with common infrastructures can jointly assist each other in designing upgrades and trouble-shooting problems. Outstanding examples of joint purchasing activities include:

- Creation of a Wisconsin Technical College System Information and Telecommunications Systems Consortium formed by the 16 districts and state office to serve as a coordination point for cooperative purchasing of hardware, software, and related training.
- Identification of ways in which technical college purchasing requirements can be more directly built into state government bids to permit the districts to make better use of state contracts to eliminate administrative costs of conducting a district bidding process and to better utilize the combined purchasing power of the University of Wisconsin System and WTCS.
- Centralization of the process of negotiating rights for video-based courses, interactive video courseware, and other instructional materials on behalf of the 16 districts. These materials are used by districts in broadcast and cable television systems, College by Cassette, as well as other alternative delivery systems to allow students to more easily take technical college courses.
- Initiation by the districts and the state foundation of a new effort to provide group insurance program in the areas of property, liability, boiler, director's and officers' liability, umbrella liability, and workers compensation.

PROGRAMS AND ENROLLMENTS

The WTCS offers students a wide variety of opportunities to enroll in educational programs leading to an associate degree, technical diploma, or technical certificate. In addition, the WTCS provides related instruction for registered apprenticeships for adults, instruction in adult basic education that may lead to awarding of a high school diploma, high school equivalency diploma, or a general education development (GED) certificate, and short-term vocational and technical courses that prepare persons for new jobs, update their existing skills, or expand their skill base.

The WTCS offers 174 different types of associate degrees in 548 individual programs throughout the state. The WTCS also offers an additional 111 different types of one- and two-year technical diploma programs and 49 short-term vocational programs at numerous locations around the state. In keeping with the WTCS focus on occupational education and training, most of these degree and diploma programs are designed to prepare students for employment in a particular occupational area.

State board approval is required prior to implementation of all associate degree programs and vocational diploma programs of one or two years in length. State board ratification of the state director's approval is required of diploma programs of less than one year in length and apprenticeship programs.

In addition to exercising program and course approval for specific associate degree and technical diploma programs by district, the state board establishes general criteria for occupational programs. These criteria include:

1. Associate degree in applied sciences or applied arts (64 to 72 semester credits)
    a) Occupational-specific courses directly related to the occupation (minimum of 32 credits);
    b) Occupational-supportive courses that provide a foundation for the occupational content, including mathematics and science (minimum of 11 credits);
    c) General education courses (minimum of 15 credits);
    d) Elective course requirements (minimum of 6 credits).
2. Vocational diploma programs (short-term, one- and two-year) (2 to 70 vocational credits)
    a) Occupational-specific courses (70 to 100 percent of total program credits);

b) Occupational-supportive/general education courses (maximum of 30 percent of total program credits)
3. Technical certificates
   a) May be awarded at the option of local districts for participation or attendance at WTCS adult and continuing education courses, seminars, etc.
   b) Three technical college districts are authorized by statute to offer a separate college transfer program. This program provides liberal arts instruction leading to an associate of arts degree. The program includes college-level courses paralleling the freshman and sophomore years of instruction that would be offered through a conventional community or four-year college liberal arts program.

WTCS students are counted by programs and courses. Enrollment data are generally computed and analyzed in terms of headcounts and full-time equivalents. Many students enroll in multiple courses that may be in more than one instructional area or aid category. As a result, duplicate enrollments are possible across categories.

Table 1
Enrollments: Headcount and FTEs by Aid Category
(State Totals)

Program Year	College Parellel	Associate Degree	Vocational Diploma	Vocational Adult	Non-Postsecondary*	Community Services	Totals**
1997-88							
Headcount	16,937	98,572	97,858	257,567	76,562	18,259	431,405
FTEs	4,678	31,095	15,694	5,090	6,607	430	56,987
1996-97							
Headcount	16,199	100,341	97,839	260,324		17,150	434,885
FTEs	4,424	31,229	14,596	4,865		397	55,511
1995-96							
Headcount	16,937	98,572	97,858	257,567		18,259	431,405
FTEs	4,678	31,095	15,694	5,090		430	56,987
1994-95							
Headcount	17,826	100,593	98,639	258,024		20,214	434,780
FTEs	4,945	32,042	16,330	5,366		473	59,156
1993-94							
Headcount	17,709	104,027	96,495	259,410		22,177	438,396
FTEs	4,907	33,238	16,598	5,436		536	60,715

*Category added in 1997-98. Category includes Basic Education, the Hearing Impaired Program, and the Visually Impaired Program.
**Unduplicated

Table 2									
Enrollments: Headcount and FTEs by Academic Division (State Totals)									
Program Year	Agriculture	Business/ Marketing	Graphics	Home Economics	Industrial	Service/ Health	Technical/TV	General Education	Total*
1997-98									
Headcount	8,221	125,421	4,875	59.989	41,315	111,341	13,549	135,323	439,068
FTEs	1,222	16,502	1,216	2,541	6,046	11,601	4,098	13,269	56,588

*Unduplicated

The WTCS has been a key partner in the design and implementation of Wisconsin's nationally acclaimed Tech Prep and School-to Work program. Tech Prep, implemented in all high school districts in the state, helps young people early in their high school programs to identify and complete the more challenging coursework they need to succeed in postsecondary education and training. A goal of the Tech Prep program is to increase the number of high school graduates entering the WTCS directly after high school. The Tech Prep program has emphasized the development of applied and integrated curriculum at the high school level and articulation of these high school courses with technical college occupational programs. The Youth Apprenticeship program, in contrast, permits interested high school juniors and seniors with identified career goals to participate in a structured program of classroom instruction tied to learning experiences in one or more workplaces. High school juniors and seniors may also participate in a more limited one-year program offering a structured cooperative education experience tied to mastery of industry-specified skill competencies In either case, the students are expected to master specified skill competencies in the workplace. Upon completion of the program, students receive a high school diploma, a certificate identifying the skill competencies they have attained, and technical college credit for the skills and knowledge they acquire. Although some students who participate in work-based learning or tech prep enter the workplace directly upon graduation, most seek additional technical training or transfer to a four-year degree program.

Other programmatic initiatives include joint funding of the development of the Wisconsin Instructional Design System (WIDS), creation of teaching innovation centers, increased incorporation of work-based learning in the associate degree curriculum. WIDS is computer/video software that can be used by districts to design performance-based curriculum. It also can be used to create study guides and training manuals that include core abilities, competencies, performance standards, learning objectives, learning activities, and performance assessment statements. Teaching innovation centers are campus-based efforts to assist technical college instructors in becoming familiar with newly emerging instructional technologies and to incorporated these learning technologies into the delivery of technical college instruction. Two existing centers are funded through district and faculty union contributions. Similar centers are envisioned for all sixteen districts. Work-based learning is a key component of many occupational training programs. In many programs, classroom instruction is capped with a clinical or workplace experience. The WTCS is attempting to better coordinate classroom instruction with the needs of employers, to increase the amount of time associate degree students spend in work-based learning, and to develop more programs in which students gain experience in actual work settings earlier in the instructional program.

ECONOMIC DEVELOPMENT

Wisconsin has long had a strategy of promoting economic development through investing in the development of its human resources. The major contribution of the WTCS to economic development in Wisconsin is through occupationally related education and training. In addition, the WTCS provides direct assistance to individual firms through contracts for customized training and technical assistance and works with other state agencies, business and industry, and organized labor to develop, promote, and implement economic and workforce development initiatives in Wisconsin.

Currently, Wisconsin's technical colleges are the primary deliverers of skilled occupational training in Wisconsin. The WTCS provides not only initial job training and education for more than 130,000 new labor market entrants each year, but also skill training and retraining for more than 250,000 incumbent workers annually. Wisconsin employers turn to the WTCS to meet their needs for technical training, workplace literacy, continuous quality improvement, and managing technological change in the workplace. In 1997, about 88,000 workers obtained customized training through contracts between their employers and their local technical college. Of the more than $13.6 million spent by business and industry on technical college training each year, about 85% provides job-related training to enhance the skills of Wisconsin's workforce.

In addition to its regular instructional programs, the WTCS provides firms with access to customized training. Instructional resources can be mobilized within a relatively short time frame to provide customized, worksite training tailored to the needs of employers and potential employers when and where needed. Alternatively, programs can be provided at one of the 46 campuses or though any of hundreds of outreach centers across the state. WTCS districts provide a variety of community services that contribute directly to economic development in Wisconsin. These include:

- Federal procurement contract assistance;
- Meeting, conference space and facilitation, and teleconferencing;
- International trade and export assistance;
- Technical assistance;
- Development of proposals for business seeking state training funds
- Business incubators and industrial park development;
- Entrepreneurial instruction; and
- Participation in education, business, labor, and government consortia, councils, planning commissions, and local economic development agencies.

The Wisconsin Manufacturing Extension Partnership (WMEP) is the most recent example of statewide cooperation and collaboration among the WTCS, the University of Wisconsin System, the Wisconsin Department of Commerce, business, industry, and organized labor to further economic development in the state. WMEP is operated by a non-profit corporation in partnership with the National Institute of Standards and Technology of the U.S. Department of Commerce to provide modernization services to small to mid-sized manufacturers. The WTCS is a founding partner of WMEP and provides funding and institutional homes for most of WMEP's 50 field agents. These field agents work with small to mid-sized manufacturers in their respective regions of the state to assess current operations, develop strategies for modernization, and identify resources to fund these efforts. Training and technical assistance to carry out these projects may come from the WTCS, other educational institutions, or private consultants.

ACCOUNTABILITY

The WTCS has take a three-pronged approach to increasing the system's accountability. These efforts involve the active participation state

and district board members, state and district staff faculty and student representatives, as well as members of the business community, organized labor, and state policymakers. The WTCS has engaged in a year-long visioning process to renew and reaffirm the WTCS's commitment to:
- being the premier provider of technical education;
- developing individuals who apply knowledge and skills to enhance quality of life and boost economic vitality; and
- extending learning beyond the classroom and throughout life.

In addition, the state board has adopted and district administrators have endorsed
- strategic goals and directions for the WTCS. These include:
- increasing to 25% the percentage of high school graduates immediately choosing to enter a technical college;
- enhancing public perceptions of the WTCS as the education provider of first choice in Wisconsin;
- fully integrating technology in the delivery of education to meet the learning needs of students; and
- expanding programs and activities to address the learning needs of incumbent workers, under-served populations (especially minorities), and those entering the job market with minimal skills.

Finally, the WTCS participates in ongoing activities to assess and enhance institutional effectiveness. In part, these activities have arisen out of a desire to find better ways to serve customers in a time of tightening resources. These efforts have also arisen in response to growing demands for accountability, changing employer needs, federal and state mandates, changing accreditation requirements, and a renewed interest in demonstrating quality.

The institutional effectiveness model is a systemwide effort, identifying core indicators that can be used by individual technical colleges to assess student achievement and the overall performance of an institution, respond to external accountability demands and North Central Association accreditation requirements, and meet federal and state reporting requirements. The WTCS has identified seventeen core indicators of effectiveness through a process involving multiple groups and a variety of information sources. Sources of expertise about measuring institutional effectiveness in the WTCS included focus groups with key stakeholders, surveys of staff perceptions, individual interviews with knowledgeable individuals, systemwide workshops, federal and state policies and legislation, and North

Central Association accreditation guidelines. The core indicators of effectiveness fall into four broad categories:
- Student achievement and satisfaction;
- Employer satisfaction;
- Organizational quality; and
- Public perception and satisfaction.

FOR ADDITIONAL INFORMATION, PLEASE CONTACT:
Edward Chin
State Director and Executive Officer
Wisconsin Technical College System Board
310 Price Place
P. O. Box 7874
Madison, Wisconsin 53707
Telephone: (608) 266-1770 (voice)
            (608) 266-2483 (TTY)
Fax: (608) 266-1690

WYOMING

Thomas C. Henry, Executive Director
and
William H. Lovejoy, Dean of Information, Planning, and Analysis
Wyoming Community College Commission

OVERVIEW

Casper College was the first of the state's community colleges to be established under the Junior College Bill enacted by the 1945 legislature. Subsequently, and conceived as University of Wyoming extension centers, colleges were established in Powell (Northwest College) in 1946, Sheridan (Northern Wyoming Community College District) in 1948, and Torrington (Eastern Wyoming College) in 1948.

The 1951 Legislature extended the system of higher education by establishing the Community College Commission. In addition to the four established colleges, three more were founded at Rock Springs (Western Wyoming Community College) in 1959, Riverton (Central Wyoming College) in 1966, and Cheyenne (Laramie County Community College) in 1968.

Since its creation, the Commission has had its mission and range of responsibility altered several times. Enabling legislation for the community colleges and the Commission in 1985 added major duties. And after a management audit of the system, the 1991 Legislature assigned additional responsibilities to the Commission.

Today, the Community College system consists of the Commission and seven local college districts located throughout the state. Each college district is comprised of a single county, and the sixteen counties without districts are divided into the service areas of the colleges.

The mission of the college system, defined in statute, is"…open access institutions focusing on academic transfer programs, career and occupational programs, developmental and basic skills instruction, adult and continuing education, economic development training, public and community services programming and student support services."

COORDINATION

The Community College Commission is mandated by statute to "ensure the operation and maintenance of the Wyoming Community College System in a coordinated, efficient and effective manner." The Commission consists of seven members appointed by the governor with approval of the senate for four-year terms, with a two-term limit. No more than four members may be from the same political party. The governor and the state superintendent of public instruction are ex-officio non-voting members of the commission. The commission is required to meet at least quarterly. An agency staff of eleven professional personnel assists the commission and is located in Cheyenne.

Prior to1985, commissioners were generally representative of the post-secondary institutions in the state. After that legislative session, revisions to statute strengthened the oversight role of the commission, and commissioners were expected to represent the broader interest of the state and of taxpayers.

While the legislation stressed a primary role of ensuring the efficient and effective operations, other responsibilities are enumerated. For one, the commission must allocate and account for fiscal resources provided by the legislature. The body is responsible for the approval or disapproval of academic and vocational-technical programs at the colleges. The development and maintenance of an effective management information system that provides accurate information about the colleges and the system is a primary duty.

Legislation passed in 1989 required the commission to develop a funding distribution formula that would provide for greater equity among the colleges. The 1991 Legislature provided additional budgetary responsibility with a greater emphasis on coordination and accountability. Comprehensive educational needs assessments, the assessment of student outcomes, the adoption of standard financial accounting, facilities inventory standards, and the establishment of tuition policies were among the additional charges made to the commission.

The commission's oversight responsibility, including Wyoming Public Television, gives it a wide-ranging clientele—local college trustees, administrators, faculty, support staff and students.

GOVERNANCE

Each of the seven college districts is a body corporate and comprises a community college district in the State of Wyoming. A local board of trustees elected by the voters residing in the district (county) governs each district.

The local board may hold property and be a party to suits and contracts. Among the board's duties is the requirement to prescribe and enforce rules and regulations for its own government, though such rules and regulations may not be inconsistent with the rules and regulations of the Wyoming Community College Commission. Local college boards prescribe graduation requirements, report revenues and expenses of the college district, submit reports as required by the commission, appoint a chief administrative officer, and assess the required number of mills on the assessed valuation of the district.

FUNDING

The operations of the community colleges are financed through a combination of local, institutional, and state resources. Local resources include a mandatory four-mill levy on the assessed valuation of the property within the district if a college is to receive state assistance, along with a portion of the motor vehicle tax and other specified local taxes. Institutional resources include tuition, fees, investment income and other miscellaneous income. Local and institutional resources are supplemented by a state appropriation provided by the legislature from the state's general fund.

Wyoming operates on a biennium budgeting basis. The colleges are required, however, to prepare annual budgets identifying revenue and expenditures in a format utilizing the accounting standards of the National Association of College and University Business Officers (NACUBO). All funds and expenditures are incorporated in the current fund budget, with the operating budget a subset of the current fund budget

Program expenditures within the operating budget are reported by instruction, research; public service, academic support, student services, institutional support, operation and maintenance of plant, and scholarships and fellowships. Series expenditures are reported by salaries, benefits, operating expenses, and capital outlay.

Either revenue or general obligation bonds fund the construction of college facilities. The debt service for revenue bonds is funded from fees collected from operation of the facility. Debt service for general obligation bonds is derived from an annual mill levy of up to four mills on the valuation of the property within the district for projects that have been approved by the electorate.

The commission implemented a fund distribution formula for the 1991-92 biennium. Budget requests made to the governor and the legislature are based upon budgeted expenditures, formula enrollment, and allowable square feet.

The primary factors in the distribution formula are average full-time-equivalency enrollment and allowable square feet. A complex set of formulas within the model breaks down enrollment by total, by levels of instruction—lecture, laboratory, high technology. The square foot allowance is generated from the budgeted expenditures for plant maintenance and operation and corrected for increases or decreases in allowable square feet. An instruction allowance is generated from budgeted expenditures for instruction and corrected for increases or decreases in formula average FTE.

Sources of funding for the formula include state appropriation, local taxes, tuition, and other miscellaneous sources. Student fees and continuing education and community services fees are excluded from the formula but are a part of the budget authority of each college that is set by the Commission.

The commission is required by statute to set a uniform rate for the system. The rate for full-time resident students for the 1998-99 academic year is $485 per semester, with out-of-state tuition triple the in-state rate. Student fees are set by local districts and vary among the colleges.

Budget expenditures for the 1999-00 biennium by source of funding are:

State	60.6%
Local	16.7%
Institutional	21.6%

PROGRAMS AND ENROLLMENT

The Wyoming Community College Commission is required to review and approve or disapprove academic and vocational-technical programs. Statute outlines criteria based on a program's relationship to student demand, excessive duplication, or lack of cost effectiveness. To date, the agency has relied on program reviews conducted and submitted by the colleges to meet its mandate.

Each of the colleges offers a full component of academic and vocational-technical programs that were approved by the commission. Each college awards associate of arts, associate of science, and associate of applied science degrees. One college offers an associate of applied arts degree and one offers an associate of business degree. All colleges offer a certificate of completion in specialized occupational programs and one college awards a diploma.

Enrollment data are collected by credit headcount, by credit full-time equivalency (FTE) and by noncredit headcount. Enrollment reports are submitted at the close of summer, fall, and spring instructional periods by each college of compilation into a system report. Credit enrolment data are summed for the three terms and divided by two to generate an annual enrollment.

In Wyoming, by statute, each FTE represents 12 hours of credit earned in a semester. Annual FTE enrollment for the college system in 1997-98 was 14,114.

Credit enrollment by headcount showed that part-time students out-numbered full-time students by almost two to one. Forty-six percent of the students are less than 25 years of age. Fifty-one percent fall within the age range of 25-59 years and the final three percent are over sixty years of age. Nearly two-thirds of all students are enrolled in a community college located in their county of residence. Thirty percent of all enrollees attended a college located in a county other than their county of residence. The remaining seven percent of the students came from out-of-state.

Students who have declared a major are reported as either academic transfer or vocational-technical, with the balance reported as undecided. The undecided category accounted for over one-third of the student head-count during 1996-97. Forty-three percent of the students indicated that they were enrolled in an academic transfer program and 21% reported themselves as vocational-technical students

Data for students enrolled in non-credit courses are reported as an annual figure by unduplicated noncredit headcount. For the report year, the non-credit headcount totaled 24,076. Two-thirds of the noncredit students were enrolled in community services programs while one-third were enrolled in continuing education courses.

Student enrollment for Adult Basic Education, General Education Development, and English as a Second Language courses is reported by student contact hours. ABE students accounted for 52% of the total. For comparative purposes only, if contact hours were converted to Full-time Equivalency, the enrollment would be 161 FTE.

During the past decade, the system-wide FTE enrollment increased steadily for five years, peaking in 1991-92 at 14,691. In the last five years, enrollment has remained relatively stable, and over the ten-year period, the increase was 1.5%. It is projected that the enrollment will continue to remain stable or possibly decline over the next several years. The student demographics have not changed significantly over the decade. Wyoming community colleges tend to enroll more females than males, have a nearly equal mix of traditional and non-traditional students, consist of mostly in-state students, and reflect the ethnic mix of the population in that students from minority groups are few in number. It is unlikely that the student profile will change over the next decade.

ECONOMIC AND WORKFORCE DEVELOPMENT

One of the responsibilities defined in the mission statement of the community colleges is economic development training. Each college meets this mandate on an individual basis as the need arises in its service area to train workers in existing businesses or to train the workforce for a business that comes into the community.

In 1995, the governor, by executive order, appointed the state Workforce Development Council, renamed in 1998 the Human Resource Investment Council. The council is charged with the development of a State Plan for Workforce Development. The community college system assumes an active role through council membership of the commission's executive director and one of the college presidents.

In 1998, the governor recommended, and the legislature approved and funded a Business Development Council. As of this date, the council is involved in organizing itself.

In March, 1996, the commission adopted a model for workforce development that places the seven community colleges as the centers for delivery of workforce development. The model represents a plan for integrated employment and training services to be offered through a workforce development system made up of regional partnerships among communities, local businesses, human resource agencies, schools and community. It proposes that the community college system be designated to provide for a series of regional One-Stop Career, Training/Education and Placement Centers. The centers will be open-entry/open-exit and provide for in both academic and technical training, skills development and support services aimed at making customers successful in both life and job skills.

Working with the Wyoming Department of Family Services, the commission assisted in the development of welfare reform legislation that included an educational component. Through a memorandum of understanding with the Wyoming Department of Family Services, the commission contracted with Laramie County Community College for a pilot skills center program that was benchmarked in 1997-98. The program proved viable and has been extended into the next fiscal year.

COMMUNITY COLLEGE COMMISSION MISSION

The community colleges in Wyoming are governed by local control. It is a principle that the commission endorses, and the administration of the colleges is left to the local governing boards.

The mission of the Wyoming Community College Commission is coordination, advocacy, and accountability for the community college system on behalf of the people of the State of Wyoming

In support of that mission, the commission is involved currently in several ongoing developmental projects. Though the implementation of a system-level management information system was legislated in 1985, such a MIS has not been completed. Accurate and reliable information about the community colleges is necessary for the governor, the legislature, and the commission to assess the efficient and effective operation of the colleges, as mandated. A composite database of college system data elements is under development and will be utilized in formula funding, program review, strategic plan measurement, and reporting to constituencies.

The funding distribution formula in use since 1991 may have outlived its intended objectives. The current formula rewards the addition of square footage of FTE enrolment to a college. In an era of stable or declining enrollments, the increasing use of distance education technology, and an emphasis on performance outcomes, those factors are less than satisfactory. The commission has retained the National Center for Higher Education Management systems for assistance in creating a possible new formula that might be implemented with the next biennium.

In addition to updating its rules in areas of fiscal, facilities, and information management, the commission is also evaluating rules in the arenas of program review, approval, and disapproval. Since the primary goal of the Commission and the colleges is the delivery of pertinent and effective program offerings to students, a credible methodology for evaluating programs is necessary.

Integral to all of the above is a Strategic Plan that the Commission adopted in 1997. A dynamic document, the Plan outlines goals and objectives and the measurements that will be utilized to assess progress. The focus is on indicators and student outcomes, and it is anticipated that those measurements will assist the Commission, the Governor, and the legislature in evaluating the State's investment in community college education and making informed decisions about future funding of the system.

FOR ADDITIONAL INFORMATION, PLEASE CONTACT:
Thomas Henry, Executive Director
Wyoming Community College Commission
2020 Carey Avenue, Eighth Floor
Cheyenne, Wyoming 82002
Telephone: (307) 777-7763
Fax: (307) 777-6567
E-mail: thenry@antelope.wcc.edu

ABOUT THE AUTHORS

Terrence A. Tollefson is Professor, Department of Educational Leadership and Policy Analysis, East Tennessee State University, Johnson City, Tennessee. He previously taught at North Carolina State University, where he was editor of *Community College Review*. He earned his Ph.D. in education from the University of Michigan. He worked many years as a community college administrator, including service as a Director of Curriculum at Oakland Community College in Michigan, Associate Vice President for Planning and Policy in the North Carolina Department of Community Colleges, and State Director of Community Colleges in New Jersey and Colorado. This is his third experience as co-author/co-editor of a book on state systems of community colleges, and he also has numerous journal articles and other publications in the same field. Terry has two children, Brad and Michelle, and four grandchildren, Lindsay, Kara, Kevin and Sam.

Rick L. Garrett, currently Vice President of Instructional Services at Mayland Community College in Spruce Pine, North Carolina, was formerly Associate Vice president for Technical and General Education at Florence-Darlington Technical College in Florence, South Carolina. Rick received his doctorate in Adult and Community College Education from North Carolina State University and is the author of a number of journal articles. Through his work at four different two-year colleges in two different states and through conducting two national studies on community college governance, Rick has gained a broad perspective regarding the function and operations of state community college systems. He enjoys living in the Northwestern mountains of North Carolina with his wife Billie and son Zachary.

William G. Ingram is Senior Vice President and Chief Instructional Officer at Durham Technical Community College in Durham, North Carolina. He previously served as Director of Continuing Education Programs, Director of Off-Campus Programs, and Dean of Technical and Vocational Programs at that institution. He also served as Special Assistant to the Dean of Instruction at Southeastern Community College in Whiteville, North Carolina. He holds both the Master of Science degree and the Doctorate in Education degree in Adult and Community College Education from North Carolina State University. With Terrence A. Tollefson he was co-author of "Local Autonomy is Alive and Well: The Results of a National Study of Effective Decision-Making Authority in State Community College Systems" in the *Community College Journal of Research and Practice* (196, 20(2). Bill and his wife, Ann, are the parents of two children, Christine Elizabeth and David.